Globalisation and the Asia-Pacific

The Asian economic crisis of the late 1990s has brought to the fore debates over the contested meanings of globalisation in the Asia-Pacific.

Bringing together internationally renowned, interdisciplinary scholars, this book explores various dimensions of globalisation, and evaluates their relationship to development processes in the Asia-Pacific region. *Globalisation and the Asia-Pacific* provides diverse accounts of how globalisation is being experienced, understood, managed and resisted at various scales in relation to economic, social, cultural and political change in the region. This collection will provide invaluable analyses for those involved in political science, human geography, sociology, international political economy, development studies, anthropology, Asian studies and economics.

The Editors: Kris Olds is Lecturer in Geography at the National University of Singapore; Peter Dicken is Professor of Economic Geography at the University of Manchester. At the National University of Singapore, Philip F. Kelly is Assistant Professor in Southeast Asian Studies, Lily Kong is Associate Professor in Geography and Henry Wai-chung Yeung is Assistant Professor in Geography.

The Contributors: Peter Dicken, Arif Dirlik, Dean Forbes, Jonathan Friedman, Nina Glick Schiller, Richard Higgott, Bob Jessop, Philip F. Kelly, Lily Kong, James H. Mittelman, Kris Olds, Cayetano W. Paderanga Jr, Saskia Sassen, Ngai-Ling Sum, Nigel Thrift, Henry Wai-chung Yeung.

Routledge/Warwick Studies in Globalisation

Edited by Richard Higgott and published in association with the Centre for the Study of Globalisation and Regionalisation, University of Warwick

What is globalisation and does it matter? How can we measure it? What are its policy implications? The Centre for the Study of Globalisation and Regionalisation at the University of Warwick is an international site for the study of key questions such as these in the theory and practice of globalisation and regionalisation. Its agenda is avowedly interdisciplinary. The work of the Centre will be showcased in this new series.

This series comprises two strands:

Routledge/Warwick Studies in Globalisation is a forum for innovative new research intended for a high-level specialist readership, and the titles will be available in hardback only. Titles include:

1. Non-State Actors and Authority in the Global System
Edited by Richard Higgott, Geoffrey Underhill and Andreas Bieler

Warwick Studies in Globalisation addresses the needs of students and teachers, and the titles will be published in hardback and paperback. Titles include:

1. Globalisation and the Asia-Pacific
Contested Territories
Edited by Kris Olds, Peter Dicken, Philip F. Kelly, Lily Kong and Henry Wai-chung Yeung

Globalisation and the Asia-Pacific

Contested territories

Edited by Kris Olds, Peter Dicken, Philip F. Kelly, Lily Kong and Henry Wai-chung Yeung

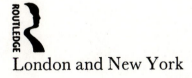

London and New York

First published 1999 by Routledge
11 New Fetter Lane, London EC4P 4EE

Simultaneously published in the USA and Canada
by Routledge
29 West 35th Street, New York, NY 10001

Typeset in Baskerville by
BC Typesetting, Bristol
Printed and bound in Great Britain by
MPG Books Ltd, Bodmin

British Library Cataloguing in Publication Data
A catalogue record for this book is available from the British Library

Library of Congress Cataloging in Publication Data
Globalisation and the Asia Pacific: contested territories/edited by
    Kris Olds . . . [et al.].
        p.   cm. – (Warwick studies in globalisation)
    From a workshop at the National University of Singapore, 1997.
    Includes bibliographical references and index.
    1. Asia–Foreign economic relations–Pacific Area.   2. Pacific
Area–Foreign economic relations–Asia.   3. Asia–Commerce–Pacific
Area.   4. Pacific Area–Commerce–Asia.   I. Olds, Kris, 1961–   .
    II. Series.
    HF1583.Z4P335   1999
337.509–dc21   93-31539
                                                                CIP

ISBN 0-415-19919-0 (hbk)
ISBN 0-415-19920-4 (pbk)

Contents

Illustrations

Figures

Tables

Contributors

Peter Dicken is Professor of Economic Geography at the University of Manchester and was Visiting Professor at the Department of Geography, National University of Singapore in 1997. He has held visiting appointments in the United States, Canada, Mexico, Australia and Hong Kong. His research interests are in global economic change, the spatial behaviour and strategies of transnational corporations, foreign direct investment (notably Japanese FDI) and economic change in Europe and East and South East Asia. He is author of several books and numerous papers on these themes, including *Global Shift: Transforming the World Economy* (3rd edn, 1998). He has also acted as consultant to the UNCTAD Programme on Transnational Corporations.

Arif Dirlik is Professor of History at Duke University, USA, where he specialises in Modern Chinese History. His research and writing ranges from the history of the modern Chinese Revolution to problems of the Pacific region to cultural criticism. His most recent publications include *What is in a Rim? Critical Perspectives on the Pacific Region Idea* (ed., 2nd rev edn, 1998); *The Postcolonial Aura: Third World Criticism in the Age of Global Capitalism* (1997); *China and Postmodernism* (ed., with Zhang Xudong, special issue of *boundary 2*); *Critical Perspectives on Mao Zedong's Thought* (ed., with Paul Healy and Nick Knight, 1997); *Asia Pacific as Space of Cultural Production* (ed., with Rob Wilson, 1995); *After the Revolution: Waking to Global Capitalism* (1994).

Dean Forbes is Professor in the School of Geography, Population and Environmental Management at Flinders University, Adelaide, Australia. He is chair of the Flinders University International Board and the Alumni Association and is an elected member of the Academy of Social Sciences in Australia. His current research work is on postcolonial representations of Pacific Asia and the large cities of Indonesia and Vietnam. He is author of *Asian Metropolis* (1996), and co-editor of *Multiculturalism, Difference and Postmodernism* (1993).

Jonathan Friedman is Professor of Social Anthropology at the University of Lund. He has done research on Southeast Asia, the Pacific and more specifically Hawaii. His theoretical work is concentrated on the study of long-term historical processes, theories of social reproduction and the relation between global process and cultural identity. He has been president of the European Society of Oceanists and has editorial functions on several journals, e.g. *Identities, Critique of Anthropology, Review of International Political Economy*. Among his books are, *Cultural Identity and Global Process* (1994); (ed.) *Consumption and Identity* (1994); *System Structure and Contradiction in the Evolution of 'Asiatic' Social Formations* (1972, in press with new introduction 1997); (ed., with Ulla Hasager) *Hawaii: Return to Nationhood* (1995); (ed., with James Carrier) *Melanesian Modernities* (1996) and (ed., with Scott Lash) *Modernity and Identity* (1992).

Nina Glick Schiller is Associate Professor of Anthropology at the University of New Hampshire. She is Editor of *Identities, Global Studies in Culture and Power*. Since 1987, Glick Schiller has begun to examine the transnational practices of immigrants settled into the United States. She co-edited *Towards A Transnational Perspective On Migration: Race, Class, Ethnicity, and Nationalism Reconsidered* and co-authored *Nations Unbound: Transnational Projects, Postcolonial Predicaments, and Deterritorialised Nation-States*. Glick Schiller has also published a series of articles exploring the Haitian experience of migration, the connection between race and nation and the relationship between past and present transnational migrations and nation-states.

Richard Higgott, formerly Professor at the University of Manchester and the Australian National University, is now Professor of International Political Economy and Director of the UK's Economic and Social Research Council Centre for the Study of Globalisation and Regionalisation at the University of Warwick. He is Editor of *The Pacific Review* and current research interests are in comparative regionalism and the evolution of international economic policy coordination. He is author and editor of numerous books including *Political Development Theory; Relocating Middle Powers: Australia and Canada in an Evolving World Order; Pacific Economic Relations: Cooperation or Conflict?* and numerous articles and book chapters. He is a member of the European Group of the Council for Security Cooperation in the Asia Pacific and the Steering Committee of the UK–Korea Forum.

Bob Jessop is Professor of Sociology at Lancaster University, United Kingdom. He was previously in the Department of Government, University of Essex, and has held visiting appointments in Australia, Canada, Columbia, Denmark, Germany, Italy, Taiwan and the USA. His principal fields of research are social theory, state theory, comparative political economy and European politics; he has also written on post-socialism in

Eastern and Central Europe and has an active interest in East Asian political economy and states. His current funded research project concerns the restructuring of welfare states in Scandinavia, Britain and Germany. His principal publications include: *The Capitalist State* (1982); *Nicos Poulantzas* (1985); *Thatcherism* (1988); *State Theory* (1990); *The Politics of Flexibility* (1991) and *Strategic Choice and Path-Dependency in Post-Socialism* (1995). He has also published more than 60 journal articles and 70 contributions to edited scholarly volumes.

Philip F. Kelly is Assistant Professor in Southeast Asian Studies at the National University of Singapore and has held research positions at the University of British Columbia and the University of the Philippines. His research focuses on the political economy of development in Southeast Asia and the politics of globalisation. He is the author of *Landscapes of Globalisation: Human Geographies of Economic Change in the Philippines* (forthcoming).

Lily Kong is Associate Professor at the Department of Geography, Vice-Dean, Faculty of Arts and Social Sciences and Assistant Director, Office of Research, National University of Singapore. She is a social and cultural geographer with research interests in religion, popular culture, nature and heritage. She is currently developing research on issues of identity as people relocate in a rapidly globalising world. She has published in *inter alia, Transactions, Institute of British Geographers, Progress in Human Geography, Environment and Planning D: Society and Space, Area, Habitat International, Political Geography* and *Urban Studies*.

James H. Mittelman is Professor in the School of International Service, American University, Washington DC. He is also the current holder of the Pok Rafeah Chair in International Studies and Distinguished Visiting Professor, Institute of Malaysian and International Studies, Universiti Kebangsaan Malaysia. In addition, he has been appointed as a Member at the Institute for Advanced Study in Princeton. His most recent books are, as editor and contributor, *Globalisation: Critical Reflections* (1996); as co-author with Mustapha Kamal Pasha, *Out from Underdevelopment Revisited: Changing Global Structures and the Remaking of the Third World* (1997); and as co-editor with Stephen Gill and contributor, *Innovation and Transformation in International Studies* (1997).

Kris Olds is Lecturer at the Department of Geography, National University of Singapore. He has recently worked at the University of Bristol, University of British Columbia, and held visiting appointments at Tongji University and the Chinese University of Hong Kong. His research focuses on globalisation and urban change in the Pacific Rim. He is the author of *Globalisation and Urban Change: Capital, Culture and Pacific Rim Mega-Projects* (forthcoming), and co-editor of *The Globalisation of Chinese Business Firms* (1999).

Cayetano W. Paderanga Jr, is currently a member of the Monetary Board of the Bangko Sentral ng Philippines. He is on leave from the School of Economics of the University of the Philippines where he is the Bienvenido M. Gonzales Professor of Economics. Since receiving his Ph.D from Stanford University in 1979, he has taught at the University of the Philippines and the University of Western Ontario. From 1990 to 1992, he was the Secretary of Socio-Economic Planning and Director-General of the Philippine National Economic and Development Authority (NEDA). With his present position as Monetary Board Member, he undertakes research on open economy, fiscal and monetary issues. Among his recent works are *A Note on Philippine Financial Openness (forthcoming)*; *The Philippines in the Emerging World Environment: Globalisation at a Glance* (ed., 1997); *Labor Absorption over the Philippine Economic Cycle* (1996); *Economic Interdependence and Macroeconomic Coordination* (1996); *Building Bureaucratic Capability* (1996); *Philippine Financial Management: 1980–1995* (1996); *Debt Management in the Philippines* (1995); *Monetary Management: the Philippine Experience* (1994) and *The Theory and Practice of Investment Programmes in the Philippines* (1994).

Saskia Sassen, formerly of Columbia University, is Professor of Sociology at the University of Chicago. She is the author of numerous articles and books. Her most recent books are *Globalisation and Its Discontents: Selected Essays* (1998); *Cities in a World Economy* (1994), with recent translations in German and Italian and *Losing Control? Sovereignty in an Age of Globalisation* (1996). Several translations of her book *The Global City* appeared in 1996, among them with Descartes Cie. (Paris) and Cliomedia (Torino). Fischer Verlag (Frankfurt) has just published her *Migranten, Siedler, Fluchtlinge*. She is currently completing *Immigration Policy in the Global Economy: From National Crisis to Multilateral Management*, sponsored by the Twentieth Century Fund, and continuing her research project 'Governance and Accountability in a Global Economy'. She has also launched a new project on 'Cities and their Cross-border Networks' sponsored by the United Nations University. In 1996–7 she was a Scholar at the Centre for Advanced Research in Stanford, California.

Ngai-Ling Sum is Simon Research Fellow at the International Centre for Labour Studies, University of Manchester. She has research interests in globalisation/regionalisation, trans-border regions, political economy of newly-industrialising countries and the relationship between political economy and identity politics. She is on the Editorial Board of *The Pacific Review*. Her most recent publications include articles and book reviews in *Economy and Society*, *New Political Economy*, *Millennium*, *Emergo*, and *Journal of International Development*. She has also contributed to edited volumes including *Fragmented Asia* (1996); *Regionalism and World Order* (1996); *Beyond Markets and Hierarchy* (1997); *Dynamic Asia* (1998) and *Demystifying Globalisation* (1998). She is currently working on a book entitled *Capitalism in East Asian Newly-Industrialising Countries: A Regulationist Perspective*. She is also co-editing a book (with Markus Perkmann) on *Globalisation and Cross-Border Regions* (1998).

Nigel Thrift is Professor of Geography, University of Bristol, UK. He is the author, co-author or editor of numerous books and articles on issues including transnational corporations, globalisation, identity, money, regional development, the city of London and socialist urbanisation. Titles include *Money/Space: Geographies of Monetary Transformation* (1997); *Spatial Formations* (1996); *Mapping the Subject. Geographies of Cultural Transformation* (1995); *Globalisation, Institutions and Regional Development in Europe* (1994) and *Money, Power and Space* (1993).

Henry Wai-chung Yeung is Assistant Professor at the Department of Geography, National University of Singapore. He has held visiting appointments at the Institute of Southeast Asian Studies, Singapore and the Centre of Asian Studies, University of Hong Kong. His research interests include the geography of transnational corporations, Asian firms and their overseas operations and Chinese business networks in the Asia-Pacific region. He has conducted extensive research on Hong Kong firms in Southeast Asia and published widely on transnational corporations from developing countries, in particular Hong Kong and Asian Newly Industrialised Economies. He is author of *Transnational Corporations and Business Networks: Hong Kong Firms in the ASEAN Region* (1998) and editor of *The Globalisation of Business Firms from Emerging Economies* (1999) and co-editor of *The Globalisation of Chinese Business Firms* (1999).

Routledge/Warwick Studies in Globalisation
Series preface

The Centre for the Study of Globalisation and Regionalisation (CSGR) at the University of Warwick opened for business with its inaugural conference entitled Non-State Actors and Authority in the Global System in October 1997. Funded by the Economic and Social Research Council of the UK with an initial grant of over £2.5 million, the Centre is rapidly becoming an international site for the study of key issues in the theory and practice of globalisation and regionalisation. Its agenda is avowedly interdisciplinary with research staff from international relations, political science, economics, law and sociology holding appointments or visiting appointments in the Centre. The Centre is committed to scholarly excellence but also strives to be problem-solving in methodological orientation.

Three broad categories of activity inform and underwrite the research programme of the Centre. (i) What is globalisation? (ii) Can we measure its impacts? If so, how? (iii) What are its policy implications? Understandings of globalisation are seen to be multi-dimensional – political, economic, cultural, and ideological – so CSGR sees globalisation in at least two broad ways: first, as the emergence of a set of sequences and processes that are increasingly unhindered by territorial or jurisdictional barriers and that enhance the spread of trans-border practices in economic, political, cultural and social domains, and second, as a discourse of political and economic knowledge offering one view of how to make the post-modern world manageable. For many, globalisation as 'knowledge' constitutes a new reality. Centre research will ask what kinds of constraints globalisation poses for independent policy initiative on the part of national policy-makers and under what conditions these constraints are enhanced or mitigated.

Within these broad contexts empirical work at CSGR focuses on (i) particular regional projects in Europe, North America and the Asia-Pacific; (ii) the enhancement of international institutions, rules and policy competence on questions of trade competition and international finance and investment; (iii) normative questions about governance, sovereignty, democratisation and policy-making under constraints of globalisation. Indeed, Centre research is sensitive to the wider normative nature of many of these questions, especially in research into the counter-tendencies towards, or sites of resistance to, globalisation at regional and local levels that give rise to different understandings of the importance of space and territoriality.

Globalisation and the Asia-Pacific: Contested territories is the first volume in this Series. Kris Olds and his colleagues from the National University of Singapore and the University of Manchester have brought together a set of high-quality research essays addressing most aspects of the research agenda of CSGR. Specifically, this volume demonstrates the multifaceted nature of globalisation and, using the Asia-Pacific as its main geographic focus, the manner in which regionalisation and globalisation exist in a dialectical relationship in the contemporary era.

Richard Higgott
Director, CSGR

Acknowledgements

This book is the product of a workshop on 'The Logic(s) of Globalisation' held at the National University of Singapore (NUS), on 3–5 December 1997. We wish to acknowledge the support provided by the National University of Singapore (via RP 970013, 'Singapore's Global Reach'); the Centre for Advanced Studies (NUS); the ESRC-funded Centre for the Study of Globalisation and Regionalisation; University of Warwick and the School for Policy Studies, University of Bristol. In addition, exemplary assistance was provided by Elen Sia in the organisation of the workshop and in the preparation of the book. Finally, we would like to acknowledge the continual support provided by the former Head of the Department of Geography (NUS), Teo Siew Eng, Richard Higgott (University of Warwick) and Victoria Smith (Routledge).

1 Questions in a crisis

The contested meanings of globalisation in the Asia-Pacific

Philip F. Kelly and Kris Olds

Introduction

A preoccupation with the 'global' has become one of the emblematic – almost obsessive – characteristics of our time. National political leaders, in particular, are increasingly adopting a global rhetoric to justify the economic (and often social) policy stance of their governments. Such rhetoric depicts globalisation as an unstoppable, unidirectional force that will inevitably transform economies and societies. Singapore's Deputy Prime Minister Lee Hsien Loong lucidly expressed this widespread sentiment in a speech to policy makers and analysts in Washington DC in May 1998:

> Globalisation, fostered by free flow of information and rapid progress in technology, is a driving force that no country can turn back. It does impose market discipline on the participants, which can be harsh, but is the mechanism that drives progress and prosperity.
>
> (*Straits Times*, 8 May 1998: 67)

At the same time as politicians, journalists and analysts have joined the global bandwagon, virtually all of the social sciences have concurrently developed their own 'take' on the processes of globalisation. We now see an avalanche of books and articles on the subject. During the five-year period between 1980 and 1984, the *Social Sciences Citation Index* identified a mere 13 books or papers dealing with 'globalisation'. In the five years from 1992–6, however, the number had grown to 581. In 1996 alone, the number of globalisation items reached 211. If we were to add all the other related works, the remarkable growth and recent acceleration in the quantity of the 'global' literature would be even more apparent. There are good reasons to be sceptical about such a bandwagon, but we believe that there is also a need to add to this debate.

The first reason essentially defines the purpose of this book. So much of the theoretical discourse on globalisation has emerged from Western contexts, and yet the processes, and the rhetoric, of globalisation have arguably worked with most transformative power in the Asia-Pacific region. But globalisation has not been uncontested, and across the region a series of contradictory tendencies are apparent in popular representations of globalisation: it has been 'the' route to economic triumph, but also the root of economic crisis; it has been resisted as an insidious process of undermining 'Asian values', but courted as a source of social change that produces cosmopolitan and reflexive citizens; and finally, it has been heralded as the end of the nation-state, and yet assiduously promoted by many states within the region.

In seeking to explore some of these contradictions in this volume we have not, however, sought to find an 'Asian voice' or 'Asia-Pacific perspective' on globalisation – the contributors currently work in Asia, Europe, North America and Australia. Instead, each contributor explicitly considers the meanings and implications of globalisation for the Asia-Pacific region or some part of it. It is worth noting that in using the regional label of Asia-Pacific we have consciously chosen one of the more egregious regional constructions currently in circulation. As much as globalisation itself, the 'Asia-Pacific' is a contested territory (Dirlik 1993b; also see Higgott, this volume). There is, however, a certain utility in its vagueness. Perhaps more than any other world region, the boundaries of the Asia-Pacific are indeterminate and open to contestation and social construction. In using it to define the main geographical anchor of this book we therefore avoid the need to place definitive boundaries on the locus of our attention. To focus on 'Southeast Asia' or 'East Asia' would imply that globalisation represents an exogenous force impacting upon a definitive region. As we will discuss later, a key element in contemporary processes of globalisation is not the impact of 'global' processes upon another clearly defined scale, but instead the relativisation of scale. By focusing on the Asia-Pacific, the openness and fluidity of the regional construct is acknowledged and its linkages with other scales – the global, the state, the city, the firm, the personal, etc. – are more readily explicated. Thus each chapter, while taking globalisation as its starting point, also attempts to bring other scales of analysis into the picture. As a result, this is neither a book about the Asia-Pacific region *per se*, nor is it purely a decontextualised debate about the reality or merits of globalisation. Instead, it stands as a collection of diverse accounts of how globalisation is being experienced, understood, managed and resisted at various scales within the Asia-Pacific region. This 'multi-scalar' approach is also reflected in the structure of the book. The first part, 'Global discourses', addresses theoretical themes which take the global scale as their starting point, but explore its theoretical and political implications in various dimensions. In the second part, 'Regional reformations', sub-global regional spaces become the locus of analysis, but once again processes that transcend this fluid scale are examined in the context of the Asia-Pacific region. 'Reterritorialising the state' then considers the implications of globalisation for the scale of the nation-state, while the final part, 'Global lives', explores some of the implications of globalisation processes for social life and cultural identity.

Two other aims define the goals of this book. The first is to examine critically the concept of globalisation and its political, economic and cultural consequences. Unlike some of its predecessors on the intellectual catwalk of the social sciences – notably 'postmodernism' – globalisation holds a great deal more purchase in policy circles and has been popularised in far more imaginative ways. This discourse of globalisation goes further than the simple description of contemporary social change; it also carries with it the power to shape material reality via the practical politics of policy formulation and implementation (Gibson-Graham 1996; Kayatekin and Ruccio 1998; Kelly 1999; Leyshon 1997). It can construct a view of geographical space that implies the deferral of political options to the global scale. In effect, globalisation 'itself has become a political force, helping to create the institutional realities it purportedly merely describes' (Piven 1995: 8). Thus there is a peculiar reflexivity in the ways globalisation is represented and experienced. As Paul Hirst (1997: 424) points out, globalisation is not just a fashionable idea, it is a concept with consequences. The contributions collected together here, then, do not simply describe, and certainly do not celebrate, globalisation; instead, they explore the complex meanings of the concept and the ways in which it might be rethought with greater rigour.

The final overall purpose of this book is to bring an interdisciplinary approach to bear upon the processes of globalisation in the Asia-Pacific region. While the literature on globalisation now consists of a number of distinct, though overlapping, approaches (economic, cultural, political, social), most of the academic debate still tends to occur within relatively sealed disciplinary compartments. Such compartments are becoming increasingly anachronistic as authors from 'grey zones' such as international political economy, economic geography and cultural studies draw intellectual stimulus from varied sources. An important purpose of this collection of essays, then, is to gather together multiple perspectives on globalisation from a wide range of scholars who are transcending their 'traditional' backgrounds in disciplines such as anthropology, economics, geography, history, planning, politics and sociology. In this way, the chapters reflect the diversity of processes that have become enmeshed in the broader idea of globalisation, including issues of cultural identity, cultural production, political institutions, manufacturing production, financial flows, migration and urbanisation.

The contributions gathered here were written during a period when debates over the meaning and consequences of globalisation in the Asia-Pacific were magnified by the economic crisis and social unrest spreading through East and Southeast Asia in 1997 and 1998. The 'Asian financial crisis', as it has come to be known, has fostered a heightened sense that globalisation implies the loss of control over the effective regulation of national economies and the diminished influence of societies over their own destinies. It has become much easier for actors in the Asia-Pacific region to imagine the direct and indirect 'discipline' that can be imposed by 'global' financial markets, multilateral institutions such as the International

Table 1.1 FDI inflows to East and Southeast Asia, by host economy, 1985–97 (billions of dollars)

Country	1985–90 (Annual average)	1991	1992	1993	1994	1995	1996	1997
High human development								
Singapore	2.952	4.887	2.204	4.686	5.480	6.912	9.440	n/a
Malaysia	1.054	3.998	5.183	5.006	4.342	4.132	5.300	3.8[b]
Hong Kong	1.597	0.538	2.051	1.667	2.000	2.100	2.500	n/a
Thailand	1.017	2.014	2.114	1.730	1.322	2.003	2.426	2.5[a]
Korea, Republic of	0.705	1.180	0.727	0.588	0.809	1.776	2.308	3.1
Taiwan	0.879	1.271	0.879	0.917	1.375	1.559	1.402	n/a
Japan	0.375	1.730	2.756	0.210	0.888	0.041	0.220	n/a
Brunei Darussalam	–	0.001	0.004	0.014	0.006	0.007	0.009	n/a
Totals	8.579	15.619	15.918	14.944	16.276	18.53	23.686	n/a
Medium human development								
China	2.654	4.366	11.156	27.515	33.787	35.849	42.300	45.3
Indonesia	0.551	1.482	1.777	2.004	2.109	4.348	7.960	4.1[a]
Vietnam	0.03	0.229	0.385	0.523	0.742	2.000	2.156	n/a
Philippines	0.413	0.544	0.228	1.238	1.591	1.478	1.408	2.9[a]
Low human development								
Cambodia	0.028	–	0.033	0.054	0.069	0.151	0.350	n/a
Myanmar	0.028	0.238	0.171	0.149	0.91	0.115	0.100	n/a
Korea, People's Republic	0.095	–	0.042	0.006	0.007	0.003	0.004	n/a

Source: Compiled from UNCTAD (1997) and International Chamber of Commerce and UNCTAD (1998) http://www.unicc.org/unctad/en/pressref/bg9802en.htm, accessed 13 May 1998.
Notes:
a Estimates.   b Not including reinvested earnings.

Monetary Fund (IMF), global superpowers (the US) and private entities such as international credit ratings agencies (Moody's or Standard and Poor's).

While the issues that are examined in this book have been brought to the fore during the economic crisis of 1997–8, recent events do not represent the beginning (and certainly not the end) of the discussion over globalisation in the region. Rather, the crisis simply provides a starting point for more 'fundamental' debates about globalisation in the Asia-Pacific. Discussions on the underlying causes and potential solutions to the Asian economic crisis have heightened awareness of several key themes that will be explored in greater theoretical and empirical depth in this volume. In the next section of this introductory chapter, then, we will provide a brief outline of the experiences of globalisation that the 1997–8 crisis precipitated. Subsequently, we broaden the discussion to highlight some of the wider issues and enduring themes relating to globalisation in the Asia-Pacific that have emerged from the crisis and which weave their way through the chapters in this book.

National crises, regional crisis, global crisis

An account of the financial crisis of 1997–8 inevitably reads as a rather economistic interpretation of what globalisation means. The papers in this collection, as we have already pointed out, take a much broader view of globalisation, but as we will argue, the questions which emerge from the financial crisis go far beyond the confines of economic processes and policy. As a starting point, however, the story of the Asian economic crisis runs something like this.

Southeast Asian growth (especially in Malaysia and Thailand, latterly in Indonesia and the Philippines) has been fuelled by inflows of foreign direct investment from other Asian economies, notably Japan and the 'Asian NICs' – Taiwan, South Korea, Singapore and Hong Kong. While the flows of investment grew throughout the 1980s, they accelerated considerably in the 1990s, especially in countries such as Indonesia (see Table 1.1).

The impetus for this transborder flow of investment was the decreasing global competitiveness of companies in source countries, their need to relocate to lower cost locations, and their efforts to gain footholds in emerging markets (UNCTAD 1997). Southeast Asian nations responded with liberalised financial sectors, industrial location incentives, high domestic interest rates (to attract portfolio investment), and a dollar peg to insure investors against currency devaluation (Bello 1997a; UNCTAD 1997: 79–85). In addition, the 1990s saw a rapid expansion of foreign portfolio equity investment and private lending in the Asian region (UNCTAD 1997: 112). Attracted by the 'dynamism' of these economies, net capital inflows (long-term debt, foreign direct investment, and equity purchases) to the Asia Pacific region increased from US$25 billion in 1990 to over US$110 billion in 1996 (Greenspan

1997). This created what Walden Bello (1997b) calls 'fast-track capitalism', with rapid industrialisation and ballooning capital markets.

Much of the inflowing capital did not, however, find its way into productive agricultural or industrial sectors, but instead gravitated towards the stock market, consumer financing and real estate. These sectors boomed, while commodity and manufactured exports, the mainstays of national economies in Southeast Asia, became less competitive in the global market place. Domestic financial sectors were making capital liberally available, but regulation of lending standards was lax and many institutions were making loans on the basis of already inflated assets in a circular process that led to further appreciation. While this virtuous circle continued to inflate, financial institutions were borrowing in US dollars and lending in local currency (Radelet and Sachs 1998). But since 1995 the dollar had been appreciating against world currencies – gaining 50 per cent against the Yen between 1995 and 1997 and Southeast Asian currencies were going up with it.

The circle was broken in July 1997. The proximate causes may have been a global slowdown in the semiconductor industry in 1996, a strengthening dollar, low wage competition and currency devaluation in China, or rising wage costs in Asia – all of which caused exports to stagnate in 1996 and 1997 (Corsetti *et al.* 1998; Radelet and Sachs 1998; Wade and Veneroso 1998a). Thus while Singapore, Hong Kong, Taiwan and China all maintained positive current account balances in 1996, Indonesia, the Philippines, South Korea, Malaysia and Thailand saw deficits of between 4 and 8 per cent of GDP (*The Economist*, 7 March 1998). But whatever the stimulus for panic, when global financial managers detected a disparity between exchange rates and global competitiveness, institutional investors and speculators began to move capital out. The Thai government of Chavalit Yongchaiyudh, having given repeated assurances that it would resolutely defend the currency against any speculative attack, finally conceded defeat after spending over US$9 billion of the country's foreign currency reserves. On 2 July 1997, the Thai baht was allowed to float against the US dollar and immediately lost 15–20 per cent of its market value.

Other Southeast Asian economies were based on similar but not identical foundations – including broadly pegged exchange rates, banks with over-exposure in the property sector, huge unhedged short-term foreign loans, a lack of 'transparency' and regulation in the financial sector, and sluggish export receipts – and their currencies came under similar pressures. A financial contagion spread across the region, fuelled to some extent by fears of declining competitiveness against economies with already devalued currencies and similar problems in financial regulation, but also by less rational sentiments of self-fulfilling panic concerning the movement of the market. The situation was also exacerbated by domestic investors quickly seeking to hedge their foreign currency exposure by buying dollars. By mid-October, the Indonesian and Thai currencies had lost over 30 per cent of their value against the dollar since July, and the Malaysian ringgit and Philippine peso more than 20 per cent (IMF 1998).

By November 1997 the crisis had spread to South Korea where investors detected a similarly problematic set of debt structures among industrial conglomerates. In particular, the politically motivated nature of some lending and the massive short-term foreign debt provided cause for concern (in June 1997 South Korean short-term foreign debt amounted to more than three times the country's foreign exchange reserves, and by December 1997 it was fourteen times (*The Economist*, 7 March 1998; Wade and Veneroso 1998a).

As the months passed, side-shows to the main drama unfolded and fanned market sentiment against the region. In August and September 1997, Prime Minister Mahathir of Malaysia engaged in a public debate with New York investment banker George Soros (among others) over the morality and merits of currency trading and speculative investment. With each new salvo, currency and stock markets dipped still lower. Meanwhile in Indonesia, political pressure on President Suharto mounted as he played a cat-and-mouse game with the IMF, which was applying pressure for economic and political reforms.

By the end of 1997, Thailand, Indonesia and South Korea had signed bailout packages with the IMF in an attempt to resuscitate ailing capital markets that were no longer capable of repaying bloated dollar loans to foreign banks, or servicing the needs of productive local enterprises. In the first quarter of 1998, Indonesian exporters were in dire straits as foreign banks refused to accept letters of credit from Indonesian institutions, even when guaranteed by the national government. Thus export manufacturers were unable to import raw materials. The IMF's strategies of insisting on increased fiscal surpluses in countries where budgets where already in surplus and cloaking its negotiations in secrecy while demanding transparency from recipients, led to criticism of the institution from various quarters.

In Indonesia, and to a lesser extent Thailand, the financial turmoil cum economic crisis also turned into a political crisis. IMF conditions became the key to 'market confidence', but these conditions conflicted with embedded political-economic power structures and vested interests. Growing hardship and latent dissatisfaction erupted into outright hostility in urban areas across Indonesia and among many middle-class urbanites in Bangkok. In Thailand, a new government was installed in November 1997, but in Indonesia social unrest continued after Suharto's 're-election' in March 1998 to a seventh five-year term in office. Anger was directed against the Suharto regime itself, and against ethnic Chinese Indonesians who have frequently borne the brunt of 'pribumi' (ethnic Malay) frustrations. This social unrest translated into increasing flows of illegal immigrants from Indonesia, causing fears in Singapore and Malaysia of a massive influx if conditions worsened. Finally, as tensions mounted and unrest intensified on the streets of Jakarta and other cities, Suharto announced his imminent resignation on 19 May and then his immediate replacement by B. J. Habibie on 21 May. Whilst the links between the volatile nature of the global financial system and such violent political turmoil may not be direct, they surely cannot be denied. As Kristof noted in the *International Herald Tribune*:

> when Mr. Suharto pledged in a sober television address to the nation on Tuesday [19 May] that he would step down from office, the force that had led to this stage was not a Communist insurgency but a conspiracy of far more potent subversives: capitalism, markets and globalisation. Instead of hiding in the jungle, they established a fifth column in glass-and-steel towers in the major cities, and Mr. Suharto's security forces never figured out how to handcuff or torture them into submission . . . His sophisticated military equipment can detect a guerilla in the jungle of East Timor at night, but it was unable to discern bad bank loans or prop up a tumbling currency.
>
> (Kristof 20 May 1998)

Interpreting the crisis

This simple sketch of the financial crisis leaves plenty that is open to interpretation and debate. Some commentators noted that poor investment decisions by financial intermediaries in Asia were being punished, but the sources of that capital (predominantly Western banks) were enjoying the full attention of the IMF to ensure that their loans were repaid. Others raised the possibility that the discipline and surveillance of the IMF in the region represented little more than a thinly veiled attempt by American/Western capital to crack the protectionist and monopolistic shell still enveloping many economies (Lim *et al.* 1998). Under this interpretation, the crisis represents not just a vulnerability to globalised capital flows, but also an attempt to globalise certain financial practices and systems of economic regulation – hence the imposition of a particular 'brand' of capitalism. In general, however, interpretations of the crisis seem to fall within four distinct categories.

The first focuses on the 'crony capitalism' and market interference that supposedly suffuses all economic transactions in 'Asia' (usually homogenised from afar). MIT economist Paul Krugman, for example, has emphasised a theory of moral hazard and asset inflation to explain the high levels of investment in overvalued assets such as land that characterised the Thai crisis story in particular. Essentially, his argument amounts to an indictment of 'crony capitalism' wherein loans were made on the basis of connections rather than economic viability and where lenders were safe in the knowledge that the government would bear the cost of failure – in Krugman's (1998a) words, a strategy of 'heads I win, tails somebody else loses'. Regulation was lax, and insufficient penalties existed for 'financial intermediaries' who were making bad loans (see also Lim 1997; Krugman 1998b). A second, but similar, interpretation focuses more broadly on financial market regulation, particularly at the national level. In testimony to the US Congress, for example, Alan Greenspan (1997, 1998), Chairman of the US Federal Reserve, identified the roots of the crisis as lying in the economic mismanagement of affected countries where market signals had not been allowed to cause adjustments in exchange rates and had thus delayed devaluation until the bubble burst in spectacular fashion. In this view, the problem is perhaps caused by crony capitalism, but the ultimate reason is a failure to allow 'market' mechanisms to allocate savings and investments in 'efficient' ways. In both 'moral hazard' and 'market failure' explanations, the crisis is ultimately a 'good thing' because it will shake out the inefficiencies of politically motivated interference in capital markets and expose economies to a healthy global discipline. To move this process along, the solution is to be found in IMF prescriptions for more transparent accounting procedures, tighter monitoring and regulation of the financial sector, and liberalised ownership restrictions.

A third interpretation focuses on the role of panic in the crisis, and particularly the contributory effect of the IMF. Radelet and Sachs (1998), for example, argue that the intensity and extent of the capital flight from the region was irrational. While economic 'fundamentals' (savings, budget surpluses, flexible labour markets, low taxation) remained sound, a precipitous loss of confidence in the financial sector was caused, or at least exacerbated, by IMF analyses declaring profound problems and the imperative of closing down financial institutions. Sachs (1997) suggests that in Thailand and Indonesia in particular the IMF should have worked to maintain a functioning credit system to service the productive export economy, rather than shutting down numerous financial institutions and undermining confidence in others.

A fourth interpretation views the crisis as reflecting broader structural issues which present fundamental problems and contradictions in the ways in which global capitalism is organised. The roots of the crisis can be viewed not as a reflection of domestic regulatory imperfections, but as a consequence of the level of globalisation to which Asian economies have exposed themselves. Bello (1997a, 1997b) suggests that the exposure of Asian economies to global capital flows inevitably left them vulnerable to the vagaries of the international financial system – to paraphrase Bello, an addiction to capital led to a 'ten-year high' and then the present-day 'withdrawal trauma' they are experiencing. On a somewhat related note, Prime Minister Mahathir of Malaysia has repeatedly argued for greater control over international financial transactions and speculative trading (Lim *et al.* 1998). The corollary of this perspective is that the global economic system should be modified to reduce the power of capital to flow freely between economies.

From crisis to fundamentals

Most analyses of the crisis to date have focused on its strictly economic dimensions and its implications for our theoretical understanding of, narrowly speaking, currency crises and more broadly, the strengths and weaknesses of the 'East Asian Miracle'. At least some of the interpretations of the crisis imply, however, that questions need to be asked beyond the immediate issues of moral hazard, financial sector management and exchange rate adjustments, and even beyond broader issues of economic structure and regulation. They also touch upon deeper structural questions concerning how countries in the Asia Pacific region articulate with economic processes operative at a global scale, and how the region will deal with questions of global integration, global governance and developmental destinies (both economic and cultural).

The 'Asian Miracle' was never just about economics, and debates over its causes and consequences have always been interwoven with discussions of cultural identity, political reform, environmental impacts and human development. Thus the 'end of the miracle' raises questions that go beyond the events of the crisis and their proximate causes. It is just beginning to force some more fundamental questions about globalisation and its significance in the Asia-Pacific region to the top of the political and intellectual agenda. Furthermore, these are questions that have an enduring relevance, beyond the current period of hardship and uncertainty, in a region where globalisation has been both a set of economic, political and cultural processes and a discourse to legitimise certain developmental strategies. We would suggest that emerging from the crisis are four interrelated issues. These are the issues that weave their way through the chapters in this book.

The first issue relates to the processes of linkage and integration that are forming within the Asia-Pacific region and between the region and the rest of the world. These are the material processes constituted by actors such as state institutions, firms, individuals, civil society associations and supra-state bodies. They are manifested in flows of commodities, capital, information, images and people, and frameworks of linkage such as regulatory organisations, transnational corporations and other intermediaries. Contrary to the more outlandish boosterist claims of a new global era, such linkages are not especially novel. The *longue durée* of history provides ample evidence of the evolving linkages within and beyond the region, forged by traders, migrants, refugees, missionaries, colonisers, creditors, tourists and investors (see, for example Petri 1993; Reid 1988, 1993). Contemporary processes therefore represent a continuation of, rather than an abrupt aberration from, past trends.

The processes through which social relations across global space have been stretched and deepened have, however, seen both qualitative and quantitative changes in recent decades. The technologies – broadly conceived – of linkage have developed in fields such as freight movement, telecommunications, labour mobility, air transport, finance, electronic media and cultural exchange to the extent that some commentators see a new paradigm of social relations emerging (see, for example, Castells 1996). These material processes of linkage underpin all of the contributions to this book, but the chapters by Bob Jessop, Saskia Sassen, Nina Glick Schiller, Cayetano Paderanga Jr and Jonathan Friedman, in particular, reflect upon new frameworks of interaction.

Such linkages need not necessarily, however, imply a globalising condition. As several chapters also point out, there are strong trends towards regionalisation rather than globalisation, both in terms of economy and identity. This is essentially Dicken and Yeung's point in their chapter, which highlights the key role that Asian firms play in the market-driven process of Asia-Pacific regionalisation. Ngai-ling Sum's examination of new trans-border relations in East Asia echoes this view, as does Richard Higgott's exploration of the evolution of regional identity in East Asia. Higgott's chapter points out that the crisis has engendered differential spins to regional identity formation. At the scale of Asia-Pacific, the crisis has led to the eruption of lingering tensions between world powers such as the United States and regional powers such as Malaysia. The façade of an 'Asia-Pacific' identity (however tenuous) has been further fractured by the political fallout of the Asian economic crisis, though regional identity at the scale of 'East Asia' appears to be strengthening on some levels.

The second issue relates to the impacts and desirability of globalisation in the interrelated spheres of economics, culture and politics. If globalisation is taken to be the intensification and extensification of social relations across space, then in itself it is neither positive nor negative. Taking the example of capital flows, there are good reasons to be sceptical of the simple equation of openness with economic success, and as Paderanga argues in his chapter, financial integration presents profound problems for macro-economic managers. But it is undoubtedly also true that inter- and intra-regional flows of investment have been fundamental in fuelling the region's development process through the provision of new sources of capital in resource-constrained environments (see Dicken and Yeung, this volume). In a very different context, Mittelman notes the environmental costs of globalised capitalism but highlights the benefits of globalising civil society for environmental activists in Southeast Asia.

Other chapters develop the contradictory tendencies and impacts of globalisation and regionalisation. Lily Kong's chapter, for example, draws upon detailed empirical research in Beijing to provide a picture of how regionalisation is leading to the formation of new, ambivalent, 'Chinese' identities among Singaporeans migrating to China. Nina Glick Schiller's chapter develops an historical perspective on the complex issue of citizenship in a globalising era, highlighting the changing role of the national state in facilitating the emergence of transnational identities. Dean Forbes uses two films by the Vietnamese/French director Tran Anh Hung (*The Scent of Green Papaya*, and *Cyclo*) to juxtapose the ongoing quotidian aspects of urban life in Vietnam with the wider context of global events. Meanwhile, Jonathan Friedman attempts to incorporate the broader sweep of shifting global hegemonies with individual experiences of class, ethnic and national identities. Each of these chapters effectively attempts to ground the impacts of globalisation in the personal, reinforcing Giddens' (1996) interpretation of globalisation as both an 'in here' as well as an 'out there' phenomenon.

The impacts of globalisation in diverse dimensions of social life mean that the question of whether globalisation is 'desirable' is a complex one. For every politician, business group, or institution in favour of globalisation (in economic terms, read liberalisation), there are critics who feel the negative impacts of globalisation are unevenly felt by workers, women, the ecosystem and so on. From personal experience evident in Paderanga's chapter, and from theoretically informed observation in the case of Jessop, Higgott and Sassen, several authors raise questions concerning the desirability of shaping development policy in a context where public (and more democratically legitimate) institutions are ill-equipped to understand and shape the global flows that are unleashed under the neo-liberal form of globalisation that is currently dominant. Arif Dirlik too questions the incorporation of the Asia-Pacific region into a development trajectory under globalised capitalism. The impact, he believes, is a process of change that leads to the commodification of place and the diminution, if not obliteration, of local forms of knowledge and resources. Dirlik's argument is that we need to support the development of place-based imaginations that reflect the basic needs of all sectors of society in the Asia-Pacific region.

The third broad issue concerning globalisation in the Asia-Pacific region relates to the construction of globalisation as a discourse and the impact of such constructions on the materialisation of the processes that constitute globalisation. As many of the chapters in this book recognise, there is a complex relationship between the material and the discursive, between hard reality of, for example, trade flows, and other realities of ideas, language, and representation. As we have noted earlier, globalisation epitomises this ambiguity in that it both describes a set of qualitative changes in the processes linking the destinies of people and places across the world, but at the same time the idea of globalisation (as an inexorable force) is deployed for political purposes and is used to legitimise specific development strategies. As Dirlik, Jessop and Sassen suggest in their chapters, such a discourse is informed by normative premises that ultimately focus on the requirements of global capital. The discourse implies that the Asia-Pacific should change (and be changed) to better suit the needs of global capital in a volatile era. Indeed, as Dirlik notes, globalisation has in many ways become the successor to the developmental paradigm of modernisation, and while it might have shed the teleological baggage of the latter, it is no less universalising. This is not to suggest, however, some kind of conspiracy hatched in the boardrooms of Wall Street – such discourses are also indigenised by many different levels of the state in the Asia-Pacific region. This point is highlighted in Jessop's and Sum's chapters on the 'discursive naturalisation' of globalised forms of territory (e.g. the 'region-state' of Southern China), and in Dean Forbes' discussion of representations of the Pacific Asian metropolis. Forbes notes that Singapore's desire to become a global/hub city is signified not only in its infrastructure programmes, but also in the state's relentless development and propagation of images and concepts to suggest its role as both a regional and global command and control centre.

Academics and the private sector also play a key role in developing the discourses that give globalisation its normative power. The community of globalisation 'intellectuals' have produced what Susan Roberts calls a 'strategic globalisation discourse' which is, in her opinion, central to the 'totalising strategic gaze through which TNCs represent, frame (and claim) their world' (cited in Leyshon 1997: 143). This is an issue closely related to Nigel Thrift's chapter on the globalisation of the system of business knowledge (see also Thrift 1996a, 1998a). Thrift focuses on the practical forms of theory used in business (including the rise of 'reflexive management theory'), and the transfer/translation of this knowledge to Asia. His discussion blends well with other discussions by Leyshon (1997) and Bhagwati (1998) concerning the largely private-sector discourses of globalisation that wield such influence in the Asia-Pacific region and elsewhere. As Leyshon (1997: 144) notes:

> Although the globalisation discourse may well be flawed and based upon a mixture of poor social science, hyperbole, exaggeration and corporate desire, it works as a discourse because it has a highly receptive audience within the offices and boardrooms of the international business community. It is in this sense a self-affirming and self-propagating discourse . . . It successfully articulates a feeling within management circles that 'something has changed' in the global economy, and which needs to be responded to by rethinking the way in which their businesses are organised. Thus it is both an explanation and a programme of action.

In short, most of the authors in this book feel people need to be more aware of the discursive construction of globalisation by different communities as they seek to fulfil their agendas in the pursuit of power.

The fourth key issue in understanding the complex and contested meaning of globalisation in the Asia-Pacific region relates to the scale at which social processes can be understood. Perhaps the key contemporary characteristic of economic, cultural and political change is that such processes can no longer be understood with reference to a particular scale in isolation. Neither the individual, the city, the nation, nor the region, unproblematically 'contain' social processes. Instead processes operate across scales and the question then becomes how we can go about understanding these processes if our scalar terms of reference have been destabilised. As Jessop argues in his chapter, one way of describing this complexity is through the notion of the 'relativisation of scale'. Thus, for example, the Asian economic crisis rests within the 'Asian region' neither in terms of its causes, consequences nor solutions. One of the key causes of the crisis was the tendency of Asian firms to over-borrow on a short-term basis from international (especially Japanese) banks. Decisions to borrow were shaped by an array of factors at a variety of interrelated scales: local (firm strategy), national (regulatory structures), regional (rapidly developing economies and bull markets) and global (aggressive international banking practices in the context of deregulation, competition and overaccumulation). In short, the crisis, like many processes of social change in the Asia-Pacific region, was driven by, in Jessop's terms, a 'multi-scalar, multi-temporal, and multi-centric series of processes operating in specific structural contexts'.

Several other chapters clearly demonstrate the multi-scalar dynamics of change in the region. Dicken and Yeung, for example, show how international regulatory structures, state strategy and ethnic identity affect the insertion of Asian firms into the regional and global economy. Similarly, Paderanga's chapter is equally concerned with the operation of global financial markets as with the inner workings of the national monetary bodies that shape the interface of the national economy (in his case the Philippines) with the global financial system.

The basic challenge that the relativisation of scale presents is to understand and represent processes of change in the Asia-Pacific region in ways that both transcend and link different scales. This is not to suggest that all scales are equally important, but instead that no one scale must be privileged – least of all the 'global' – in our understandings of social change. This point relates directly to the challenges of governance in a globalising era. The literature on globalisation makes much of the anachronistic role of the nation-state in contemporary economic governance. This preoccupation has perhaps been rather ethnocentric, drawing on the experiences and concerns of well-established and powerful nation-states (though see Weiss 1997 for a more balanced perspective). As several chapters in this volume point out, especially those under the heading 'Reterritorialising the State', the nation-state's role is being reworked, but certainly not revoked. The national scale represents one among several relevant levels at which contemporary change can be understood, managed, and contested. Furthermore, as Jonathan Friedman points out, the role of the nation-state might well be seen as regionally distinct – with a process of class and ethnic fragmentation occurring in the industrialised global 'core', but with the active consolidation and integration of disparate identities in the emergent nations of East and Southeast Asia.

Conclusion

Each of the four issues identified above has been accentuated by the economic crisis in East and Southeast Asia. The events of 1997–8 have laid bare some of the ways in which the region is embedded within new spatial structures of economic interaction at both regional and global scales. At the same time, the impacts and desirability of this global interdependency have become even more hotly contested. In the university campuses of Indonesia, the streets of Bangkok, the factories of South Korea and the corridors of power of Malaysia, the volatilities and vulnerabilities now associated with economic globalisation are leading to questions over its desirability as a development strategy. But still the discursive power of globalisation both legitimises, and is upheld by, the financial muscle of the IMF and many nation-states in the Asia-Pacific. As we have attempted to show briefly in this chapter, the economic costs of the 1997–8 financial crisis raise broader questions concerning the meaning of globalisation in the Asia-Pacific. While recent events have focused attention on the financial dimensions of globalisation and issues of national economic autonomy, continuing processes of integration clearly incorporate social, cultural and political spheres. The Asian economic crisis highlights enduring issues that stretch far beyond the time horizons of panicked currency markets and cyclically depressed growth rates to include questions about how the people, places and institutions of the Asia-Pacific region might better understand, manage and contest their deepening integration into the global space of flows. It is these questions that the chapters in this volume seek to address.

Part I

Global discourses

2   Reflections on globalisation and its (il)logic(s)

Bob Jessop

This chapter critically addresses globalisation in four ways: (a) contesting the often unstated assumption that globalisation comprises a coherent causal mechanism – or set of causal mechanisms – rather than a complex, chaotic, and overdetermined outcome of a multiscalar, multitemporal, and multicentric series of processes operating in specific structural contexts; (b) questioning the intellectual and practical search for 'the' primary scale – whether global, triadic, national, regional, or urban – around which the world economy is currently organised as if this would somehow be directly analogous to the primacy of the national scale in the thirty years of postwar growth in the circuits of Atlantic Fordism; (c) relating the resulting 'relativisation of scale', i.e. the absence of a dominant nodal point in managing interscalar relations, to some basic contradictions and dilemmas of capitalism, the changing bases of accumulation, the changing relation between the economic and political and the increased competitive importance of the social embeddedness of economic activities; and (d) noting how these problems are being addressed through economic and political projects oriented to different scales – with little consensus as yet on how these projects and scales might be reconciled.

Globalisation: a 'chaotic concept'

Globalisation is generally better interpreted as the complex resultant of many different processes than as a distinctive causal process in its own right. It is misleading to explain specific events and phenomena in terms of the process of 'globalisation', pointless to subsume anything or everything under the umbrella of 'globalisation', and unhelpful to seek to link anything and everything to 'globalisation' as if this somehow conveys more insight than alternative rubrics could. Indeed many phenomena subsumed thereunder would be more adequately and clearly analysed in terms of other notions, such as internationalisation or liberalisation (cf. Scholte 1997). To introduce some order into this chaos requires careful conceptual analysis as well as concern with real causal mechanisms and how they are actualised in given circumstances.

Before presenting my own solution, I address two other approaches. The first cites statistics allegedly showing that the current level of globalisation (or internationalisation) is similar to 1913 (or thereabouts) and/or that no economic trends over the last two decades justify claims about a major break in capitalist development. The second argues that, even today, few, if any, genuinely global companies exist. Even large firms usually have a clearly defined national home base, especially for core activities; and, when they are active abroad, firms (especially smaller transnationals) operate mostly in one triad region. Such data are said to indicate, at best, a further step in the internationalisation of firms' activities, rather than a shift to a qualitatively different stage which could justifiably be termed globalisation.

Whilst these approaches certainly help to decompose and demystify the concept of globalisation, some problems still remain. Thus, regarding the 1913–90s comparison: (a) many more activities in the global economy having been commodified since 1913, similar formal statistics probably involve quite different proportions of the formal and informal economies combined; (b) as international labour mobility before 1913 was greater than today, there was less asymmetry between 'immobile' labour power and 'mobile' capital (Rodrik 1997: 35); (c) as pre-1913 states did not provide universal social welfare and collective consumption, there was little pressure on the 'social wage' *qua* international cost of production; (d) dynastic empires in Europe before 1913 and European colonial empires overseas up to and beyond 1945 are quite different forms of pluri-national space from today's triadic and cross-border regions; (e) the rise of East Asian trading economies and, even more, their increasing intra-regional integration, make capitalism more multicentric compared to 1913; (f) the main forms of internationalisation in trade, finance, indirect and direct investment, services and R&D have been changing as has the relative weight of these different domains in overall global flows;[1] (g) the impact of increasing internationalisation for firms and states depends on whether it occurs during upswing phases in hegemonic cycles, associated with increased openness, or downswing phases (when protectionism gains support) and on whether it is associated with economic expansion or contraction in specific economic or political spaces within the world economy – the period up to 1913 saw economic expansion under British hegemony, the 1980s and early 1990s have seen mixed fortunes during a period of crisis in US hegemony (Altvater and Mahnkopf 1997: 27);[2] (h) the dominant forms of corporate organisation differ due to technological, organisational, and other changes; (i) forms of competition, the dynamic of competitiveness, the degree of reflexiveness of competitive strategies, and their spatial and temporal horizons, are also different; (j) economic and political actors do not generally compare the 1990s with 1913 but with periods they have actually experienced – thus the level of internationalisation is novel insofar as it feels novel and, at least as compared to the heyday of Atlantic Fordism, they are not wholly mistaken.[3]

Regarding the more ideal-typical comparisons of full globalisation and the more limited nature of internationalisation, one must distinguish between firms' actual place-boundedness and the possible extension of their spatial and temporal horizons of action. Firms may well be rooted largely in one place for material production and social reproduction but still take account of far broader 'market conditions'. The rhythm of many economic activities has also accelerated so that, to be competitive, firms must often react over far shorter time horizons. In some cases, the faster a firm's reactions, the more rooted it might become (see below). Similarly, the capacity of finance houses to operate globally often depends significantly on some core activities being rooted locally (see Sassen, this volume; also see Sassen 1996a; Storper 1997).

These arguments already move us some way from mystificatory or confused analyses of globalisation. The following comments are meant as another step. For, if adequately re-specified, trends towards globalisation can certainly help situate and interpret current changes in the spatial scale of economic (and other) institutions, organisations, and strategies. Nonetheless, while outlining a general framework to study globalisation, my focus below is on tendencies towards economic globalisation.

Structurally, globalisation would exist in so far as co-variation of relevant activities becomes more global in extent and/or the speed of that covariation on a global scale increases. Thus defined, global interdependence typically results from processes on various spatial scales, operates differently in each functional subsystem, involves complex and tangled causal hierarchies rather than a simple, unilinear, bottom-up or top-down movement and often displays an eccentric 'nesting' or interpenetration of different scales of social organisation. As an emergent property deriving from these diverse processes, however, and as one reacting back on their subsequent development, globalisation is both a structural and structuring phenomenon. Conversely, to the extent that global co-variation is weakened (perhaps due to the emergence – or resurgence – of coherent regions with their own relatively autonomous accumulation regimes) and/or its speed slackens (perhaps due to structural contradictions or forms of resistance which brake or reverse the effects of global integration), one could talk about counter-tendencies to globalisation.

This approach clearly implies that globalisation develops unevenly across space and time. Indeed it can be said to involve both 'time-space distantiation' and 'time-space compression'. Time-space distantiation stretches social relations over time and space so that they can be controlled or coordinated over longer periods of time (including into the ever more distant future) and over longer distances, greater areas, or more scales of activity. In this regard, then, globalisation results from increasing spatial distantiation reflected in the growing spatial reach of divisions of labour in different fields and is enabled by new material and social technologies of transportation, communication, command, control and intelligence. Conversely, time-space

compression involves the intensification of 'discrete' events in real time[4] and/
or increased velocity of material and immaterial flows over a given distance.
This is linked to changing material and social technologies enabling more
precise control over ever shorter periods of action as well as 'the conquest
of space by time'. Differential abilities to stretch and/or compress time and
space help to shape power and resistance in the emerging global order. Thus
the power of hypermobile forms of finance capital depends on their unique
capacity to compress their own decision-making time (e.g. through split-
second computerised trading) whilst continuing to extend and consolidate
their global reach. The proposed 'Tobin tax' on short-term financial transactions might be one way to reduce this power by encouraging hypermobile
financial capital to adopt longer-term horizons of action. This might also
encourage greater consonance between financial and productive capital
flows. This brings us to the strategic dimension of globalisation.

Strategically, globalisation refers to actors' attempts to promote the global
coordination of activities on a continuing basis within (but not necessarily
across) different institutional orders or functional systems. Such attempts
can be pursued through different material and social technologies on the
interpersonal, interorganisational, interinstitutional, or intersystemic levels.
Examples could include: interpersonal networking (e.g. the Chinese
diaspora); strategic alliances orchestrated by transnational enterprises
(alliances which may include more local or regionally-based firms as well as
not-for-profit organisations); the institutional design of 'international
regimes' to govern particular fields of action; and projects for world government or global governance. The forms of coordination proposed for globalisation vary widely and none are guaranteed to succeed – witness the market-
led globalisation favoured by the World Bank, the horizontal 'global
governance' favoured by proponents (especially NGOs) of international
regimes, and plans for more top-down interstatal (or even world) government.

Thus viewed, what is generally labelled nowadays as 'economic globalisation' rarely, if ever, involves full structural integration and strategic
coordination across the globe. Processes included under this rubric actually
include: (a) internationalisation of national economic spaces through
growing penetration (inward flows) and extraversion (outward flows); (b)
formation of regional economic blocs embracing several national economies –
including, most notably, the formation of various formally organised blocs
in the triadic regions of North America, Europe, and East Asia – and the
development of formal links between these blocs – notably through the Asia-
Pacific Economic Cooperation (APEC) forum, the New Transatlantic
Agenda, and the Asia-Europe Meetings; (c) growth of more 'local internationalisation' or 'virtual regions' through the development of economic
ties between contiguous or non-contiguous local and regional authorities in
different national economies – ties which often by-pass the level of the
national state but may also be sponsored by the latter; (d) extension and
deepening of multinationalisation as multinational companies and trans-

national banks move from limited economic activities abroad to more comprehensive and worldwide strategies, sometimes extending to 'global localisation' whereby firms pursue a global strategy based on exploiting and/ or adjusting to local differences; (e) widening and deepening of international regimes covering economic and economically relevant issues; and (f) emergence of globalisation proper through the introduction and acceptance of global norms and standards, the development of globally integrated markets together with globally oriented strategies, and 'deracinated' firms with no evident national operational base. In each case these processes could be said to promote the structural integration and/or strategic coordination of the economy on a global scale. But their dispersed, fragmented, highly mediated, and partial dynamic means that they are far from producing an homogenised, evenly developing world economy. On the contrary, the various processes involved in globalisation actually re-order – across economic spaces on different spatial scales – place-based differences and complementarities as the basis for dynamic competitive advantages.

In this context I conclude that globalisation is better interpreted as the most inclusive 'structural context' in which processes on other economic scales can be identified and interrelated and/or as the broadest 'horizon of action' to which accumulation strategies and economic projects can be directed. Interpreted as structural context, globalisation should be seen as an emergent, evolutionary phenomenon resulting from economic processes on many scales rather than as a distinctive causal mechanism in its own right. Thus its nature depends critically on sub-global processes. This is seen in the continuing (if often transformed) significance of the local, urban, cross-border, national and macro-regional as substantive sites of real economic activities. And it is also seen in new place-based competitive strategies to articulate other scales with the global to maximise relatively local advantages – strategies such as glocalisation, 'glurbanisation',[5] or international localisation. Smaller scales are also key sites of counter-tendencies and resistance to globalisation.[6] Likewise, regarded as an horizon of action, globalisation means thinking globally, even if acting locally, on an urban scale, regionally or triadically. For one need not be omnipresent to insert oneself favourably into the global division of labour. Nonetheless one must increasingly reflect strategically on the spatial and scalar implications of global processes. This is why such convinced globalisers as Porter (1990) or Ohmae (1995) stress the need to promote the competitive advantage of nations or regions respectively in order to maximise the benefits of globalisation. Nonetheless, while globalising trends certainly exist both in the structural and strategic senses, they will not – indeed, I would argue, cannot – culminate in a fully global world. This is due to the illogic(s) of globalisation (its internal contradictions), to various external structural limits to globalisation (including its relation to other scales of action), and to various forms of resistance. Before considering these limits, however, let me first address some aspects of the relation between globalisation and the 'relativisation of scale'.

The relativisation of scale

In the 'thirty glorious years' of postwar economic expansion, the dominant scale of organisation in growing capitalist economies was the national. Thus national economies were the taken-for-granted objects of economic management in Atlantic Fordism, the 'trading nations' of East Asia, and Latin American import-substitution strategies. This taken-for-grantedness actually depended on quite specific material and ideological foundations which could not themselves be taken for granted. Thus the 'naturalisation' of the structural congruence (or spatio-temporal coincidence) of national economies, national states, and national societies was grounded in postwar reconstruction in Europe, in the national security state in East Asia and in critiques of dependency in Latin America; and, in each case, the national framework was also supported by various (typically asymmetrical) international regimes and alliances which had to be put in place. Continued reproduction of these different forms of structured complementarity depended in turn on the discovery of forms of economic management, regularisation, and governance which could provide a 'spatio-temporal' fix (or a 'time-space envelope', Sum, this volume) within which to at least partially resolve the contradictions and dilemmas of the capital relation. Nonetheless, because the contradictory dynamic of accumulation and its resulting struggles always escape attempts to fix them within any given spatio-temporally anchored institutional framework, any and all such solutions are bound to be unstable and provisional. This is particularly evident in the case of the national scale that predominated in the organisation of postwar economic expansion. For this has since been undermined in many different ways, including the various multiscalar, multitemporal processes that contribute to 'globalisation'.

In response to these changes, views of 'naturalness' seem to have bifurcated from the 'national' towards the global economy and different types of subnational economy. This is clear in the discovery of the 'always-already-there' local, urban, and regional economies as well as new discourses about the emerging significance of the 'global' as the 'natural' scale of economic organisation. Arguments about 'triads' are also sometimes presented as if they are a 'natural' development and extension of the regional scale. In this context, then, we are witnessing a proliferation of spatial scales (whether terrestrial, territorial or telematic), their relative dissociation in complex tangled hierarchies (rather than a simple nesting of scales), and an increasingly convoluted mix of interscalar strategies as various economic and political forces seek the most favourable conditions for their insertion into the changing international order. At least in comparison with the boom years of Atlantic Fordism, this phenomenon can usefully be described as the 'relativisation of scale'. For, although the national scale has lost the taken-for-granted primacy it held in the economic and political organisation of Atlantic Fordism, no other scale of economic and political organisation (whether the 'global' or the 'local', the 'urban' or the 'triadic') has acquired a similar primacy in the current 'after-Fordist' period. There is no new privileged scale around which other levels are now being organised to ensure structured coherence within and across scales. Instead we find growing unstructured complexity as different scales of economic organisation are consolidated structurally and/or approached strategically as so many competing objects of economic management, regularisation or governance. This is also reflected in the former heartlands of Atlantic Fordism, its semi-peripheries in Southern Europe and the more peripheral regions that became its production platforms. The leading East Asian economies also now emphasise the role of technopoles, megalopolises, growth triangles or polygons and other scales of action alongside national plans or, in Hong Kong's case, the apparent simplicities of 'positive non-intervention' in a semi-sovereign city-state. There are also regionalisation trends in Latin America as well as moves towards hemispheric integration.

Some theorists explain newly emerging regions as based on 'natural economic territories' which have been allowed to re-emerge or develop with the decline of the national state as an economic as well as political 'power container'. It is certainly remarkable how older, cross-border trading blocs re-emerged after the Cold War. One might also interpret the rise of 'Greater China' or attempts to build a 'Greater Shanghai' in this context. But 'natural economic territories' are discursively 'naturalised' as well as being economically and politically constructed. Whether any given space is seen as natural or not depends, for example, on views about the dominant modes of economic competition and the factors which promote structural competitiveness. A Ricardian interpretation (based on factor-driven growth in open economies) would lead one to identify different 'NETs' and economic strategies from those implied in a 'Listian' account (based on protectionist 'catch-up' investment dynamics promoted by a national state concerned with its economic and politico-military security). Likewise, a Keynesian interpretation (based on securing the interdependent conditions for mass production economies of scale and mass consumption) would imply different 'NETs' and economic strategies from a Schumpeterian account (based on securing the conditions for systemic competitiveness and permanent innovation).

This affects how one analyses the re-articulation of different spatial scales. There is no pre-given set of places, spaces or scales that are merely being re-ordered. Instead, new places are emerging, new spaces are being created, new scales of organisation are being developed, and new horizons of action are being imagined – all in the light of new forms of (understanding) competition. This situation is complicated by the eccentricity or 'debordering' of spatial scales relative to the early and boom years of Atlantic Fordism.[7] Thus larger territorial units have come to contain a decreasing proportion of the activities of smaller units in their borders so that the latter can no longer be seen as 'nested' within the former in the manner of so many Russian dolls. This is particularly clear in the emerging network of global cities which, *qua* network, is not contained within any given national territory. Another example is the growth of cross-border regions. In short, past scalar fixes, as well as past spatial fixes, are becoming unstable.

The present 'relativisation of scale' clearly involves very different opportunities and threats for economic, political, and social forces compared to the period when the national scale could be taken for granted as primary. It is associated with actions both to exploit and resist the processes producing globalisation. Thus economic actors may engage in strategic alliances to extend their global reach or seek protection from global competition behind various protective barriers. Likewise, as these complex and contradictory processes unfold, states on various levels tackle the domestic repercussions of global restructuring through their involvement in identifying and managing the many different processes contributing to what currently passes as 'globalisation'. In the absence of a new primary scale which can serve as a nodal point for the management of interscalar relations, however, the predominant trend is a continuing 'global–local' disorder rather than the re-regularisation of capital accumulation in and across different spatial scales (cf. Peck and Tickell 1994).

The contradictions of capital accumulation

Capital accumulation depends essentially on the market-mediated exploitation of wage-labour. For, while markets mediate the search for added value, they cannot themselves produce it. Moreover, the very process of commodification rooted in the spread of the market mechanism generates contradictions which cannot be resolved by that mechanism itself. For example, the commodity is both an exchange-value and a use-value; the worker is both an abstract unit of labour power substitutable by other such units (or, indeed, other factors of production) and a concrete individual with specific skills, knowledge and creativity; the wage is both a cost of production and a source of demand; money functions both as an international currency and as national money; productive capital is both abstract value in motion (notably in the form of realised profits available for re-investment) and a concrete stock of time- and place-specific assets in the course of being valorised; and so forth. These structural contradictions are always present in the capital relation but they can assume different forms in different contexts. They can also prove more or less manageable depending on the specific 'spatio-temporal fixes' and the nature of the institutionalised class compromises with which they are from time to time associated. It is in disrupting past fixes and compromises without providing a new structured coherence for continued capital accumulation that neo-liberal forms of globalisation appear to be so threatening to many capitalist – let alone other – interests.

In contrast, it was in managing, at least for a while, such contradictions that the Keynesian welfare national state (or KWNS) made its distinctive contribution to the Atlantic Fordist regime. This benefited from a spatio-territorial matrix based on the congruence between national economy, national state, national citizenship and national society; and from institutions relatively well adapted to combining the tasks of securing full employment and economic growth and managing national electoral cycles. This spatio-temporal fix enabled a specific resolution of the contradictions of capital accumulation as they were expressed under Fordism. Thus, within relatively closed national economies which had been institutionally-discursively consti-tuted as the primary objects of economic management, national states aimed to achieve full employment by treating wages primarily as a source of (domestic) demand and managed their budgets on the assumption that money circulated primarily as national money. The diffusion of mass produc-tion (and its economies of scale) through expanding Fordist firms as well as the development of collective bargaining indexed to productivity and prices were the primary means through which wages as a cost of production were brought under control. And the combination of the Bretton Woods monetary regime and the GATT trade regime meant that the (still limited) circulation of free-floating international currencies need not seriously disturb Keynesian economic management through state control over the national money. Welfare rights based on national citizenship helped to generalise norms of mass consumption and thereby contributed to full employment levels of demand; and they were sustained in turn by an institutionalised compromise involving Fordist unions and Fordist firms. Securing full employment and extending welfare rights were in turn important axes of party political com-petition. Finally, we should note that some costs of the Fordist compromise and the KWNS were borne within Fordist societies themselves by the relative decline of small and medium firms, by workers employed in disadvantaged parts of segmented labour markets and by women subject to the dual burden of paid and domestic labour. Other costs were borne beyond Fordist societies by economic and political spaces that were integrated into international regimes (such as those for cheap oil or migrant labour) necessary to Atlantic Fordism's continued growth.

As capitalist development undermined the national economy as an object of state management (especially through internationalisation of trade, invest-ment and finance), some familiar expressions of the underlying contradictions of capitalism emerged with renewed force. Thus the wage (both individual and social) came increasingly to be seen as an international cost of production rather than as a source of domestic demand; and money has increasingly come to circulate as an international currency and has thereby weakened Keynesian economic demand management on a national level. This shift in the primary aspect of the contradiction in the money form is related to the tendency for the dynamic of industrial capital to be subordinated to the hypermobile logic of financial capital and the tendency for returns on money capital to exceed those on productive capital. At the same time the relative exhaustion of the Atlantic Fordist growth dynamic posed problems of productivity growth and market saturation (which combine to intensify an emerging fiscal crisis of the state) and problems of how best to manage the transition to the next long wave of economic expansion (which entails changes in the temporal horizons of state economic intervention and thus in the forms and mechanisms of such intervention). The crisis of US hegemony is also reflected in struggles over the shaping of new international regimes and the extent to which they should serve particular American interests rather than the interests of capitalism more generally.[8] In addition, new conflicts and/or forms of struggle have emerged which escape stabilisation within existing structural forms: two major examples are the crisis of corporatism and the rise of new social movements. New problems have also emerged, such as pollution and new categories of risk, which are not easily managed, regularised or governed within the old forms. Finally we should note that, relative to the growth phase of Atlantic Fordism, some contradictions have increased in importance and/or acquired new forms.

The illogic(s) of globalisation

Viewed in terms of the overall dynamic of capitalism, there is both a logic and an illogic to globalisation. Thus Marx and Engels noted 150 years ago in *The Manifesto of the Communist Party* (1848) that the logic of capitalism points to the formation of a single world market. But their own work also indicated that the fundamental contradictions of capitalism might prevent the full realisation of globalisation and thereby ensure that any attempts to move in this direction are inherently unstable. This is especially clear in the impact of the neo-liberal form of globalisation on the forms of appearance of the structural contradictions and strategic dilemmas inherent in capital accumulation. Neo-liberalism could well be described as the hegemonic strategy for economic globalisation due to its support by leading international economic bodies (such as the OECD, IMF and World Bank), its primacy in the United States (the still undisputed capitalist hegemon) and in other anglophone countries (notably Britain, Australia, New Zealand and Canada), the significance of neo-liberal policy adjustments (even in the absence of a more radical neo-liberal regime change) in most other advanced capitalist economies and its paradigmatic status for restructuring the post-socialist economies and integrating them into the global economy. But even a hegemonic strategy can prove irrational and, despite its pretensions to represent the general interest, serve to promote only particular and one-sided interests in a blinkered and short-termist manner.

This point can be elaborated by considering how current neo-liberal trends in globalisation increase the importance of the first side of each of the contradictions mentioned in the preceding section. These trends reinforce the abstract-formal moment of exchange value in these structural forms at the expense of the substantive-material moment of use value. For it is capital in these abstract moments that is most easily disembedded from specific places and thereby freed to 'flow' freely through space and time.[9] However, in each of its more concrete moments, capital has its own particular productive and reproductive requirements. These can often be materialised only in specific types of spatio-temporal location. This leads to a general tension between neo-liberal demands to accelerate the flow of abstract (money) capital through an increasingly disembedded space and the need for the more concrete forms of capital to be 'fixed' in time and place as well as embedded in specific social relations as a condition for their valorisation. Brenner has expressed this well:

> No matter how rapidly turnover times are accelerated, the moment of territorialisation remains endemic to capital, a basic structural feature of its circulation process. Capital remains as dependent as ever upon relatively fixed, place-bound technological-institutional ensembles in which technology, the means of production, forms of industrial organisation and labor-power are productively combined to create and extract surplus-value. The processes of apparent deterritorialisation associated with economic globalisation and the massive growth of finance capital since the early 1980s are therefore only one dimension of a more complex, unevenly articulated process of global sociospatial restructuring in which the reterritorialisation of both cities and states has played a constitutive role.
>
> (Brenner 1997: 11–12)

Indeed, even where the two forms are relatively de-coupled as distinct fractions of capital, a concrete 'spatio-temporal fix' is still needed to enable disembedded capital to flow more easily (Harvey 1982). In the case of global finance capital, of course, the grid of global cities (Sassen 1996a) provides this 'fix'. Moreover, since abstract capital or 'capital in general' cannot be valorised without the continuing valorisation of at least some particular capitals (as well as, perhaps, through competition, uneven development, and 'gales of creative destruction', the devalorisation of others), this general tension inevitably creates a whole series of contradictions and dilemmas.

I have already considered some of these contradictions in the context of the crisis of Atlantic Fordism and the KWNS and will shortly comment briefly on their manifestation in the so-called 'Asian crisis'. But now I want to consider two specific new forms of contradiction and dilemmas that have emerged in the present period of 'after-Fordist' accumulation. The first problem is evident in the paradox noted by Veltz (1996: 12) that '(t)he most advanced economies function more and more in terms of the extra-economic'. The paradox rests on the increasing interdependence between the economic and extra-economic factors making for structural or systemic competitiveness. For this generates major new contradictions that affect the spatial and temporal organisation of accumulation. Thus, temporally, there is a major contradiction between short-term economic calculation (especially in financial flows) and the long-term dynamic of 'real competition' rooted in resources (skills, trust, collective mastery of techniques, economies of agglomeration and size) which take years to create, stabilise and reproduce. And, spatially, there is a fundamental contradiction between the economy considered as a pure space of flows and the economy as a territorially and/or socially embedded system of extra-economic as well as economic resources and competencies. This poses new dilemmas for stabilising the capital relation over an expanding range of scales and over increasingly compressed as well as extended temporal horizons of action.

Another emerging major contradiction in the after-Fordist (or, at least, the post-industrial) accumulation regime is that between the information economy and the information society. Whereas the former is concerned with the private appropriation of knowledge in the form of 'intellectual property rights' so that it can become the basis for monopoly rents and national competitiveness (and is thereby subject to many of the tendencies towards market failure long recognised in studies of the 'economics of information'), the latter is concerned with broadening public access to knowledge as a source of personal empowerment and the expansion of the public sphere.

The re-emergence and transformation of the basic contradictions inherent in the capital relation generate fundamental problems of collective action as well as more or less acute dilemmas for individual economic or political actors. One such dilemma concerns the balance between de-skilling, hire-and-fire, and de-localising strategies and re-skilling, investment in human capital and mobilising the tacit social knowledge found in particular localities. For many firms, these and the other dilemmas generated by the contradictory nature of the capital relation are relatively easy to resolve at the individual firm level because of the nature of their inputs, products or markets (e.g., Storper 1997). But, despite claims for the superiority of the market mechanism, the pursuit of individual solutions need not produce a coherent collective solution even in the long run.

Likewise, as the crisis of the KWNS developed, political actors initally faced the false dilemma of mounting a one-sided attack on wages as a cost of production or providing one-sided support for wages as a source of national economic demand. An analogous dilemma in this context was that between abandoning demand management in favour of monetarism (national or international) and an equally one-sided resort to 'Keynesianism in one country' and subsidies for crisis-hit industries. This in turn was linked to the choice between a one-sided liberalisation of economies (especially financial markets) that would reinforce the dissociation of financial and industrial capital and the pursuit of neo-mercantilist or protectionist strategies that might force greater cooperation on to these two fractions of capital. A related dilemma within the KWNS framework was between retrenching the welfare state and attacking the social wage as a cost of international production and defending welfare employment, public services and transfers without regard to their impact on international competitiveness. What unified these opposed but equally false solutions to the crisis of Atlantic Fordism and the KWNS was their one-sided emphasis on tackling one or other moment of the contra-dictions in different structural forms. They differed in opting for unilateral commitment to reinvigorating the national scale of economic and political organisation or else unconditionally supporting (or surrendering to) the illogic of abstract capital in unrestricted global motion. The policy debate has since gone beyond this global–national framework as the search intensifies for some other scale on which the structural contradictions and strategic dilemmas might again be reconciled through an appropriate spatio-temporal fix and institutionalised compromise for an extended period.

This is where more general collective action problems become significant in both the economic and political domains. Economically, they are reflected in conflicts between the requirements of 'capital in general' and the interests of particular capitals. This conflict is always subject to hegemonic struggles over specific accumulation strategies, always depends on particular spatio-temporal fixes which cannot be guaranteed, and is often secured in practice only through trial-and-error experimentation which reveals the requirements of capital in general more through continued failure than sustained success (see Jessop 1990). Politically, collective action problems occur in the conflict between the state's economic functions (especially for securing certain con-ditions for the valorisation of capital and the social reproduction of labour power) and its overall political responsibility for maintaining social cohesion in a socially divided, pluralistic social formation. Together these problems create formidable meta-governance problems in securing a 'requisite variety' in the forms of economic management, regularisation, and governance and modulating these different forms with 'requisite irony' in the recognition that most attempts at economic management, regularisation and governance fail but that non-intervention is itself a form of intervention which has its own limitations and its own forms of failure.

An excursus on the Asian crisis

Given this volume's concern with globalisation and Asia-Pacific, it may be worth relating my analysis to the 'Asian Crisis'. This notion needs just as much deconstruction and de-mystification as the concept of globalisation but, rather than undertake that task here, I will simply note some aspects that can be illuminated by my earlier comments.

Important aspects of the so-called 'crisis' have been produced by the 'illogic(s) of globalisation'. In particular, the neo-liberal emphasis on encouraging global flows of disembedded capital has contributed significantly to the form and dynamic of the crisis – especially by helping to undermine the relative 'structured coherence' that existed between the East Asian export-oriented economies, their national security developmental states and the regional geo-politics of the Cold War period. Export-oriented growth prioritises the wage as an international cost of production at the expense of its role in generating domestic demand; this is reinforced where the wage rela-tion can be subordinated to an exportist and workfarist (rather than welfare) logic through a strong national security state that also restricts opportunities for organisation in favour of workers' economic, political and social rights. The catch-up dynamic of most East Asian economies also privileges the allocation of credit according to long-term growth priorities and hence the subordination of the national money (and international aid or loans) to investment rather than consumption. This also requires a strong develop-mental state and/or close coordination between banking and industrial capi-tals that are mobilised behind the national accumulation strategy. In this sense we can characterise the initial mode of regulation in most East Asian newly industrialising economies in ideal-typical terms as a 'Listian Workfare National State' (or LWNS) – the exception being what one might, by analogy, describe as a more 'Ricardian Workfare Colonial Regime' in Hong Kong.[10]

As export-led growth continued in the LWNS, however, it became harder to maintain the initial economic, political, and social institutional fix with its relative 'structured coherence' around the national scale. Pressures developed to move towards more Schumpeterian (innovation and competitiveness-oriented) forms of economic intervention and workfare as well as to address problems of domestic demand and social welfare. Satisfying these pressures would require major institutional changes in the economy and state that would inevitably threaten certain sectors of the dominant economic and political elites. This has contributed in turn to an emerging crisis in state forms and political domination. Such problems have been particularly acute in the second-tier East Asian newly industrialised economies (NIEs), which have experienced a much faster catch-up process, more rapid integration into the emerging regional as well as global division of labour, and greater economic, social and political stresses due to uneven development.

This brief account helps us interpret the differential impact of 'globalisa-tion' on the East Asian economies. Two aspects are worth noting: first, the increasing cost pressures in the East Asian economies as they compete with each other and even newer NIEs in the region (such as China and Vietnam) for market share, seek to cover the costs of new rounds of investment and technological innovation, cope with the appreciation of the dollar to which their national monies are pegged and address workers' demands for higher wages and social welfare benefits; and, second, the de-stabilisation of national systems of credit allocation through the attempted global imposition of liberalisation and deregulation, the use of short-term dollar-denominated foreign credits to finance long-term investment, the additional inflow of short-term speculative 'hot money', and the search for easier profits in land, property and stock market speculation (not to mention intensified political corruption) as compared to industrial production. These two sets of factors – both more closely linked to the private than public sector – made the East Asian economies (especially second-tier NIEs) increasingly vulnerable to currency speculation despite their having what orthodox economists are usually pleased to call strong underlying 'fundamentals', namely, high domestic savings, budget surpluses, low inflation and good growth prospects. Unsurprisingly, then, the crisis itself was triggered by the collapse of financial bubbles previously generated by hypermobile speculative capital (aided and abetted, of course, by local economic and political forces) rather than by long-term balance of trade problems.

Hong Kong, Singapore, and Taiwan, the three first-tier East Asian economies with the strongest trading accounts and foreign exchange reserves, were less affected than their brother-dragon South Korea, with its deeper-rooted institutional crisis as well as short-term debt problems. Second-tier NIEs (notably Thailand, Indonesia, Malaysia and the Philippines) have suffered even more due to their more acute combination of foreign debt and domestic institutional crises. Of those East Asian economies affected, the so-called 'IMF-3' (South Korea, Thailand and Indonesia) will be drawn furthest into the 'illogic' of globalisation as a result of the IMF and World Bank's 'neo-liberal' conditionalities and structural adjustment programmes – unless a different escape route from the crisis can be constructed on a regional scale, beginning with a 'dollar-free' regional currency regime and the deepening of the intra-regional division of labour and associated intra-regional trade. Such a solution is, of course, unacceptable to the IMF and the United States. But it is surely worth noting here the increasing worries among western economic and political elites about the possible adverse impacts of the IMF's neo-liberal debt regime on global demand and hence on growth in Western economies themselves.

The illogic(s) of globalisation and the political economy of scale

This excursus serves to illustrate some of the problems involved in the political economy of scale. This concept refers to the strategic selectivity of the inter-scalar division of labour and to struggles to shape this selectivity. For present purposes the relations between capital and the state are most significant – relations which involve far more than a simple opposition between capital's search to reduce its place-dependency and the state's search to fix capital inside its own territory. For increasingly open economies mean that national states can no longer act as if their main task is to manage and defend their respective 'national economies'. Instead they must increasingly manage the re-articulation of scales in a period marked by the 'relativisation of scale'. The respective needs of capital and the state are reflected in a variable mix of institutional forms and governance mechanisms involved in stabilising specific economic spaces in however provisional, partial and temporary a manner in the face of continuing volatility, market failures and economic (and other) conflicts. Moreover, for various reasons, a key role in economic governance in this regard still falls to the state system. Indeed, in the absence of supranational states in the triads (let alone within the global economy as a whole) with powers equivalent to those of the national state, we find constantly renewed attempts by the latter to re-claim power for themselves by managing the relationship among different scales of economic and political organisation. This is evident not only in the formation of the triads but on all other scales too.

As the global economic hierarchy is redefined we find increased emphasis on three supra-national growth poles that exclude significant areas of the globe. These are based on the regional hegemonies of the USA, Japan and Germany and reflected in attempts to create the North American Free Trade Area, European Economic Space, and some form of Asian Pacific Economic Cooperation. Each of these in turn has its own spatial and scalar divisions of labour and associated tangled hierarchies of space and place. There is already a material basis to these triadic developments, of course, with a growing intensity of intrabloc trade (most marked in the European Union but also seen in the other two triads) and/or further deepening of the interregional division of labour within each bloc. This development may eventually come to provide a new privileged scale on which to begin the re-regularisation of capital accumulation and thereby limit the illogic of the neo-liberal forms of globalisation. For this to happen, however, the dominance of neo-liberalism in two of the three triads (America and Europe) must first be reversed and new forms of spatio-temporal governance be developed.

Recent celebration of 'triad power' should not, however, blind us to three other important tendencies: (a) the growing interpenetration of the so-called triad powers themselves as they seek to develop and to deepen specific complementarities and as multinationals headquartered in each triad form strategic alliances with partners in others; (b) shifts in the spatial hierarchies within each triad due to uneven development – reflected not only in shifts among 'national economies' but also in the rise and fall of regions, new forms of 'north–south' divide and so forth; and (c) the re-emergence of regional and local economies within some national economies or, in some cases, cross-cutting national borders – whether such resurgence is part of the overall globalisation process and/or develops in reaction to it. All of these changes have their own material and/or strategic bases and thus contribute to the complex ongoing re-articulation of global–regional–national–local economies.

These complexities point in turn to the potential for alliance strategies among states on similar or different regional scales (e.g., the European Union, whether as an intergovernmental organisation of nation-states or a 'Europe of the regions') to secure the basis for economic and political survival as the imperatives of structural competitiveness on a global scale make themselves felt. Others may call for protectionism on different scales as past regional and local modes of growth are disrupted (ranging from 'Fortress Europe' to 'new localisms', from the Sao Paulo Forum or the People's Plan for the Twenty-First Century to the informal economic self-organisation of shanty towns). Nonetheless, in general terms, as noted by Mittelman, '(r)egionalism in the 1990s is not to be considered as a movement toward territorially based autarkies as it was during the 1930s. Rather, it represents concentration of political and economic power competing in the global economy, with multiple interregional and intraregional flows' (Mittelman 1996b: 190).

These alliances will vary with the position of the economies concerned in the global hierarchy. Thus, whilst a small open economy (whether capitalist, post-socialist, or socialist) might seek closer integration with the dominant economic power in its immediate triadic growth pole, the dominant power might seek not only selectively to bind neighbouring economies into its strategic economic orbit but also to enter alliances with other dominant triad powers. An alternative strategy for a small open economy is to seek niche markets in the global economy (perhaps through encouraging strategic alliances with key firms in each triad region) or to form regional alliances with other small economies (whether they share borders or not) as a basis of increasing their economic capacities and leverage.

A further scale of action that is emerging (or re-emerging) also seems to cut across conventional geo-economic and geo-political hierarchies. This is the urban scale. There are three significant changes occurring here: (a) the vast expansion of the size and scale of leading cities within urban hierarchies so that they become larger metropolitan or regional entities with several centres (on extended metropolitan regions and urban corridors in Pacific Asia, see also Forbes, this volume); (b) an increasing structural integration and strategic orientation of cities' activities beyond national space – an orientation which creates potential conflicts with the national state as some cities become potential 'regional states' less oriented to their respective national hinterlands than to their ties with cities and economic spaces abroad (witness the increasing use of the 'hub' and 'network' metaphors); and, paradoxically, (c) the growing role of some leading cities (rather than, as hitherto, specific firms or sectors) as state-sponsored and state-protected 'national champions' in the face of intensifying international competition.

It is in this last context that we can speak of 'glurbanisation' as a trend analogous to 'glocalisation'. Whereas the latter refers to individual firms' strategies to build global advantage by exploiting local differences, the former would refer to a local or national state's strategies to build global advantage by restructuring urban spaces to enhance their international competitiveness. Moreover, with the increasing interest in dynamic competitive advantages and the bases of structural and/or systemic competitiveness, the extra-economic dimensions of cities have also come to be increasingly significant in urban entrepreneurial strategies. So-called 'natural' economic factor endowments become less important (despite the continuing path-dependent aspects of the positioning of places in urban hierarchies); and socially constructed, socially regularised and socially embedded factors have become more important for interurban competitiveness. Thus 'entrepreneurial cities' must not only position themselves in the economic sphere but also in the extra-economic spheres that are so important nowadays to effective structural or systemic competition. In doing so, moreover, they continue to reproduce local differences that enable transnational firms to pursue their own 'glocalisation' strategies. An analogous process can be found on the regional and cross-border levels.

An important aspect of each of these different spatial scale strategies is their concern to limit competition within the region (structured coherence) through market-oriented cooperation as the basis of more effective competition beyond the relevant spatial scale. The spatial scale on which these compromises will be struck is shaped in part by the nature of commodity chains and economic clusters, by associated spatial externalities (including district, proximity and synergy aspects of agglomeration economies), and by the existing forms of social embeddedness of economic relations and learning processes (cf. Porter 1990; Camagni 1995; Messner 1996; Smith 1988).

The existence of regional projects is no guarantee, of course, that real economic spaces with a 'structured coherence' and sustainable competitive advantages will emerge. Apart from any doubts one might have about current projects in particular cases, scepticism is also prompted by the failure of various interwar proposals for regional federations in Europe (in the Balkan, Baltic or Danubian regions) due to divergent economic and/or political interests; by the checkered record of regional cooperation agreements among developing countries (ranging from free trade areas to economic communities); and by the problems involved in the development of bodies such as ASEAN (The Association of Southeast Asian Nations) and APEC. These difficulties in launching and consolidating new regional blocs reflect the complex cooperative–competitive–conflictual relations that are involved in any regional bloc and the 'geo-governance' tensions to which they give rise. In short they raise problems of economic coordination within economic spaces identified as manageable from the viewpoint of a given spatio-temporal accumulation strategy and between the relevant economic actors and the extra-economic forces whose cooperation is needed to support that strategy. There is no reason to expect that all the factors needed for a successful regional or local strategy will be found within the borders of the economic space that provides its primary location.

Conclusions

I have argued that globalisation is not a single causal mechanism but a complex and even contradictory trend resulting from many causal processes.

I am not denying the evidence for increasing structural interdependence on a global scale in many different fields nor for the increasing importance of the global as the most extensive strategic horizon of action for ever more actors. But we must decompose globalisation into its various constitutive processes and also consider the counter-tendencies that hinder its complete realisation. There are objective limits to economic globalisation due to capital's need not only to disembed economic relations from their old social integument but also to re-embed them into new supportive social relations. Indeed, as Veltz has recently argued, hard economic calculation increasingly rests on mobilising soft social resources, which are irreducible to the economic and resistant to such calculation (1996: 16).

Economic globalisation is a contradictory phenomenon that necessarily produces, as its support, a space of flows and, as its nemesis, the importance of place, a source of objective and subjective resistance. The neo-liberal form of globalisation which is currently dominant (but has by no means become hegemonic in all quarters) finds it particularly difficult to manage this balance between the abstract-formal moments of global accumulation and its concrete-material moments. It is this inability to reconcile these moments on a global scale that generates the continued search for a 'spatio-temporal fix' and institutionalised compromise on less inclusive scales which can provide the basis for a favourable insertion into the changing global economic hierarchy and for social cohesion within the relevant economic, political and social space. While many believe that this 'fix' and its associated compromise will eventually be found at a triadic level, the discursive and institutional conditions for this have not yet been established. Nor are they likely to be as long as the neo-liberal strategy predominates globally and within two of the triad regions. In this context, national states remain key players despite the challenge to the taken-for-grantedness of the national scale that has been introduced by the various processes contributing to globalisation. Thus national states seek in different, competing and often conflictual ways to organise the continuing development of globalisation–regionalisation and deal with its repercussions at the national level. In this context regions, sub-regions, and cross-border regions can have both positive and negative effects. They provide important means for national economies to be favourably inserted into the emerging global economy (hence their emerging role as 'national champions'); but their very insertion into that economy can also further fragment national economies and societies and create alternative foci of identity and political legitimacy. It is the paradoxes, dilemmas, contradictions and identity conflicts thereby engendered that make analysis of the logic(s) and illogic(s) of globalisation such a rich topic for research.

Notes

1 Thus there was less international competition in identical or similar products before 1913 and trade mostly involved noncompeting products, such as primary products exchanged for manufactured goods (Rodrik 1997: 35). The role of FDI is much greater relative to portfolio investment; wholesale global financial markets are now as significant as national financial markets; and portfolio investments are becoming more arcane (Zysman *et al.* 1997: 46–7).

2 Thus a better comparison is the 1980–90s and the interwar period – when economic and hegemonic crises led to protectionism (cf. Williamson 1996: 19).

3 The experience of the small open economies integrated into the circuits of Atlantic Fordism differs in this regard, of course, from that of larger national economies such as the USA, France, or Germany. This was already reflected in their respective forms of state economic intervention and their articulation with welfare policies.

4 This can occur either by reducing the time a given 'event' takes to produce within a given spatial frame of action; or by increasing the ability to discriminate more steps in an 'event' and so enhancing opportunities to modify its course or outcome by intervening into the event as it happens.

5 Whereas 'glocalisation' is a firm-level strategy, 'glurbanisation' involves the increasing orientation of city strategies (or strategies for cities) to their place within the global urban hierarchy.

6 This is evident from the rise of social movements based on localism, various 'tribalisms', or resurgent nationalism as well as movements (sometimes the same movements) resistant in different ways to globalisation (see the chapters by Dirlik and Mittelman, this volume).

7 This qualification is important because of the above-mentioned arguments about earlier levels of internationalisation or globalisation.

8 This contrasts with the period of postwar international reconstruction when the new international regimes established under American hegemony served broader interests in capital accumulation.

9 The temporal dimension of flow is captured in the metaphors of 'liquidity' and 'stickiness'.

10 For a discussion of the Ricardian Workfare Regime in relation to Hong Kong, see Sum (1998).

3   Globalism and the politics of place

Arif Dirlik

The past decade has witnessed the irruption of place consciousness into social and political analysis. Place consciousness, one recent philosophical inquiry suggests, is integral to human existence, for it is nearly impossible to 'imagine what it would be like if there were no places in the world' (Casey 1993: ix). On the other hand, places are not given, but are produced by human activity, which implies that how we imagine and conceive places is a historical problem. In its most recent manifestation, place consciousness is closely linked to, and appears as the radical other of that other conspicuous phenomenon of the last decade, globalism.

It is becoming daily more evident that globalisation is on its way to replacing the earlier modernisation discourse as a paradigm, as well as a social imaginary. The new paradigm breaks with modernisation in significant ways, most notably in abandoning the spatial and temporal teleology that informed the latter. Basic to it is recognition that while participation in the global capitalist economy is a condition of globalisation, global futures no longer require motion towards a Euro-American model of modernity. At the same time, however, globalisation shares with its predecessor its most fundamental premise: that unbridled development is the fate of humankind. Most importantly, globalisation may represent the universalisation of this developmentalism in its capitalist form.

While globalisation as paradigm responds to a real world situation, therefore, it does not merely describe the world as its advocates seem to pretend, but, much like the earlier modernisation discourse, seeks to transform the world in accordance with a vision that is derivative of capitalist modernity. For all its incoherence, globalisation discourse articulates a reconfiguration of relations of economic and political power globally, that in its hegemony rules out the thinking of alternatives to its developmentalist premises. Even criticism of globalisation discourse, to the extent that it does not confront these fundamental premises, only contributes to the consolidation of its hegemony.

This is where place consciousness comes in. While there is nothing new about place consciousness, it too has acquired renewed visibility in recent years as globalisation ironically has made places more visible in its own contradictory motions, which at once incorporate and marginalise places. For the same reason, places offer critical vantage points from which to sort out the contradictions of globalisation. To the extent that contemporary place consciousness is entangled in globalisation, places offer a counter-paradigm for grasping contemporary realities. The idea of place, too, is discursive, informed by normative premises that challenge the vision of globalisation with an alternative vision that focuses not on the off-ground operations of global capital, with all its institutional and cultural accoutrements, but on the concrete conditions of everyday life. Given that globalisation, in its various economic, political and cultural consequences, has brought places face-to-face with the operations of capital, places offer not only vantage points for a fundamental critique of globalism, but also locations for new kinds of radical political activity that reaffirm the priorities of everyday life against the abstract developmentalism of capitalist modernity.

I inquire below into the relationship between globalism and place consciousness, and the implications of this relationship for contemporary configurations of the ways in which we seek to grasp the world. The discussion has three goals. The first is to bring some terminological clarity to discussions of place, which I find somewhat confusing in their juxtapositions of the global and the local, or the spatial and the place-based, while using such terms as local, spatial and place-based interchangeably. Second, on the basis of such clarification, I seek to rephrase the problem of the global and the local, specifically, to address a certain asymmetry in the formulation of the relationship between the two. Finally, I will make a case for a specifically place-based consciousness, by considering the implications of places for conceptions of development, for categories of social analysis such as class, gender and ethnicity, and for the ways in which we deal with questions of culture in cultural criticism. I will suggest on the basis of these three sets of questions that it may be best to conceive of places and place-based consciousness not as a legacy of history or geography, but as a project that is devoted to the creation and construction of new contexts for thinking about politics and the production of knowledge.

Global/local: spatial/place-based

For all their supposed concrete referentiality, the global and the local are terms that derive their meanings from each other, rather than from reference to any specifically describable spatiality. The term 'global', used as a signifier for certain processes (economic, political, social and cultural), obviously does not refer to the globe as a representation of the whole world conceived geometrically. Not only are large parts of the world left out of those processes, but even in those parts of the world that are included in the processes, the processes appear as pathways in networks of one kind or another that leave untouched or even reduce to marginality significant surfaces of what is implied by a term such as global.[1] The global, therefore, is something more than national or regional, but it is by no means descriptive of any whole; at its most abstractly discursive, it may refer to anything other than the local. Projected on to realms beyond that of the physically geographic, such as realms of culture and psychology, it is also not universal.[2] To burden it with further complications, it is in constant motion.

The global, nevertheless, would seem in our day to call into question spaces defined by the political boundaries of the nation, which has called into question the meaning of its spatial other, the local. The local in an earlier usage derived its meaning from its contradiction to the national, or the universal. Increasingly, however, the local derives its meaning from its juxtaposition to the global. The very uncertainty about the meaning of the global condemns it to ambiguity. Unless the boundaries of the local may be drawn by fiat, as in national administrative structures, which are blurred by globalisation, however, the local is as difficult to locate as the global which endows it with meaning. Hence, unlike in an earlier day when the local derived its meaning from the national, it is not surprising to find that nations and entire extra-national regions may qualify as referents for the local.

It is not surprising, given the conflation of the language of space and place with that of the global and the local, that those terms too should be imbued through and through with the ambiguities of the latter juxtaposition. In much of the discussion about places, 'local', 'spatial', and 'place-based' are used interchangeably. The conflation is not just intellectual; it is also, and even more deeply, political. The very conceptualisation of globalism is revealed upon closer examination to be a kind of spaceless and timeless operation, which rather than render it vacuous as a concept, ironically bolsters its pretensions to a new kind of universalism, rendering it into a point of departure for all other spatialisations. It is not very surprising that anything less than the global should be mobilised in juxtaposition to it as its other, confounding the possibility of profound differences among the spatial, the local and the place-based. Thus it becomes possible to speak of the spatial, the local and the place-based in the same breath, forgetting that while the local derives its meaning from the global, spatial itself derives its meaning from a parallel with globality, and stands in the same oppositional relationship to the place-based as the global does to the local. This confounding of terminology may be illustrated concretely through Doreen Massey's influential theorisation of a socialised conception of place. As she puts it in a recent work,

> If . . . the spatial is thought of in the context of space-time and as formed out of social interrelations at all scales, then one view of a place is as a particular appreciation of those relations, a particular moment in those networks of social relations and understandings . . . But the particular mix of social relations which are thus part of what defines the uniqueness of any place is by no means all included within that place itself. Importantly, it includes relations which stretch beyond – the global as

part of what constitutes the local, the outside as part of the inside. Such a view of place challenges any possibility of claims to internal histories or to timeless identities. The identities of places are always unfixed, contested and multiple. Places viewed in this way are open and porous.

(Massey 1994: 5)

That place consciousness does not of necessity require spatial boundedness or the exclusion of the extra – local, temporal stasis, or social homogeneity are important reminders that these putative characteristics of place consciousness were more a fabrication of modernist prejudice than a description of the realities of premodern (and modern) local societies. On the other hand, this critique of the marginalisation of places in a modernist radicalism does not quite abolish the problematic of place; places may not be 'place-bound', but the abolition of the distinction between place-based and spatial reintroduces an ambiguity at another level by denying the distinctiveness of the place-based: the effort to salvage place ends up by declaring that there is nothing special about place after all. Massey's conceptualisation needs to be amended by a further critique of the spatialisation of places which is overly zealous, I think, in disassociating place from fixed location. This is where ecological conceptions of place, which are almost totally absent from these discussions (and marginalised by them in the preoccupation with the 'social construction of space') have some crucial insights to contribute by once again bringing nature (even if it is only a 'myth of nature') into the conceptualisation of place.

The ecological conception insists that an important aspect of the concept of place is its groundedness in topography.[3] Most theoretical discussions of place of which I am aware (including Massey's) take place within the context of urban geography and sociology, with the consequence that this aspect of place consciousness disappears into the background. Ecologically conceived discussions of places, by contrast, are of necessity attentive to questions of the fixity of places and the limitations set on the production of place by its immediate environment.[4]

The topographical grounding of place immediately points to a second question, that of boundaries. If place is not enclosed within exclusive boundaries, can the concept of space therefore dispense with the problem of boundaries? Massey's reconceptualisation of space and place in terms of social relations (the spatial is social relations 'stretched out' (Massey 1994: 2)) is quite fruitful. Without some delimitation of how far social relations may be 'stretched out', however, place may be meaningless, especially in these days of diasporas where even kinship relations, for example, may be stretched out over the globe, making place indistinguishable from the global. This may be the reason that, for all her effort at specifying place, Massey's discussion continues to use place-based, spatial and local interchangeably, where place is on occasion equated with the territory of the nation.[5] Here, too, attention to the groundedness of places in ecology and topography is important. This is not to return to some kind of geographic determinism or bounded notion of place, but to suggest that any intellectually and politically critical notion of place must recognise some notion of boundary; porosity of boundaries is not the same as the abolition of boundaries.

Groundedness, which is not the same as immutable fixity, and some measure of definition by flexible and porous boundaries, I suggest, are crucial to any conceptualisation of place and place-based consciousness. Place as metaphor suggests groundedness from below, and a flexible and porous boundary around it, without closing out the extra-local, all the way to the global. What is important about the metaphor is that it calls for a definition of what is to be included in the place from within the place-some control over the conduct and organisation of everyday life – rather than from above, from those placeless abstractions such as capital, the nation-state, and their discursive expressions in the realm of theory.

Place conceived as project provides a context in which we may reformulate the ways in which we think of spaces presently. What the project may be is best enunciated through a consideration of the implications of place or place-based consciousness for the categories through which the modernist project expresses itself: development, categories of social analysis and culture. But first a reformulation of the problem that recognises the intractability of the problem of the local and the global, or the place-based and the spatial.

Hybridity and contradiction: the unity of the global and the local

There is an asymmetry in almost all discussions of the problem of the global and the local. It is in the relegation of the local to subordinate status against the global, which is also associated with the universal. This almost inevitably issues in the objectification of the local which must then be explained or defended. What if the global were local, or place-based, just as the local or place-based were global?

This is the question raised in a central way by Latour (1993) who addresses the question of the global and the local as part of a broader project of deconstructing modernity (i.e. Western modernity), which was made possible by dividing humans from non-humans (culture/nature), that in turn enabled another divide, the West and the Rest (Us and Them). These two divides that underlie 'the modern constitution', as he puts it, necessitated procedures of 'purification' and 'translation' (separating the various realms in thought, followed by mediating their relationships) which ironically was to result in the proliferation of hybrids, negating the whole project of modernity. The global and the local provide just such a case of hybridity which, in their separation, enable an illusion of the universal against the parochial, in the process disguising its own affinities with the pre- and the non-modern:

Just as the adjectives 'natural' and 'social' designate representations of that which are natural nor social in themselves, so the words 'local' and 'global' offer points of view on networks that are by nature neither local nor global, but are more or less long and more or less connected. What I have called the modern exoticism consists in taking these two pairs of oppositions as what defines our world and what would set us apart from all others.

(Latour 1993: 122)

For Latour, the metaphor of the network assumes a crucial epistemological part in questioning not only the division between the global and the local, but the very idea of a distinct modernity, for 'the moderns have simply invented longer networks by enlisting a certain type of nonhumans' (Latour 1993: 117). He observes, moreover, that 'as concepts, "local" and "global" work well for surfaces and geometry, but very badly for networks and topology' (Latour 1993: 119). His own conception of the relationship between the global and the local is expressed through the deceptively simple 'railroad model':

Is a railroad local or global? Neither. It is local at all points, since you always find sleepers and railroad workers, and you have stations and automatic ticket machines scattered along the way. Yet it is global, since it takes you from Madrid to Berlin or from Brest to Vladivostok. However, it is not universal enough to take you just anywhere.

(Latour 1993: 117)

If the railroad is neither local nor global, it is arguably though not necessarily both local and global. In conflating the two, Latour's goal is to bring down to size claims to globality, and attendant epistemological claims to universality. That Latour uses the metaphor of the railroad to illustrate his argument, instead of, say, the footpath or the airplane, may alert us immediately to some of the problems in his conceptualisation of networks, and his suppression of historicity in deconstructing modernity. But it may be fruitful for the moment to pursue the line of thought he offers where the global and the local are concerned.

The ultimate indistinguishability of the global and the local may be more pertinent presently, as a distinctive characteristic of the regime of global capitalism. 'Glocal' expresses cogently what Latour has in mind by the hybridity of the global and the local. The question here is whether or not hybridity, as Latour proposes, provides a resolution of these problems. Hybridity itself as a concept, no less in Latour's than in postcolonial conceptualisations, is a static resolution of the problem of difference in naturalised boundaries, that does not recognise the contradictions produced by hybridity, the ways in which hybridity produces its own structural contexts, and how those contexts, themselves products of human activity, come to delimit the resolution of the problems it presents.

In spite of this problem, Latour's phrasing of the problem of the local and the global yields an important conclusion: that the question of the local cannot be eliminated or marginalised without an equal elimination or marginalisation of the global, which restores to the problematic of the local/ global a symmetry that is missing from most discussions. If the local is not to be conceived without reference to the global, it is possible to suggest that the global cannot exist without the local, which is the location for its producers and consumers of commodities, not to speak of the transnational institutions themselves. With the significant exception of finance capital, which indeed moves increasingly in cyberspaces, most operations of global capital are located in places; what, after all are the 'commodity chains' of flexible production but networks of production? Even the mystifying procedures of corporate decision-making power is located somewhere (which is an additional reason for caution against the mystification of transnationality, see the chapters by Sassen and Jessop, this volume).

The question then is not the confrontation of the global and the local, but of different configurations of 'glocality'. Instead of assigning some phenomena to the realm of the global and others to the realm of the local, it may be necessary to recognise that in other than the most exceptional cases, these phenomena are all both local and global, but that they are not all local and global in the same way. Such recognition may also help clarify what is distinctive about place-based thinking or imagination. The task that follows immediately is to inquire into the meaningfulness of any social analysis that does not take place seriously as not just a location for, but as a determinant of the ways in which we think social categories.

Place in social and cultural analysis

Massey's (1994) reminder that what makes a place unique is a 'particular mix of social relations' is well taken but one-sided. If places are socially produced, as Lefebvre (1991: 68–99) tells us, and are not merely preordained locations where things happen, the production of place includes as part of its very constitution the production of that 'particular mix of social relations', which implies that social relations, and the categories in terms of which we conceive them, make sense most if we conceive them in terms of place-based manifestations, if not only in place-bound ways. That particular mix, in turn, produces the particular set of structures that give concrete meaning to social relations represented in categories of class, gender, race, etc. – and place itself. This has become more and more inescapable as (a) the production of places under Global Capitalism (as either creation or destruction) become a condition of life, and (b) dissatisfaction with this situation has led to the questioning of the hegemonic implications of concepts divorced from places.

Most conspicuous in this regard are questions that have been raised concerning what Escobar (1995) calls 'development discourse'. Development discourse, assuming universality for its own particular definitions of poverty and wealth, stagnation and progress, and ultimately what constitutes a good life, has led to an invasion of the world by Euro-American capitalism (now joined by others), which ultimately has had destructive consequences for societies and natures (Escobar 1995). In a similar vein, Pigg (1992: 491–513) argues in a recent article that essential to the development discourse is an erasure of differences, in her case, the erasure of differences between living villages in Nepal to create a 'generic village' that is more easily comprehended by developmentalist bureaucrats (foreign or Nepalese), and lend themselves more easily to development schemes directed from afar. The erasure of difference, however, is not the responsibility just of far-away development bureaucrats, because it is 'localised' through the complicity of the state, and native leaders who have internalised the culture of developmentalism, which is a problem that is not peculiar to Nepal but describes the complicity in erasing differences of all modernising nation-states. Indeed, it is difficult to say in historical hindsight which has been the bigger problem in the creation of such generic categories: a voracious capitalism ever invading places or a nation-state inventing homogeneities. This may be a moot question ultimately because the complicity of state and capital (or, in the case of existing socialisms, of state and managerial bureaucrats) extends over the history of modernity. Closer attention to difference, which implies closer attention to place, leads Escobar to conclude that while developmentalism has already destroyed much (in Latin America), it has not destroyed everything, and the hybrid forms that place-based native traditions have forced on a universalist developmentalism may yet provide alternative ways of thinking about life and change against a development discourse that recognises no exterior (Escobar 1995: 217–22). Place in any case is essential to the critique of developmentalism, and imagining alternatives to it.

The questioning of developmentalist universalism, which is one aspect, albeit a fundamental one, of the questioning of universalist social categories inevitably raises questions about the universality of categories of social analysis, which are all products of the same modernity that produced developmentalism, and are implicated in it one way or another. In this case, however, there is greater complexity to both the sources of such questioning, and to its consequences, which has played a major part in the debates over the global and the local, the spatial and the place-based. Are classes conceivable without reference to places? Are genders, races and ethnicities? Is the obliviousness to places in the use of such categories responsible for the rendering of critical categories into instruments of hegemony? The sources of such questions are complex, because the questions do not arise unmediated from the conditions of capitalism or the state, but are mediated by differences that emerge simultaneously with the enunciation of the categories themselves: for instance, questions of gender and race in class, questions of race and class in gender, questions of gender and class in race. Place appears as one more such critical question.[6]

Ironically, the emphasis on place in social analysis may be more important than ever as globalisation transnationalises classes and genders, but not equally among all groups. It may be more valid than ever to speak of transnational classes or a transnational feminism, but effective participation in transnationality is restricted for the most part to the elite in various societies, and further distances them from their immediate environments (see Friedman, this volume). Even in the case of these groups, however, attention to place is important to reveal the contradictions in the very processes of transnationalisation.

The consequences are also complex. Places that define themselves in terms of communities, or some kind of 'place-bound' (I use this term intentionally) identity, also end up disguising and suppressing inequalities and oppressions that are internal to place. The ease with which 'communities' blame internal dissension on outside agitators has the obviousness of a cliché. Social categories such as class, gender and race are divisive against the self-image of the community. Could the inequalities that they articulate be faced, let alone resolved, without a sense of the categories as universals? On the other hand, viewed from supracommunity perspective, these categories are also integrative, providing bonds between places, that may be the only defence against supraplace forces (of capital and the state) playing communities against one another to maximise their own powers.

It may be because such categories have assumed hegemonic implications in their complicity with supra-place power that place has begun to intrude insistently into their constitution. But the structural conditions of global capitalism, and the gradual abandonment by nation-states of the responsibilities they had assumed briefly for remedying spatial inequalities in national territories, have done much to underline the placedness of categories of social analysis; because such abandonment has brought places face to face with capital without the intermediation of the state, set places against one another in the competition for attracting capital and, in the process, revealed the fracturing of categories of social analysis along place differences. Hence the arguments heard frequently these days are that classes and class relations are best understood in their place-based manifestations, that gender has a place aspect to it that is not addressed in its qualifications by class and race, that ethnicity which has been globalised in contemporary diasporic motions needs to be understood also in terms of places, which is where different ethnicities confront one another, and that race, which has always been a meaningless category, carries different meanings in different locations. The questioning of hegemony that place makes possible is not an alternative to, but an additional moment – albeit a most fundamental one – in the questioning of the hegemony of homogenising abstractions, this time directed at the very anti-hegemonic categories themselves.

Finally, the question of culture, and the organisation and transmission of knowledge that is an integral part of any conceptualisation of culture as a dynamic force. If we are to engage the question of culture in any anti-hegemonic, critical sense, can we dispense with places? I realise that the notion of culture has been used for long to imprison places, to render place-bound cultural identities into markers of backwardness, which then has provided the excuse for opening them up to 'civilisation' – global and national. But having gone through the latter process already, is it time once again to reaffirm culture as a place-based (not place-bound) phenomenon? Culture being a prime weapon in the struggles over hegemony, the question has a particular urgency in this, the age of global capitalism.

The recent attack on Area Studies in the United States illustrates the changing relationship between culture and knowledge (see Dirlik 1997). Area Studies were themselves products of the post-Second World War mapping of the world to answer the needs of US hegemony, that drew upon an earlier Orientalist culturalism to organise knowledge of the world. Such organisation of knowledge is no longer sufficient to sustain hegemony, as globalisation scrambles areas (and already has rendered irrelevant the more comprehensive tripartite division of the world in the Three Worlds paradigm). While the legacies of Orientalism have by no means been abolished, it has become increasingly difficult to speak of distinct cultural areas, or even of national cultures, as a transnational culture industry invades the world. It is culture at its most localised levels that confronts, is transformed by, and appropriates the culture industry's globalised messages – which are more often than not tailored to satisfy local markets, and produce new localisations even as they undermine the possibility of any serious autonomy in the production of culture. Even more radical in its consequences, however, is globalisation in the knowledge industry, which is unhindered by marketing needs (see Thrift, this volume). The so-called 'rational choice' approach to the world, which nourishes off the globalisation of economic, social, political and environmental problems, leads the attack on Area Studies on the grounds that the problems of the world may no longer be resolved at the level of regions, areas and nations. While this is reasonable enough, what often remains unremarked is that the universalist claims of Euro-American scientism, of which 'rational choice' theory is but one expression, in erasing local knowledge, continues an earlier modernisationist tradition of expanding the power of one form of knowledge over others, and sustains a Euro-American hegemony even as it professes a new kind of cosmopolitanism – which proceeds, at best, by cannibalising other ways of knowing, only to make them irrelevant. What go unquestioned by this new scientism are the developmentalist premises of globalisation. Its very legitimacy, in fact, depends on its ability to confront the problems created by development.

My point here is not to defend Area Studies, but rather to point out that to substitute globalisation or rational choice (or even cultural studies) is to replace one form of hegemony with another that is more appropriate to the times. The insistence on culture areas in the mapping of the world, whether promoted by Samuel Huntington, Jiang Zemin or Lee Kuan Yew, falls back upon earlier Orientalist or nationalist reifications of culture, that under the guise of repudiating Eurocentrism misrepresent the reconfiguring of the world by a Global Capitalism which is global precisely because it is no longer shaped by a Eurocentric teleology. Areas such as East or Southeast Asia, or even the latecomer Pacific, are being reconfigured in ways that do indeed render irrelevant the way they had been mapped earlier. The reconfiguration does not of necessity produce a condition of globality, or one form of knowledge that is acceptable across the board (see Jessop, this volume) (except in limited areas), but points to new contradictions that are products of a globalised capitalism and not just hangovers from the past. Globalisation produces its own regionalisations. It is also important to note that globality in one realm, such as the economic, does not automatically imply globality in other realms, such as the political and the cultural. The relationships, in other words, are not smoothly functional, but relationships of contradiction between different network alignments, networks and surfaces, unities and fragmentations.

What is at issue in sorting out these contradictions, I would like to suggest, is not the confrontation between globalisation and areas (or nations), but rather an issue of long-standing historical significance: universalism versus particularism in grasping the world. For those who are unwilling to buy into the ideology of either Area Studies or Globalisation, and see in them different hegemonies appropriate to the different historical circumstances of capitalism, the question that emerges is what kind of knowledge is appropriate to counter this new form of hegemony. We may abandon Area Studies, as they were an expression of an earlier form of hegemony, but may we therefore abandon place-based knowledge without resigning to the hegemony of a global capitalism? Have particular forms of knowledge become irrelevant with globalisation? Or is globalisation producing new kinds of particularisms so that place-based knowledge is of the first order of significance – not in terms of some pristine place-bound purity, but simply as a way to reappropriate places as a condition of living under changed historical circumstances? There is much evidence in the contemporary world to justify a positive response to these questions, much of it negative and even deadly in consequence, which further calls into question particularistic forms of knowledge. On the other hand, if such evidence points to the operations of the universalist claims of global capitalism, and the forms of knowledge appropriate to it, is it particularism that is to bear the burden, or globalisation that in its operations sets different kinds of knowledge against one another in deadly confrontation? Is it possible that the solution to these dilemmas may lie not in confronting globalisation with areas, or nations, but rather in shifting the grounds for the discussion?

In the midst of a 'globalism' craze, it may be important to consider what it is that a place-based imagination has to offer, and what may be the conceptualisation of places that contributes the most to this end. It seems to me that it is necessary, to begin with, to 'place' globalism so as to counteract its mystification of its own location. The agenda of globalism, which seeks further to erase difference even while eulogising the latter, gives away its continuities with earlier discourses of development. If globalism is more efficient as a developmentalist ideology, it is because it seeks to conceal, with some success, that this agenda is set still within the old locations of power, but now with the complicity of Third World states, corporations, intellectuals and experts, who are allowed increasingly to participate in the discourse and processes of development; partly as an unavoidable consequence of their incorporation into a global capitalism, and partly because their participation is deemed to be necessary to the efficient operation of transnationalism. The condition of their participation, nevertheless, is their internalisation of the knowledge and norms of the system. It follows that the stress on place also entails the reconceptualisation of those societies not only against First World domination, but also against the domination of places by nation-states, and against transnationalised classes, genders, ethnicities (e.g. 'diasporic identi-ties') and so forth.

The second aspect is that, under such conditions, places have come to face the operations of global power more directly, as nation-states become more complicit in globalism, and abandon gradually the task they had assumed earlier of mediating the global and the local. In contrast to, say, earlier ideol-ogies of national liberation that rested in the nation-state the responsibility for the defence of places, places now must fend for themselves. This is not to say that the nation-state has become irrelevant, or that it should be conceded to the forces of globalism. But it is more urgent than ever to 'place' the nation-state itself, demystify its claims, and organise against it, if only as a means to resuscitate the connection between place and nation – this time from below. It is also necessary, to this end, to reconsider relations between places, between places and trans-place or supra-place organisational forms, and, finally, across national boundaries, to imagine alternative possibilities in the reorganisation of spaces.

A defence of place

The discussion above indicates, I hope, that the defence or advocacy of place-based imagination here is not a product of a utopian project, but a response to a very real systemic crisis. To speak of places, and new forms of politics informed by places, therefore, is to answer a need for new ways to reorganise political space, which of necessity may be contingent in form, but nevertheless address problems of a systemic nature.

In our day, places become visible in many guises, which may not be very surprising, as the very structural and ideological incoherence of a globalised capitalism has rendered places incoherent as well. I have argued above that places may be incomprehensible without reference to globalisation, which implies that they should partake also of all the contradictions of global capitalism. In fact, places may articulate those contradictions most sharply where they pertain to the conditions of everyday life. These many contradictions may be grouped under two headings that represent the extremes in the relationship of places to globalisation: the marginalisation of places and their incorporation into capitalism (Dirlik 1994b and 1998).

Contrary to claims implicit in the term itself, globalisation proceeds not by encompassing the globe, but by marginalising large areas that are irrelevant to the operations of capital. While these areas include continents like Africa, which as a 'basket-case' is deemed to be quite irrelevant to globalisation, they also include places within the earlier First and Second Worlds that prove to be unsuitable for investment and production. It was the marginalisation of earlier industrial cities in England that first prompted geographers like Doreen Massey to focus attention on places in the early 1980s. As 'flexible production' got under way, the insecurities it created for local communities were responsible in the United States and elsewhere for greater attention to localities and their unpredictable fates under the new regime of production. On an international scale, the movement of capital from place to place (not just nations but locations within nations) has brought place consciousness to the foreground.

Place consciousness has been reinforced by the 'downsizing' of nation-state functions with the neo-Liberal ideology that seeks to accommodate, and provide political leadership to, global capitalism. The dismantling of the welfare state where it only had a weak foundation (as in the US), or in socialist societies, has created a situation where places have to fend for themselves. Ironically, this has helped strengthen place consciousness in such a way as to reinforce the plea for attention to places of political forces such as ecological activists, who have long argued for the ecologically destructive and socially negative consequences of unbridled capitalist development. But it has also made for a more complicated political situation. Socially and politically progressive attention to places these days is often apt to be indistinguishable from place-based movements that blame 'foreigners', native or otherwise, who take jobs away somewhere else, that are oblivious to the fact that such shifts take place within the invisible boundaries of transnational corporations. Whether in its radical or reactionary guise, response to political downsizing calls for greater attention to places, and new kinds of social practices.

Places have also become visible through incorporation into global capitalism. Transnational corporations, which otherwise have little concern for places, nevertheless find it in their interests to 'domesticate' themselves in terms of their marketing operations, but not necessarily in their responsibilities to the communities in which they are 'domesticated'. But they promote the ideology of place nevertheless. Local communities in their turn advertise themselves so as to get in on the pathways of capital. Place is no longer where one lives, but also a commodity to be marketed. It is surely a postmodern phenomenon that a Chinese village, collectivised under socialism but privatised under the so-called Reform regime, recollectivises in response to the pressures of incorporation into capitalism, only to go ahead and globalise by investing in global futures (see Nathan and Kelkan 1997).

It is not surprising, given these complexities, that the advocacy of place presently should cover a broad spectrum socially and politically. They range from indigenous, ecological and social movements (informed widely by women's concerns) around the world that articulate basic concerns for survival in their reaffirmation of spirit, nature and place against developmentalism, to urban movements that seek to protect neighbourhoods, to recollectivisation efforts in China within the context of relations to global markets, to elitist communitarian movements and militia movements of displaced farmers in the US that also draw on earlier religious values. Politically, they cover the whole range from place-based anarchism to right-wing elitism.

It is those movements, including indigenism, that have reasserted the priority of abolishing the alienation of humans from nature, with a corresponding reevaluation of relationships between humans that in my view offer the most radical and possibly the only meaningful criticism of modernist developmentalism – as long as they avoid reification of nature and society, of essentialised communitarianism, and of constructed tradition, and instead view their undertaking as projects without naturalising them.[7]

The questions raised by indigenous alternatives are compelling because they are fundamental. Most importantly, can there be any meaning to the discussion of place without a simultaneous and uncompromising repudiation of the very idea of development? The question immediately invites a second one that is equally basic: if places isolated from one another must be condemned to manipulation from the outside, is there any point in discussing place without also bringing in new forms of supra-place relationships as an alternative to existing institutional mechanisms, whether of capital or the nation-state? The transformation of place, in other words, may be inconceivable without a simultaneous transformation of space because place and space, while analytically distinct, are nevertheless linked in intimate ways.

I would like here to return to the statement I made above about phenomena being inextricably global and local, but that they are not global and local in the same way. While Latour and Escobar use the concept of hybridity with close attention to its structural contexts and consequences, there is nevertheless a constant possibility imbedded in the concept itself of slippage into a dehistoricised and decontextualised localisation of encounters between place and space. Escobar struggles with this problem explicitly but, I think, without a clear resolution, because he is unwilling to confront the question that the possibility of alternative developments he perceives in hybridisation may be prefigured already by the development discourse of which he is critical. He is conscious of differences between different kinds of hybridities, and even the possibility that the static, naturalised, concept of hybridity may suppress the contradictions presented by difference; but he nevertheless stops short of engaging these differences, and hybridity itself, in terms of their internal contradictions, which themselves are inextricable from the contradiction between the inside and the outside, as is implicit in the globalisation of the local, and the localisation of the global. The contradiction is both structural and historical.

Hybridity does not offer a resolution of contradictions between the global and the place-based, but itself begs resolution. Under conditions of 'unequal exchange', the resolution itself is likely to be more in favour of space over place, of abstract power over concrete everyday existence, where the former may even produce the 'differences' of the latter in a process of maximising its power while mystifying its location. This is where the insistence on groundedness, fixity, and the 'myth of nature' assume strategic significance if counter-resolutions to the contradictions of hybridity are to be even conceivable; for they point to the reconquest of space by place as an irreducible goal. This is also where indigenism, and other movements inspired by it, assume an unprecedented significance, both in their reaffirmation of groundedness in land, and in the possibilities that they may offer in the restructuring of space.

By way of conclusion

The defence of place invokes mixed reactions. Where it is not dismissed for its utopianism, it evokes a certain anxiety. To speak of places is to invite suspicions of parochialism, reaction and backwardness. In the United States, it is to bring back the ghost of Pat Buchanan, whose economic nationalism created a scare for a brief while in 1996 among both liberals and conservatives, reminding them of the need to pay greater attention to 'neighbourhoods'.[8]

It is also remarkable, however, that places have emerged as locations for new kinds of social and political activity. Places seem to be on everybody's mind these days because globalisation has brought place consciousness to the foreground in thinking of alternatives to the uncertainties and ravages of unbridled capitalist development. While it is possible to challenge the claims of globalisation from a number of perspectives – as in the case of the region-based critiques undertaken by many of the contributors to this volume – it is places, where the new political economy invades everyday life, that offer possibilities of criticism that is both comprehensive, and productive of new visions of economic and political welfare. Given the politically mixed consequences of place consciousness, I would like to conclude here by briefly addressing three questions that may be crucial to distinguishing progressive from reactionary forms of place-based politics.

First is the question of places in this conceptualisation. I hope it is clear from the discussion above that my conceptualisation of place does not presuppose any pristine untouchability to places. Places all along have been subject to transformation, more so today possibly than any time before. Any radical project of place must insist both on the openness of places to the outside world, and on the need to transform places to resolve questions of inequality that are internal to them. On the other hand, essential to place consciousness is recognition of the diversity of places (especially but not restricted to urban versus rural places), which requires local solutions to place problems, rather than the imposition of an abstract blueprint.

Second is the question of development. Recognition of the integrity of place necessitates a critique of developmentalism, especially of capitalist developmentalism as an earlier socialist developmentalism is no longer an issue. But the critique of developmentalism as represented most recently by the globalisation paradigm should not be confused with the repudiation of change or development *per se*. Those who see in this kind of advocacy a regression to the past should be reminded that the so-called development they enjoy is still not shared by the majority of humankind, who experience globalisation as exploitation and marginalisation. Even for the 'globalised', development under the regime of globalisation brings with it new uncertainties and insecurities, as was evidenced recently by the so-called 'economic melt-down' in East and Southeast Asia, which immediately brought to the surface a lurking consciousness of the contradictions within global capitalism, reviving in the process a supposedly forgotten language of nationalism and colonial domination. The crisis most importantly dramatised the need to control the one truly global (and destructive) constituent of contemporary capitalism, finance capital. It was interesting to this writer that at least one Southeast Asian leader, King Bhumibol Adulyadej of Thailand, responded to the crisis by urging Thais to return to a 'self-sufficient' economy that gave priority to the subsistence needs of the people – although the King was also quick to point out that, 'Modern economists may say that my theory on a self-sufficient economy is outdated and we should replace it with the Western theory of trade' (*The Straits Times* 6 December 1997). Such is the hegemony of capitalist developmentalism that something so simple as the affirmation of attention to human needs should appear backward, and call for apologetic justification. It is this hegemony that needs to be challenged, to secure development that is consonant with human welfare both socially and environmentally. Places are an indispensable point of departure for such a challenge.

The third question is political. The advocacy of place consciousness does not mean the repudiation of political action and organisation at other levels. Jessop (this volume) has pointed to the different levels of governance required in a post-Fordist global system. While most attention focuses on global or regional organisations that are dear to the hearts of global managers, little is said on the consequences of such organisations for people on the ground level. Whether we speak of labour unions, or environmental organisations, or global management, it is more important than ever to consider the way they appear from the bottom up – which is crucial to restoring democracy to everyday life. The point is not to reject action or organisation at these 'higher' levels, but whether such action or organisation is top-down or bottom-up. In this regard, it is also important to reconsider easy dismissals of the nation. As the leader of a well-known contemporary insurgent movement has remarked recently, the destruction of the nation-state may be in the interests of global capital, but it is not in the interests of the people at large who still need the nation-state for their protection; not the state that devotes itself to the management of global capital, but a state that grows out of popular reorganisation from the bottom up (Marcos 1997). Places are the logical point of departure for such reorganisation; not in their fragmentation but in translocal (or, in John Brown Childs' words, 'transcommunal') alliances that are crucial both to their survival, and to the creation of a more democratic economic, social and political life.

That these are difficult tasks does not, therefore, make the advocacy of place a utopian project; at least no more utopian than the promise of globalisation under the regime of global capital. The difference between the two is not a difference between reality and utopia, but a difference in the power to determine the course of human existence. Place-consciousness is in some ways little more than the reaffirmation of the claims of everyday life and welfare against their abstraction in projects of globalisation. It would be no mean achievement if it were to contribute only to the restoration of priority to those claims in thinking about human futures.

A post-script on Hong Kong

In a book on the contemporary global economy published in 1992, *Brave Modern World*, the distinguished French historian of China, Jean Chesneaux, described the contemporary economy as an 'off-ground' economy. It was off-ground because its operations were divorced from the lives of the people that it shaped economically and politically. Chesneaux used Hong Kong as a metaphor for such an economy, not only because Hong Kong as a global city was a hub of the global economy, but also because one could get around in Hong Kong through the many fly-overs without ever having to touch the ground.

Hong Kong is indeed a global city, where it may be difficult to conceive of places as an alternative to globality. And yet, I think Chesneaux was off the mark, in 1992 anyway. We have probably erred in the past in not noticing the many ways in which people who inhabit this global hub may have felt about it. What is remarkable, however, is the emergence of an articulated place consciousness in Hong Kong in response to the political pressures of the last decade. It is as if, once given the chance to express themselves, the people of Hong Kong have become deeply aware of Hong Kong as a place, and even of places within Hong Kong. Hong Kong is still a global city, but the globality now finds a counterpoint in the claims to a particular Hong Kong culture, a particular Hong Kong identity, and Hong Kong as a place of memory that distinguish the people of Hong Kong from other locations on the globe, as well as within the new political space of the People's Republic of China in which Hong Kong has been relocated. Ping-Kwan Leung captures this contrapuntal relationship when he queries: 'can we not seek our own space in the midst of this endless refraction of images and light?' (Leung 1997: 104)

Being on the boundaries of global capitalism and the Chinese nation-state may have sharpened this place consciousness. But we should not overlook the intimate relationship between the new awareness of place, and the calls for democratic participation, which reinforce one another in the assertion of everyday life claims against the abstract demands of capital and the nation-state.

Notes

1 The network character of globalisation has been analysed in depth recently by Castells (1996). It is not that globalisation has no effects outside the networks, but such effects may best be conceived as 'inductive' effects of networks. We need also to underline that marginalisation is not simply of 'areas', but more importantly of people, who may be marginalised even at their locations within the networks. For a critique of what many among the globalisers have come to describe as the '20 : 80 society' (that is 20 per cent of the population necessary, the rest redundant), see, Martin and Schumann (1997).

2 My distinctions here between the global and the universal, and surface and network, owe much to the discussion of the problem of modernity in Latour (1993).

3 For a critical discussion of efforts to reconcile Marxism to 'green' thought, see Castree (1995).

4 Such discussions are voluminous, and represent a spectrum from the bizarre to the eminently sensible. For a sampling of reasoned defences of ecologically conceived places, see Dobson (1991).

5 For example, Massey (1994: 8) describes national liberation movements as 'the classic case of place-based struggles', ignoring the part nationalism has played in erasing places.

6 I should stress here that 'placing' categories is intended to complicate and refine analysis, not to abolish the categories. My intention here is quite different from that underlying a recent (1996) collection, *Putting Class in Its Place: Worker Identities in East Asia*, edited by Elizabeth J. Perry. While the editor and the contributors profess similar goals to mine here, most of the essays end up rendering the question of class largely irrelevant, partly because their positivistic understanding of class does not allow for much complexity.

7 I am quite cognizant in the discussion below of the existence of different notions of what indigenous futures should be. Indigenism, too, is a discourse that is subject to interpretation from different ideological perspectives. For a harshly critical perspective, see Elizabeth Rata, 'The Theory of Tribal-Capitalism', unpublished conference paper (I am grateful to Ravi Palat for bringing the piece to my attention, and to Dr. Rata for permission to quote it). On the other hand, it seems to me that indigenism as a paradigm is important both for the affirmation of place, and for the possibilities it suggests for rebuilding society from the bottom up. Indigenous peoples have the advantage over the rest of us in their ability to name those who are corrupt, and betray the community, which is more than we can say about the condition of life in general under global capitalism. For an interesting essay on the relevance of indigenous forms of organisation to confronting contemporary problems, see Brown Childs (1994).

8 While some of the media referred derisively (and revealingly) to Pat Buchanan's 'pitchforked peasants', others saw a lesson in Buchanan's appeal to attend more closely to places. See Friedman (1996).

4   The globalisation of the system of business knowledge

Nigel Thrift

Capitalist firms exist in a world which they increasingly regard as inherently uncertain, and that regard in itself helps bring about such a world (Thrift 1996c). How, then, can firms establish some control of these wayward circumstances? In this chapter, I want to argue that this vision of uncertainty has pushed those who run capitalist firms into taking a 'theoretical' turn but, as I shall make clear, this is a turn towards a quite particular form of theory.

I will pursue the ramifications of this theoretical turn in three ways in this chapter. In the first part of the chapter, I want to consider the practical forms of theory, based upon the dictates of the moment, that are crucial to the running of capitalist organisations. But then in the second part of the chapter I want to suggest that this bedrock of day-to-day mobilisations is being affected by the rise of reflexive management theory. This is a form of 'virtualism' (Carrier and Miller 1998) that, as I will point out, has its own self-reproducing institutional dimension, which is itself undergoing its own form of globalisation. Then, in the third section I will underline this point by lighting on the example of Asia. I want to show the way in which, as the institutional infrastructure of this more reflexive capitalism expands and settles into the conduct of Asian business, it is helping to bring about new business practices. A brief conclusion reflects on the likely impact of the recent economic events in Asia on the genesis of this institutional infrastructure.

The practicalities of capitalism

How, then, might we think about theory 'in' capitalism, rather than of the theories about capitalism that abound? Let us start with a picture: Hans Holbein's famous painting of The Ambassadors (1533). In this painting is a sign of the new confidence in business and trade, a sign that is also one of the reasons for that confidence. The sign, placed significantly under the globe, is one of the first books for business people, a German work the cover of which translates as 'A New and Well Grounded Instruction in All Merchant's Arithmetic in Three Books compiled by Peter Apian, Astronomer in Ordinary at Ingolstadt' (Latour 1988; Conley 1996; Foister *et al.* 1997).

Academics have treated this and similar signs as betokening the first stirrings of political economy. And, being academics, they have tended to see the birth of political economy as a pivotal event: the beginnings of a discourse, a textual outfitting of the world which constitutes notions of economy (Foucault 1970). Similarly, they have tended to assume that one of the descendants of political economy – economics – is the theoretical language of business. They have thought that, over the years, economics has provided the theoretical backbone of business. Thus, the world is made into a reflection of theory.

But I have become less and less convinced by this kind of story. No one can deny that political economy, and then economics, have been important through recent history but I am not at all sure how important they have been in business. They are important as discursive elements of states, justifying action in producing arenas that the state enacts as 'economic'. On the whole, however, I think that capitalist firms play to different drums. I make this judgement for four reasons.

First, much economics has never been quite as important in business as is often made out to be. It is true that economics is taught to MBA students, sometimes in profusion, as at the hard-line economics business schools like Stanford, and at many German business schools. It is also true that many business people have been taught some formal economics. But what strikes me is how little economics is ever used in business. The exception is financial economics. This is used in financial markets and is one of the backbones of corporate finance; more generally it appears in audit operations and in standard measures like ROCE (return on capital employed). But much of economics seems to me to function as legitimisation, a discursive principle which can be referred to, but that often bears about as much relation to the conduct of business as the high court judge does to the shoplifter.

The second reason is that capitalist business is performative (Thrift 1997). By this I mean that it is a practical order that is constantly in action, based in the irreversible time of strategy (Bourdieu 1977). Whilst it has its contemplative aspects, based in the time of learned knowledge, it is chiefly an order of the moment, and a means of crafting the moment. Tasks have to be carried out. Reports have to be made. Plans for the next two years cannot be made in two years' time. There is no 'if only . . .' (Boden 1994).

The third reason is that capitalist business is based in a material culture that ranges from the vast number of intermediaries required to produce trade, through the wide range of means of recording and summarising business, to the different layouts of buildings that discipline workers' bodies. These devices and arrangements are not an aid to capitalism; they are a fundamental part of what capitalism is. My point here is hardly unusual, for there are elements of it in the work of Braudel, and more recently it has been taken up by actor-network theorists (Latour 1986, 1993). However, only recently have researchers begun to work through its consequences.

The fourth and final reason is that capitalist business is based in a notion of 'theory' that is of a different order from more formal theory. It is based on problematisation and problem spaces rather than a succession of scholarly theories which roll by and are judged according to particular criteria of correctness. The difficulty is that academics tend to marginalise and demean such theory on a number of grounds: its lack of formality; its source in social groups that are regarded as practical rather than theoretical; its closeness to technological devices; its allegiance to the empirical; its fixation on the moment. In turn, however, the denigration of such theory can be seen as a problem for more formal notions of theory since,

> these problematising voices tend not to be much concerned with 'epochal' theories or systems, or with abstract conceptions of society and yet, some suggest, it is these voices that have often proved decisive, setting the terms under which sociological theories can place themselves 'in the time' or, alternatively, shaping the criteria which strip their Truthfulness away.
>
> (Osborne and Rose 1997: 90)

So, I want to interpret the sign of Peter Apian's book in a different way; not as one of the first sightings of political economy, but as the basis of a more specific set of practical skills concerning what I will call the promotion of intelligence about competence within specific problem spaces. Such thinking on 'how to solve' specific problems, usually by modest example, has a long but only partially-told history in business, and more generally (Osborne and Rose 1997).

I argue that, in the sphere of business, three different but related variants of this practical theory exist, each with its own specialist communities which produce and disperse these intelligences and competences. Such communities include not only specific kinds of people but also specific kinds of devices, vital parts of the means of producing and distributing intelligence. Elsewhere, these spheres have been called by terms like 'regimes of calculation' (for example, Porter 1995). For my purposes, however, this conjures up too great a sense of a pursuit of objectivity through numerical means. I prefer, then, to call them 'theoretical networks'.

The first such theoretical network I have called bookkeeping. Until recently, the history of accounting was something of a backwater, but in the last ten years it has grown markedly, which makes it easier to present a brief history of this network. The early growth was based on three practices. The first of these was the abacus or counting board.

By the late eleventh and twelfth centuries, treatises on elementary calculations were, by and large, treatises on the use of the counting board, and there was a new word, abacus, meaning to compute. In the sixteenth century counting boards were so common that Martin Luther could offhandedly refer to them to illustrate the compatibility of spiritual egalitarianism and obedience to one's betters (Crosby 1996: 44). But the counting board was a device for computing not recording:

> Its users of necessity erased their steps as they calculated, making it impossible to locate mistakes in the process except by going back to the beginning and repeating the whole sequence. As for permanently writing down the answers, that was done in Roman numerals.
>
> (Crosby 1996: 111)

Thus, another important practice, which allowed not only better calculation but also better recording, was imported from Arabic Spain in the twelfth century. This was calculation using Arabic numerals, called 'pen reckoning'. Even given the usefulness of these numerals, it took three hundred years for them to become current throughout western Europe, even though they allowed calculating and recording to be done with the same symbols, and did not erase themselves as calculation occurred, and so could be checked.

The final element of this first theoretical network is double-entry bookkeeping. Living in a blizzard of transactions as they did, merchants and other business people had to have some sense of how to track each transaction. This problem was solved by the evolution of a two-column system of debits and credits, probably originating in Venice at the end of the thirteenth century. This was supplemented by the practice of entering each entry twice, keeping what was, in effect, a double account. This procedure spread across Europe, chiefly through manuals and bookkeeping practice.

Nowadays, the bookkeeping network is most often associated with the computer but it is important to understand the extent to which automated practices of bookkeeping have evolved gradually. Tabulating and calculating machines were introduced in the 1880s into accounting departments, later supplemented by punch-card systems and various electro-mechanical devices for sorting and analysis were also used (Yates 1994). Thus, by the time the computer appeared, the protocols of automated bookkeeping had already been established.

A second theoretical network consists of the crystallisation of organisational practice in written procedures, as codes and algorithms, organisational values, opinions and rhetorics, as well as skills, are frozen into devices like operating manuals, company rules and procedures, company handbooks, posters and the like. The network has its origin in two devices. The first is instruction manuals dating from the sixteenth century. These are the first attempts to objectify practical knowledge (Thrift 1984). The second is the recording and compiling of lists, and then reports, which collect and draw up information that could not have been written down hitherto.

> List-making has frequently been seen as one of the fundamental activities of advanced human society necessary for coordinating activity across time and space, and it is associated with the development of complex

organisational structures and infrastructures (Yates and Orlikowski 1992). Similarly, the creation of lists brings with it substantial political and conceptual changes in the classes of things that they inventory (Bowker and Star 1994: 188–9). Thus, Jack Goody (1971, 1987) has argued that the first written records are lists of things; Michel Foucault (1970) and Patrick Tort (1989) have claimed that the production of lists revolutionised science in the nineteenth century and led directly to modern science; Latour (1987) has proclaimed that the prime job of the bureaucrat is to compile lists that can be shuffled and compared. These authors have helped turn our attention away from dazzling end-products of list-making in the various forms of Hammurabi's code, mythologies, the theory of evolution, the welfare state and so on. They have instead described the work involved in making these productions possible. They have done so by dusting off the archives and discovered piles and piles of lowly, dull, mechanical lists.

These list-making activities were measurably boosted by the new office technologies which were produced from the mid-nineteenth century onwards. Thus,

> mass-produced typewriters appeared in 1874, aimed at a large market of court reporters, authors and other specialised users. Typewriters operated by experienced typists could produce documents at three times the rate of pen and paper, thus increasing the speed and lowering the cost of producing them. Beginning in the 1880s and 1890s, firms adopted the typewriter just in time to slow the already rising costs of their increased internal and external written communication.
>
> (Yates 1994: 32)

At the same time, prepared forms became common. These reduced the time spent recording information and encouraged consistency and made it easier to retrieve information. (Around 1900, the tab function was added to typewriters precisely in order to aid the typist in typing tables and filling out forms.) Duplicating activity was also becoming easier. Carbon paper, hectographs and stencils were used to produce large numbers of copies, culminating in the invention of the mimeograph in the late 1890s. Filing systems also became more common, with the introduction of vertical filing at the Chicago World's Fair in 1893. In turn, these inventions allowed the production of systems of indexing and organising that were much lauded in management periodicals and textbooks. The card file also became more common and had many of the same effects. Thus, by the time of the computer, many business procedures, codes and algorithms had already emerged and needed only to be adapted to the new medium (Pellegram 1997).

In some cases values, opinions, rhetorics and skills are frozen in the written word or number, but it is just as likely that they are encapsulated in visual representations. These are the graphs, maps, charts and diagrams that envision the organisation and give it its position in the 'economy' (Buck-Morss 1995). For example,

> graphs were widely adopted in the early twentieth century to make information more accessible and compelling to those using it. While graphic representations of data had existed for at least a century, they had been used primarily for government statistics and later for experimental data in science and engineering. Advocated by systematisers and engineers-turned-managers, graphs gained considerable popularity as a way to make the information gathered and analysed available to decision-makers in an efficient and compelling form.
>
> (Yates 1994: 32)

Visual representation keeps evolving. Much has been made of the impact of the computer but perhaps the most potent tools of the last few decades have been the humble flipchart, the overhead projector, and the slide projector, all used in a vast number of different situations to produce, organise and represent the thinking of groups. That said, in the last twenty years, a new crystallisation of organisational practice has become possible through the development of computer software of a bewildering range and variety, which imposes standards but also offers choices. In turn, software has become intelligent in its own right, and capable of producing complex representations.

The third network is the most recent, even though its pre-history can be traced back to Robert Owen or to Quakers like the Cadburys and Rowntrees. Its modern origin is usually identified as managerial experiments in the 1940s and 1950s in Britain and the United States arising out of psychology. In Britain, it emerged from the work of psychologists like C. S. Myers and Elliott Jacques at the Tavistock Institute, as well as the work of Eric Trist on coalmines in Haighmoor. In the United States it emerged from the invention of training groups and the founding of the National Training Laboratories (NTL) by psychologists like Lewin, Lippitt, MacGregor and Argyris, in Bethel, which then spread widely.

From these beginnings there developed an alternative tradition of management, one that stresses human interaction and self-fulfilment as general elements of organisational success. Indeed, one might argue that this network has, to a considerable degree, developed in direct opposition to the other two networks, as a conscious effort to supplement, extend or even undermine them. Kleiner (1996) shows how this network was built up in piecemeal fashion from all manner of sources until the 1970s, dependent upon the enthusiasms of particular managers and corporate whim. But in the period since the 1970s, it has become highly successful as the inculcation of 'soft' management skills like team leadership, creativity, emotional thinking and the like.

This third network has been successful for a number of reasons. To begin with it was able to find a home in institutional bases like business schools and, increasingly, management consulting firms. Then, it was able to promote itself through the media, to which it is strongly linked, especially through inspirational books for managers, business and the like (Thrift 1997; Micklethwait and Wooldridge 1996; Crainer 1997a; Carrier 1996). Again, it has been able to produce believers who have considerable investments in the network, especially in the human-resources sector which it has largely driven. And, finally, it has been able to produce and make general its own interactional devices. These include all manner of transactional trainings and therapies (Heelas 1996; Brown 1997), as well as far more mundane but equally effective means of interaction. Thus, business lunches and seminars and conferences are now regarded as a background hum in business; but they all had to be invented. For example, social events and seminars as means of selling to businesses were probably invented by Marvin Bower of McKinsey as a way of selling services. The first such event was held in 1940 and was called a 'clinic dinner'. Conferences about business strategy (which are also marketing tools) probably originated with Bruce Henderson of Boston Consulting in the 1960s. They were used as a means of starting or maintaining relations with top corporate management (O'Shea and Madigan 1997).

Reflexive capitalism

Capitalist 'theory' is of a practical bent. However, it is interesting that, over the last thirty years or so, capitalist business increasingly has taken a more reflexive, 'theoretical' turn. This turn is not a total one. It is concentrated in larger firms and the more dynamic of the smaller ones. But that it exists can no longer be doubted.

Some words of caution are necessary, however. First, much of what I will describe here has direct antecedents in practical theory. Thus the seminar, which is now so essential to the practices of reflexive capitalism, is an outgrowth of previous practices. Similarly, many of the books and guides that circulate in such profusion in business are really only developments of company procedures and guides. Second, reflexive theory and practical theory remain closely linked. Whilst the language of the reflexive turn is often stratospheric, the fact is that it has to be connected to practical theory if it is to be sold on in quantity. In other words, reflexive theory is likely to be commoditised at an early stage and must stand up to the rigours of the market.

The reflexive turn is based on a body of management theory which has arisen from a number of sources. To begin with, management theory has clearly had a long history of its own. For example, even at the turn of the twentieth century there was the systematic management movement in the United States and, a little later, the scientific management of F. W. Taylor; the *Management Review* was founded in 1918; the *Harvard Business Review* in

1922; the American Management Association in 1925. By the end of the First World War, Arthur D. Little, originally an engineering firm, included management advice amongst its services; James McKinsey started his consulting firm in 1925.

Arguably, however, management theory came into its own after the Second World War through the incorporation of a large and eclectic body of knowledge. This included organisation theory, economics and actual business practice (including, most especially, the use of case studies as exemplars of success) on one side, and on the other it included 'softer' sources of inspiration, including sociology and psychology. Currently, its most visible manifestation is the 'business fad' (Huczynski 1993; Shapiro 1995; Thrift 1997). In the past, such fads have included management by objective, quality circles, just-in-time manufacturing and, most famously of late, business process re-engineering (Hammer and Champy 1993; Coulson-Thomas 1994) and core competences (Hamel and Prahalad 1994). More recent fads have included the balanced scorecard (Kaplan and Norton 1997), the living company (de Geuss 1997), and, most particularly, knowledge as capital (Nonaka and Takeuchi 1995). For example, 1997 saw at least three books published with exactly the same title: *Intellectual Capital*. These marketable philosophies are the basic quanta of business knowledge. They are the means of tapping the moment by creating the spirit of the moment. They are

> part of a tried and tested formula that evolved after Tom Peters, a McKinsey and Co consultant, gathered wealth and fame in the wake of *In Search of Excellence*, published some 15 years ago and the most successful business book of modern times. The response: Get an article in the *Harvard Business Review*, pump it up into a book, pray for a best-seller, then market the idea for all it is worth through a consultancy company.
> (O'Shea and Madigan 1997: 189)

Whilst fads come round like the seasons, they are only the most visible part of the system of reflexive business knowledge. Many other knowledges circulate as well, chiefly through the constant, unremitting hum of courses and seminars.

How has this autopoetic system been able to come about? There are four different reasons. The first of these is an interlocking institutional arrangement that I have described elswhere (Thrift 1997). It consists, to begin with, of the business school. Business schools have, of course, existed for some time: Wharton, the first business school, was set up at the University of Pennsylvania in 1881; the University of Chicago and the University of California both established undergraduate schools of commerce in 1899; Stern (New York), Amos Tuck (Dartmouth) and Harvard followed in the next decade (Mark 1987; Micklethwait and Wooldridge 1996). However, they have boomed since the 1960s and now more than 75,000 students are awarded MBAs every year in America – fifteen times the number in 1960. Every year

250,000 people around the world sit the GMAT entrance examination for MBA courses (Micklethwait and Wooldridge 1996). The business school has produced new, more reflexive knowledge in a number of ways. To begin with, it has systematised and then reproduced existing business knowledge. For example, the case-study method at one time so beloved of Harvard Business School is able to be used as a means of reflecting back on business. Then, it has synthesised existing academic knowledge and fed it into businesses. For example, the primary route for much organisation theory into business has been from journals like the *Administrative Science Quarterly* into the business school and so into business. And, finally, it has produced new knowledge by producing fresh modes of interchange and knowledge creation. For example, the presence of more MBA students who already have business experience means that academic knowledge is tested against that experience.

Another element of the institutional arrangement supporting reflexive capitalism is the management consultancy, which, like the business school, has grown massively since the 1960s. Consultants trade in reflexive knowledge and do so more and more conspicuously. For example, Arthur Andersen, with revenues of $5,300 million in 1996 and an international staff of about 38,000 consultants, has its own 'university', the former girls' school at St Charles, Illinois which is now known as Andersen Consulting College. There, it trains consultants by the thousands and, increasingly, promotes conferences and video conferences. And, since Andersen believes in the growth of an 'infocosm', consultants communicate through a computer communications system called Knowledge X-Change, aimed at integrating the organisation's business knowledge. Most recently, it has established a 'thought leadership' centre near its technology centre in Palo Alto. But there is a rub:

> Whatever the product – downsising, growth, or something else – consultants need to sell ideas. The problem is that what consulting has to sell isn't always new, and certainly isn't always fresh. It is an unusual industry because it builds its knowledge base at the expense of its clients. From a more critical perspective, it is not much of a stretch to say that consulting companies make a lot of money collecting experience from their clients, which they turn around and sell in other forms, sometimes not very well disguised, to other clients.
>
> (O'Shea and Madigan 1997: 13)

A final element of the institutional arrangement supporting reflexive capitalism is the management guru. Though they had existed before – Peter Drucker being a case in point – management gurus came into their own in the early 1980s with the rise of new types of high-energy management theorists, led by Tom Peters (Micklethwait and Wooldridge 1996). Many of these consultants now have their own, very successful consulting companies (as in the case of Michael Porter's Company, Monitor). Management gurus are high-profile embodiments of management fads, whose business is to produce and, more importantly, to communicate these fads by performatively energising their audiences.

Thus far I have described the first general reason for the rise of reflexive capitalism, the institutional framework that supports it. A second reason has been the growth of the business media. Reflexive business theory is intimately associated with those media, for management has become a cultural industry. In particular, business fads depend upon media to make them visible and generate their audiences (Jackson 1997a). This link has, of course, been present for a long time. For example, Marvin Bower published a handbook of McKinsey management philosophy, *Supplementing Successful Management*, in the 1940s. However, the significant association of business theory with the media dates from the success of Peters and Waterman's *In Search of Excellence*, published in 1982, the book that demonstrated the size of the market. Since then, each year has seen a flood of management books, tapes and videos.

In 1991 McGraw-Hill published 25 (business) titles; in 1996 it published 110. Marketing budgets at the esteemed Harvard Business School Press are estimated to have almost doubled in the last four years. In the UK alone 2,931 business titles were published in 1996, compared with a paltry 771 in 1975 (Crainer 1997b: 38). Sometimes ghost-written, the books can relate management to almost any aspect of human life, from jazz (Kao 1997) to computer hacking (Phillips 1997).

The business media consist of a number of institutions. To begin with, there are the various institutions that publish books, business journals and the business pages of other periodicals. And, increasingly, there are the producers of radio and television programmes and videos. For management theory to spread, it must become interwoven with the media, and books that sell widely taken on their own momentum, becoming the subject of presentations by business gurus and being actively marketed by the management consultants who have been involved in producing them. Similarly, increasing numbers of journals are being published by management consultants in order to spread their ideas, such as the *McKinsey Quarterly*, *Strategy and Business* (Booz and Allen) and *Transformations* (Gemini). Another set of institutions consists of media consultants and press officers who interact with the media, attempting to sell ideas to it. A symbolic date for this set of institutions was the appointment, in 1980, of a press officer by Bain and Company, the last significant consulting firm to resist the press. Even they were forced to recognise the necessity of media publicity, a necessity underlined by the recent, widespread use of advertising by some management consultants; Robert Duboff of Mercer Management says that 'ten years ago, if I'd suggested we advertise, I'd have been shot; five years ago I'd have been whipped' (Wooldridge 1997: 16). Then, finally, there is the audience for business ideas. About this audience we know very little (see Thrift 1997), but there can be no doubt that it is extensive and rapidly growing.

A third reason for the development of reflexive capitalism has been the growth of new business practices, as well as the transformation of some older ones. Of these, three stand out. One is the area of human resources. Human resources managers have become a staple of most firms since the 1970s. Another is the growth of marketing, spurred on by the simultaneous growth of computers and psychology. In particular, since the beginnings of consumer psychology in the 1940s and 1950s, marketing has taken on a more clearly psychological tinge (see Miller and Rose 1997). The final practice is the growth of interest in leadership, communication and other 'soft skills'. Recently, for example, there has been much interest in emotions and emotional leadership (e.g. Cooper and Sawaf 1997).

A fourth reason is simply momentum. Once a system becomes autopoetic it has its own push. For example, more and more people in business have been taught reflexive management in business schools, and they provide a ready audience for related management ideas. Again, such people are likely to demand reflexive management when they attain positions of responsibility, and thus pull in more people skilled in reflexive theory. Similarly, a growing number of managers have themselves worked in management consultancies and, in any case, 'bosses who have had a taste of management theory, either at business schools or working for consultancies, may be more inclined to listen to consultants than those who have not' (Wooldridge 1997: 4).

The globalisation of business knowledge

What is clear is that reflexive capitalism is rapidly globalising, together with the management ideas that mobilise it. It is worth considering in more detail how it is journeying and, in order to achieve this, in this section of the chapter, I want to concentrate on the example of Asia, both in order to demonstrate the ways in which reflexive capitalism can make its way in a different milieu and the way in which this different milieu has begun to change a number of its practices.

Of course, Asia has a number of business traditions that depart from conventional Western practice. To begin with, for thousands of years it has had extensive trade networks. For hundreds of years it has had significant theoretical networks, based on the use of the abacus and on indigenous forms of bookkeeping, which are only now being analysed fully (Goody 1996). Its economic ethics (such as 'rationality') have been varied, and though they may have been based on the family more than have Occidental economic ethics, equally, as Carrier (1995), Goody (1996) and others have pointed out, this depiction has often suited both East and West as signals of their difference (as for example, in notions of collectivist and individualist spirits of capitalism).

While Asia's business history has been a different one, it is worth remembering that this is a relative judgement. Asia has still shared much of its economic history with the rest of the world: it has never been a closed economic zone. Thus, it is no surprise that Asia has been drawn into the practices of reflexive capitalism. Foreign multinational corporations have moved into the region en masse. Meanwhile, Asian firms have experienced a massive increase in physical and electronic communication, and therefore in general interconnection. They have experienced the problems of economic success, such as the increasing scale of business organisations, the need to ensure management succession in what have been family-run firms (see Dicken and Yeung, this volume; Dumaine 1997; Hiscock 1997a, 1997b), and a general shortage of managers. In these circumstances, it is perhaps not surprising to find the reproduction of the institutional set-up of reflexive capitalism in Asia.

The business school is a fairly recent invention in Asia, with most dating from the late 1960s or 1970s. Until recently the demand for MBAs could not have been satisfied from within Asia and especially the United States: for example, Blanck (1992) found that in 1988 more than 50 per cent of the foreign students in the US came from Asia with China, Taiwan and Japan being the leading sending countries with 25,000 to 30,000 students each; many of these students were clearly studying for MBAs. But Asia now has more and more business schools, some of them freestanding, others mounting courses jointly with prominent Western business schools. The number of schools and courses is expanding all the time, and more and more Asians are attending them, as well as the large number of Asian business colleges, distance learning schemes and the like that offer credentials. Many of the schools are wildly over-subscribed, even though their fees are often well above average national incomes. For example, in India in 1996, 40,000 students took the entrance examinations for the six Indian Institutes of Management (at Ahmedabad, Calcutta, Lucknow, Bangalore, Calicut and Indore) but only 1,000 were accepted (*Financial Times* 1997: iv). In China in the same year, there were 4,000 applicants for a twenty-month MBA course at the China Europe International Business School in Shanghai, but only 65 were accepted (Micklethwait and Wooldridge 1996; the number accepted on to the course increased to 120 in 1997).

The management consultant is another important part of the institutional arrangement in Asia. Until recently, expansion into Asia has been rather haphazard often associated as much with the expansion of the plants and offices of foreign multinational corporations as with a search for indigenous businesses. It is no surprise then, that the expansion plans of most large management consultant firms in the region are uneven. For example, market penetration is still low in Japan. Further, these expansion plans face a number of problems when it comes to serving indigenous businesses. First, establishing an intangible product in a market dominated by family firms who have often been suspicious of playing outside is difficult. It can take a decade or more to establish a profitable branch office that is staffed by locals (Wooldridge 1997: 6). Second, recruitment and retention of staff is difficult when well-qualified people are scarce, and when training local recruits increases their market value and makes them difficult to keep. Third, while it is necessary to keep a balance of Western and local employees, it is not always easy to do so, as many clients in emerging markets would rather take advice from foreigners. In particular, 'Chinese family companies tend to put more faith in grey-haired Westerners than in Chinese MBAs just out of business school' (Wooldridge 1997: 6). Fourth, it is difficult for consultants to publicise their activities: many Asian clients do not like their names used in firm publicity. In spite of these problems, management consultancies are expanding rapidly in Asia. For example, Andersen Consulting now has 4,000 people in Asia while McKinsey's Indian Office is the company's fastest-growing (Micklethwait and Wooldridge 1996).

Management gurus also are becoming influential in Asia. Indeed, for many, it is one of their most important stamping grounds, as typified by books that are tailored to the market, like Naisbitt's *Megatrends Asia*. A number of superstar gurus regularly tour the region. For example, Tom Peters currently charges $95,000 for a one-day seminar that usually lasts about seven hours (Crainer 1997a).

For many western gurus, Asian speaking tours offer much the same entice-ments that the musical variety do for elderly rock stars. The money is good ($25,000 a seminar), the audience large and relatively uncritical, and there is also a chance that you can find an Asian anecdote or two to spice up your performances back home (Micklethwait and Wooldridge 1996: 57).

Finally, Asian business media are extensive. Apart from business-oriented newspapers, the region contains a large and lively battery of magazine titles such as *Asia Inc.*, as well as a large market for Western business titles.

Three kinds of ideas have been circulated in Asia by this mix of periodicals, travelling gurus, consulting firms and the like. One is the standard self-improvement theme, which emphasises leadership, self-discipline, and other skills and books on this theme sell well. For example, Zhang Ruimin is the President and Chair of the Chinese Haier Group, which employs 13,000 people in plants in China, Malaysia, Indonesia and the Philippines, chiefly in the manufacture of home appliances. The Haier Group is known for its aggressive management style, which has made Zhang Ruimin into one of the few famous managers in China (*The Economist*, 20 December 1997: 119). He told the *Financial Times* (3 November 1997: 16) that he has a profound interest in US business thinking – an avid reader of Western business books, Mr Zhang has just finished Peter Senge's *The Fifth Discipline*, which he appreciated for its emphasis on what he describes as the idea of 'a people-nurturing business'.

Another set of ideas has been the round of business fads and fashions. For example, the bible of business process re-engineering, *Re-engineering the Corporation* (Hammer and Champy 1993), has sold 17 million copies world-wide, including 5 million copies in Asia. Whilst few companies have taken up the approach lock, stock and barrel there have been Asian examples.

The third set of ideas has been based on the success of Asian and especially Japanese, businesses (see, most recently, Hampden-Turner and Trompenaars 1997). In turn, these ideas have spawned Asian management gurus. The most noted are from Japan, such as Kenichi Ohmae (a former McKinsey employee) and, more recently, Ikujiro Nonaka, whose book with Hirotaka Takeuchi, *The Knowledge-Creating Company*, has become a business best-seller. However, not only the Japanese business experience has been drawn upon. So has the Korean experience (as in the work of Chan Kim, now at INSEAD) and the Chinese experience (Wee *et al.* 1991; Kotkin 1991).

We can argue about the relative influence of these three kinds of idea on Asian managers, but that they are beginning to have an effect seems less open to dispute. For example, in a massive pan-Asian survey of business people in 1995 roughly half of the respondents had bought a book by a Western management writer in the previous two years (although it was noticeable that roughly the same proportion admitted that they had not finished reading it) (Micklethwait and Wooldridge 1996: 57).

In turn, increasingly these ideas can no longer be seen as a purely Western cultural form. They are being produced simultaneously in many parts of the world as the institutions of an increasingly reflexive capitalism.

Conclusion

The recent linked economic crises in Asia will obviously have their effect on the growth of the system of reflexive business knowledge in the region. On one reading, these crises will produce a considerable set back as many of the institutions of reflexive management theory suffer through the general lack of demand, and as indigenous firms collapse back on their own practices, retreating into the familiar. But there is another reading. This is that the crises will only hasten the growth of the system of reflexive business knowledge, and for three reasons. First, even before the crises, Asian business was adopting Western management practices. Even the most patriarchal of large family-run Asian businesses have been hiring professional managers for some time now. For example,

> [Richard] Li tells how he recently had to choose between two managers in one of his Asian operations. One was old school – very loyal but with no specific skills, the other knew the industry and was creative and bicultural. Li fired the former and gave the job to the one with specific knowledge. Says he: 'it is much more difficult in Asia to remove top managers. But when you have a dramatic technological change or a sharp change in a market then I believe the model of change makes it necessary to fire someone.
>
> (Dumaine 1997: 8)

Second, many commentators believe that these crises demonstrate some of the weaknesses, as well as the strengths, of certain Asian business practices (such as the use and reliance upon informal social networks). In other words, more formal management techniques (and advice) are needed if Asian firms are to survive and prosper. Third, adoption of Western management techniques and advice may well become the *quid pro quo* for response by creditors.

The net result is probably that, as the Asian economic crises bite, the long march of reflexive capitalism into Asia will continue. Indeed its momentum may even be strengthened with the result that some of the pervasive practices of neo-liberalism become even more embedded in the global economy (Biersteker 1995; Thrift 1998b).

Acknowledgements

This chapter is a shortened and recast form of the chapter 'Virtual Capitalism' published in James Carrier and Daniel Miller (eds) *Virtualism: The New Political Economy*, Oxford: Berg and is reprinted here with permission. I would like to thank Peter Dicken and Kris Olds for their extensive comments on the paper which helped enormously in redrafting it for this volume.

5 Resisting globalisation
Environmental politics in Eastern Asia

James H. Mittelman

Introduction

Not all types of environmental degradation are of recent origin or global in scope – some are long established and local.[1] Even so, unsustainable transformation of the environment under globalisation differs from environmental damage in previous epochs. Although contemporary environmental abuses have their antecedents in earlier periods of history, globalisation coincides with new environmental problems such as global warming, depletion of the ozone layer, acute loss of biodiversity, and forms of transboundary pollution (e.g. acid rain). These problems have emerged not singly but together. Moreover, certain ecological problems are clearly the result of global cross-border flows, as with the kinds of groundwater contamination, leaching and long-term health threats traceable to the import of hazardous wastes.

Large-scale growth in world economic output since the 1970s has not only quickened the breakdown of the global resource base, but also upset the planet's regenerative system, including its equilibrium among different forms of life and their support structures. A large part of the explanation is that deregulation and liberalisation mean more global pressure to lower environmental standards (although there are of course counterpressures). In the absence of stringent regulations and effective enforcement mechanisms, fear and insecurity about the planet's future are on the rise.

With hypercompetition for profits reaching a global level, the market is breaching nature's limits. Yet nature's protest, its signals of breakdown, provide an opening. Rather than reify the environment, it is important to resist the ontological distinction between humans and nature, a dualism rooted in modern thought since Descartes. If so, humankind and nature may be viewed interactively as 'a single causal stream' (Rosenau 1997: 190–1). The environment may then be understood as political space, a critical venue where civil society is voicing its concerns. As such, the environment represents a marker where, to varying degrees, popular resistance to globalisation is evident. Slicing across party, class, gender, race and ethnicity, environmental politics offers a useful entry point for assessing counterglobalisation.

Accordingly, the questions that frame this study are: What are the specific sites of environmental resistance to globalisation? Who are the agents of resistance? What strategies are adopted? And to what extent are they localised or regionalised and globalised? In other words, is there evidence to demonstrate the stirrings of counterglobalisation?

In attempting to answer these questions, I will show the complex layering of different modes of resistance politics. My chief concern is organised environmental responses to globalisation, though not to the exclusion of other types of resistance. For reasons that will be elaborated in the next section, I am especially interested in direct environmental initiatives – solid patterns and cumulative action – but also in the soft, or latent, forms of protest that may or may not sufficiently harden so as to eventually challenge global structures. Attention will be given to submerged forms of resistance insofar as they are emerging into networks. A major goal in this chapter is to explore theoretical propositions on the meaning of resistance and to bring to light the diversity of environmental politics in encounters with globalising processes.

My research strategy is to locate globalising tendencies in environmental resistance in Eastern (i.e. East and Southeast) Asia, an internally diverse subregion, and notwithstanding economic turbulence that began in 1997, an epicentre of globalisation. The evidential material adduced here illustrates the myriad ways that environmental groups organise, and offers fresh and original examples of emerging resistance. For the purposes of academic research, it would be desirable to separate the domain of resistance to globalisation from resistance to other forms of hierarchical power relations, but they cannot be neatly divided. Rather, spheres of resistance surrounding the environment, labour standards, women's issues, human rights, etc. merge and interpenetrate. One can, however, identify certain emphases in consciousness and action as a basis for analysing potential transformations in world order (Mittelman 1997b).

This chapter considers, but in no way romanticises, the voices of the subjects of globalisation who are engaged in environmental resistance politics. Not at all limited to perceptual evidence, it draws on both documentary research and interviews in Japan, Malaysia, Philippines, Singapore, and Vietnam. It was of course impossible to hold interviews or do other types of fieldwork in all of the countries in Eastern Asia. I had ample opportunity to talk formally and informally with people in international and indigenous non-governmental organisations (NGOs),[2] businesses, state agencies, universities and the media. The interviewees were selected with reference to categories deemed theoretically central to environmental resistance politics and identified in the next section of this chapter. In carrying out research in countries where civil society is of recent origin and relatively thin, I sought out the leading activists pursuing environmental objectives (though they may also mobilise around other causes pertaining to social justice) and challenging global structures either directly or indirectly. Of course, the proximate issues vary from one case to another – e.g. from deforestation to toxic waste – but in all instances involve transborder problems.

To enter the crucible of resistance politics, I first explore the characteristics of environmental resistance politics. The next section turns to the sources of popular resistance, followed by a discussion of the agents who are challenging macro structures. Inquiry then focuses on the sites of resistance and, finally, weighs the efficacy of multilayered strategies.

Characteristics of environmental resistance politics

The environment is not a single phenomenon, and, as implied above, may be viewed from different vantage points: a series of interactions between the human and physical worlds; a site of resistance; and a social construction that is contested. In terms of the third approach, it is important to note that attitudes to nature are always changing, are bound to time and place, and initially reflect the dominant culture. In fact, the relationship between nature and culture has been rapidly and variously transformed around the world. This is not new, but technological innovations and hypercompetition accelerate the trend. Moreover, a hallmark of globalisation is the explosion of cultural pluralism (Mittelman 1996a and 1997a), and some cultural conflicts linked to imbalances in power relations find expression in environmental ideologies, understood as systems of representation of a definite group or class.

The environment may be construed as a set of alternative moral forces forming ideological representations. Submerged responses to environmental use (or abuse) may in turn be transformed into organised political resistance that props up its counterideologies – a problematic explored by the master theorists of resistance. Elsewhere, Christine Chin and I (1997) have sought to explicate theories of resistance by critically examining competing conceptualisations: resistance as counterhegemony (Gramsci 1971), resistance as infrapolitics (Scott 1990), and resistance as countermovements (Polanyi 1957). Without rehearsing our analysis here, I merely want to position myself within this triad so as to offer a way to examine environmental resistance politics.

Needless to say, all three frameworks have great explanatory power. Their merits do not require elaboration here, but a few critical comments are in order. A Marxist who subscribed to the view that class conflict is the motor of history, Gramsci differed from Marx in allowing considerable autonomy for consciousness, which helps to understand the cultural dimensions of resistance. Nonetheless, a drawback to Gramsci's two-pronged conceptualisation of resistance (his notion of wars of movement and position) is that in both cases, the objective is to take control of state power. With globalisation, however, resistance may or may not target the state. If one of the roles of the state today is to provide the domestic economy with greater access to global capital, then the state is a part of the whole matrix of globalisation. To rotate the holders of state power may not alleviate the problems that ignited resistance in the first place. Accordingly, Gramsci's conceptualisation must be stretched at the turn of the century to include other types of actors and different paces in which consciousness develops. To be sure, Gramsci's own writings on civil society are fragmentary and sometimes incongruent. Yet one may still profitably invoke Gramsci's formulations on changing power relations within civil society and the dynamics of culture for building theory to explain resistance to globalisation.

Like Gramsci, Scott turns attention to the culture of resistance. His emphasis on 'infrapolitical' activities that range from footdragging, squatting, gossip, and jokes to the formation of dissident subcultures offers a subtle way to probe everyday responses to globalising processes. Nevertheless, the limitation to Scott's probing of covert acts is that the wide gamut of forms of resistance he suggests is a catch-all. Not only are they highly diffuse, but also they may make little overall impact on power relations. This problem in Scott's framework is revealed in the very first line of his 1990 book. The aphorism he selects to open it is an Ethiopian proverb: 'When the great lord passes the wise peasant bows deeply and farts.' Yet how much political impact does farting really have? How much effect do footdragging, squatting, gossip and other forms of uncoordinated resistance actually have on environmental problems such as global warming and deterioriation of the ozone layer? Where is the evidence to demonstrate that countless microscopic activities will ultimately amount to a shift in macrostructures? Although these acts, even when multiplied, may not topple regimes, they often signal weaknesses in a regime's legitimacy and can help undermine forms of authority.

It might be argued that these subversive measures do add up, for they are cumulative. But it seems fair to ask, if the consequences are fully felt only in the *longue durée*, how long will that be? As the eruption of multiple environmental crises patently shows, nature is already voiding its subordination to the market economy (Harries-Jones *et al.* 1992).[3] By all indications, it will not wait for the *longue durée* to resolve the matter. Whereas it is right to be alert to the subtexts of resistance and thus the potential for transformation, the question is: how and under what conditions do submerged forms of resistance coalesce and genuinely contest globalising structures? Conversely, it is important to specify the conditions that prevent the crystallisation of resistance politics. What factors facilitate and hinder the stiffening of resistance?

Few contemporary scholars (with notable exceptions including Shaw 1994; Walker 1994; Sklair 1994 and 1997) have attempted to theorise the connections between social movements and world politics. It should be recalled that master thinkers such as Gramsci and Polanyi offered traces of a finely grained analysis of the emergence of social movements within the global political economy of their times. Turning attention to the Owenites and Chartists, Polanyi underlined that 'both movements comprised hundreds of thousands of craftsmen and artisans, labourers and working people, with their vast

following ranked among the biggest social movements in modern history'
(1957: 167). It was Polanyi's insight that the dialectic of movement and
countermovement advances understanding of resistance. He remained stead-
fast in emphasising the role that concrete economic and social institutions
play in historical transformation. Polanyi was above all concerned with the
specific institutional arrangements by which particular societies ensure their
livelihood. Following from Polanyi's contribution, an area of enquiry that
needs to be extended is: as societies try to protect themselves against the traumatic effects of the market, including what Polanyi (1957: 157) regarded as
'the disintegration of the cultural environment', how do submerged
expressions of resistance solidify and actually take shape as countermovements? In this vein, a Polanyian framework may be readily applied to the
relationship between political economy and ecology (Bernard 1997). In fact,
writing more than a half century ago, Polanyi (1957, originally published in
1944) himself registered grave concern over the disembeddedness of markets
not only from society but also from nature. To extrapolate from Polanyi
(1968), the error of economic rationalism is to vest an economistic culture
with an economistic logic. A science of economics subordinates the science of
nature. The interactions between humans and their natural surroundings
thus carry 'meanings', and there may be counteracting forces at work.

For a condition in which economics subordinates both nature and society,
and hence creates market society, the antidote is re-embedding (see Dirlik,
this volume). But in practice, what does it really mean to reground economics
in nature and social relations? Posing this question underscores the elemental
dilemma in resistance politics today. The challenge is even greater than in
Polanyi's time – and requires an extension of his framework – because globalisation involves a disjuncture between an increasingly integrated world
economy, or deterritorialisation, and the territoriality of nation-states based
on the principle of sovereignty. The search for a formula for re-embedding
has clearly given rise to different political projects, and is a contested issue.
To examine these projects, let us first identify sources of popular environmental resistance so that we can then delineate the work of agents for
change, especially the politically organised wings of civil society. What must
then be taken into account is whether these wings fall into any sort of
formation.

Forms and sources of popular environmental resistance

The targets of environmental resistance may be direct and assume a tangible
form, or indirect in the sense of process. The issue, at bottom, is control:
control of land, species, forests, marine life, labour and ideology. Evident
today is a clash between advocates of a modern-day, neoliberal variant of
the trickle-down approach, which holds that the first task is to grow the
economy and then one can attend to distribution and equity, and proponents
of alternatives that stress the need for community-based development and

the linkage between economic reform and social policy (e.g. 'social forestry'). In other words, access to resources is reinforced or challenged by different ideologies; but the dominant one is reform understood as growth before equity. Although from one individual to another, my interviewees' terminology differed, this same point was made several times over. In a joint interview that centred on forestry, an interviewee punctuated it by proclaiming: 'The root causes are in social structures reinforced by the development paradigm. The paradigm is the villain' (del Castillo 1996; Rebugio 1996).

The resisters adopt time and space perspectives consonant with their own sense of dignity and interests, which at present is a matter of sheer survival for many. Under varied conditions, agents establish political spaces where they can resist globalising structures and craft alternative strategies.

Sites of resistance

With globalisation, politics is being redefined. Civil society transcending the state, if only in an incipient manner, is emerging as a major site of contestation where diverse groups seek to restructure politics, including its time-space dimensions. In a Braudelian sense of time, shared mental frameworks, including paradigms, are shifting, and borders are being redrawn not only in a formal way, but also in terms of real transboundary flows of population, information, knowledge, technology and other products.

The concept of civil society has its roots in the European intellectual tradition, especially the Scottish Enlightenment of the seventeenth and eighteenth centuries, and Western political culture. As the idea is often used in the West, civil society has Hegelian overtones. In this manner, it is regarded as that realm of associational life above the individual and below the state (Wapner 1996). However, for many activists who seek to build an alternative order, the concept is contested and perhaps more in line with Gramsci's notion that 'between the economic structure and the state with its legislation and coercion stands civil society' (Gramsci 1971: 208). The boundaries, however, are blurred and must be negotiated. The way that groups represent themselves, civil society is thus both outside and inside the state. In other words, for Gramsci, the state itself, especially in its interactions with civil society, becomes a terrain of struggle. Indeed today, some of the leaders of civil society occupy important positions in state agencies. This poses an ethical dilemma for the 'independent' organs of civil society.

The state–civil society complex varies dramatically from one context to another, and there are many different kinds of civil society. In some cases, the state monopolises resources, but there are other permutations. In many parts of the non-Western world, claims emerging from civil society were not a feature of political life before recent decades, and the idea was transported from the West. Aside from self-help societies and local charities, a dense web of private, associational life did not exist in Japan and most other areas outside the West before the 1960s and 1970s. In fact, it is generally absent in

Vietnam today, where environmentalists work with a ministry and find little scope for private initiatives outside the state. There is only a handful of Vietnamese environmental NGOs, each one small, based in Hanoi and lacking autonomy. Environmental groups also face severe constraints in Singapore and Malaysia, but the conditions differ and beget a distinctive mix of strategies.

There have been tentative attempts by Singaporean environmentalists, a multiclass group but mainly professionals, administrators and managers, to open up political space and test the state's rhetoric about tolerance. Most notably, the Nature Society of Singapore (NSS), founded over 30 years ago as the Singapore branch of the Malayan Nature Society, has contested government policy within stringent parameters. Inasmuch as NGOs in Singapore are subject to restraining legislation such as the Societies Act and deregistration, which effectively bans their operations, as well as court proceedings, the NSS has represented its actions as 'constructive dialogue'. Comprised of about 2,000 members, the NSS has engaged in letter-writing campaigns, designed a master plan for conservation, and commissioned its own environmental impact assessments (Ho 1997b). The NSS also takes the initiative and submits proposals to the government, even though most of them – perhaps 99 per cent – are rejected. The most extreme move involved enlisting up to 25,000 signatures for a petition and submitting it to the appropriate authority. A major constraint is that the NSS and Singapore's few other environmental groups, which are mainly involved in school activities, risk losing credibility with the state – and thus facing sanctions – if they work with NGOs in other countries. Apart from sharing information, there is little transnational collaboration. Even so, tussles over environmental projects have contributed to important changes in land use: converting 87 hectares zoned for an agro-technology park to a bird sanctuary at Sungei Buloh, shelving plans for a golf course at the Lower Pierce reserve catchment area, and the diversion of a proposed Mass Rapid Transit line so that it would not disrupt the natural habitat of bird life in Senoko (Ho 1997a; Rodan 1996: 106–7; Kong 1994). Notwithstanding coercive rule and co-optation wrought by a post-colonial transformation from poverty to economic well being, and despite a culture that values 'consensus', not dissent, clearly there are fledgling attempts to expand civil society and, however tenuously, to foster resistance.

As in Singapore, civil society in Malaysia is constrained by economic co-optation, draconian laws such as the Internal Security Act (a relic of colonialism that permits detention without trial), and intimidation against environmental activism, including Prime Minister Mahathir Mohamad's rhetoric about 'green imperialism'. So too the state requires NGO registration, controls access to the media, and is dominated by one party, which not only penetrates deeply into society, but also is extremely shrewd in mixing coercion and consent (the ingredients of a hegemonic constellation, in Gramsci's sense, so long as the latter is the predominant element). The holders of state power have nipped off elements of checks and balances – e.g. by eroding the prerogatives of farmers associations and other semi-autonomous structures in the rural areas. Ideological representations – issues of race, language, and religion – have deflected attention from critical problems, including environmental degradation. Nevertheless, there have been bottom-up actions by environmentalists – mobilisation in kampung (villages) around acid pollution, protests over radioactive waste, residence issues concerning trees in Cheras, and logging blockades in Sarawak (Gurmit 1997). A handful of environmental organisations – including the Environmental Protection Society, the Malayan Nature Society, Sahabat Alam Malaysia, and the Centre for Environment, Technology and Development, Malaysia, as well as various consumer associations – have established space for low-key agitation and 'critical collaboration' with the government.

In contrast, a robust civil society has developed in the Philippines, and there are vibrant activities elsewhere – for example, in Thailand and South Korea. A highly politicised Philippine civil society emerged in the context of mobilisation: through armed struggles against Spanish colonialism, US domination, and martial rule. Between the different kinds of civil society activities, illustrated above, environmentalists in other countries push the limits but are ever mindful of the consequences of not respecting them. In all instances, the concrete institutions of civil society, specific to countries and regions, are crucial.

The agents

It is direct and organised action at five levels of civil society that seems to have the greatest impact and bear the most potential for resisting globalisation. A host of international environmental organisations such as Greenpeace, Friends of the Earth, and the World Wildlife Fund work closely with indigenous groups or have local affiliates under their aegis (see Wapner 1996). Most of the former are based in the West, and may or may not have the same agenda as their partners in the Third World (Brosius 1997; Eccleston 1996; Eccleston and Potter 1996). In some cases, those on the ground express reservations about the discrepant priorities of external bodies. At the second level of generality are national coalitions or networks such as the Caucus of Development NGO Networks, an umbrella organisation of 14 major development NGO networks in the Philippines. Its objective is to serve as a network of networks (Songco 1996). Together, these coalitions encompass nearly 3,000 individual organisations. An important research need is to map these coalition structures. Essentially, this is a web-like realm of functionally specialised organisations that link many NGOs, associations, societies, and so on, as well as share a common agenda and set of priorities.

Third, individual NGOs at a national level play multiple roles. They are catalysts that strive to facilitate action, often by advocacy, mobilising resources, and providing expertise: skills in local administration, legal drafting, accounting and other forms of training, as well as research on specific issues. In honing their mission and carrying out research, NGOs require, and indeed seek, analytical paradigms. Swept up in transformations of their livelihoods and modes of existence, leaders of civil society are searching for an understanding of these conditions. Notions such as trickle-down economics, participatory development, and community organising are all born out of paradigms. Yet, with globalisation, more compelling explanations are sought, especially in order to help generate means of action.

Next, although the idiom varies from one country to another, grassroots organisations are engaged in the actual implementation of projects. People's organisations (POs) in the Philippines, for example, are grassroots bodies involved in collective action. They may or may not seek the assistance of NGOs. Finally, civil society also includes a large swathe of unheard masses who are unorganised but not unconcerned citizens, for they too are stakeholders. They can be mobilised around issues of severe environmental degradation, and have been incited to join campaigns to block such activities as illegal logging and the dumping of toxic wastes. Religious leaders, from Catholic bishops to the mufti, have indeed implored their followers to stop ecological destruction. The influence of Buddhism, Christianity, Confucianism, Hinduism, Islam and other religions runs deep in Asian environmental resistance politics, but extends farther down in a context such as the Philippines than in, say, Singapore.

In the Philippines, the Church sometimes serves as an alternative power structure or may help to establish one. Through their sermons, parish priests have rallied the masses to self-organise and to take action such as blocking illegal logging in the Philippine countryside. They have made moral and practical appeals, explaining that 'God created the trees, but the trees are being cut down'. One priest even called on the people to revive their tradition of head-hunting, and this threat was used against the loggers and their collaborators in local government (de Guzman 1996; Dacumos 1996).

Drawing on different support bases of privileged and underprivileged elements, civil society crosscuts class structures, but the roots of the contemporary environmental movement, at least in the more economically advanced areas, are implanted in the privileged sector. Again, it is important to underscore the wide variation from one context to another. In Japan, for example, lawyers, some of them doing pro bono work in other countries in Eastern Asia, as well as intellectuals, have played a leading role in the environmental movement, though the middle classes and many working-class people have mobilised around consumer issues. In some other Eastern Asian countries, environmental politics for the many is linked to matters of livelihood and, thus, social justice, not ecocentric causes – conserving nature for its own sake – as in parts of the 'developed' world (though eco-dhamma, or Green Buddhism, in Thailand may be an exception).

A power structure has emerged within the environmental movement. Groups are arrayed according to size of staff as well as the number of projects undertaken; scope and type of activities; and human and financial resources. In terms of access to resources in Eastern Asia, the organs of civil society have little connection to regional international organisations. For the most part, the formal regional infrastructure to support civil society projects is weak. The Association of Southeast Asian Nations (ASEAN) is largely remote from the day-to-day activities of civil society. Part of the explanation is that different political coalitions are dominant in each country and embrace diverse paradigms, some of which discourage the development of civil society. Another factor is the power relationship between North and South. In civil society in Eastern Asia, ties to Northern governmental and non-governmental institutions are stronger than are links within the sub-regions themselves. Surely regional and subregional international organisations have not developed clear environmental policies, and the United Nations Environmental Programme has not had the capacity to connect to civil society.

In the practice of environmental resistance politics, several problems have arisen. A large NGO bureaucracy has mushroomed, and individual NGOs have established a sense of territoriality. There is no formal code of ethics that governs or mitigates competition among NGOs. More conversation among different institutions in civil society is a good thing, but can there be too much diversity? Sometimes schisms emerge – for example, between the conservationists and those who stress the link between environment and development – over fundamental aims or resources. Bilateral and multilateral aid donors generally offer an environmental package. Implementation of their projects on the ground produces an island effect: isolated initiatives that are not effectively interrelated. Embeddedness in the local social structure is often lacking. Nationally based NGOs can serve as proxies for international agencies, with little or no organic connection to the roots of society. Frequently, there is a pizza effect as well: environmental programmes are spread on top of one another without any overall design (Braganza 1996). In fact, some of the institutions in civil society are not really civil-society driven, but corporate- or state-driven, for they are held accountable to their sponsors and have little autonomy.

Closely related, there is the question of co-optation. Under what conditions do or should grassroots movements accept or rebuff funding, and who is setting the agenda? In a proposed reversal of the classical dependency syndrome built into aid packages and structural adjustment programmes, some organs of civil society have proposed systematically monitoring international agencies and other donors. There is also the ethical dilemma, anticipated by Gramsci over a half century ago, of whether to contest elections in government, and become part of the state, rather than serve as a countervailing source of pressure and perhaps as a social conscience that raises ethical issues. Even if leaders of civil society do not take government posts, the dangers of state substitution and parallelism arise. Government agencies and interstate organisations are essentially subcontracting some of their work to

NGOs. The institutions of civil society thus perform certain functions normally executed by the state, and sometimes carry them out more efficiently than do the politicians and bureaucrats. Nonetheless, there are serious differences over strategies appropriate for contesting globalisation, a wide variety of which has been deployed.

Core strategies of resistance

There is not a single model of resistance, but globalisation is transforming the parameters, redefining the constraints, and upping the environmental ante, especially for future generations. Innovative strategies specifically crafted to resist globalisation, a set of processes detailed elsewhere (Mittelman 1996), are not merely stabs in the dark at an amorphous phenomenon. Some – by no means, all – groups that are self-organising have engaged in self-conscious strategising about countering globalisation. These resisters have thought out the question: what kind of political interventions can be adopted to subject neoliberal globalisation, often mediated by national and local programmes, to social control? Four core strategies seem most important, and are being employed individually or in combination.

Inasmuch as globalisation embraces, and is facilitated by, technological advances, resistance involves developing new knowledge structures. Simply put, a precondition for resisting globalisation is to understand it. Hence the importance of the chain of education–research–information. What some educators are striving to reclaim and transmit is indigenous and traditional knowledge about the environment, which is seen as but one part of building research capacity through networks in an effort to comprehend the dynamics of globalisation. The objective of environmental education is to generate information for action, share it with the public, and channel it to the media so as to challenge globalising forces that jeopardise the public interest. In short, an appreciation for the strategic importance of knowledge generation is not new, but what is novel are the linkages suggested in knowledge production and diffusion as well as perhaps the method to point towards an alternative paradigm. If only in a very preliminary way, it may be possible to piece together a method of developing knowledge for resistance politics: deciphering the codes of domination, exposing the fault lines of power structures, identifying the pressure points for action, and fashioning images for counter-identification (Zawiah 1994: 16–18).

The second core strategy is scaling up: an increase in the scope of operations. More specifically, it is a process whereby groups within civil society broaden their impact by building links with other sectors and extending their reach beyond the local area. Asked what scaling up means in practice, two leaders of civil society, interviewed jointly, stressed 'expanding the level of operations in the field' and 'having a strong voice at the policy level to influence government' (Morales 1996; Serrano 1996). Another activist explained scaling up resistance in terms of the different time horizons of globalisation.

Unlike the resistance that seeks to strike immediately at concrete manifestations of globalisation, scaling up takes a longer span of time. It involves synergising different skills and capacities as well as building spaces to contest globalisation (dela Torre 1996; for a concrete illustration and analysis, see Kelly 1997).

Translated into practice, scaling up can entail establishing multisectoral fora beyond the barangay, the basic unit in the Philippines, or coordinating among several sectors so as to paralyse a city or stop plans for, say, opening casinos. Operationally, however, it seems that when resisters try to scale up, the parametric transformation wrought by globalisation, especially the ideology of neoliberalism, obfuscates its dynamics. Insofar as globalisation's architecture is perceived as too big for local life, it causes disorientation. In some cases, the ambiguity rendered by globalising structures precipitates a paradoxical reaction, which is not to scale up but to scale down. This backlash is an attempt to erect a fortress around the community, to localise rather than to engage the forces of globalisation. Indeed, there is good reason to try to assert local control, particularly in places and spheres of activity where globalisation involves the most acute forms of loss of control. To be sure, the more local groups extend to the global arena, the greater the temptation to conform to global norms. Nonetheless, the quickening speed of environmental degradation, its irreversibility in some cases, and its transnational reach suggest that by itself, scaling down is not a sufficient means to protect nature's endowment.

Third, resisters seek to thrust out in order to gain wider latitude for direct voluntary action. Earlier, reference was made to top-down forms of market-driven and state-led regionalism. In response, regionalism at the base may be either bilateral or multilateral among organisations and movements, and may thrust globally to forge links with civil societies in other regions as well. Although sometimes circumspect about 'going regional' or 'going global' because of fear of being eclipsed or losing control, especially to large Northern partners, Southern NGOs are increasingly aware of the potential advantages of transnational collaboration (Eccleston 1996: 82). In Eastern Asia, the strategy of thrusting out draws significantly on the experience of the Philippines, given the density and relative maturity of civil society there. Its NGO sector has been invited to share experiences with its counterparts in other countries. In dialogue with the representatives of civil society elsewhere, Philippine NGOs have also been involved in monitoring international financial institutions such as the Asian Development Bank and the World Bank, with the goal of fashioning sustainable and alternative policies.

In terms of regional alternatives, the People's Plan for the Twenty-first Century (PP21) is a process that began in Japan in 1989. A coalition of grassroots movements and action groups brought together 360 activists from various countries to meet with thousands of Japanese members of civil society. They sought to establish goals and strategies based on modelling alternative social relations, not direct struggle with state structures. Following a meeting with representatives from six Central American countries, a second PP21 forum was held in Thailand in 1992, and basic concepts were hammered out. Efforts are underway to breathe life into the idea of 'transborder participatory democracy', and consideration is being given to the implications of living according to the strictures of a 'single, global division of labor', a hierarchy that spawns 'inter-people conflicts and antagonism'. As well as conferences, workshops and electronic communication, the PP21 process includes a secretariat based in Tokyo and a quarterly review, AMPO (Muto 1994 and 1996; Inoue 1996).

Engaging regional processes is a space that popular movements in Eastern Asia have sought to establish. For example, environmental organisations in Indonesia, Malaysia, and the Philippines have set up the Climate Action Network, with its own secretariat. In 1995–6, environmental NGOs requested observer status in ASEAN, and were rebuffed on the ground that there is no such mechanism. When this bid was scotched, the NGOs argued that inasmuch as other international institutions, including the United Nations, provide access for people's organisations, ASEAN should do so too. Then in 1997, the members of the Climate Action Network wrote to the ministers of the environment in their respective countries asking for the opportunity to address them, and were told that the officials did not have time for a hearing (Gurmit 1997).

Popular movements in Eastern Asia have also targeted the Asia Pacific Economic Cooperation (APEC) process of governance by summitry and its agenda of deepening and broadening liberalisation policies, which can be far reaching: APEC's 18 members account for about 56 per cent of the world's Gross Domestic Product and 46 per cent of its exports. Working across borders, people's movements took aim at the 1996 APEC summit in Manila. First, they held a preparatory meeting in Kyoto, and mounted parallel NGO fora in various countries, yielding specific resolutions and action points designed to oppose member-governments' trade and investment regimes that damage the environment and transgress people's rights. Preparations entailed pre-summit fact-finding missions to various locales so that delegates themselves could study precisely how forms of integration affect communities and their modes of livelihood. The documentation included a critique of 'the breakneck pace and unilateral character' of blanket liberalisation, especially in terms of its impact on the most vulnerable sectors and the environment, and took issue with the way that the APEC provisions 'dissociate economic issues from their social implications and effects' (Proposed Philippine PO–NGO Position 1996). Women have contested 'APEC opportunities that will fast track our rapidly shifting economic environment' (National Council of Women of the Philippines 1996). In light of a labour market structured along gender lines and the consequences for women and children, delegates called for, among other things, government financing for 'a social welfare agenda to soften globalisation's adverse effects' (Women's Forum 1996). Although probably unintentional, the pre-summit Forum's message seemed to bear shrill – hardly modulated – overtones of a Polanyian analysis; it assailed APEC for its 'anti-democratic, unaccountable and untransparent' free trade processes, and stressed the need to protect the people from 'the ravages of market forces' (Manila People's Forum on APEC 1996).

Without exaggerating the importance of the above instance, there are important lessons to be derived. A market-driven, state-led process – APEC – has catalysed intercourse among resistance movements in different countries, and grassroots organisations have set a regional agenda, one very different from that of state power holders. For example, in contrast to the latter's thrust grassroots groups emphasise the need to link trade and investment, on the one hand, and social policy, on the other. Additionally, this process of resistance not only ties the substate level to the state level, but also elucidates key interactions between regionalism and globalisation.

A fourth strategy of resistance builds innovative relationships between social movements in order directly to engage the market and establish an alternative, sustainable ecological system. In 1986, farmers from Negros Island in the Philippines and Japanese consumer cooperatives, large organisations whose members sought a substitute for the chemically laden products sold on the market, began to trade with one another. Negros grassroots communities searched for a basis to transform the island's sugar-monoculture plantation economy into an integrated system of agriculture, industry and finance. They have fundamentally attempted to remake the economy through the mutual exchange of products and services in a cyclic manner. This project includes a transborder North-South trading system whereby an autonomous association of small farmers delivers chemical-free bananas to Japanese consumer associations of nearly one million people. The Negros growers have developed organic agriculture and set the price of bananas three times higher than the market price of bananas produced by transnational corporations on Mindanao Island. The elevated price, which consumers gladly pay for chemical-free products, amounts to a reverse transfer of value from the North to the South (Hotta 1996; Muto and Kothari n.d.).

At a Tokyo meeting of representatives of the two organisations, I was struck by their class membership – small farmers from Negros and Japanese workers, many of them in the service sector and mostly in the lower reaches of the middle class. Together, these groups have sought to resist not the market economy but market society. They have established an alternative circuit of capital under social control – what Polanyi regarded as re-embedding the market in society and nature. This project includes cross-visits between the two communities so that social and political ties are generalised beyond trading relations. The strategy is a transboundary initiative that breaks out of the cage of the nation-state, and so do other initiatives by risk takers who strive to build social capital.

Community forestry is another example of movement-to-movement relationships that are meant to offer a sustainable alternative to the conventional market system. To substitute non-timber products such as rattan, vines and river resources for wood, links are being forged between corporations, NGOs, and associations of direct producers (Tengco 1996). Without going into further detail, it is apparent that patterns of organised resistance are deepening, leading to multilayering strategies employed according to the varied ways that globalising trends affect individual countries and regions. Such efforts may be suggestive in terms of alternative means of governing the environment.

Fledgling tendencies

This moment in history is producing strong disjunctures. Most important for the purposes of this discussion, globalisation's hegemonic project is neoliberalism, and liberal democracy cannot keep pace with its spread. In the space opened by this disjuncture, resistance to neoliberal globalisation is mounting, but thus far has had a limited impact. This resistance is a spur to redefine politics, to allow more space for non-state politics. Within civil society, one of the reasons for forming coalitions and networks is to foster more democratic politics. However, upscaling and linking these associations does not of course solve the problem of hierarchical power relations integral to top-down globalisation. As a political vehicle countering globalisation, environmental resistance movements run on many engines. They can both follow and lead the state.

On the basis of the foregoing research findings, it is possible to identify five trends – micro counterglobalising activities, if you will: (1) In light of the diversity of experiences and contexts, many environmental initiatives are issue-oriented and subject-specific. At present, most environmental struggles are localised. (2) Nonetheless, there is a putting together of modest resistance activities based on the forging of overlapping alliances and networks within and between regions. (3) Environmental movements have implicitly adopted a policy of parallelism – i.e. replicating in one context resistance strategies that have proven successful elsewhere. (4) The core strategies are positive, not a negation, in the sense of engagement; they do not evade – delink from – either the market or the state. (5) The resistance is accumulating critical venues such as cultural integrity and ancestral domain, finding openings, and establishing political space.

Quite clearly, it would be wrong to celebrate these Polanyian counterforces. One might even call them what Polanyi (1957: 239) regarded as a 'move' rather than movements to indicate the proto forms by which social forces 'waxed and waned' and ultimately gave birth to a political organisation that begot a transformation of a particular kind. Although some of today's counterforces are federating, surely environmental resistance movements are anything but coherent. Perhaps a high level of coherence is a desideratum that should be balanced against another consideration, namely that civil society feeds on diversity (Serrano 1994: 309). Also, given the impediments to organising, regional and interregional solidarity from below is a ways off. Regional and global civil societies are, at best, nascent and highly uneven.

At the end of the day, the impetus for resistance politics is not only material or technological, but decidedly intertwined with the environmental ethic of protecting people and their diverse ways of life against quickening market forces. The words of a Jesuit priest engaged in environmental struggles in the Philippines give pause: 'Spirituality is associated with suffering. This landscape bleeds. This is a suffering landscape' (Walpole 1996). The force of this message drives a powerful spiritual question in the path of neoliberal globalisation: Must the environment be experienced negatively, as a constraint, in terms of destruction, rather than as beauty to be relished and preserved? Posing the dilemma in this way raises the political issue of who should be entrusted, or empowered, to look after the public good.

Notes

1 This chapter draws on my 'Globalisation and Environmental Resistance Politics', *Third World Quarterly* 19, 5 (1998). It incorporates research findings from my large-scale, cross-regional project, including 75 interviews with environmental activists, undertaken in nine countries in Eastern Asia and Southern Africa over six years (Mittelman 2000). For awards that enabled me to carry out the fieldwork, I owe a debt of gratitude to the Professional Staff Congress of the City University of New York and the World Society Foundation. For institutional support for the component on Asia, I acknowledge the School of International Service, American University; the Institute of Southeast Asian Studies, Singapore; and the Institute of Malaysian and International Studies, Universiti Kebangsaan Malaysia. At my home university, Paul Wapner generously shared materials and offered guidance in exploring the extensive scholarly literature on environmental politics. Special thanks are due to two assistants who played a key role in different phases of the research on Asia: Juliet Litterer and Ashwini Tambe in Washington DC. I am indebted as well as to other colleagues who facilitated this study, especially Jorge Emmanuel, Akihiko Kimijima, Francisco Magno, Leonor Magtolis-Briones and Chito Salazar. I am grateful for critical comments on drafts of this chapter, provided by Glenn Adler, Linda J. Yarr, and the editors of this book. All errors, of course, remain mine alone.
2 In keeping with conventional practice, I use the term 'NGO', but with reservation. NGO is an unfortunate construct since, by definition, it is a negation, and the frame of reference is solely the state.
3 This formulation embodies a departure from the Cartesian dualism of humankind and nature.

Part II
Regional reformations

6 The political economy of globalisation in East Asia

The salience of 'region building'

Richard Higgott

Introduction

The currency and stock market collapses in East Asia of 1997–8 (especially Thailand, Indonesia, South Korea and Malaysia) have made it difficult for some Western analysts to disguise a certain *Schadenfreude* at the discomfort that comes in the wake of the escalating hubris – encapsulated in the 'Asian Way' and 'Asian Miracle' clichés – that accompanied East Asian growth throughout the 1990s. But narrowly economistic readings of these events ignore other secular trends that may even be consolidated by the economic shocks. One such trend is the prospect of continued development of an 'East Asian' as opposed to 'Asia-Pacific' understanding of region. To argue this case flies in the face of conventional realist wisdom that in times of crisis the national urge to act independently comes to the fore. But, it will be an argument of this chapter that the enhancement of greater collective regional understanding in the wake of the economic crisis is not incompatible with the desire for strengthened national decision making autonomy in the face of crisis.

The chapter combines a theoretical reading of the relationship between globalisation and regionalisation with some empirical evidence for the importance of region building in East Asia, both before and after the economic shocks of 1997–8. Section one focuses on the trend towards regionalism which is argued not to be contradictory to globalisation but integral to it. It is in the relationship between globalisation and regionalisation that the distinction between *de facto* 'economic integration' and *de jure* 'political institutionalisation' – what we might call a 'political economy perspective' – offers heuristic insights.

Section two focuses on the importance of 'identity' as a yet little understood dimension of the contemporary regional urge. Given the domination of economic explanations of regionalism, identity questions – or more precisely, the move towards greater shared regional understanding in a range of policy areas – are neither amenable to quantitative analysis nor parsimonious theorising and fall into the analytical 'too hard box'. But the salience of regional policy building – what we might call the 'sociological or constructivist perspective' on regionalism – is indissoluble from the enhanced economic activity that is part of the overall structural transformation taking place in the global economy.

The Asia-Pacific, and East Asia in particular, is the least institutionally developed of the three regional pillars of the contemporary global order when contrasted with Europe and North America. Thus they offer the best laboratory in which to demonstrate the salience of identity building. Section three, the most tentative section of the chapter, argues that the trend towards region building will not axiomatically be curtailed by recent economic woes, and that there is some evidence of regional 'learning' arising from the crisis that may well consolidate the economic policy coordination that gathered pace in the 1980s.

This chapter accepts the problematic nature of globalisation and offers a twofold definition of the concept as: (i) the emergence of a set of sequences and processes increasingly less hindered by territorial or jurisdictional barriers and one that enhances the spread of trans-border practices in economic, political, cultural and social domains; and (ii) as a discourse of political knowledge offering one view – perhaps the dominant one among powerful decision making elite – of how to make the postmodern world manageable. For many, globalisation as knowledge constitutes a rationalisation of government that challenges the language and imagery of a state-centric world and defines the limits of the possible.

Accompanying this discourse of globalisation is a discourse of regionalisation. Regionalisation is a contested term which scholars and practitioners have traditionally understood as interstate activity ranging from nascent policy coordination of the kind taking place in the Asia-Pacific through to the full blown integration of states within a common market as in the development of the European Union (EU) over the last forty years. This is too simple. We must contend with at least three interactive and evolving processes that represent intermediary stages in the relationship between the state and globalisation, giving rise to new forms of regional geo-governance:

1   *de facto* economic integration (at both global and regional levels) and *de jure* processes of regional institutionalised governance;
2   emerging (vertical) meso-levels of authority between the state and the global order (trans or supra-national regionalisation) and between the state and the local level (sub-national regionalisation);
3   emerging (horizontal) authority across extant territorial jurisdictions (Natural Economic Territories or growth triangles).

The political economy of globalisation and regionalisation

Some analysts (Hirst and Thompson 1996; Cable 1995) have suggested that globalisation – as the increased ratio of international trade to GDP or that of

FDI to domestic investment – is exaggerated and that the integration of the international economy is little more advanced post-1980 than it was pre-1914. Maybe, but this misses the larger point. There has been growth in both internationalisation and regionalisation of production, and finance; the increasing importance of the NIEs over the last 30 years, notwithstanding the crisis, has brought a change in the international division of labour; the EU, North America and the East Asian NIEs now have more equal shares of world trade than at the end of the Second World War; FDI has exhibited stronger regional as well as global tendencies; market (corporate) power has grown at the expense of state authority; governmental autonomy has been mitigated and the role of the state is changed as other salient actors emerge. These include global actors such as the IMF, the World Bank and the WTO as well as a range of sub-national regional actors.

The tendency for authority to shift – both upwards and downwards – and the increased role for a variegated range of actors, and different levels of loyalty, was identified over two decades ago by Hedley Bull (1977: 245) as the 'new medievalism' as an alternative to the modern Westphalian state system of the last 300 or so years. But we should not lose sight of the fact that the 'new medievalism' is a metaphor, albeit one which recognises that the globalisation of the international economy does not take place in isolation from change in the role of the state as the dominant actor in this system when faced with the emergence of competing authorities and multiple notions of loyalty and identity (see also the chapters by Jessop, Paderanga and Sassen, this volume). In the absence of satisfactory global structures, the development of regional structures becomes salient.

But 'regionness' varies by policy issue and by what the dominant actors in a given group of countries, at a given time, see as their priorities. Shared historical, linguistic and/or cultural characteristics traditionally define a region, but with the attempts to construct understandings of region around the Pacific Ocean, these factors have lost some salience. While there may be structural incentives to regional cooperation (proximity, dramatic techno-logical and economic growth and enhanced interaction flowing from it) regions are socially constructed – they need positive social and political action to advance them.

The most basic definitions of economic regionalism are those of 'closed' and 'open' regionalism. The European Union is held by economists as the exemplar of closed regionalism, concerned with economic liberalisation for a large protected market but reinforced by a centralised hierarchy of power and a common internal rules-based regime managed by strong institutional structures exhibiting socio-political as well as economic objectives. Counter arguments suggest regionalism mitigates economic nationalism, and provides for the codification, transparency and regulation of trade. Open regionalism, a fashionable if illusive concept, finds its exemplar in the development of APEC. Defined as 'regional economic integration without discrimination against outsiders', it is institutionally informal and liberalisation is advanced by a process of 'concerted unilateralism'. Advocates claim it offers a foundation upon which proliferating regional arrangements and the multilateral trading system can be reconciled (Garnaut 1997).

The role for regions

We should see a trend towards regionalisation as an intermediary stage in the relationship between states and the global economy. If globalisation is both a set of processes and an ideology of economic management, then regionalism in East Asia and the Pacific is a manifestation of globalisation. But regionalism is a dual level project. At the *de facto* level it has been firm-led and network-led within markets and the principal actors are networks of regional firms and corporations giving rise to a regionalisation of production in an East Asian context as foreign direct investment from Japan, Korea and Taiwan became increasingly important throughout the 1980s and the 1990s in underwriting development in Southeast Asia (see Dicken and Yeung, this volume). *De facto* regionalisation has not been policy driven by governments. At the same time, the system of exchange – that is the trading relationship – continued to exhibit a strong Asia-Pacific regional complexion in which the United States represented the largest market for the products of the major trading states of East Asia.

At the *de jure* level it is 'statist' institutional cooperation and it can take a number of forms – for example, loosely agreed, or institutionally sanctioned trade commitments between states geared towards enhanced cooperation of either a binding or non binding nature. This is a government-led process with the principal actors drawn from trans-regional policy communities made up of public and private sector managers from the political, bureaucratic and research communities of the states of the region. Track two organisations such as the Pacific Economic Cooperation Council (PECC) and the Council for Security Cooperation in the Asia-Pacific (CSCAP) provide the intellectual support system for a nascent regional architecture of intergovernmental bodies such as Asia-Pacific Economic Cooperation Forum (APEC) in the economic domain and the ASEAN Regional Forum (ARF) in the security domain.

Globalisation has had the effect of changing the 'rules of the game' in the struggle for competitive advantage among firms within, as well as between, countries and regions. As such, globalisation has been a spur to regionalisation of both a private (*de facto*) nature and public (*de jure*) nature. States have introduced regionalisation policies to enhance the credibility of regional members *vis-à-vis* external actors, especially sources of FDI. Entering regional agreements provides policy discipline – often in the face of domestic opposition – the aim of which is to make up collectively in the region for diminished domestic policy autonomy. These processes do not take place in a uniform fashion. Broad brush distinctions exist – Europe as a multilevel mode of regionalist governance, North America as a Hub and Spoke exercise in governance, and the Asia-Pacific as an emerging, but still looser institutional, market-led system of regional cooperation.

The debate on the dialectic of globalisation and regionalism proliferates. For too long, this debate has focused on trade policy matters – notably whether the emergence of regional trading arrangements support, or detract from, an open/liberal trading regime. An excessive concentration on the political economy of trade has led to a neglect of the political economy of capital mobility and the less tangible question of regional identity building. Both, as the crisis in East Asia shows, have been ignored at considerable cost.

The dramatic deregulation of the international financial system in the 1980s saw competition to attract FDI become more intense. The Single Integrated Market and NAFTA increased demand for FDI. In addition, after the Cold War, Eastern Europe joined finance hungry China and Southeast Asia in the search for FDI. Only by offering regional inducements, argue many analysts, could one region expect to compete successfully against another. In short, a need to persuade global firms of the virtue of region X over Y as a site for FDI spurs regionalisation. In sum, it was not only the internationalisation of investment but also the regionalisation of investment that helped change the nature of manufacturing and trade patterns throughout the 1980s and 1990s.

This point has been illustrated in exemplary fashion by the recent history of East Asia (taken to mean both Southeast and Northeast Asia). The late 1980s and early 1990s saw FDI take on a strong regional character as Northeast Asia (Japan, South Korea and Taiwan) became the major investor in ASEAN. Indeed, while Japanese FDI decreased by nearly 40 per cent overall between 1989 and 1994, investment in ASEAN grew by 17.7 per cent (Bowles 1997). The pattern for production reinforces the point. In 1995, over 10 per cent of Japanese-owned companies' total output was produced outside of Japan, compared with 4 per cent in 1986. While this growth was a global phenomenon for Japanese companies, the growth in imports of consumer goods into Japan from Japanese-owned factories in Asia was more striking. Between 1992 and 1996, imports from foreign subsidiaries rose from 4 to 14 per cent of imports overall. Whilst almost everything made by Japanese companies in the USA was sold there, a growing proportion of the product of their Asian subsidiaries was imported into Japan (Hatch and Yamamura 1996).

What will the effect of the economic down turn in East Asia be on this pattern of development? The evidence of early 1998 would suggest that while the strength of this trend is likely to weaken in the wake of the crisis, its nature will remain unchanged. By February 1998 all 19 of Japan's major trading houses in Southeast Asia had experienced sharp drops in regional business and many had begun to scale down investment and production. In automobiles, Nissan, Toyota and Daihatsu and in electronics Hitachi and Matsushita cut back activity sharply in 1998. Significantly, however, none expressed an intention to withdraw from the region and all aspire to keep their affiliates afloat pending a return to stronger economic times (*The Nikkei Weekly* 9 February 1998: 18).

Globalisation is a stronger structural force than regionalisation – especially the need to conform to a liberal orthodoxy and the preferences of multi-national corporations within regions. Globalisation further enhances region-alism by encouraging collective action problem solving. But while the changing nature of the global economy provides the structural context for change, it is still governments that are the agents of institutional co-operation. Policy emerges from a wider community of actors that exhibit a common neo-liberal ideology underpinning regional decision making processes.

For example, throughout the 1990s 'open regionalism' and market-led integration – the themes of APEC – have been impeccable in protesting their faith in a neo-classical theory of free trade. Increased exposure to the effects of international markets, in both trade and investment, required not only domestic policy adjustments, but also generated a desire by regional policy elites to address these problems collectively. Having been historically slower than the USA and European states to recognise the international dimensions of adjustment via collective action, the growing interest of Asian NIEs in enhanced regional economic cooperation represented a new stage in their international economic understanding. But while the increased activity of APEC and ASEAN in the 1990s suggests regional learning has been occurring, the implication to be drawn from the crisis of 1997 is that it has not been quick enough nor substantial enough. The question is whether the crisis might spur or impede enhanced regional economic dialogue.

Explaining regionalism in Asia: from rationialism to social constructivism?

The previous section outlined a political economy approach to region build-ing. It is, rightly so, the dominant explanatory approach. But it is insufficient. Ideas shape agendas and ideational factors must now inform understanding of region-construction more than in the past. This assertion finds support in the European regional experience. It also finds support in the Asia-Pacific in recent years. The last decade has seen a convergence in the dominant ideas system under-writing policy change in both regions. Specifically, ideas under-writing policy making on questions of regional cooperation have largely drawn their epistemological strength from a neo-liberal ideology (Gill 1995).

In a European policy context this is detailed in the development of the Single Market Programme. In the Asia-Pacific it has led to the development of a policy commitment to market led open regionalism. The source of these ideas is to be found not simply in the interests identified by policy making elite, but also in the ideational influence of a wider community of like minded corporate sector actors, scholars, research brokers and practitioners (both public and private) engaged in the definition of regional identities, problems and putative proposals for their resolution.

For members of the Asia-Pacific policy making elite, open regionalism took on the status of a normatively good thing throughout the boom years of the 1990s. That it was not popular in all sections of the Asia-Pacific policy community – *pace* the views of Malaysian Prime Minister Dr Mohammed Mahathir – did not detract from its growing importance as an agenda setting metaphor in the debate about regionalism under multilateralism after the Uruguay Round (Dieter 1997). APEC is a creature of economic liberalism and open regionalism is the dominant discourse on economic region building in the Asia-Pacific. The narrative of APEC is a political construct as well as an economic one.

But if the notion of open regionalism provided the ideational underpinnings of the economic policy dialogue across the Asia-Pacific throughout the 1980s, it did not do so in an uncontested manner. Equally important has been the development of a sense of regional identity in a more tightly defined East Asian context. APEC can be seen as an Asia-Pacific region-wide exercise in dialogue with aspirations to become the vehicle for setting regional economic policy for the twenty-first century. But it is not the only voice of region in the Asia-Pacific. The East Asian Economic Caucus (EAEC) or the 'Asia 10'[1] is an East Asian response to APEC motivated by state-centred understandings of political interest. The governing elite of Asia, given a history of conflict, might not think of each other as natural partners, but an effect of globalisation has been the evolution of regional cooperative dialogues. A policy community of the principal players (public and private) has become gradually normatively wedded to a regional dialogue on liberalisation.

Economic literature explains collective action problems but it is not adept at dealing with the causal relationship between power and purpose on the one hand or identity and interest on the other. Inter-subjective explanation is invariably seen as secondary to rationalist utility maximising understandings of interest, geographical proximity and gravity models of intra-regional trade. But economic theory alone cannot explain enhanced regional dialogue and nascent institutionalisation. Interests change with learning, persuasion, knowledge and ideology (see Adler and Crawford 1991). Policy is not structurally determined. The history of East Asia prior to the 1997 crises demonstrated that strict rationalist assumptions about utility maximisation were too parsimonious. Perception and interpretative practices also play a role in shaping regional actor preferences.

Specifically, the activities of the Asia-Pacific trans-regional policy elite between 1989 and 1997 demonstrated how a shared, context-specific understanding of region amongst these elites was developing alongside the consolidation of economic indicators of region. From a more socio-constructivist position, national interest is the outcome of a combination of both power and values. APEC, and more so the EAEC, need to be understood not only as rationalistic but also processes that may defy the rationalist logic underpinning realist and liberal–institutionalist approaches to cooperation.

The EAEC represents an alternative politico-ideational construction to APEC (Higgott and Stubbs 1995). It reflects the development of regional 'intersubjective structures' constituted by some '. . . shared understandings, expectations and social knowledge embedded in international institutions and threat complexes, in terms of which states define (some of) their identities and interests' (Wendt 1994: 389). As a consequence, new institutional structures of region have been laid down that are not just the outcome of rational utility maximising. We may be witnessing the internalisation of 'new understandings and roles . . . [and] . . . shared commitments to social norms' (Wendt 1992: 417) developing out of the very practices of enhanced regional economic dialogue.

Institutional structures, of course, vary as to degree, kind and context. While not unaware of the longer-term welfare benefits of greater cooperation, Asian leaders are often seduced by the short-term gains to be had from regional non-cooperation. State building in Asia takes precedence over the 'pooling' of sovereignty to advance policy coordination. Thus we must ask if the material and ideational structures in the Asia-Pacific provide incentives for collective regional problem solving? Specifically in need of investigation is (i) the degree to which the dynamic economic density that had been developing up until 1997 and the degree to which a more benign security environment had emerged since the end of the Cold War provided a more positive context within which new discursive strategies of regional economic and security cooperation might flourish and (ii) the degree to which enhanced interaction – even recent economic vicissitudes – strengthen or inhibit incentives for policy making elites to identify with one another in the interest of policy coordination?

It is not inevitable that states of the region will continue to consolidate collective interests. Historical experience does not support a claim for greater regional identification. But systemic interaction in the Asia-Pacific prior to the crisis had influenced the attitudes of policy makers to some important regional questions. Boldly stated, identity became a factor in interregional relations (Dirlik 1993a). Lest there be doubt about its salience, consider briefly two counterfactual cases in European and Asian region building.

Turkey and Australia both demonstrate high economic interdependence with their regional partners. In patterns of both trade and FDI they exhibit strong *de facto* economic integration into the EU and East Asia. Yet, Turkey's formal membership of the EU has to-date been blocked – the reasons for this are only secondarily economic, a lack of a European cultural identity being the 'real' reason (Wensley 1997) – and Australia, notwithstanding its economic complementarity and strenuous efforts to build bridges, has not realised significant formal links with its East Asian neighbours. Australia is not part of the EAEC and has to date failed to gain admission to ASEM. Worse, its 'Asian pretensions' have, on occasion, been ridiculed (Higgott and Nossal 1997).

These two cases suggest the importance of an 'imagined' or 'invented' understanding of region. Regions are cognitively constructed as much as they are determined historically, geographically or economically. This cognitive process in East Asia is not deep. There is an absence of other than an instrumental or tactical commitment to cooperation. There is no collective objective comparable to a 'European Ideal' or 'deepening' (Higgott 1997b). Despite Eurosceptic resistance, 'Europe' exists in substance. 'Asia' does not.

But the identification of European and North American economic space and policy positions has fostered the identification of distinct Asian policy positions. Just as the European Commission, via the Cecchini Report, developed a 'distinct discursive strategy . . . to place the idea of Europe as an economic entity on the agenda' (Rosamond 1996), so too the regional and international diplomacy of Asia and the Pacific in the closing stages of the twentieth century reflects the evolution of discursive strategies by different groups of actors with multilevel regional agendas. Serious processes of regional cooperation are being attempted (Mack and Ravenhill 1994). Since the end of the Cold War the regional allies of the two major protagonists have explored different – more multilateral – approaches to their regional foreign policy environments In so doing, the notion of 'region' has become more important than in the past.

Without over-stating the case, it is necessary to think about the invention of region or, more modestly, a set of significant sources of regional dialogue giving rise to multiple over-lapping and intertwined institutions that form the basis of a regional architecture of enhanced cooperation and nascent regional problem solving capability where none has previously existed. There is no one *de jure* voice of region. Region is defined by membership and by issue. In institutional terms there are three basic voices of region:

1   *Southeast Asia*, articulated via ASEAN and bodies such as the ASEAN Free Trade Area and the ASEAN Regional Forum;
2   *East Asia,* increasingly articulated through the discussions of the East Asian Economic Caucus (EAEC, that is ASEAN plus Japan, South Korea and the PRC) that are also involved in the Asia Europe Meeting (ASEM) process
3   the *Asia-Pacific,* articulated via APEC with added 'Western voices' from the USA, Canada, Australia and New Zealand.

None of these groupings are without internal tensions (they lack the formal 'legalised' structures of the EU) but nor have they been incapable of articulating a range of specific policy positions. Examples can be found in the economic domain in the activities of bodies such as AFTA, the East Asia Economic Caucus (EAEC), Asia Pacific Economic Corporation (APEC) and the development of a range of NETS or growth triangles; in the political/security domain in the activities of ASEAN and the ARF; in interregional relations via the inauguration and development of the ASEM process. These exercises in social learning are more important than many outside observers assume.

Within a tripartite regional policy community – consisting of key actors within the corporate, governmental/bureaucratic and research communities of bodies like the Pacific Basin Economic Council (PBEC), the Pacific Economic Cooperation Council (PECC), the Pacific Business Forum (PBF) and APEC initiatives such as the Eminent Persons Group (EPG) – actors are emerging similar to those identified in the European context such as the European Roundtable of Industrialists (Cowles 1995). Interaction in Asia is not as deep as in Europe and policy learning is still at the instrumental end of a instrumental–cognitive spectrum with no roots in the civil societies of the member states. The regionalisation of many institutional or social practices and relationships is still resisted, although this resistance is often stronger at the rhetorical level than in practice.

But Asian objections to European legal-formalism aside, institutions have played a stronger regional role throughout the 1990s. Many states have adhered positively to the norms and institutional principles set out by the WTO, often in a manner greater than they publicly acknowledge. While the notion of Asia as a focal point for identity exists only in the minds of a small number of the most devoted members of that transnational community of Asia-Pacific scholars and practitioners, this is not the point. Especially in the economic domain, an 'Asian regional approach' to problem solving is a manifestation of Asian intent and capability to enhance regional positions. The development of 'Asian positions' on some issues reflects the interactive relationship between globalisation and regionalisation. Policy elites implement policy within a context of global understanding – in so doing, they often reflect policy positions and interests informed by a 'neo-liberal' discourse. The regionalisation of these positions had been enhancing East Asian bargaining strength within wider global contexts.

For example, a harmonisation of opinion amongst Asian states developed throughout the mid-1990s *vis-à-vis* US attitudes to labour standards. Any reservations about policies became less important than who was advancing them. Policy makers in Japan may have felt ill at ease with the labour policies pursued by some Southeast Asia states, but were less impressed by 'intrusive' American and European, pressure on these issues. Similarly, some ASEAN states have been uneasy with the admission of Myannmar to their ranks, but they have refused to make common cause with Europeans on the issue.

For some, the 'Asian way' to diplomacy is a more precise concept than the all embracing notion of 'Asian values' (Amitav 1997). It is seen as a way of stemming the intrusion of Western value systems without having to reject economic and technological modernisation. It implies resistance to the hegemony of the USA's 'Asia-Pacific' discursive strategy. To the extent that an 'Asian Way' to diplomacy has meaning, it is as much by how it is responded to by actors exogenous to the region as to how it harmonises the behaviour of actors within the region. Outsiders feel obliged to define their policies to individual East Asian states in regionalist terms. Such socio-political aims may seem 'fuzzy', but they are no less significant because they do not lend themselves to quantitative analysis. Cognition and ideas are important in the identification of regional communities.

We are in the early stages of a set of multiple responses to globalisation. The variation in the forms that regionalisation may take are wide ranging and may give rise to *ad hoc*, more or less rule governed and institutionalised contexts for adjustment. Adjustment to recent economic crises in East Asia will be determined by the logics of globalisation on the one hand, but also by emerging regional tendencies and influences on the other. These mixed levels of regional dialogue – and the projection of Asian voices into the wider international context – have had both theoretical and policy implications. At a theoretical level, the development of regional identities and the evolution of trans-regional policy communities with a growing commonality of interests over a range of areas, can take us beyond realist understandings of the foreign policy process in the Asia-Pacific. In addition to the primacy of 'interest' we need also to pay attention to the manner in which systemic interaction amongst policy elites taking place within fora such as APEC, ASEAN and the EAEC may generate collective responses to international issues. This interaction constructs new and multiple understandings of identity among regional elites, some immediate implications of which are discussed in the next section.

Globalisation, the politics of resentment and region building: some lessons from the currency crises of 1997–8

Realist policy analysts would dismiss the theoretical argumentation of the preceding section. Surely, financial crises, stock market shake-outs, environmental disasters, ongoing security problems on the Korean Peninsula and in the South China Sea and the prospects of instability and dislocation arising from first-generation political transition in many countries confirm the continued salience of realist analysis. But recent realist readings of East Asia fail to acknowledge the regionalisation of these factors and the manner in which there is a growing desire to solve or, importantly for the modest argument of this chapter, attempt to solve problems collectively. This can even be illustrated since 1997. The currency crises were both global and regional in scope and policy response. Their impact on Asia and the responses called forth tell us something about differing understandings of region that are emerging in East Asia and the Pacific.

The popular, Western view of the behaviour of the US and the IMF in the wake of the economic crisis in East Asia is that the IMF has effectively bailed out South Korea, Thailand and Indonesia after they got themselves into trouble largely by acts of their own making. That the acts may have been, in large part at least, of their own making is not contested. That US and the international financial institutions have saved the day – and will be duly recognised and appreciated for doing so – is contested.

There is an alternative reading, which sees the crisis as being as much the product of excessive deregulation of the financial markets – that allowed Asian firms to engage in massive overseas borrowing in the first instance – as it was the result of corrupt, or incompetent Asian borrowers (see Higgott 1998). If the optimism that generated the high inflows of capital to the region was excessive, then so, too, has been the market panic that saw the process reversed in a few short months. Those international investors who thought the East Asian NIEs could do no wrong until early 1997 appeared after that date to think they could do no right, thus causing panic and the ensuing currency and business collapses well beyond what the underlying economic situation has warranted.[2]

This analysis is not a defence of the grosser infelicities of Asian business culture, rather, it is as a starting point for thinking about regional political responses to the economic crisis and especially longer-term Asian responses to Western neo-liberal (IMF) approaches to reform – domestic austerity and financial restructuring. If the USA and the IMF have their way, then such a model of liberalisation, replacing the Asian, developmental statist 'high debt model', may come into place overtime.

Alternatively, it could also see a hardening nationalist resistance to neo-liberalism. For what has been challenged in the crisis of the East Asian NIES in the late twentieth century is the very model on which they have built their success. This is not only as an economic crisis, but also an 'ideas battle'. No sooner is one bout of triumphalism over – having 'won' the Cold War against Soviet style collectivism – than liberalism is protesting its superiority over the so-called 'Asian' model. This may not play well in the long run and can expect to fuel Asian resentment at the policy responses it has been forced to adopt.

That the Asian model would have changed after the end of the Cold War anyway does not undermine the prospects for growing resentment in the region. During the Cold War US willingness to supply capital and open its markets for a largely one way flow of exports was predicated on the consideration of containing communism. By the late 1980s, that geo-strategic window of opportunity – used so well by South Korea especially – was closing rapidly. In a more benign environment, American concerns that its allies were free riding saw an increasing clamour for change within the US policy community. Regional economic trade liberalisation and financial deregulation were to be the American pay-off for a continued Asian security presence.

As a consequence, those socio-political practices of the Asian model that were acceptable for security reasons during the Cold War – exclusionary politics, nepotism and the blurred lines of authority between political and economic power – now clash more violently with the interests of private capital in search of greater market share and profits in an era of deregulation. Most East Asian political leaders recognised that the currency and stock market collapses arose from a combination of property booms and other bad investments on the one hand and mismanagement, corruption and inefficiency in both public and private decision making sectors – especially the cosy relationship between governments and business – on the other. The Southeast Asian middle classes hold their political and economic elite accountable for the mess and even though so-called 'crony capitalism' is an insufficient explanation of the magnitude of the crisis, it is recognised that adjustment will be painful and require 'creative destruction'.

Thus the real question, in both the short and longer term, is the degree to which regional economic and political leaders will be willing, and/or able, to grasp the nettle of economic adjustment in an era of potential political instability that will accompany the generational transition processes in many countries. This remains an open and multidimensional question, but there is evidence to point towards a 'regionalisation of thinking' on these issues supportive of the broader argument advanced in this chapter.

For example, the main donors for the initial financial adjustment package to stem the haemorrhage of the Thai economy in late 1997 were Japan ($4 billion) Korea and Taiwan ($2 billion) Australia and the PRC ($1 billion) were all from the region. Their motives may have been mixed but this is less important than their demonstrable desire to be involved in the process. All states in their own ways were attempting to consolidate their regional positions in both an economic *(de facto)* and political *(de jure)* fashion. This process of 'regional supportiveness' – albeit largely gesture politics – continued throughout 1998.

Conversely, not only did the US refuse to support the package, it also opposed regional calls to set up a Japan led $100 billion 'Asian only' bailout. This generated considerable regional resentment towards the US which in turn galvanised the USA and the IMF (for purposes here the two are indistinguishable) into strongly reasserting their position that adjustment funds not under the direct or indirect control of the IMF might not be 'properly used'. Their desire to control adjustment funding has to-date prevailed. But, in so doing, the seeds of polarisation of the Asian and Caucasian members of APEC may have been sown. The exhortatory liberalisation rhetoric of the November 1997 Vancouver APEC summit only superficially concealed a deeper schism between the states on the two edges of the Pacific.

The turmoil of 1997–8 reinforced the notion of the Asia-Pacific region as an artificial construction, the long-term salience of which may well have been affected by the regional resentment at US dominated policy responses to the crisis. IMF style solutions to reform may represent defensible economic theory, but they also reflect US power as a threat to extant patterns of political and economic power in the region. Asian policy elites may take, digest and implement their adjustment medicine, but in looking to the future, the liberal agenda of APEC is likely to resonate less with regional decision-makers.

Moreover, Asian leaders are developing dialogues that may lead to new forms of cooperation. ASEAN finance ministers meeting in Manila (1–2 December 1997) agreed a framework whereby member states would engage in the mutual surveillance of each other's economies. This agreement, unthinkable prior to the crisis, demonstrates a desire to enhance regional policy making capabilities. While it was anchored within the existing international financial institutional context, the Manila framework represents a contribution to regional institutional economic architecture that fits no existing model.

The ambivalent relationship that has always existed between the states of East Asia and the USA (and US-led institutions) has been brought into sharp relief by the collapse of the East Asian currencies and the subsequent process of international intervention. As time progresses, the nature of the bailout seems increasingly problematic to Asian elites. For many the crisis appears to have presented the IMF with the opportunity to open East Asian economies, pave the way for international banks to make inroads into the region's banking sector and for US firms to achieve unprecedented market access (see Khor 1998: 29).

Most resented of all is a widely held view that there is a double standard present in the IMF insistence that regional governments not rescue local financial institutions, while at the same time insisting that they guarantee the repayment of international loans, thus alleviating foreign lending houses from 'moral hazard'. To the educated populations of the crisis-hit countries, this is local entrepreneurs paying for their mistakes while foreign investors are underwritten at local expense, thus undermining the legitimacy of the externally coerced policy recommendations from the IMF. For Asian elites, the real bailout has not been of their economies but of the foreign investment houses.

Conclusion

The preceding section represents an alternative reading of the economic crisis to that found in mainstream Western policy analysis. But perception counts and this one resonates at the heart of the East Asian public and private sector policy making community in 1998. If it has substance it can be expected to have longer-term implications for the international relations of the Asia-Pacific region. The economic meltdown of 1997–8 is seen as the darker side of globalisation, and not just in the more vocal states such as Malaysia. *The Bangkok Post* (9 December 1997: 3) argued for example, that 'the juggernaut of globalisation' must not become a vehicle of a 'global monoculture.'

In addition, the nature of the IMF reforms has brought the North-South divide back into the open in the relationship between the Caucasian and Asian members of APEC. For many Asians, it was never eradicated from the Pacific dialogue anyway. Resentment and resistance exists not only within the domestic polities of the region, but also in the trans-regional policy making communities that, imbued with the neo-liberal ethos, had been striding towards greater harmonisation of economic policy making across the Asia-Pacific within APEC. The crisis may make the gap across the Pacific greater rather than smaller. A putative regional economic grouping – like the East Asia Economic Caucus – may prove more conducive to the interests of the regional policy elite in the long term than APEC. Unlike APEC, EAEC is unambiguously 'regional' and may be a more sympathetic venue for East Asia's political leaders – especially if their domestic political positions become more precarious over the next few years if the crises do not abate.

Considering regionalism in historical perspective, we can see that in the 1950s and 1960s it was intended to give LDCs some preferential trading arrangements that would enhance independence for the South in what was seen as the exploitative North-South dichotomy of the immediate post-colonial period. By the late 1980s and early 1990s, and in contrast to the earlier period, regionalism was seen by the dynamic economies of East Asia not as a way of isolating states from the effects of the global economy but as a way of incorporating them into it on more favourable terms. Especially, it was a way of enhancing access to global capital flows. Notwithstanding that regional policy elites of Asia have learned much from the events of 1997–8 – and that the nature of the continued moves towards regional economic cooperation will be conditioned by this experience – it is unlikely that the downturn is going to make the continued enhancement of regional economic cooperation any less an imperative.

If the regional currency crisis is to provide a positive learning experience at the multilateral level it must trigger a discussion of the assumption that the unfettered movement of capital (especially short-term lending) is axio-matically a good thing. As even the *Financial Times* (16 January 1998: 18) noted, globalisation requires the development of institutional capability for prudential regulation in these areas. While most policy analysts recognise this is best pursued at the global level, regional level initiatives can be expected to evolve. Asian desires to enhance supervision of private cross border flows, especially FDI, can be expected to grow in the wake of recent experiences. In a post-hegemonic era there is no 'lender of last resort'. They will look to regional self-help as much as to institutional resolution of these issues at the global level.

The events of 1997–8 have been some of the most traumatic experienced in Asia since the Cold War confrontations in the 1950s and 1960s. They have, in the short term, side-tracked policy elites from the dialogue activities that became increasingly popular throughout the first half of the 1990s. But as the crisis recedes and the policy elite begins to think again about the regional cooperative agenda, the events of 1997–8 will offer analytical perspective. We can expect the development of multilevel regionalism in Asia to continue. East Asia will be at the core of the new regionalism. The Asia-Pacific, as constituted by the membership of the APEC, will form the outer shell. Broad economic philosophies, principally liberal in nature, will continue to under-pin both the inner core and outer shell – especially a commitment to freer and open trade and the multilateral trading system. But there will be a different regional spin towards these issues that will reflect Asian experience and which may lead to enhanced East Asian regional policy responses to the major global economic questions of our time.

Notes

1 The Asian states represented at the first two ASEM meetings – Bangkok, March 1996 and London, April 1998 – were seven members of ASEAN (Brunei, Indonesia, Malaysia, the Philippines, Singapore, Thailand and Vietnam) and the Northeast Asian states of Japan, South Korea and the People's Republic of China.
2 Between 1994 and 1996 net private inflows into Indonesia, Korea, Malaysia, Thailand and the Philippines grew from $48 billion to $93 billion. The figure for 1997 was *minus* $12 billion (*The Financial Times* 16 February 1998: 21).

7 Investing in the future

East and Southeast Asian firms in the global economy

Peter Dicken and Henry Wai-chung Yeung

Introduction

Although the nature and extent of globalisation is contested within the social science literature, one phenomenon on which all sides agree is the significance of the emergence of East and Southeast Asia as a major component of the post-war global economic map. Without doubt, this has been the major change in the international division of labour. The aim of this chapter is to explore the specific role of firms from within the region itself in this process and to consider their likely future trajectories. Given the region's economic significance, it is somewhat paradoxical that, at least until very recently, little scholarly or popular attention was devoted to East and Southeast Asian business firms, other than those from Japan.[1] Outside the sphere of Asian business organisation specialists, such firms were generally regarded as being of very limited significance. After all, it was widely believed, the East and Southeast Asian economies were essentially dominated, either directly through foreign investment, or indirectly through various forms of subcontracting relationships, by foreign firms. Even when it was recognised that some Asian firms were themselves becoming international in their scope, they were generally caricatured, rather patronisingly, as 'Third World multinationals' (Wells 1983; Aggarwal, forthcoming; cf. Yeung 1994a).

Although, today, that position has changed substantially there is still a very limited understanding of the highly diversified nature, significance, and behaviour of firms from the Asian region (see Yeung 1994b). Certainly in the West, where competitive bidding for internationally mobile investment is especially intense, an extremely simplistic conception of the 'Asian firm' has gained currency. Asian firms, it is widely believed, and fervently hoped – or feared – will follow the 'Japanese' model and increasingly invest in North America and Europe. The recent, widely-publicised, cases of major investment decisions by some Korean and Taiwanese firms in Europe (primarily in the UK) and North America have tended to reinforce this view (Wesson 1990; McDermott 1992; Dent and Randerson 1996; UNCTAD 1996a). Such perceptions have a significance far beyond the parochial boundaries

of those communities anxious to attract Asian firms. They raise the fundamental question of the nature of Asian firms and their role within the global
economy.

The uncertainty generated by the recent financial turmoil in Asia during
the second half of 1997 and through 1998 does not lessen the significance of
this issue, but it does, of course, make it more difficult to make unequivocal
statements about likely future trends. Although nobody can ascertain the
depth and temporal extent of the crisis – and views vary widely on this (see
chapters by Higgott, Paderanga and Sassen in this volume) – it will, without
question, impact upon the nature of Asia's involvement in the global economy
and upon the scale and location of firms' investment decisions. We will comment on these issues at appropriate points within the chapter. The primary
objective of this chapter therefore is to examine contemporary patterns and
processes of international involvement by Asian business firms.[2] We make no
attempt to address the broader issues of the nature of Asian firms in general
or to explore how they might relate to the conventional, Western-centric
models of business organisation (see Whitley 1992; Hamilton 1996a).
Although our primary focus is upon non-Japanese Asian firms we will make
some brief comments on the nature of internationalisation by Japanese firms
in order to provide a regionally specific benchmark.

The chapter is organised in the following way. In the first section, we provide the broad context of international involvement by Asian firms by outlining recent trends in international trade and in foreign direct investment
within the global economy, with particular reference to Asian Foreign
Direct Investment (FDI). In the second – and most substantive – part of the
chapter, we focus specifically on the internationalisation of Asian firms at a
global and a regional scale. Our primary focus is on firms from the four 'first-
tier' Newly Industrialised Economies (NIEs) (Hong Kong, Korea, Singapore
and Taiwan) with a particular emphasis on ethnic Chinese business networks
because they play a dominant role in the economic organisation of three of
these NIEs and other emerging economies in Southeast Asia. Finally, we
attempt to connect this essentially empirical analysis into the conceptual and
policy debates concerning regionalisation and the changing position of East
and Southeast Asia in the global economy.

The global context: trends in international trade and Asian foreign direct investment

Asian NIEs as sources of manufactured exports

Trade, particularly exports, is the most important modality of Asian firm's
involvement in the global economy. It is through their spectacular growth as
exporters of particular kinds of manufactured goods to the industrialised
economies that their impact has been most keenly felt. Increasingly, such
penetration of industrialised country markets has become a focus of political

friction between exporting and importing countries, articulated both inside and outside the framework of the General Agreement on Tariffs and Trade (GATT) and later the World Trade Organisation (WTO). The story is well-known and needs not be repeated in detail here (UNCTAD 1996b). Suffice it to say that the eight leading Asian economies outside Japan (Hong Kong, Korea, Singapore, Taiwan, China, Malaysia, Indonesia and Thailand) increased their share of world manufactured exports from 1.5 per cent in 1963 to 20 per cent in 1995 (Dicken 1998: Table 2.6).

However, we should not forget the other side of the import penetration coin. The East and South East Asian NIEs are not just export generators. They are increasingly important as markets for imports. In fact, they make up one of the fastest growing markets in the world. The region's share of global GDP virtually doubled between 1976 and 1995 (to 25 per cent of the world total). In terms of imports, the share of the world total accounted for by the East and South East Asian NIEs increased from 10 per cent in 1984 to 17 per cent in 1994. In contrast, the combined market size of North America, the European Union, and Japan fell from 52 per cent to 47 per cent. Hence, we must lose the habit of seeing the East and South East Asian NIEs as merely the generators of cheap exports. Not only are the first-tier NIEs producing increasingly sophisticated goods but also together with their neighbours, they are now major global markets.

Of course, the recent economic crisis in Asia will have a substantial effect on the size and growth of Asian markets, at least in the short term. Estimates of the magnitude of this effect vary considerably. Forecasts published by *The Economist* (7 March 1998: Chart 3) show a wide variation in the rate of slowdown between individual Asian countries. Virtually all the region's economies were forecast to have markedly slower rates of GDP growth in 1998 (with especially steep falls in Indonesia, South Korea and Thailand from positive growth rates prior to 1998 to negative in 1998) but with some recovery in 1999. Of course, these estimates are sensitive to the assumptions on which they are based. Nevertheless, the extreme apocalyptic views of some Western commentators seem unlikely to materialise.

> Doomsayers now predict a decade of lost growth in East Asia, like the one that Latin America went through after its debt crisis in the early 1980s. To express certainty about the future is always foolish, but such gloom looks premature . . . If governments put their economic houses in order, East Asia's growth might average 5–6 per cent a year over the next decade rather than 7–8 per cent over the past decade . . . it would still be twice as fast as the average in the rich industrial countries.
>
> (*The Economist*, 7 March 1998)

In fact, when expressed in purchasing-power parities (PPPs), the decline in the size of Asian countries' GDPs is put in much clearer perspective and is not as dramatic. Of course, this will still have an impact on these countries' propensities to import.

This raises the question of the effect of the economic crisis on the overall trade position of the Asian economies. The massive devaluations of some of these countries' currencies potentially makes their exports cheaper and much more competitive in world markets. Indeed, the idea that the Asian NIEs will be able to export their way out of crisis is widely held. But how quickly and how far that is possible will depend on two key factors. First, there must be markets able and willing to absorb any major increase in exports. In effect, this means the United States and Europe. Given the bullish market sentiments in the US, the primary export market for many Asian economies, the potential for rapid recovery among some Asian export-oriented economies is bright. Second, the ability to generate the exports themselves depends upon their manufacturers having access to liquid capital and credit to buy the materials and other inputs needed. In the early stages of the crisis, at least, this was a major problem. There are apparently some concerted efforts to resolve the problem, as evident in the recent collaboration of various national banks and the IMF (see Higgott, this volume).

Prior to the onset of the economic crisis, the relative importance of individual Asian markets to Asian firms has shown some significant changes between the mid-1980s and the mid-1990s. In Figure 7.1, the East and South

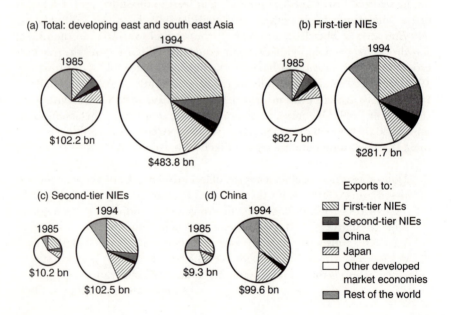

Figure 7.1 The trade network of East and Southeast Asian NIEs
(*Source:* based on data in UNCTAD (1996b) *Trade and Development Report, 1996,* Table 24)

East Asian NIEs are divided into three categories: the 'first tier NIEs' (Hong Kong, Korea, Singapore, Taiwan), the 'second tier NIEs' (Indonesia, Malaysia, Philippines, Thailand) and China. It also reflects the evolving intra-regional division of labour within East and South East Asia, an issue we discuss later in this chapter. The changing export structure of these three groups reflects the intra-regional dynamics of the East and South East Asian region and, especially, the transition from lower-skilled, labour-intensive manufactured products to more technologically sophisticated products by the first tier NIEs.

Asia as a source of foreign direct investment

In aggregate terms, between 1986 and 1990, total world FDI outflows grew at an average annual rate of 28 per cent and cumulative FDI stocks at a rate of 20 per cent a year compared with a growth rate of world exports of 14 per cent. One calculation suggests that world FDI during the 1980s grew more than four times faster than world GNP (UNCTAD 1996c: 4). The early 1990s' recession reduced the FDI growth rates significantly, but by the mid-1990s the upward trend had resumed to reach a record of $315 billion in inflows and $318 billion in outflows in 1995.

Globally, the Asian NIEs are far less significant as foreign direct investors than they are as exporters. With the notable exception of Japan and Korea, East and Southeast Asian countries have been primarily destinations for FDI.[3] Although only one-quarter of global FDI goes to developing countries, almost 60 per cent of the developing country total goes to East and Southeast Asia (with China taking 19 per cent). Nevertheless, this position has been changing quite rapidly, though unevenly, in the past ten years, as firms from Asian NIEs have become increasingly transnational. Although more than 90 per cent of global FDI still originates from the developed economies, the developing countries' share has more than doubled since 1985 to around 8 per cent of the world total. Four-fifths of all developing country FDI originates from just seven countries (UNCTAD 1996c). As Figure 7.2 shows, six of those seven are Asian NIEs. Clearly, the nature of these Asian NIEs' articulation with the global economy has been changing to a very considerable degree.

Japanese FDI

Among Asian firms as a whole, it is undoubtedly TNCs from Japan that have spearheaded the geographical spread of their foreign involvement. This is hardly surprising, of course, since Japan emerged as the most powerful economic force from Asia in the post-Second World War period. Indeed, outward FDI from Japan to non-Asian locations has a very long history. In Europe, for example, the first Japanese FDI was made during the late nineteenth century (Mason 1992; Dicken *et al.* 1997). This early wave of

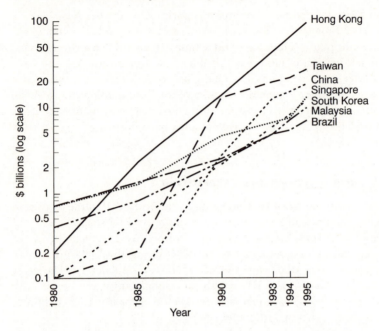

Figure 7.2 Foreign direct investment from Newly Industrialising Economies, 1980–95 (*Source:* based on data in UNCTAD (1995) *World Investment Report, 1995*, Annex Table 4; UNCTAD (1996) *World Investment Report, 1996*, Annex Table 4)

Japanese FDI in Europe was led by the general trading companies (*sogo shosha*) and other service firms; Japanese manufacturing TNCs did not appear in Europe and North America until very much later. The growth of Japanese FDI had completed its first phase by the late 1970s. Geographically, it was fairly evenly distributed throughout the Triad regions by the late 1970s. The 1980s represented a second phase in the proliferation of Japanese FDI when North America and Europe received disproportionately more Japanese FDI than Asia. As shown in Table 7.1, by 1987, Japanese FDI in North America (US$9.6 billion) and E. C. (US$3.6 billion) had surpassed East and Southeast Asia (US$2.1 billion) by a significant amount. Asia, as a destination for intra-regional investment flows, managed to capture some 11 per cent of total Japanese FDI flows. This trend of 'globalisation' of Japanese FDI continued until the collapse of the Japanese 'bubble economy' in the early 1990s.

It must be emphasised, however, that not all Japanese TNCs are globalising their production networks. Table 7.1 shows that during the post-bubble period, Japanese FDI flows to North America and the EC were reduced substantially from 49 per cent and 23 per cent of total respectively in 1993 to 41 per cent and 10 per cent of total in 1996. On the other hand, Japanese

FDI flows to Asia increased dramatically from 11 per cent of total in 1993 to 36 per cent in 1996. Most Japanese firms continue to extend their linkages and production networks into East and Southeast Asia, creating extremely complex intra-regional production chains and networks. As such, they provide perhaps the most important force for economic integration in Asia (Hatch and Yamamura 1996; Katzenstein and Shiraishi 1997; Dicken and Miyamachi 1998).

FDI from Asian NIEs

The emergence of TNCs from other Asian countries is, of course, a very recent phenomenon. Yet, as we pointed out in the introduction to this chapter, it has become a focus of significant policy interest in the West. In this section, we draw together what is a very disparate and messy set of statistical data[4] to present as full a picture as possible of the overall pattern of Asian FDI. In the next section we offer some explanations of these patterns based upon a more disaggregated, firm-based perspective.[5]

Table 7.2 shows the geographical distribution of outward FDI from the Asian NIEs for two different time periods: 1988 and the mid-1990s. By 1988, more than half of the total outward FDI stocks from Hong Kong, Singapore, and Thailand went to East, South and Southeast Asia. To a large extent, outflows of FDI from these three Asian developing countries were intra-regional in their geographical focus (see also Yeung 1994b). On the other hand, more than half of the FDI stocks from South Korea and Taiwan were located in developed countries, in particular the US. It must be noted, however, that these investments were highly sector- and place-specific. A significant amount of Korean and Taiwanese FDI stocks went into such high-tech sectors as electronics. This sectoral-specificity explains the large quantum of FDI stocks in the US *vis-à-vis* other host countries. The overall geographical pattern of Asian FDI in 1988, therefore, was one in which although all of the source countries' investment had a strong Asian dimension there were indications that, in the case of South Korea and Taiwan, a more 'global' trend might be emerging. It was tempting to see this as a process of following the Japanese model of FDI. How far has that trend developed? Have firms from the other Asian NIEs followed a similar pattern?

When the 1988 data are compared with the mid-1990s data in Table 7.2,[6] one can observe that TNCs from the Asian NIEs have tended to invest overwhelmingly within the Asian region itself – a pattern we define as 'regionalisation'. In particular, FDI stocks from Hong Kong up to the end of 1993 remained largely concentrated in Asia at US$47 billion (94 per cent of the total). The absence of data for Western Europe as a destination does not significantly affect this observation because Hong Kong's FDI in Western Europe is not very substantial in aggregate terms, although there are some important Hong Kong investments in Europe. Malaysia, as an emerging Asian NIE, had 57 per cent of its equity investment abroad located in Asia

Table 7.1 Japanese FDI flows by host regions (in percentage share)

Region	1987	1988	1989	1990	1991	1992	1993	1994	1995	1996
USA	49.4	55.4	48.1	53.3	49.5	51.8	49.3	34.5	39.1	40.5
EC	18.4	16.9	22.1	23.0	26.0	19.6	23.1	15.8	14.4	10.4
East and SE Asia	10.5	7.9	11.3	10.2	9.0	11.7	11.1	19.2	23.0	35.6
NIEs	8.6	6.1	7.8	5.5	3.3	3.6	2.1	9.0	7.9	11.1
Other countries	21.7	19.8	18.5	13.5	15.5	16.9	16.5	30.5	23.5	13.5
World total in US$ millions	19,519	34,210	44,130	48,024	30,726	17,222	13,714	17,938	22,284	29,805

Source: Based on Bank of Japan (various years), *Balance of Payments Statistics*, compiled by Eric Ramstetter.

during the 1991–6 period. The other two Triad regions, North America and Western Europe, received respectively only 13 per cent and 8 per cent during the same period. Compared to the 1988 data, direct equity investments from Singapore at the end of 1995 also did not show a greater locational preference for North America (5.5 per cent) or Western Europe (10 per cent). Regionalisation is again the dominant trend among Singaporean TNCs.

Reversing the trends of the 1980s, cumulative outward FDI from South Korea and Taiwan showed a stronger preference for the Asian region by the mid-1990s. By 1995, Asia was the largest recipient of Korean and Taiwanese FDI, at 43 per cent and 39 per cent respectively. During the same period, only Thailand had more outward FDI in developed countries than in the mid-1980s. By 1996, some 33 per cent of Thailand's outward FDI went to developed countries, compared to 24 per cent in 1988. This increase was largely accounted for by increasing Thai investment in Western Europe.

Strategies and organisation of production by Asian firms

The aggregate FDI data presented in Table 7.2 reveal a variety of geographical tendencies by non-Japanese Asian firms. Broadly, such tendencies can be described as the reflection of firms pursuing either 'globalising' or 'regionalising' strategies. Our view is that 'regionalising' strategies are significantly more powerful than 'globalising' strategies among such firms. In the following sections, we use firm-specific data to explain why we believe this to be so.

The FDI data in Table 7.2 indicate that non-Japanese Asian TNCs, particularly those from South Korea and Taiwan, show some 'globalising' tendencies. The most significant cases are the four leading *chaebol* from South Korea (Samsung, LG, Hyundai and Daewoo), and Taiwanese firms such as Acer. In the last ten years, each of these firms have moved very quickly to develop a direct presence in North America and, more recently, in Europe. The pattern closely follows that of the Japanese in the 1970s and 1980s and is driven by very similar motives: to cope with non-tariff barriers and to get closer to specific markets/technologies. Although differing in detail, each of the major Korean *chaebol* has begun to follow a similarly ambitious globalising route. As such, they have come to be seen as the first in a supposed new wave of Asian TNCs, following in the footsteps of the Japanese and, by extrapolation, seen as being highly desirable targets for investment promotion agencies in the west. The effect of the recent Asian financial crisis, especially for Korean firms, has been to force at least some of them to delay the implementation of some of their major European investments. For example, Korean LG's £1.6 billion investment in Newport, South Wales, will go ahead despite the meltdown in South Korea, but the project will be implemented over longer phases (Nicholas Phelps, personal communication, 28 March 1998). We believe, however, that the effect is far from uniform.

Table 7.2 Geographical distribution of outward Foreign Direct Investment from Asian Newly Industrialised and Industrialising Economies in 1988* and the mid-1990s (in percentage share)

Country/Region	Hong Kong[a]	Singapore[b]	South Korea[c]	Taiwan[d]	Thailand[e]
Developed countries					
1988	12.0	23.0	56.0	71.0	24.0
Mid-1990s	6.0	20.0	45.0	34.0	33.0
North America					
1988	10.0	2.9	44.0	61.0	23.0
Mid-1990s	5.3	5.5	31.0	27.0	24.0
Western Europe					
1988	–	13.0	3.7	–	0.3
Mid-1990s	–	10.0	10.0	5.5	–
Developing countries					
1988	88.0	77.0	45.0	29.0	76.0
Mid-1990s	94.0	57.0	55.0	66.0	57.0

East, South and Southeast Asia					
1988	88.0	64.0	23.0	24.0	75.0
Mid-1990s	94.0	57.0	43.0	38.6	55.0
Total	US$mil	US$mil	US$mil	US$mil	Bt$mil
1988	13,952 (100)	1,407 (100)	1,119 (100)	704 (100)	212 (100)
Mid-1990s	50,141 (100)	36,866 (100)	10,225 (100)	10,254 (100)	55,934 (100)

Notes and sources:

a Data for the early 1990s are obtained on the basis of inward stock attributed to Hong Kong up to 1993 in the various host countries (US$mil).
  Source: Low et al. (1996: Table 2).

b Data refer to the cumulative stock of Singapore's direct equity investment abroad as of end of 1995 (US$mil).
  Source: Department of Statistics (1997), *Yearbook of Statistics Singapore, 1996*, Singapore: DOS.

c Data represent cumulative flows of realised investment abroad from 1968 to 1995 (US$mil).
  Source: Bank of Korea (1996), *Overseas Direct Investment Statistics Yearbook*, Seoul: Bank of Korea.

d Data refer to cumulative approved outward investment from 1952 to 1995 (US$mil).
  Source: Ministry of Economic Affairs, Taiwan (1996), *Statistics on Outward Investment*, Taipei: MEA.

e Data represent cumulative net flows of Thai equity investment abroad from 1987 to September 1996 (Bt$mil).
  Source: Bank of Thailand (various years), *Quarterly Bulletin*, Bangkok: Bank of Thailand.

* 1988 is chosen because data in US$millions are available from UNCTC (1992: various country tables).

Well into the crisis (in March 1998), for example, it was reported that ten Taiwanese electronics companies were actively seeking production sites in Britain (*The Sunday Times*, 15 March 1998). But even supposing that the effect of the crisis on the non-Asian investment plans of Korean companies in particular is relatively short-lived and that the planned investments are implemented, we doubt that the experience of the major Korean firms is a likely template for the internationalisation of most other Asian firms. Indeed, we would argue that the recent Asian economic crisis would further reinforce the regionalisation tendencies of Asian firms. The reasons for this assertion are explored in the next section.

Regional networks of production chains

One of the main reasons why most non-Japanese Asian TNCs may not follow the Japanese (and Korean *chaebol*) trajectory of building a large direct presence in North America and Western Europe is that these emerging Asian firms are increasingly capable of organising much more sophisticated production chains at a regional, rather than a global, scale. At the same time, the globalisation of economic activities has led to a more complex business environment and sharper competition. All these changes together present a dilemma to emerging Asian firms because the coordination and configuration of production chains has become the key to creating and sustaining competitive advantage. In addition, the barriers – social, cultural and political – to establishing a significant presence in North American and, especially European, markets are substantial. Hence, to many emerging Asian TNCs, the 'regional solution' is a much more attractive strategy for competition and growth for two main reasons.

First, the Asia Pacific region has been a growth region since the late 1970s and is expected to lead the growth of the global economy in the next millennium, despite the current turmoil. Many countries in the region have either emerging markets or relatively low costs of production. The regional market and production location thus provide an opportunity for Asian firms to grow and establish their market position. In order to tap into the emerging markets in Asia, some Asian TNCs focus on organising their regional production networks to maximise location-specific advantages. For example, the Gold Peak Group, an electrical and electronics TNC from Hong Kong, has production facilities strategically configured in the region (*South China Morning Post*, 25 February 1994: 15–18).

While the emerging regional market represents Gold Peak's primary location-specific advantage, other TNCs from the Asian NIEs configure their production facilities in the region to exploit cost advantage. Indeed, cost leadership continues to be the key competitive strategy employed by leading TNCs from Asian NIEs. In the apparel industry, most Asian firms (particularly those from Hong Kong) rely on a geographically dispersed configuration of their production chains within the Asian region in order to reach low cost production sites and to circumvent quota restrictions. Cost advantage in Asia, however, is more than confined to labour-intensive industries only. In high-tech sectors, such leading Asian TNCs as Acer, Hyundai, LG, Samsung and Tatung also rely on cost advantage to capture market shares from their competitors in the Triad regions, including Japan. For example, using technology licensed from Japan since the late 1980s, South Korean *chaebols* have managed to capture about 20 per cent of the worldwide market for computer memory chips (Angel 1994: 20). Indeed, by 1996, Korea had become the world's third leading producer of semi-conductors (Dicken 1998: 356). To sustain their cost advantage, many of these firms search actively for locations which offer lower overall costs of production and which fit well into their networks of production chains. Often, Asian industrialising countries are chosen because of their geographical proximity to the home countries and their positive attitude towards foreign investment.

Second, the 'regional solution' is also preferred by emerging TNCs from Asian NIEs that lack ownership-specific advantages to compete with global TNCs in their 'home turf', i.e. in North America and Western Europe. This phenomenon applies particularly to services TNCs from the Asian NIEs that specialise in the downstream activities of production chains. On the one hand, many of these service TNCs, from the retail sector to the financial sector, have neither sufficient capital nor strong brand names to compete with leading TNCs in the global market. With very few exceptions, Asian consumer- and business-service TNCs confine themselves to establishing operations within the region (see Yeung 1998a, 1998b). The recent crisis in Asia tends to further enhance this regional focus of Asian service firms. On the other hand, these Asian TNCs are reluctant to go beyond the Asian region because their competitive advantage is largely embedded in the regional economy. They are mostly Asian firms with international operations, rather than international firms with Asian operations. As will be evident in the next section on Chinese business networks, many Asian TNCs find it difficult to replicate or transfer their distinctive network advantage to other regions of the global economy. In today's context of a changing global economy, globalisation is best seen as an idealised option whereas regionalisation is a much more realistic strategy for most Asian firms.

Regionalisation and Chinese business networks

We argue that because many TNCs from the Asian NIEs (other than South Korea) are owned and managed by ethnic Chinese, they find it more advantageous to regionalise their operations into other Asian countries to tap into pre-existing business networks or to develop new network relationships (see also Yeung 1997a, 1997b, 1998b; Olds and Yeung 1998, 1999). The recent Asian economic crisis has not put ethnic Chinese business firms under siege. Rather, it opens windows of opportunities for these firms to strengthen further

Table 7.3 Major ethnic Chinese Transnational Corporations from East and Southeast Asia

Company/Group name	Major shareholder (ethnic Chinese)	Country of origin	Estimated net worth[a] (US$ billion)	Major operations abroad
Cheung Kong Holding	Li Ka-shing	Hong Kong	5.8	Husky Oil (Canada) Pacific Place Project (Vancouver)
Cathay Life Insurance	Tsai family	Taiwan	7.5	–
Hong Leong Group	Kwek Leng Beng Quek Leng Chan	Singapore Malaysia	2.0 2.1	CDL Hotels (worldwide) Dao Heng Bank (HK)
Salim Group Lippo Group	Liem Sioe Liong Mochtar Riady	Indonesia Indonesia	3.0 6.0 (assets)	First Pacific Group (HK) Lippo Banks (worldwide)
Kerry Group	Robert Kuok	Malaysia/Hong Kong	2.1	Shangri-la Hotels (Asia) TVB International (Asia)
Charoen Pokphand Group	Chearavanont family	Thailand	5.3	CP Pokphand (HK and China) Telecom Asia (Asia)
Fortune Tobacco	Lucio Tan	Philippines	1.7	Eton Properties (HK)

Source:
[a] East Asia Analytical Unit (1995: Table 6.1)

their regional business networks and alliances with local and foreign firms (Yeung 1998c, 1999a). To understand the key actors in these ethnic Chinese business networks, we turn to Table 7.3 which provides some useful insights into the international operations of several major ethnic Chinese TNCs from East and Southeast Asia. It is clear that Asia remains the most important region for their cross-border operations. The only two exceptions are CDL Hotels International (controlled by the Hong Leong Group) from Singapore and Lippo Banks (controlled by the Lippo Group) from Indonesia. A large proportion of Hong Leong's business empire, however, is located in Singapore and Malaysia, due to the historical legacy of the founders' (Kwek/Quek) families (see Yeung, 1998a, 1999b).

What then explains the reticence of ethnic Chinese to venture beyond the Asian region? We believe that although the obstacles to establishing a direct presence outside Asia may be considerable, the development of a regional business network in Asia is indeed preferable because many Chinese business firms in Asia are firmly embedded in their social and institutional contexts. It becomes difficult for them not only to give up privileged access to markets and information in Asia, but also to transplant their business networks successfully in the other Triad regions. To begin with, the competitive advantage of Chinese business firms from East and Southeast Asia is embedded in their capabilities in network formation and exploitation. These capabilities, in turn, are both culturally and economically determined. Culturally, Chinese business traditionally relies on business networks to facilitate transactions and circumvent host country discrimination. This networking capability historically underscores the competitiveness of Chinese business firms *vis-à-vis* Western firms in China (Hamilton 1996b; Weidenbaum and Hughes 1996).

The cultural explanation of 'Overseas Chinese' business success has recently been questioned because of its inherent methodological pitfalls expressed in parochialism, exclusive focus on Chinese business, and the lack of comparative analysis of familism in other ethnic groups (Greenhalgh 1994; Hodder 1996; Dirlik 1997). It is equally important, therefore, to examine the economic tendencies of Chinese business firms. Economically, Chinese business firms tend to engage in industries and/or sectors that promise relatively quick returns on investment (e.g. retail and wholesale trade, property development, finance and so on). Cultures *per se* do not explain the success or failure of particular communities or forms of organisations. Rather, it is a combination of cultural traditions and economic practices within the broader context of global changes that explains the outcome of economic competition. For example, it is often argued that Chinese business firms in Southeast Asia engage in political–economic alliances in specific countries in order to obtain privileged access to markets and resources. When these firms internationalise their operations, such political–economic alliances will not provide a significant source of competitive advantage except that they enable these Chinese business firms to build up sufficient capital and market bases in their home countries, thereby enabling cross-border acquisitions. For example, the rapid expansion and diversification of the Salim Group (Table 7.3), in the past three decades, was, to a certain extent, facilitated by the personal patronage of former President Suharto of Indonesia (Sato 1993).

To internationalise beyond the Asian region, Chinese business firms would need to transfer some, if not all, of their business networks in order to compensate for their relative lack of ownership-specific advantages. This was the case of Japanese TNCs in their early phase of internationalisation when the *sogo shosha* served as the *de facto* distributor of goods and products for Japanese manufacturing TNCs. In the later phase of the internationalisation of Japanese *keiretsu*, Japanese transplants were established in North America and Western Europe to enable *keiretsu* members to benefit from group and organisational synergy. Japanese transplants in North America and Western Europe, however, are not without their critics (Elgar and Smith 1994; Munday *et al.* 1995; Williams *et al.* 1992). This points to the grave difficulties of transplanting business networks to host countries which have different social and institutional structures (Hu 1995).

The political economy of regionalisation

Our argument, then, is that Asian firms are regionalising, rather than globalising, because of their capabilities to organise production networks at a regional scale and because of their embeddedness in the social and institutional contexts of the Asian regional economy. One major influence on the behaviour of Asian firms is their domestic (home-country) context, especially the state's role in shaping the regionalisation of their national firms. Through macro-organisational strategies and the establishment of favourable national institutional structures, nation-states can directly affect the capabilities and competitiveness of their national firms in the global economy (Dunning 1995). The regulatory capacity of nation-states can also impinge on the spatial behaviour of TNCs (Dicken 1992, 1994). It has been argued, for example, that the globalisation of Japanese firms is an outcome of the macro-organisational strategy of the Japanese government in the postwar period (Dunning 1993).

In developing Asian countries, the state is a potent influence, particularly when it is actively pursuing either an import-substitution or export-promotion policy (Wade 1990). The state serves both as a constraint and an enabling mechanism to the regionalisation of national firms (Yeung 1994b). In recent years, none of the Asian NIEs has been as active in promoting the regionalisation of national firms as has Singapore. Since 1993, the state has launched an aggressive regionalisation drive through which Singaporean firms are encouraged to invest in other Asian countries (Yeung 1998d, 1999c). The state has not only created favourable institutional conditions for this regionalisation effort (cf. Japan), but also has taken key initiatives to ensure its success. This largely state-driven process is spearheaded by government-linked corporations (GLCs) such as Temasek Holdings, Singapore Technologies and the Keppel Group. Institutional support is provided through incentives offered by various state agencies and through active promotion abroad by key politicians. It is hoped that regionalisation will give Singapore's economy an 'external wing' in order to maintain its competitiveness in the regional and global economy and to reduce its dependence on foreign capital and overseas markets for long-term economic survival.

The data in Table 7.2 indicate that the state's regionalisation programme has achieved some success insofar as the absolute level of Singaporean investment has increased massively and a significant proportion of this total outward FDI (at US$36.9 billion) continued to flow into the Asian region in 1995. In addition, two of the top 50 TNCs from developing countries in 1994 were GLCs from Singapore: Keppel Corporation and Singapore Telecom Ltd. We will illustrate the political economy of Singapore's regionalisation drive with the case of Keppel Corporation and its operations in Asia. Keppel Shipyard Pte Ltd was incorporated in 1968 as a separate ship repairing operation for the Port of Singapore Authority, to form a wholly state-owned enterprise. From a modest beginning, it has grown into one of the largest and most widely diversified industrial conglomerates in Singapore, including nine public listed companies and over 140 active subsidiaries (Low *et al.* 1993: 459–65).

In May 1994, Keppel led a consortium of 19 Singapore companies to form the Singapore-Suzhou Township Development Company (SSTDC). This idea of developing a township and bringing a Singapore style of economic management to China was first mooted by the former Prime Minister, Lee Kuan Yew, when he met China's senior leader Deng Xiaoping during his visit to Singapore in 1978 (Tan 1995; Tan 1997/1998). After a long period of discussion, China's State Council approved this innovative concept. Numerous top level official visits were exchanged between the two countries to identify a suitable site. Suzhou, in China's Jiangsu province, was finally chosen after a state visit led by Singapore's current Prime Minister, Goh Chok Tong, his deputies and other top officials. On 26 February 1994, the Singapore Government, represented by Senior Minister Lee Kuan Yew, signed an agreement with China's Vice Premier Li Lanqing to transfer 'software' to Suzhou. This 'software' comprises economic development and public administration expertise. It involves the Singapore state in taking the lead to develop an industrial township in China (Economic Development Board 1995: 20–21). This case study of Keppel Corporation demonstrates how the state in Singapore has tried to lead the regionalisation drive by taking a direct equity stake in large infrastructural development projects in the region and by employing interstate relationships to raise the profile and image of its investment projects (Cartier 1995; Lu and Zhu 1995; Yeung 1998d).

Some implications

A number of implications follow from our analysis of Asian international investment. Here we focus on just three related issues: (1) the nature of the internationalisation process; (2) the nature of the intra-regional economic system in Asia; and (3) the possible future direction of Asian international involvement within the global economy.

First, the analysis throws some light on the nature of the internationalisation process itself and the difficulty of applying simple labels to immensely complex and diverse processes and forms. Although we have argued that the majority of Asian firms are internationalising primarily within the Asian region itself, the forms such 'regionalisation' takes are extremely varied. Similarly, the actual strategies pursued by those allegedly 'globalising' firms (notably Japanese, Korean and, to a lesser extent, some Taiwanese firms) are also far from uniform. Hence, the internationalisation processes of Asian firms (including Japanese firms) and their concrete, locationally-specific forms cannot be encapsulated within such broad dichotomous concepts as 'globalisation' or 'regionalisation'.

Indeed the terms 'globalisation' and 'regionalisation' need to be more carefully specified and distinguished from that of 'internationalisation'. In so doing, it is important to emphasise that we are concerned with these processes as they apply to firms, rather than countries. In our interpretation, the 'internationalisation' of a firm's activities refers simply to their geographical dispersal across national boundaries. It is essentially a quantitative process and one which has an extremely long history. 'Globalisation', on the other hand, is much more than this (and is also much more recent); it is essentially a qualitative process, defined by the functional integration of a firm's international operations and not merely by their geographical extent. Thus, a firm which has operations distributed on a global scale may not, in fact, be globalised if its operations are not functionally integrated. It would remain, according to our definition, an 'international' firm. Hence, a globalising firm may actually be less geographically dispersed than an international firm (Hu 1992). Many of today's global firms also continue to behave differently and are embedded in their distinctive national and institutional structures (Hirst and Thompson 1996; Pauly and Reich 1997; Dicken 1998; Yeung 1998e).

Similarly, we believe that a 'regionalising' strategy should be interpreted as the functional integration of a firm's activities within a defined geographical region and not merely on their regional extent. A pure 'regionalising' strategy, then, is one in which a firm extends and integrates its activities within its home region (i.e. Asian firms within Asia; European firms within Europe). Where, in addition, a firm pursues a strategy of regionalising operations outside its home region (e.g. Asian firms with integrated operations within Europe as well as in Asia, or United States firms with integrated operations within Asia as well as in North America and Europe) then we would see this as being part of a globalising (or, as some would have it, a glocalising) strategy. These are not merely semantic points. They imply different forms of organising internationalisation and, in all likelihood, different kinds of impact on home and host economies.

Thus, we need to recognise the organisational and geographical diversity of internationalising, regionalising, and globalising processes and forms – all of which are evident at the present time – together with the multiple scales at which they are enacted. Without question, the place-specific characteristics of a firm's home environment play a very significant role. Indeed, the influence of this home environment remains extremely important in terms of how and why TNC internationalise, even when such internationalisation is of long standing (as in the case of some Japanese firms). At the same time, precisely how firms from one country articulate with a local host economy and society is a contingent process resulting in hybrid forms which bears greater or lesser traces of the firm's home environment (Abo 1996; Yeung 1998f). Hence, Asian TNCs, like TNCs in general, are emphatically not 'placeless'.[7] Thus, the idea that there is an 'Asian investment model' is as misleading as the idea of an 'Asian economic development model'. In this chapter, we have tried to illustrate some of the diversity of strategy and behaviour among different kinds of Asian TNC. Clearly, the aggregate statistical data do not allow us to make inferences about the nature of firm strategies. They cannot, for example, allow us to distinguish between the internationalisation, regionalisation or globalisation of firms. However, the qualitative data presented does allow us to make such inferences and support our argument regarding the geographical tendencies of Asian TNCs.

Second, the high degree of intra-regional investment (and trade) practised by Asian firms in Asia is not very different in its scale and intensity from that of European firms in Europe. In both regions, geographical proximity has been, and probably always will be, an extremely powerful influence on firms' investment patterns. Where intra-regional patterns in Asia and in Europe do differ is in their specific mechanisms and forms. The particular geographical, social, cultural, political, and institutional complexion of East and Southeast Asia, together with the position of the region in the global economy, produces a distinctive but complex intra-regional structure. Various attempts have been made to capture the essential dynamic of this structure, the most well-known being the so-called flying geese model[8] which portrays the economic growth and development of individual Asian countries as a Japanese-led sequential process. The flying geese model is, essentially, a product-cycle-based model in which countries move successively (and successfully) through a series of stages each of which has specific product and technological characteristics. Although continued support for the model as a 'best-fit' explanation of East Asian industrialisation has been voiced recently by Hill and Fujita (1996), we agree with Bernard and Ravenhill (1995) and with Hatch and Yamamura (1996) that it does not adequately capture reality. Contrary to the model's predictions, there is little evidence of a real 'catching up' process cascading through the various economies of the region. Rather, the situation is one in which 'Japan is actually flying further and further ahead of the regional flock. The division of labour in Asia, based on the technological capacity of each nation, is becoming more – not less – vertical' (Hatch and Yamamura 1996: 28).

Although Japan and Japanese firms undoubtedly play an enormously influential role, the Asian regional economy is connected into the broader global economy not only through Japanese-dominated production networks, but also through those of United States and, to a much lesser extent, European firms. Indeed, in some sectors – notably semiconductors and some consumer electronics, as well as in clothing manufacture – it was the activities of such non-Asian manufacturers and retailers/wholesalers which provided much of the initial impetus.[9] TNCs from Asian economies occupy varying positions within such regional production structures as Gereffi (1996) has shown. His work is important in emphasising the complex and differentiated nature of the buyer- and producer-driven production networks in which many Asian firms are embedded.

This, in effect, is the third implication of our analysis in this chapter: the possible future direction of Asian international involvement within the global economy. Here we can do no more than speculate on the basis of our analysis of the trends in, and forms of, international involvement by Asian firms and of the broader regional and global context in which such involvement occurs. This will, in our view, reinforce our position: that the dominant form of future international involvement (aside from trade) by Asian firms will be regional. For reasons spelt out in this chapter, there are very strong and enduring reasons why this is likely to be so. Some of these reasons are internal: primarily the immense advantages of operating, and further developing, regional networks based upon their socially-embedded nature (this is especially the case for Chinese business networks). It is not at all clear that such networks can easily be transferred to other parts of the world. Here, external forces come into play: the extent to which the nature of a host economy (local, national or regional) creates implicit 'barriers to entry' for such Asian firms. A 1998 survey conducted by UNCTAD and the International Chamber of Commerce shows that 74 per cent of the sample of firms from developing Asian countries expected their FDI in the region to remain unchanged in the short and medium term. A further 23 per cent expected to increase such investment in the region. Only 3 per cent of the sample predicted a decrease (cited in Dunning 1998).

A major reason why most Asian firms will probably remain 'regional' is the growing size and depth of the regional consumer market. In that sense, the position today is beginning to approach that of Europe, where the majority of international investment by European firms (other than UK firms) is located within Europe itself. Undoubtedly the current financial problems within the region will have a dampening effect on consumer demand and on the willingness and ability of Asian firms to make major investments either within the region or elsewhere.[10] It is impossible to estimate at this stage the magnitude of this effect. However, the Asian market is now many times larger and more sophisticated than it was at the time Japanese firms began to internationalise in the early 1970s. In that sense, the further growth of Japanese firms necessitated increased penetration of western markets while the growing incidence of non-tariff barriers stimulated direct investment there rather than a continuation of market-serving through exports from Japan. Of course, such barriers to Asian trade show no sign of fading away and this will inevitably influence some Asian firms to establish a direct presence in Europe and North America. Although our view is that most Asian firms will continue to prioritise the Asian region for their future investments, this does not mean that the pattern will be uniform. Again, we must emphasise the diversity inherent in the ways in which firms insert themselves in the global and regional economy. Such diversity continues to be based, in large part, on the nature and characteristics of the firm's domestic environment, particularly the role of the state.

On the other hand, there are undoubtedly some Asian firms that will attempt to follow the Japanese example in establishing a globalising strategy and locating operations in North America and Europe. There is, already, a small 'wave' of Korean and Taiwanese investment in those regions which seems likely to grow at least to some extent although, as we have seen, the current financial crisis has slowed down and, in a few cases, halted such investments, particularly by Korean firms. Our belief is that such investment will restart in at least the medium term. But that will not alter the basic fact that such firms also remain fundamentally embedded within the Asian region and continue to develop their intra-regional production networks. In our view, the number of Asian firms likely to develop a globalising strategy will be relatively small and will be strongly determined by the nature of their domestic environment as well as by the entrepreneurial characteristics of individual firms.

Notes

1 For brevity, in the remainder of this chapter we will use the collective term 'Asian firms' to denote firms from East and Southeast Asia. Firms from South Asia are not included.

2 The term 'involvement' is chosen deliberately to encompass more than the conventional notions of 'investment'.

3 The relative importance of inward FDI to Asian countries is extremely variable. Expressed as a proportion of GDP, it ranges from 72.8 per cent in the case of Singapore and 46 per cent in Malaysia down to 6.6 per cent in Taiwan, 3.3 per cent in Korea, and a minuscule 0.4 per cent in Japan.

4 The data presented in Table 7.2 need to be interpreted with care for several reasons. First, they are generated from different *home* country statistics, instead of from host country statistics. They are thus not strictly comparable in an absolute sense. Second, different home country governments use different methods of collection. The Taiwanese data, for example, are based on approved FDI, whereas most other data are based on realised equity investments abroad. Third, the FDI

data are obviously denoted in different country currencies, e.g. Thai Baht, Singapore Dollar and Malaysian Ringgit. Together, the data at best provide some broad trends of FDI from Asian NIEs rather than definitive maps of these emerging trends.

5 One may question the validity of using firm-level information to explain trends in aggregate statistics. This is however, a rather difficult question to be answered with full satisfaction. We believe that the aggregate statistics which are really hard to come by do show some interesting trends and that the firm-level data gathered from our primary research do shed some lights on the processes underlying those aggregate statistics. These underlying processes reported in the next section are abstractions of the empirical landscape of Asian firms in the global economy. It is thus as difficult for us to validate our claims as for someone to *in*validate our claims.

6 A qualification of methodology is necessary here. Though the data are not broadly comparable because they originate from different national statistics, we may ascertain the comparative percentages of geographical destinations in two time periods with reasonable certainty.

7 For a general discussion of this issue, see Dicken (1998: chapter 6).

8 The term was first introduced (in Japanese literature) in the late 1930s by Akamatsu Kaname. Recent contributions to the debate over the validity of the flying geese model include Bernard and Ravenhill (1995), Hatch and Yamamura (1996) and Hill and Fujita (1996).

9 Gereffi (1996) develops this argument within his 'global commodity chains' concept. However, it is worth recalling that the key role of non-Asian buyers was described as long ago as 1974 by Angus Hone (1974).

10 A relevant example is the liquidation of Peregrine Investment Holdings Ltd, the leading merchant bank in Asia, on 12 January 1998 because of its over-exposure to a bad loan in Indonesia (see Yeung 1999a).

8 Rethinking globalisation

Re-articulating the spatial scale and temporal horizons of trans-border spaces

Ngai-Ling Sum

Introduction and overview

Scholte (1997) suggests that 'globalisation' can refer to an increase in: (a) cross-border relations (or internationalisation); (b) open-border relations (or liberalisation); and (c) trans-border relations (or the relative uncoupling of social relations from territorial frameworks). I agree with Scholte that the third meaning is the most distinctive and useful starting point. Some scholars of globalisation in this third sense focus on the growing importance of 'the space of flows' due to, for example, the growth of global finance and trade (Corbridge and Thrift 1994; Agnew and Corbridge 1995) or the advance of information technologies (Castells 1996). Others focus on its relation to external 'threats' to sovereign 'nation-states' and their traditional *modus operandi*. There are strong and weak versions of this more 'state-centred' account. The strong version (e.g. O'Brien 1992) links this threatening 'outside' to the capacity of global finance to undermine state's monetary and fiscal powers. Scholars favouring a 'weak globalisation' (but strong internationalisation) thesis (e.g. Hirst and Thompson 1996) claim only that states' traditional roles *qua* sovereign powers or economic managers have been attenuated.

These 'space of flows' and 'state-centred' accounts have certainly enriched understandings of aspects of globalisation. But they also distract attention from the multiple and heterogeneous processes involved in the current re-articulation of spatial scales and temporal horizons (Mitchell 1997: 104); as well as from the role of other scales (and their spatio-temporal interlinkages) in the global–local interactions. Accordingly my chapter seeks to rethink globalisation in terms of a complex, tangled dialectic of changes in temporal horizons (such as the compressed-time and memory time of nations) and in spatial scales (such as global, regional, national and local scales). Such changes are especially prevalent in the making of trans-border spaces – which thereby reveal the complexities of this general form of globalisation. To this end, this chapter introduces the middle-range concepts of time-space governance and its associated capacities and tensions; it then applies these concepts to the trans-border space of 'Greater China'. This combination of theoretical and empirical analysis permits some more general conclusions on the multiscalar and multitemporal nature of globalisation.

A multitemporal and multiscalar approach: tendencies towards time-space governance

This agenda requires examining four issues: the variability and multiplicities of time, space, and scales; the re-articulation, in the wider context, of the spatial scales and temporal horizons involved in making trans-border spaces; trends towards reflexive time-space governance for managing the spatial-temporal dimensions of trans-border social relations; and tensions and reimaginations involved in the (re)making and time-space governance of trans-border spaces.

Time-space governance and its different moments

The concept of time-space governance focuses on the strategic networks of trans-border actors (both public and private) involved in coordinating and stabilising divergent trans-border modes of growth and their capacities to manage self-reflexively the material, social, discursive, and time-space dimensions of these modes of growth. These networks typically seek to promote global–regional–local competitiveness by shaping/disciplining/controlling the time-space dimensions of production and exchange (Gereffi and Korzeniewicz 1994; Adam 1994). These dimensions include the emerging temporalities-spatialities associated with 'electronic space' and the compression of social time through information and communication technologies. This approach can be developed by examining four key aspects of time-space moments in capitalist restructuring: finance, industry, commerce and culture.

First, the financial time-space moments are structured by the practices of networks of multinational banks, other financial intermediaries, and trans-local organisations. Their operations are premised on 'de-nationalised' or 'stateless' funds which are pooled and managed in an allegedly 'borderless world' (Ohmae 1990). Fund movement is coordinated virtually instantaneously in and through 'electronic space' and 'electronic time'. Temporally, such operations are oriented to the nano-seconds of computer operations; speed is related in turn to profitability and global competitiveness (Adam 1994: 100–3). Spatially, they are mediated in 'electronic space' through telecommunication practices, ranging from the humble fax through electronic data interchange to an ever more mundane Internet and electronic conferencing (Poster 1995: 26). The so-called 'information superhighway' (albeit still partial and limited) plays an increasingly important role in transmitting information and knowledge. This does not nullify social space, for global/regional/national actors from the private and public realms typically need to meet face-to-face to develop trust, establish networks, form partnerships, settle differences, engage in mutual learning and interaction (Granovetter 1985; Jarillo 1988; Camagni 1991; Conti 1993; Mayntz 1993; Storper 1997).

Second, technological/industrial time-space moments are shaped by global networks of multinational firms interacting with regional and more locally based firms within the evolving regional division of labour/knowledge. Their operations are premised on trans-border cost differentials and/or techno-logical complementarities that affect global-regional competitiveness (Simon 1995: 4). Temporally, such networks aim to produce goods in time, on time, and every time to customers wherever they may be located in the global market. To speed up innovation, reduce lead times, and coordinate time-bound schedules, firms within and beyond the region join forces in sub-contracting activities, joint ventures, strategic alliances, etc., to produce just-in-time in 'regional factories'. Likewise, since production must be closely coordinated in trans-spatial and time-bound/compressed-time schedules, new institutional and technical forms of integrating activities emerge in both social and 'electronic space'. In social space, new spatial forms cut across borders and are mediated by dense networks of private-to-private and private-to-public alliances based on complex relations of trust, competition, and policy support (Jarillo 1988; Camagni 1991, Conti 1993; Mayntz 1993; Huber 1994). These networks are also shaped by their strategic calculations of how to produce and reproduce labour across borders through skilled com-muter workers, guest and/or migrant labour. Besides social space, these links are reinforced by emerging practices in 'electronic space' whereby relevant industrial/technological information is exchanged about R&D and stages of the production process from design to manufacturing (Howell 1993). The sites which emerge in this new discourse/identity are 'regional blocs', 'growth triangles', 'growth circles', 'sub-regional economic zones', 'offshore production sites', and 'learning/technological regions' linking the regions with the global and other regional circuits (Boisier 1994; Florida 1995).

Third, commerce is influenced by networks of multinational service firms and their regional/local counterparts located in 'global-gateway' cities. These provide producer and distributive services and logistics information (i.e. insurance, legal services, consultancies, logistic management, transpor-tation, retail) that 'facilitate all economic transactions, and the driving force that stimulates the production of goods' within the 'regional chain' (Riddle 1986: 26). Such networks coordinate the time-space of global–regional and regional–local production and distributive chains. Temporally, service firms engaged in the 'supply pipeline' are managing information flows that balance cost options as well as lead- and transit-time in time-bound projects. This is increasingly coordinated in 'electronic space'. One recent development here is 'virtual ports' offering 'virtual terminal services' with papers cleared and permits issued within minutes of arrival. Increasingly, information is sub-stituted for inventory (i.e. 'virtual inventory') at the centre so that 'quick responses' can be made directly into the replenishment systems through local outsourcing or procurement (Christopher 1992: 108–24). Thus social space remains important in developing trust, forming liaisons with local sub-contractors and management, and tapping local information flows to enhance customer service.

Fourth, cultural time-space moments are influenced by social practices embedded in networks of intra- and/or cross-cultural ties. Intra-cultural practices and norms embedded in common linguistic, familial, clan, and communal ties often help to 'grease the functioning of the social networks' through practices such as gift exchange and banqueting so as to generate familial/clan/communal loyalty. This intensification of social space may help to speed up the border-crossing time across private and public spaces. Cross-cultural subjectivities and networks emerge through the consolidation of practices and norms that reduce border-crossing time between cultural spaces. This is illustrated by global entrepreneurialism, multiculturalism, and even global post-colonialism.

These time-space moments help constitute the complex terrain in which networks of agencies struggle to construct new identities and to re-order their time and space across borders. New time-space and private-public practices may consolidate into a new form of geo-economic coordination, which can be termed time-space governance. This is defined as a mode of coordination that is mediated by a multilayered network of social relations that cuts across discursive-material, time-space, private–public, and global–regional–national–local dimensions of production and exchange.

Time-space governance: objects and capacities

Discursive-material dimensions

- As circumstances change, networks of actors struggle over the best way to define objects of governance (e.g. growth and competitiveness) despite differences in their respective spatio-temporal horizons of action;
- these struggles involve re-ordering available symbols and codes and lead to new identities, interests, and strategies; and
- these generate in turn new temporal-spatial moments in social relations.

Time-space dimensions

- 'Electronic space' and its related social practices are developed by net-works of multinational banks and other financial intermediaries to pool and manage trans-spatial funds fast-in-time and fast-in-space for global competitiveness;
- practices in social and 'electronic space' coordinate networks of production-service firms to plan and manage time-bound and compressed-time projects just-in-time for global competitiveness;

- 'electronic space' and its related social practices help networks of service firms to reduce lead- and transit-time of production and distribution; and
- cultural/social practices/norms emerge to reduce the border-crossing time between cultural and/or private–public spaces.

Private–public dimensions

- These networks often link the private and public spheres to coordinate the use of their respective economic and political resources and thereby enhance the synergy of these resources within and across each of these spheres (e.g. combining disparate but complementary forces and resources for investment, labour power, information, knowledge, subsidies, etc.); and
- these often involve new scales of activity that lie beyond sovereign states (e.g. trans-local, local–regional, and local–global arrangements).

Global–regional–national–local dimensions

- Networks of global–regional–national–local actors develop mechanisms and strategies to coordinate production, finance, and trade practices across border (e.g. strategic alliances, joint ventures, subcontracting, and foreign aid);
- these networks contribute to a specific regional division of labour/ knowledge based on cost differentials and technological complementarities;
- certain nodal points (such as global-gateway cities) have a key role here in providing complex services to bridge time-space gaps in this global– regional–national–local complex of production, finance, and trade;
- specific cross-border migratory/labour flows, labour processes, and modes of (inter- as well as intra-generational) social reproduction of labour power also emerge; and
- so do trans-border social blocs which accept, support, and carry the discourses and practices beyond elites.

Such strategic networks for trans-border time-space governance could enhance: (a) joint decision-making based on information-sharing, trust, and commitment; (b) the privileged role of business and industrial interests in formulating policy; (c) capacities to deploy economic and political-bureaucratic resources, such as grants or loans (for infrastructure), authority, organisational intelligence, technology and manufacturing know-how; (d) capacities to reduce lead-times and so increase global competitiveness; (e) interactive learning among private–public actors and institutions; and (f) negotiation systems conducive to societal guidance in the region. On the other hand, such networks and structures do not arise just because they are needed;

nor, once they have emerged for whatever reason(s), do they always operate beneficially. They develop in quite specific conditions and cannot be created at will through specific policy initiatives. Moreover, once developed, they may face various coordination problems and other challenges (in short, tensions) from within and beyond the networks.

Time-space governance tensions

Such tensions are rooted in trans-border strategic practices and identities. In examining them, we must first note that not all logically possible sets of trans-border regions are likely to develop into regional modes of growth. In particular, the network of private–public actors might fail to coordinate the economic spaces in which they are located because they are too similarly endowed to permit economic complementarities. Moreover, even if conditions are initially favourable, they may change, e.g. the rising costs of particular host economies or the 'leapfrogging' behaviour of subordinate partners in a system of technology transfer. These could create tensions for the host economies/dominant partner(s) in the time-space governance network. This may prompt problems regarding information-sharing, communication, trust, and cross-cultural understanding in strategic partnerships. However, this does not mean that such networks are thin and lack the capacities to learn: they may reorganise and/or combine with other existing networks to search for a new regional division of labour/knowledge.

As for time-space governance networks based on trans-local linkages, the politics of scale may involve conflicts over national sovereignty/security, local autonomy, and corruption at different levels. Moreover, given the socially embedded character of such networks, they are also linked to other geometries of power. For example, the geo-economic identity of a trans-border space may be intercepted by global–regional hegemons, which showcase it as a geo-political hub for 'democracy' and/or a 'nationalist' powerhouse. The co-existence of geo-economic and other geometries of powers may even de-stabilise a region through a contest of different identities, which cut across a thick network of economic relations. This can be illustrated, in a preliminary way, from the development of 'Greater China' as a trans-border space.

The making of 'Greater China' as a trans-border space

This section examines how trans-border actors construct and re-articulate the temporal and spatial horizons of the trans-border space. It starts with the global–regional–national contexts of the 'Open Door' discourse in the PRC.

Global–regional–national contexts of the 'Open Door' discourse in the PRC

The emergence of 'Greater China' as a trans-border space is articulated to a wide range of global–regional changes. Globally, techno-economic changes related to the rise of information technology, international competition based on shortened product life cycles and rapid dissemination of information have influenced the rise of the 'global factory' and the expansion of specific commodity chains (Dicken 1998; Gereffi and Korzeniewicz 1994). Transnational producers from the USA, Germany and Japan coordinate diversely skilled members working simultaneously to produce a good across many sites. Such international division of labour has created opportunities for outsourcing for cheap (un-)skilled labour, component parts and raw materials. These production and exchange activities also enable private–public actors in newly-industrialising countries (e.g. Hong Kong, Singapore, Taiwan and South Korea) to explore new time-space coordinates that cut across the global–regional–national–local domains.

These economic changes are also linked to the end of the Cold War, the re-emergence of China as a regional hegemon, and changes in its own internal politics. Despite struggles over China's identity after Mao's death, its leaders (especially Deng) did succeed during the 1970s in constructing a new hegemonic project to 'build socialism with Chinese characteristics'. This created the discursive space to re-make China's time-space meanings. The 'open door' narrative introduces the global–regional into China's own national–local spaces in and through localised experiments drawing on foreign direct investment (FDI) and/or 'special domestic' investment (a term used by China to refer to capital originating from Hong Kong and Taiwan) to expand and develop new production platforms and markets. Certain pioneering sites in China came to combine socialist-capitalist subjectivities and practices in new and productive ways. These imaginative experiments won support from key party elites and coastal-provincial actors in Guangdong and Fujian. The latter actors began to demand 'special/flexible measures' to create new geo-economic time-space forms to reconnect China to the regional and global system(s).

The Party Central Committee responded in 1979 with a decentralisation strategy permitting Guangdong and Fujian to adopt 'special policies and flexible measures'. The most notable measures include: (a) commercial reform that allows enterprises or business units under central control (except those in certain areas) to be managed by the province and to enter contracts (subject to central approval) with incoming investors valued up to $3 million (extended to $10 million in 1985, $30 million in 1988); and (b) fisco-financial reform enabling provinces such as Guangdong to retain 70 per cent of export earnings after paying 30 per cent of them to central government. These reforms were especially significant for the Special Economic Zones (SEZs) in Guangdong and Fujian, Shenzhen, Zhuhai, Shantou and Xiamen. These zones are the interface of an emerging socialist-capitalist and global–regional economy. They are the 'windows' and 'laboratory' for learning advanced technology and managerial skills as well as attracting foreign investment. Foreign investment in these zones enjoys various tax incentives and exemptions, etc. Moreover, given their headstart, the provincial and local governments in Guangdong above all had great incentives to open southern China.

In response to the above emerging discourse/opportunities within China, the rise of Western protectionism, the USA's granting of the Most Favoured Nation (MFN) trade status to mainland China, and increases in domestic costs for land and labour in Hong Kong, investors from the latter were searching for new outlets. Their search was influenced by strategic images of 'Greater China'. An increasing body of literature deploys ideas about 'Greater China' (e.g. 'Chinese Economic Circle', 'South China Economic Circle', 'Chinese Economic Community', 'Coordinating System of Chinese Economies') to present an image of vibrant economic interactions in the economically, culturally, and linguistically compatible area which map Hong Kong, southern China and Taiwan as part of an imagined community of 'Greater China' (Huang 1989; Cheng 1992; Fang 1992; Fu 1992). This project relates Hong Kong/Taiwan's time and space to Chinese strategies for growth and reunification. It remaps Hong Kong and Taiwan by, firstly, encouraging 'patriotic ethnic Chinese' (*huaqiao*) to 'invest in the motherland'. This pragmatic approach consolidates Hong Kong as a 'gateway' to China, 'Greater China', and the rest of the world. It enables China to stress the spatial coherence of the region and its competitiveness in relation to global restructuring; and to ground narratives of a common 'economic future' in pragmatic networking practices without having to confront, at least in the short term, the problematic relation between nationalism and politics.

Building and consolidating time-space governance capacities in 'Greater China'

Hong Kong is now by far the biggest investor in Guangdong province, supplying 80 per cent of the FDI. The Pearl River Delta is now a major production base for its more labour-intensive products. Almost 25,000 Hong Kong manufacturing enterprises, mostly in textiles and clothing, toys and consumer electronics, have moved there to exploit low labour and rent costs. They directly employ about 3 million workers, i.e. three times the total manufacturing labour force left in Hong Kong.

Unlike Hong Kong, the Taiwanese government in the early 1980s saw few advantages and many serious Cold War risks in trading with the mainland. Commercial links were first established in 1979 but were conducted through Hong Kong. However, the appreciation of Taiwanese currency from 1986, the rising cost of land, and the high standards set by the 1984 Basic Labour Law have all made the Chinese market increasingly attractive to Taiwanese businesses. Fears of an investment strike by Taiwan capital prompted the

KMT government to replace restrictions on trade/investment with more positive state guidance. In particular, legalisation of travel and liberalisation of foreign exchange sharply accelerated the growth in trade and FDI between the two economies. In 1988, the Chinese State Council promulgated a set of 22 measures to encourage investment from Taiwan. Taiwanese capital is treated as 'special domestic capital' and can pursue business not open to foreign capital, such as banking, wholesale and retail. In January 1993, the Taiwanese government began allowing Taiwanese companies to invest not more that US$1 million in China without going through a third site. Five million Taiwanese have since visited China and 9,300 Taiwanese firms have moved production facilities there with investment of $8.6 billion at the end of 1993 (Cheng 1992: 102–5). However, for security considerations, Taipei requires that trade and movement of factors of production pass through a third site. Thus, whilst seeking to maintain its own competitive edge, Taiwan is adopting a gradual and selective open-door policy on cross-Strait economic exchanges.

Despite security apprehensions, Guangdong and Fujian, as FDI hosts, possess cheap labour and land; they also offer ready access to a vast and rapidly growing Chinese market. These coastal provinces also share a similar cultural background and common language. These cultural traits and decentralisation/coastal strategies have combined to consolidate a privileged set of networks that cross-cuts public–private, central–provincial–local, and global–regional domains within China and the 'Greater China' region. This meta-network has a key role in the emerging time-space governance of this cross-border region.

The emergence of cross-cutting networks in China

The 'open-door' policy has unleashed new central–provincial–local forces in China itself. They are mediated by a network of public, quasi-public and private institutions aiming to expand foreign economic relations and development. At the centre, they include the Ministry of Foreign Economic Relations and Trade (MOFERT) which is responsible for managing the introduction of foreign investment, new trading arrangements, and new joint ventures. The provinces of Guangdong and Fujian followed the policy of the centre in setting up their own province-level functional and line ministries. These ministries were empowered in 1985 to administer and monitor incoming investments worth less than $3 million. Unsurprisingly, local functionaries often manipulate these policies to enable them to retain the benefits of inward investment.

On this issue, I will concentrate on the emergence of elites in 'special economic zones' or 'development zones' (Nee 1992: 1–27). They largely comprise state/party officials who control township-village enterprises (TVEs) around the coastal regions. They are termed 'cadre entrepreneurs' because they serve both as managers-executives of the TVEs and party-state functionaries at the same levels (Zweig 1995: 268; Goodman 1995: 136–8; Heberer 1995: 59). They mediate private and public interests. Such cadre entrepreneurs are eager to attract overseas Chinese investment to their counties, townships or villages. Often, they encourage inward investors from Hong Kong and Taiwan to 'unbundle' their investment so that its artificially constructed component parts each fall below the threshold which would trigger central–provincial monitoring and administration. This 'unbundling' tactic enables local elites to bypass higher tiers of government and network with inward investors on their own terms.

Their networking capacities are reinforced by decentralisation/coastal strategies. These have devolved ownership rights (including utilisation and return rights) from the central to provincial and local levels. This empowers cadre entrepreneurs to network with Hong Kong and Taiwanese investors through: (a) transfer of 'utilisation rights' of assets (such as taxes, land, labour, loans, power supply, import/export licences, etc.) to the local level, where these rights enable local players to deal more flexibly with Hong Kong/Taiwanese investors; (b) transfer of rights to revenue from the utilisation of state assets to the local level also permits unofficial 'second budgets' as cadre entrepreneurs creatively shift 'taxable' items away from the central–local budgetary accounts (Oi 1992: 100; Wang 1994: 99); and (c) fiscal softness at local level due to such 'second budgets' also enables local governments to 'experiment' with new local 'growth projects', external linkages, and central–local relations. These new capacities enable the coastal provinces, their cities and counties, as well as special economic zones, to compete more effectively for Hong Kong and Taiwanese investment.

The formation of strategic networks in 'Greater China'

Capitalising on these new capacities/opportunities, Taiwan and Hong Kong traders-cum-producers are sourcing for potential Chinese partners. They draw on their linguistic affinities and kinship ties to build socio-economic connections in the region (see Kong, this volume). They also enter strategic networks with various local Chinese public, quasi-public, and private agencies in the region and consolidate them through the socio-cultural practices of '*quanxi*' (relationship). When such pre-existing relationships are absent, it may take time to cultivate new linkages and this will often involve exchanging material/informational gifts (Smart and Smart 1991; Yang 1989 and 1994; Yan 1996), taking potential partners out for dinner, karaoke, or other entertainment, inviting them to ceremonial banquets/meetings, and making donations to the community (Zhao and Aram 1995: 360). These practices are often symbolised as gestures/signs of friendship, loyalty, mutual trust and 'giving face' (a code that communicates a sense of social importance in the network). The active exchange of these gifts/favours gives boundaries and significance to *quanxi* networks. These consolidate a reliable and effective social space of relatives, friends, and business partners to be called upon for utilitarian purposes. A reliable and effective network can speed up the border-crossing time between the private and public spaces as the latter becomes more permeable to private interests. For example, pre-existing good *quanxi* can expedite access to licences, loans, raw materials, etc., from public or quasi-public organisations.

Thus the cultural time-space aspects of 'Greater China' involve the steady rise of a strategic group of actors/institutions organised in a loosely-hierarchical network that spans the private–public divide as trans-local domains. These trans-border networks are quite different in form, scope, actors, aims, and modus operandi from the transnational networks formed among Hong Kong multinationals and their economic partners in the ASEAN region or elsewhere (see Dicken and Yeung, this volume). Thus the networks at the centre of my analysis involve municipal authorities special-ising in Hong Kong/Taiwan investment, county-township cadre entre-preneurs, as well as small- and medium-sized firms from Hong Kong and Taiwan. They draw on pre-existing *quanxi* to build a flexible and open system of networking relations which allows them to build trust, obtain advice, communicate demand and gain resources at below-market prices. The form of interaction tends to be group- and not firm-based: local state-party officials, semi-public TVE, and incoming firms from Hong Kong and Taiwan all play important roles. However, this is not a horizontal market connection because it does not involve links between legally equal indi-viduals; it involves power asymmetries between actors and institutions. Nor do these networks resemble hierarchical command-economy linkages because exchanges are not mediated through authority relations between superiors and subordinates: rather, they involve informal material and administrative exchanges from which actors can exit when desired. For example, local party-state officials still control resources such as land, labour, capital and regulations; semi-public enterprises command information and contacts; and private firms control capital, managerial skills and market outlets. Given this interdependence, these public–private networks tend to form clientelist alliances that operate an interactive process of 'steering' and societal guidance. This may consolidate as a pattern of open regional collaborative networks that guide learning within 'Greater China'.

Consolidating a trans-border division of labour/knowledge in 'Greater China'

These strategic networks represent a coalition/alliance of local party/administrative officials, their entrepreneurial affiliates, and Hong Kong and Taiwanese capital. They form the social bases of support for a trans-border division of labour/knowledge for export processing in the 'Greater China' bloc. Hong Kong and Taiwan are moving up the industrial technology ladder by shifting their labour-intensive industries to low-wage and cheap-land localities in Southern China. Labour has been made available through rural de-collectivisation since 1984 and it is estimated that there are 100–150 million migrants (Wolf 1996: 14) from the inland areas. To compete for capital from Hong Kong and Taiwan, coastal communities undercut each other by providing low-cost and low-protection labour systems. Most workers, especially in the Pearl River Delta, are engaged in what one can call a highly 'flexible-taylorised' process whereby production is minutely divided, e.g. sewing, button-holing and button-stitching in the garment industry. The flexibility of this form of organisation of the labour process is further secured by adjusting hours, wage rates, a capital-controlled hire-and-fire procedure and lax interpretation of labour standards/laws in the region (Sum 1994: 90–3; 1998: 66–8). The resulting 'workhouse regions' also reproduce labour through their use of workfare shelters based on dormitory-type accommodation, subsidised meals and a trip back home for the Chinese New Year.

In response to the availability of a new labour regime in the region, 80 per cent of Hong Kong's manufacturing industries (e.g. simple electronics, toys, leather, shoe-making and watches) have moved to southern China. In the 1990s, a second wave of relocation has involved moving low-skilled white-collar work (e.g. telephone enquiry/paging service) to southern China. How-ever, manufacturing relocation is still pre-dominant in southern China. Because Hong Kong's manufacture is largely oriented to export-processing, its transfer to southern China promotes entrepot trade between the two regions.

As for Taiwan, investments before 1990 were mostly in manufacturing especially in labour-intensive industries. It was reported that Taiwan's tradi-tional industries – for instance, 80 per cent of handbag production, 90 per cent of shoemaking, and over 90 per cent of umbrella-making – have been transferred to southern China. These goods are mainly exported and some are even sent back to Taiwan. Since 1989, Taiwan's investment has included petrochemicals and machinery. Given that Taiwanese investment needs to involve a third area, most of the flows of material, people, and money targeted on southern China pass through Hong Kong. In this regard, Hong Kong is a principal trade and capital dispatch centre for Taiwanese investment in China (Sung 1997: 61–6).

The shifting of labour-intensive processes to the Pearl River Delta not only consolidates Hong Kong's entrepot role but also enhances its capacity, as a global-gateway city, to coordinate investment, trade and services in and beyond the 'Greater China' region. Thus the region's international subcon-tracting chain is mediated by a more complex network of relations within and beyond the 'Greater China' bloc that comprises: global/regional buyers, Hong Kong and/or Taiwan-owned firms, China's quasi-state trading firms in Hong Kong, state-owned firms or county/township-village enterprises in China, provincial and local governments and their subsidiaries, and local branches of ministries and their affiliates. This strategic network is coordinated by subcontracting management based in Hong Kong which involves re-articulating time-space dimensions of trans-border production and trade.

More specifically, subcontracting management involves sourcing, production, authority and distribution management. Producers-cum-traders from Hong Kong/Taiwan locate Chinese partners through formal contacts as well as informal kinship and communal ties. Exchanges of visits and/or gifts help to consolidate reliable and effective *quanxi*. This intensification of the social space helps to speed up the border-crossing time across the urban–rural as well as the ethnic divide within the subregion; and also to build the mutual trust needed for future contracts or longer-lasting arrangements (such as sub-contracting partnerships and joint ventures). The latter can involve more complex services related to legal services on production-sharing contracts, etc. After establishing the sourcing networks, the Hong Kong/Taiwan traders-cum-producers then engage in production management across time and space. This production process involves the coordination and supervision of time-bound projects dispersed over several sites with the more skill-intensive sub-processes in Hong Kong/Taiwan and the more labour-intensive ones in southern China. Production managers and quality-controllers from Hong Kong/Taiwan are at the forefront here in re-articulating spatial scales and temporal horizons in realising time-bound projects. These often involve more intensification of production practices such as finer differentiation of pre-production planning and more intensification of production schedules and monitoring. For example, Hong Kong or Taiwan-based managers make frequent visits to production sites to ensure their conformity to production schedules (Chan *et al.* 1991: 189); and quality controllers often get based in China to tighten monitoring procedures. Such practices build the capacity to coordinate trans-border production processes so that goods reach the global market just-in-time.

Also essential to this time-space governance network is the building of good relations with local/central officials and cadre entrepreneurs in China. Such strategic networking is important in reducing the border-crossing time between the private–public as well as the urban–rural divides. Here producer-cum-traders from Hong Kong/Taiwan intensify the social space through practices such as entertaining the authorities and making donations to the community. After all, these authorities still control enormous resources such as land, labour, capital and regulations. In addition to production and authority management, finished goods in the 'supply pipeline' need to be exported/distributed to the global market. Distribution management, then, involves the re-articulation of factory time and global lead time through the activities of service-based firms in the region as well as trading and customs authorities. This trans-border private–public network is coordinated in the 'electronic' and 'social space' that synchronises transport schedules, export procedures of import/export licensing, customs liaison, packaging and logistic management, etc., so that goods can be delivered just-in-time and 'right-in-place' for global/regional buyers. Practices of these kind help to speed up the transit- and pipeline-time crucial to time-bound projects. This phenomenon was described by one Hong Kong managing director of a multinational as being the three T's: time, trust and truth (personal communication). They form the basic ingredients, in the ideal case, for producing and reproducing this strategic private–public network both in social and electronic space. It is this capacity that enables Hong Kong to consolidate its emerging position as a global-gateway city providing trading and producer services (logistics, insurance, legal, banking, accounting expertise, etc.).

Similarly, the setting up of factories in southern China has gradually turned Taiwan into headquarters for higher-end production (e.g. computer monitors, desk-top and portable personal computers, motherboards, keyboards and PC mice), R&D activities, receipt of overseas orders, materials procurement, and provision of technical assistance and personnel training for plants in China. Economic and technological/financial complementarities between the partners include: (a) southern China's cheap land, trainable cheap labour, raw materials, negotiable investment packages and culturally-affiliated and FDI-friendly local cadre entrepreneurs; (b) Hong Kong's role as an entrepot and global-gateway city with good global–regional connections and knowledge in finance, trade, and production management; and (c) Taiwan's capital, applied technology on electronics, synthetic fabrics, plastic materials and the experience in administration and marketing of products (Xu 1994: 151; Chung 1997).

'Time-space governance tensions' and scale politics in 'Greater China'

My discussion of strategic cross-border networks in 'Greater China' would be incomplete without examining the tensions in this emerging form of time-space governance. But editorial constraints mean I will focus only on tensions related to the politics of scale in relation to the central–local, trans-national, and trans-local interfaces.

First, tensions may emerge between local development communities (led by cadre entrepreneurs) and the centre. Decentralisation has changed central–local fiscal relations. It weakens the fiscal leverage of central-level government over local government by reducing the latter's dependence on central revenues and investment funds relative to revenues generated by local investment and economic growth. Thus local party-state officials are less inclined to comply with superiors' wishes regarding economic activities (Wong 1991: 691–3; Walder 1994: 306). This weakening of central government is far from complete because it still controls 'recentralisation' levers, such as tightening macro-economic control, reorienting national economic policy, renegotiating resource-sharing and controlling personnel appointments. Similarly, local authorities have devised various coping strategies to deal with the centre, such as lobbying for central support, creatively interpreting central policies, flexibly implementing central measures and withholding as many funds as possible from central extraction. The use of these bargaining instruments in the tug-of-war between the central and local government is interpreted by Howell (1993) in terms of cycles of decentral-isation and recentralisation in China since 1978. This rivalry is especially intense when the size of the fiscal and economic 'pie' is shrinking. On the other hand, the central and local governments are also willing to cooperate as partners when they anticipate rapid expansion in foreign trade. In such cases, localities may encourage local enterprises to accept the centre's rules of the game in order to achieve their mutual goal of expanding exports. Thus, in the case of trade, if the goal is to build export bases for raw material production, both sides would work together to establish a joint venture.

Such central–local tensions indicate the possibility of Guangdong/southern China regional challenges to the centre. Issues may include the share of tax revenue owed to Beijing, growing independence in foreign trade and conflicts between TVEs and state-owned enterprises. Following factional struggles in the central party elite, measures were taken in 1994 to alter central–provincial relations. These comprised fiscal and investment reforms, includ-ing closer scrutiny on local government's power to grant tax exemption and to reduce both central and shared taxes. Provinces and regions responded differently. Guangdong interpreted these measures as a 'conspiracy' of state-sector interests to favour state-sector dominated provinces such as Shanghai and weaken it and southern China more generally (Cannon and Zhang 1996: 90–4). Whether or not this is so, the central government is certainly promoting new centres of economic gravity in central and northern China, e.g. Shanghai-Pudong, Bohai Region, and Dalian.

As indicated earlier, central–local conflict not only raises the question of regional challenges but is also fuelling the debate among Chinese elites over possible path(s) of reform and over continued one-party domination. For example, the tendencies towards regionalism and coastal developmental communities intensify the conflict between the reformer-cosmopolitan and reformer-nativist factions within the central elites (Ling 1996: 17). This involves struggles over China's future identity as having an economy based on 'market socialism'/'socialism with Chinese characteristics'. Such tensions have also fuelled debates on the disjuncture between market and adminis-trative reforms, the conflict between TVEs and state-owned enterprises, problems of corruption, etc.

Technology transfer in a regional division of labour/knowledge is also a site of tensions. This involves TVEs and their Hong Kong and/or Taiwanese counterparts. The latter typically import low-tech second hand equipment that is no longer profitable (or deemed too polluting) in Taiwan or Hong Kong. Unsurprisingly, the TVEs are demanding a deepening of technology transfer and the regional division of labour/knowledge. But Hong Kong and Taiwan are worried about the consequences for a 'hollowing out' of their own economies because of the relocation of more high-tech industries (e.g. computer manufacturing from Taiwan) and service sector (e.g. backroom banking services) to China. One way forward has been to re-think the future regional roles of Hong Kong and Taiwan (see below).

Private–public coordination of the different scales of action often takes the form of quasi-public people-to-people diplomacy (Clough 1993). This has generated new tensions because such trans-border networks also challenge specific identities and interests rooted in other geometries of power and time-space calculations (e.g. geo-political and nationalist ones). Thus Hong Kong not only has a geo-economic role as a 'global-gateway' for Beijing and Taiwan to attract '*huaqiao*' investments to the 'motherland', but is also presented, within Anglo-American geo-political strategic discourse, as a 'democratic hub' to be contrasted with mainland China. Chris Patten had a key role here during his Governorship but local democratic groups continue to articulate the spatio-temporal perspectives of the American hegemon and present China as a 'risk' to other nation-states in the region as well as to 'democracy', 'human rights', and other Enlightenment values (Pollock 1993: 76; Sum 1996a: 215–20 and 1996b: 55–9). Matters are further complicated by Taiwan's security concerns, the fear of over-dependence on China, and the USA's geo-political linkages with the KMT and democracy movement in the island. This can be seen in the continued lease/sale of arms to Taiwan, open support by some senators for the Taiwanese democracy movement, permission for President Lee's unofficial visit to USA in 1995, and so forth. These geo-political partnerships between US, UK, Hong Kong (e.g. Democratic Party), Taiwan (e.g. Democratic People's Party) and the geo-economic network centred on China have clearly confronted social forces at different scales with crucial tensions/dilemmas on their identities/interests (Sum 1998).

The resulting politics of scales and identity struggles not only mark the emerging trans-border space as a contested space; they also open it up as a space for re-imaginations and re-visioning. This helps guide in turn the design of institutions to recode/redirect/remap time-space governance patterns. In the 1990s, the reconstruction of 'Greater Shanghai' as a new object of governance has affected the mode of time-space governance coordination within 'Greater China'. New repositionings and re-negotiation of identities are occurring within the region (Sum 1998).

Conclusion

My case study of 'Greater China' as a trans-border space offers a preliminary account of some complex issues in transnationalism. It departs from the 'space of flows' and 'state-centred' approaches noted above and proposes a rethinking of globalisation in terms of the complex, tangled dialectic of changes in temporal horizons (such as compressed-time and memory time of nations) and spatial scales (such as global, regional, national, and local scales). Such changes are most prevalent in the making of trans-border spaces and it is here that the latter crystallise some of the complexities of this process. To capture these complexities, this chapter introduces the middle-range concept of time-space governance which draws on insights from the new regional geography, discourse analysis, institutional economics/sociology and governance theory. The concept of time-space governance helps to explore articulatory practices across different sites and scales. It also highlights the strategic terrains on which new subject positions are re-imagined. In short, the chapter emphasizes contingencies, the politics of scales between the global–regional–national–local nexus, the re-ordering of time and space in remaking social relations in the trans-border space, and the role of reflexive time-space governance and reimagination that help to sustain these relations.

Part III

Reterritorialising the state

9   Servicing the global economy

Reconfigured states and private agents[1]

Saskia Sassen

Economic globalisation represents a transformation in the territorial organisation of economic activity and of politico-economic power (Mittelman 1996a; Ruggie 1993; Jessop 1990; Hitz *et al.* 1995; Aman, Jr 1995). It contains the capacity to undo the particular form of the intersection of sovereignty and territory embedded in the modern state and the modern state-system.[2] But simply to posit, as is so often done, that economic globalisation has brought with it a declining significance of the national state *tout court*, misses some of the finer points about this transformation.

The encounter of a global actor – firm or market – with one or another instantiation of the national state can be thought of as a new frontier zone. It is not merely a dividing line between the national economy and the global economy. It is a zone of politico-economic interactions that produce new institutional forms and alter some of the old ones. Nor is it just a matter of reducing regulations or the role of government generally. For instance, in many countries, the necessity for autonomous central banks in the current global economic system has required a thickening of regulations in order to de-link central banks from the influence of the executive branch of government.

This zone of interaction is highly charged and potentially the outcomes of this interaction can make for epochal change. Why is it highly charged and significant? Because it is not simply the push by global firms and markets that is shaping the dynamics of interaction as is implied in much of the literature on the declining significance of the national state under globalisation. States are also shaping the dynamics of interaction and are doing so not merely in the form of resistance (see, e.g. various chapters in Mittelman 1996a). In doing so, however, they are reconfigured (Sassen 1996a: chapter 1). This reconfiguring is shaped both by trends towards standardisation, as is the growing convergence in the role of central banks, and by national particularities.

The tension between the weight of national specificity and the weight of the new global rules of the game is well illustrated by some aspects of the current Asian financial crisis. We are seeing different responses by the Asian countries involved in IMF 'rescue packages', signalling the weight of specific domestic institutional arrangements and leadership. At the same time, the emergent consensus in the community of states to further globalisation has created a set of specific obligations on participating states, no matter how reluctant some of these states might be.

Beyond the inadequacy of simply accepting the general proposition of a declining significance of the state, there is also the problematic acceptance of a simple quantitative measure of globalisation. Simply to focus on the fact of the often minimal share of foreign inputs in national economies overlooks, again, some of the marking features of the current phase of the global economy. It is indeed the case that in most developed countries the share of foreign in total investment, the share of international in total trade, the share of foreign in total stock market value, are all very small. However, to infer from this that economic globalisation is not really a significant issue, misses a crucial feature: the fact that most global processes materialise in national territories and do so to a large extent through national institutional arrangements, from legislative acts to firms, and are thereby not necessarily counted as 'foreign'.

Conversely, for that same reason we cannot simply assume that because a transaction takes place in national territory and in a national institutional setting it is *ipso facto* national. In my reading, the imbrication of global actors and national institutions is far more ambiguous. The case of the central banks today also illustrates another key aspect in the process whereby national economies accommodate a global economic system: a country's central bank can be a key institution for implementing – in its national economy – some of the new rules of the global game, notably some of the standards in IMF conditionality. This signals that 'national' institutions can become home to some of the operational rules of the global economic system.[3]

Here I want to focus on some of the state and non-state agents central to the operations of the global economy. The purpose is to understand the interactions between national states and global actors and the ways in which some of the dynamics that constitute the global economy operate through national institutions and in national territories. Analytically the discussion is centred in this notion of a frontier zone where many different outcomes are possible. Running through the larger project and the particular discussion here is a working hypothesis that maintains that the tension between (a) the necessary, though partial, location of globalisation in national territories, and (b) an elaborate system that has constructed the exclusive national territorial authority of sovereign states, has (c) been partly negotiated through processes of institutional de-nationalisation and the formation of privatised intermediary institutional arrangements for handling cross-border operations.[4]

Necessary instrumentalities: state and non-state centred mechanisms

Implementing today's global economic system in the context of national territorial sovereignty requires multiple policy negotiations. One of the roles of
the state *vis-à-vis* today's global economy, unlike earlier forms of the world
economy, has been to negotiate the intersection of national law and foreign
actors – whether firms, markets or supranational organisations. What makes
the current phase distinctive is, on the one hand, the existence of an enormously elaborate body of law which secures the exclusive territoriality of
national states to an extent not seen in the nineteenth century (e.g. Ruggie
1993; Kratochwil 1986), and on the other, the considerable institutionalising
of the 'rights' of non-national firms, the 'legalising' of a growing array of
cross-border transactions, and the growing, and increasingly institutionalised, participation by supranational organisations in national matters
(e.g. Rosen and McFadyen 1995; Kennedy 1992).[5] This sets up the conditions
for a necessary engagement of national states in the process of globalisation.

We generally use terms such as 'deregulation', financial and trade liberalisation, and privatisation, to describe the outcome of this negotiation. The
problem with such terms is that they only capture the withdrawal of the
state from regulating its economy. They do not register all the ways in which
the state participates in setting up the new frameworks through which
globalisation is furthered (e.g. Mittelman 1996a; Shapiro 1993); nor do they
capture the associated transformations inside the state. One way of putting it
then, would be to say that certain components of the national state operate
as necessary instrumentalities for the implementation of a global economic
system.

The starting point for my argument is that there is much more going on in
these negotiations than the concept 'deregulation' captures. 'Deregulation'
actually refers to an extremely complex set of intersections and negotiations
which, while they may preserve the integrity of national territory as a geographic condition, do transform exclusive territoriality, i.e. the national and
international frameworks through which national territory has assumed an
institutional form over the last seventy years (Sassen, forthcoming). National
territory and exclusive territoriality have corresponded tightly for much of
the recent history of the developed nation-states. (For critical accounts see,
for example, Walker 1993 and Weber 1996.)[6] Today, globalisation may be
contributing to an incipient slippage in that correspondence. Much deregulation has had the effect of promoting that slippage and giving it a legitimate
form in national legal frameworks. The reconfiguring of the institutional
encasement of national territory also brings with it the ascendance of sub-
national spaces.(See Jessop in this volume; see also Sassen's concept of global
cities; for an historical account see Taylor 1995.)

The fact that we cannot simply reduce these negotiations to the notion of
deregulation is also illustrated by the privatisation of public sector firms.

Such privatisation is not just a change in ownership status, but also a shift of regulatory functions to the private sector where they re-emerge under other forms, most notably, private corporate legal and accounting services.

Recognising the importance of place and of production – in this case the production of a system of power – helps us refocus our thinking about the global economy along these lines. The global economy needs to be implemented, reproduced, serviced, financed. It cannot be taken simply as a given, or a set of markets, or merely as a function of the power of multinational corporations and financial markets. There is a vast array of highly specialised functions that need to be executed and infrastructures that need to be secured. These have become so specialised that they can no longer be subsumed under general corporate headquarter functions. Global cities, with their complex networks of highly specialised service firms and labour markets are strategic sites for the production of these specialised functions. In this sense, global cities are one form of this embeddedness of global processes in national territories and in national institutional arrangements.[7] The role played by these strategic places in the organisation and management of the global economy, along with the fact that much investment and all financial markets, no matter how deregulated, are located somewhere, shows us that the global economy to a large extent materialises in national territories.[8]

It means, in turn, that various instantiations of the national state are inevitably involved.[9] The result is a particular set of negotiations which have the effect of leaving the geographic condition of the nation-state's territory unaltered, but do transform the institutional encasements of that geographic fact, that is, the state's territorial jurisdiction or, more abstractly, the state's exclusive territoriality. My argument is that precisely because global processes materialise to a large extent in national territories, many national states have had to become involved, even if at times peripherally, in the implementation of the global economic system and have, in this process, experienced transformations of various aspects of their institutional structure.[10]

Studying the impact of economic globalisation through the lenses of this distinction between national territory and exclusive territoriality overcomes at least two limitations evident in much research on the global economy. One of these is the notion of a zero-sum relationship between the national and the global: what the global gains the national loses, and vice versa. Partly because of my earlier research on global cities, it is quite evident to me that many global processes materialise in national territories and institutions. Thus the relationship between the global economy and the national state is far more imbricated than the notion of mutually exclusive domains suggests.

The second of these limitations has to do with a measurement question: the tendency in quantitative approaches to measure the global as the international portion of national trade, investment, financial markets and consumption. According to these measures – and we now have a growing body of evidence – the 'global', i.e. 'foreign', is an insignificant portion of most national economies, especially in the highly developed world. From there one can easily go to the inference that hence it is not even worth taking seriously.

If, however, there is more to the global economy than direct cross-border flows, then it may well be that its impact on national systems cannot be fully captured with straightforward quantitative measures. I see the global economy as a system of privatised economic power that by necessity has to operate partly through national institutions. The question then becomes what is the impact of economic globalisation on the territorial jurisdiction, or more theoretically, the exclusive territoriality of the nation-state. It requires a critical examination of an assumption evident in much of the current discussion about globalisation, to wit, that if an event takes place in a national territory it is a national event, whether a business transaction or a judiciary decision.[11]

Implementing the new norms through national institutions

On a fairly abstract level we can see the ambiguity of the distinction between 'national' and 'global' in the normative weight gained by the logic of the global capital market in setting criteria for key national economic policies (see Sassen 1996, chapter 2 for a fuller discussion). The multiple negotiations between national states and global economic actors signal that the logic of the global capital market is succeeding in imposing itself on important aspects of national economic policy making. Autonomy of the central bank, anti-inflation policies, exchange rate parity and the variety of items usually referred to as 'IMF conditionality' – all of these have become a set of norms (see Higgott, this volume). This new normativity can be seen at work in the design of the 'solution' to the Mexican economic crisis of December 1994; this crisis was described as a consequence of the global financial markets having 'lost confidence' in the government's leadership of the Mexican economy and the 'solution' was explicitly aimed at restoring that confidence.[12]

Today we see the (attempted) imposition of that same set of norms on several countries in Asia, no matter how different the underlying conditions from those of Mexico and in each of the Asian countries involved.[13] The actual architecture of the crisis may well have more to do with the aggressive attempts to globalise these economies from the outside than with their governments' leadership of these economies. Corruption, favouritism and weak banking systems were features of these economies long before the current financial crisis and throughout their period of growth, when they were much admired and put up as models for Latin America, the Caribbean and Africa. In this regard it is interesting to note, for instance, in the case of Indonesia that besides the enormous amounts of FDI, 70 per cent of turnover on the Jakarta stock market in 1995, well before the crisis, was accounted for by foreign investors; market capitalisation in that market increased by 47 per cent in 1995. This required deregulation of the financial markets. In 1995 – again, before the crisis – Indonesia also eliminated the rule necessitating joint venture with a local partner, making it possible for companies to be a 100 per cent foreign owned. But corruption and favouritism for local firms which allowed huge conglomerates to operate as monopolies, in fact kept many potential foreign owners out. We see a similar syndrome in South Korea.

In this context I read the Asian financial crisis as a dynamic that has the effect of destabilising national monopoly control of these economies and IMF conditionality as facilitating a massive transfer to foreign ownership. The outcome is further globalisation and further imposition of the new normativity attached to the logic of the global capital market. However the actual materialisation of these conditions will go through specific institutional channels and assume distinct forms in each country, with various levels of resistance and consent – whence my notion of this dynamic as having the features of a frontier zone. It is worth noting that all the Latin American countries that deregulated their financial markets had a banking system crisis. More generally, FDI in emerging markets went from $24 billion in 1990 to $90 billion in 1995. It does suggest that the 'financial crises' experienced by many of these emerging markets cannot only be a function of inadequate government performance. The globalisation of their financial markets has something to do with it. And this globalisation follows the norms of the logic of the global capital market.

Let me elaborate on this. After the Mexico crisis, there was a general collapse in emerging markets. But a mere six months later there was a sharp recovery. The trade literature describes this as a partly engineered result: international investors got together with the most creative talent in financial institutions and banks to design some of the most creative and unprecedented deals.[14] The aim was to produce assets of emerging markets attractive to the scared-off investors.

There are also more subtle ways in which globalisation operates through national institutions and in national terrains. This can be illustrated with a key feature of globalisation – privatisation.[15] Privatisation is not simply a change in ownership regime; it is also a privatising of coordination and governance functions which shift from the public to the private corporate sector. In some particular geographic situations, these developments can be captured in the image of a shift of functions and authority from Washington's government world to New York City's corporate world, from New Delhi to Bombay, from Brazilia to Sao Paulo. In most countries the national capital is also the leading financial and business centre, so this geographic image does not hold even though the institutional transfer may take place.

The key issue is this transfer of what were regulatory functions embedded in government bureaucracies to the corporate world where they re-emerge as corporate management functions or specialised corporate services. Insofar as foreign investors and foreign firms are increasingly part of this privatisation of public sector firms – and indeed, in many cases, are the main investors – we could argue that this represents not only a privatising of economic governance functions but also an incipient de-nationalising of such functions (see Sassen 1996: chapter 1). Thus while central, the role of the state in producing the legal encasements for economic activity is no longer what it was in earlier periods.

The new intermediaries

Economic globalisation has also been accompanied by the creation of new legal regimes and legal practices and the expansion and renovation of some older forms that have the effect of replacing public regulation and law with private mechanisms and sometimes even bypass national legal systems. The importance of private oversight institutions, such as credit rating agencies, has increased with the deregulation and globalisation of the financial markets. These agencies are now key institutions in the creation of order and transparency in the global capital market and have considerable power over sovereign states through their authority in rating government debt. Also the rise of international commercial arbitration as the main mechanism for resolving cross-border business disputes entails a declining importance of national courts in these matters – a privatising of this kind of justice (e.g. Salacuse 1991). Further, the new international rules for financial reporting and accounting that are to be implemented in 1998 and 1999 also relocate some national functions to a privatised international system.

All of these begin to amount to a privatised system of governance ensuring order, respect for contracts, transparency and accountability in the world of cross-border business transactions. To some extent this privatised world of governance has replaced various functions of national states in ensuring the protection of the rights of firms. This privatisation contributes to changing the dynamics and to fuelling new dynamics in the zone of interaction between national institutions and global actors. The state continues to play a crucial, but no longer exclusive, role in the production of 'legality' around new forms of economic activity.

There is a new intermediary world of strategic agents that contribute to the management and coordination of the global economy. These agents are largely, though not exclusively, private. And they have absorbed some of the international functions carried out by states in the recent past, as was the case, for instance, with international trade under predominantly protectionist regimes in the post-Second World War decades. Their role is dramatically illustrated by the case of China: When the Chinese government in 1996 issued a 100-year bond to be sold, not in Shanghai, but mostly in New York, it did not have to deal with Washington; it dealt with J. P. Morgan. This example can be repeated over and over for a broad range of countries.

Private firms in international finance, accounting and law, the new private standards for international accounting and financial reporting, and supra-national organisations such as WTO, all play strategic non-government entred governance functions. But they do so in good part inside the territory of national states.

Many of these rather abstract issues are well illustrated by the work being done to create new private international standards for accounting and financial reporting. And they can be illustrated with the aggressively innovative deals launched by the major financial services firms in the last few years to sell what had often been considered unsaleable, or at least not gradable debt, and to ensure the continuing expansion of the financial markets. The next two sub-sections briefly discuss these two issues.

The new Accounting Standards

The International Accounting Standards Committee is an independent private sector body which has been working intensely to create uniform standards to be used by business and government. It wants to bring these standards on line by 1999. In 1995 the International Organisation of Securities Commission agreed to endorse the IASC's standards and set March 1998 as the target date for completion of a body of international accounting standards. While this is a world of private actors and private standards, national states are crucial presences in the whole operation. It is worth noting that by early 1997, IASC standards had been accepted by all stock exchanges except Japan, Canada and the US – though these eventually also joined.[16]

This evolution was not without incidents that made it clear to what extent national governments and firms resisted or had difficulty accepting the concept of standards valid across borders, let alone uniform international standards as pursued by the IASC. Japan resisted changing its national accounting system, one lacking the standards of 'transparency' that have become the norm in international transactions. It was indeed Japan's reluctance to implement such standards of transparency in a wide range of business activities in conjunction with its reluctance to continue deregulating its financial sector which, it seems to me, aborted Tokyo's rise as a major international financial centre. Tokyo remained too Japanese.

The sudden turnabout by German companies, including even Deutsche Bank, and their decision to adopt international accounting standards came as a shock to Japan's finance ministry and many top businessmen. Indeed the Ministry of Finance announced not long after that it would gradually implement a whole set of measures aimed at deregulation and transparency. But the sharpest pressure for change is coming from Japan's increasing dependence on international markets and trade. Many Japanese companies have shifted production abroad; their major shareholders increasingly include US and European firms and raising capital abroad has become increasingly attractive. So by the time the Ministry of Finance decided to change policy, some Japanese companies had already begun to implement accounting standards that are closer to Anglo-American standards, the norm for most international transactions.[17]

The case of Japan is interesting because it is one of the powerful countries in the world. It has resisted implementing the IASC standards but finally had to accept under pressure from its own firms. The US stock exchange, another powerful actor, resisted even longer and insisted on having its own standards (or something approaching them) be the international norm, but eventually accepted the IAS. These are instances that illustrate the degree of contestation in the new frontier zone where the encounter of global actors and national institutions is enacted.

Working to solve financial crises

The role of the new intermediaries is also revealed in the strategic work done by leading financial services firms in the wake of the Mexico financial crisis. It might be interesting to speculate to what extent this kind of 'activism' towards ensuring growth in their industry will also be deployed in the case of the Asian countries now involved.

The events following the Mexico crisis provide us with some interesting insights about these firms' role in changing the conditions for financial operation, about the ways in which national states participated, and about the formation of a new institutionalised intermediary space. J. P. Morgan worked with Goldman Sachs and Chemical Bank to develop several innovative deals that brought back investors to Mexico's markets, as I discussed in note 14 above. Further, in July 1996, an enormous $6 billion five year deal that offered investors a Mexican floating rate note or syndicated loan – backed by oil receivables from the state oil monopoly PEMEX – was twice oversubscribed. It became somewhat of a model for asset-backed deals from Latin America, especially oil-rich Venezuela and Ecuador. Key to the high demand was that the structure had been designed to capture investment grade ratings from S&P and Moody's (it got BBB– and Baa3). This was the first Mexican deal with an investment grade. The intermediaries worked with the Mexican government, but on their terms – this was not a government-to-government deal. This secured acceptability in the new institutionalised privatised intermediary space for cross-border transactions – evidenced by the high level of oversubscription and the high ratings. And it allowed the financial markets to grow on what had been a crisis.

After the Mexico crisis and before the first signs of the Asian crisis, we see a large number of very innovative deals that contribute to further expand the volumes in the financial markets and to incorporate new sources of profit, that is, debts for sale. Typically these deals involved novel concepts of how to sell debt and what could be a saleable debt. Often the financial services firms structuring these deals also implemented minor changes in depository systems to bring them more in line with international standards. The aggressive innovating and selling on the world market of what had hitherto been thought to be too illiquid and too risky for such a sale further contributed to expand

and strengthen the institutionalisation of this intermediary space for cross-border transactions operating partly outside the interstate system.

A few examples will illustrate the range of these transactions. Argentina, working with J. P. Morgan, got investors back to its markets through a US$250 million deal for Telecom Argentina.[18] Nicaragua issued a bond backed by US treasury strips, purchased with the proceeds from the planned sale of the state telephone company. It was a success, with more demand than supply, which in turn led to a rising price. In Russia, Salomon Brothers figured out a way for foreign investors to buy the Russian Ministry of Finance bonds known as Min-Fins; these are high-yielding dollar denominated domestic securities until recently controlled by Russian investors. Salomon Brothers repackaged MinFins into a Euro-clearable asset that bypassed Russian custody and allowed access by foreign investors who are prohibited from buying assets that do not meet US custody requirements. Again, they were a success and attracted far more foreign capital than expected. In Central Europe, Bankers Trust developed an instrument – German mark based certificates – allowing investors access into the rather illiquid markets of Czekia, Hungary and Poland. In Croatia, Union Bank of Switzerland helped the first-ever float of shares by a Croatian company on the global capital market. It was 20 times oversubscribed. In Romania, Creditanstalt, with the European Bank for Reconstruction and Development coordinating, created a fund to sell majority shares in 550 companies – one-third of Romania's GDP – to attract foreign investors. In China, besides the already mentioned 100 year bond organised by J. P. Morgan, Bear Stearns was the lead in organising a $540 million dual-listed equity to privatise China's Guangshen Railways, which sold well in New York via ADRs. This deal was seen as stimulating China's capital markets. Morocco reentered the international capital market in March 1996 after a 12-year absence, under the global coordination of IFC, jointly led by Nomura. This was Morocco's first international equity issue; demand was four times higher than the issue.

These are just some of the transactions that show how the financial services firms, operating in their privatised world succeeded in mobilising new sources of capital and institutionalising new forms of selling debt/investing. Legal services firms and accounting firms are the indispensable hand-maidens in these operations.

Conclusion

The process whereby national economies accommodate global firms and markets and supranational institutions is more complex than a simple relinquishing of state powers would indicate. Much of the literature on globalisation fails to problematise this process. In the most extreme interpretations, deregulation and the declining significance of the state are seen as indicating that today's global economy spells the end of national economic sovereignty. At the other extreme, quantitative studies that show the non-national portion of national trade, investment and consumption to be very small posit that the global economy is not a significant factor for national economies.

This chapter sought to qualify both of these positions by showing that what is conceived of as a line separating the national from the global – or non-national – is actually a zone where old institutions are modified, new institutions are created, and there is much contestation and uncertain outcomes. Analytically it is a space that requires empirical and theoretical specification. This chapter seeks to contribute to this effort.

Globalisation in this conception, does not only have to do with crossing geographic borders, as is captured in measures of international investment and trade. It also has to do with the relocation of national public governance functions to transnational private arenas and with the development inside national states – through legislative acts, court rulings, executive orders – of the mechanisms necessary to accommodate the rights of global capital in what are still national territories. One overall effect is, I argue, an incipient de-nationalising of several highly specialised national institutional orders. This denationalising has to be instituted: it is one way in which the state matters under conditions of globalisation. It goes beyond its role as guarantor of the 'rights' of global capital, i.e. the protection of contracts and property rights. The state here can be conceived of as representing a technical administrative capacity which cannot be replicated at this time by any other institutional arrangement; furthermore, this is a capacity backed by military power, with global power in the case of some states.

An important theoretical and political implication is that economic globalisation has actually strengthened certain components of national states, notably those linked to international banking functions, such as ministries of finance, even as it has weakened many others. Simply submerging this fact under general observations about the declining significance of national states keeps us from seeing how the national state itself is contributing to the democratic deficit brought about by economic globalisation.

Notes

1 This chapter is part of a larger five-year project on governance and accountability in the global economy. The first phase of the larger project was partly published as the 1995 Leonard Hastings Schoff Memorial Lectures (*Losing Control? Sovereignty in an Age of Globalisation*, Columbia University Press 1996). I want to thank the Schoff Memorial Fund for their support.
2 For historical accounts of this interaction see, e.g. Hobsbawm 1975; Arrighi 1994; Berman 1995.
3 There are parallels here with a totally different sphere of state activity and transnational processes: the role of national courts in implementing instruments of the international human rights regime and the incorporation in several new national constitutions of provisions that limit the national state's presumption to represent all its people in international fora (see, e.g. Franck 1992, and generally Henkin 1990).

4 I have developed this argument elsewhere. See note 1 for sources. See also 'Territory and Territoriality' paper prepared for the Social Science Research Council Committee on Sovereignty (Sassen 1998).

5 There is a parallel here between the institutionalising of the rights of non-national economic actors with that of immigrants who have also gained rights – even though now they experience an attempt to shrink those rights. See e.g. Heisler 1986; Sassen 1998a: chapter 2.

6 There is a historically produced presumption of a unitary spatiotemporal concept of sovereignty and its exclusive institutional location in the national state. It leads to an analysis of economic globalisation that rests on standard theories about sovereignty and national states and hence sees globalisation as simply taking away from national states. If we recognise the historical specificity of this experience of sovereignty it may be easier to allow for the possibility that certain components of sovereignty have under current conditions been relocated to supra and subnational institutions, both governmental and nongovernmental institutions, and both old and newly formed institutions. The proposition that I draw out of this analysis is that we are seeing processes of incipient denationalisation of sovereignty – the partial detachment of sovereignty from the national state (see Sassen 1996: chapter 1).

7 The global city is a function of a network, and in this sense different from the old capitals of empires or the more general concept of the world city (see Sassen, forthcoming). The network of global cities today constitutes a strategic geography of centrality for the coordination and servicing of the global economy. It is a geography that cuts across the old North-South divide (it includes Sao Paulo and Bombay, for instance) and strenghtens the territorial unevenness, both inside developed and less developed countries. The corporate world of Sao Paulo and of New York gain strength, power and wealth. The world of the middle class and of the working class loses in both cities. See Friedmann (1995) for an overview.

8 For concrete applications of these propositions see, e.g. Knox and Taylor (1995); Peraldi and Perrin (1996); Hitz *et al.* (1996); Social Justice (1993). A key aspect of the spatialisation of global economic processes which I cannot develop here (but see Sassen 1998: chapter 9) is digital space. The topography for economic activities such as finance and specialised services, moves in and out of digital space. However at this time there is no purely and exclusively digital topography in any firm and in any sector. One of the interesting features about finance is that though it is one of the most digitalised and dematerialised industries, when it hits the ground it does so in some of the largest and densest concentrations of infrastructure, structures and markets for resources.

9 There is an interesting parallel here with critical accounts that seek to establish the role of the government in autonomous markets. See, for example, Paul (1994/5).

10 I cannot develop this subject here at length. But see Sassen (1996) and Sassen (1998a: chapters 2 and 10).

11 In this regard, I see the crossborder network of global cities as concentrating a significant share of institutional orders with incipient denationalisation, and hence see it as a partially denationalised – rather than internationalised – strategic geography (in progress).

12 The fact that this 'solution' brought with it the bankruptcy of middle sectors of the economy and of households, who suddenly confronted interest rates that guaranteed their bankruptcy, was not factored in the equation. The key was to secure the confidence of 'investors', that is to guarantee them a profitable return – and today 'profitable' has come to mean very high returns.

13 The data used in this and the next section come from a data set that is part of the author's project 'Governance and Accountability in the Global Economy'.

14 The $40 billion emergency loan package from the IMF and the US government and the hiring of Wall Street's top firms to refurbish its image and find ways to bring it back into the market, helped Mexico 'solve' its financial crisis. With J. P. Morgan as its financial adviser the Mexican government worked with Goldman Sachs and Chemical Bank to come up with several innovative deals. The trade literature noted, at the time, that these innovations could change the face of other emerging markets – words that now ring with foresight. Goldman organised a $1.75 billion Mexican sovereign deal in which the firm was able to persuade investors in May 1996 to swap Mexican Brady bonds collateralised with US Treasury bonds (Mexican Bradys were a component of almost any emerging market portfolio until the 1994 crisis) for a 30-year naked Mexican risk. This is in my reading quite a testimony to the aggressive innovations that characterise the financial markets and to the importance of a whole new subculture in international finance that facilitates the circulation, i.e. sale, of these instruments (see Thrift in this volume).

15 Based on a report 'The challenge of privatisation' prepared by John Nellis, senior manager of the Enterprise Reform and Privatisation section of the World Bank, revenues generated by privatisation reached $21 billion in 1995, compared with $3.5 billion in 1989, of which: 40 per cent from Europe/Central Asia; 26 per cent from East Asia/Pacific; 22 per cent from Latin America/Caribbean; 3–4 per cent from Sub-Saharan Africa, South Asia, Middle East/North Africa each. Between 1980 and 1991 in all industrialised and developing countries 6,800 firms divested. From 1990 to 1994 15 'transition' countries divested 30,740 firms. There were also 14,500 in Germany. The total for all countries reached 45,300. That is more than 6 times the number in the much longer earlier period; and they were sold in half the time.

   In the 1980s almost all investment in privatisations was FDI; by 1991 there was an enormous increase in total volume of investment and in the share of portfolio investment – about 40 per cent; by 1994, it had reached 60 per cent. The Mexico peso crisis slowed down privatisations in Latin America, but they have now picked up again. In East Asia privatisations have tended to be few in numbers but huge in size: Indonesia and Malaysia saw two of the biggest deals with the sale of PT Telekom and Petronas Gas ($1.1 billion in revenues for the latter). According to *The Economist* privatisation revenues from 1985 to 1995 in Britain were $85 billion; France, almost $34 billion; Italy $17 billion; Netherlands about $10 billion; Spain about $9 billion; Germany under $5 billion. Overall the European Union in 1994, one of the highest years, had $34 billion in privatisation sales.

16 One of the issues for the US has been that it considers its own standards more stringent than the new standards being proposed. It is also the case that Anglo-American standards have emerged as *de facto* international standards over the last few years, thereby greatly expanding the market for Anglo-American firms.

17 Japanese firms interested in operating outside Japan had already recognised that not adhering to Anglo American accounting standards would crowd them out of the global market. It has become necessary for firms from any country who want to work internationally to adjust to the most widely accepted standards in the world or not be a player in the world financial market. For example, lenders on the interbank market charge Japanese banks higher interest rates due to opaque accounting and insufficient disclosure of bad debts; Daiwa bank was expelled from the US for hiding losses for 11 years. Indeed, the only Japanese financial institution listed on the New York Stock Exchange, The Bank of Tokyo-Mitsubishi Bank, conformed to US accounting standards (the world's most stringent) long before the Japanese government's decision to adopt international standards, and in 1996 raised $2 billion with an international convertible bond issue. The

dominance first of Anglo-American standards and now of the new international standards is one component of the new normativity derived from the logic of the global capital market.

18 Again, it was an innovative instrument, functioning as a bond for the first four years – paying 10 per cent a year – and subsequently becoming shares in Telecom Agentina. As in the Mexican deal, the trade literature saw this as an innovative concept that might become a model for other offerings.

10 Globalisation and the limits to national economic management

Cayetano Paderanga Jr

The Asian currency crisis of 1997–8 has made a world of difference to national economic management in the region. In the first half of 1997, the case for keeping the economy open to the outside world was not difficult to make. The Asian dragons, Chile, and the emerging countries of Southeast Asia had been doing very well for the previous few years. Asia was expected to dominate the world's economic developments for at least the first part of the twenty-first century. That encouraging picture has become open to question. As of the middle of 1998, Southeast Asia is still experiencing the turmoil of currency adjustments. The economic outlook for the region, while still positive, is no longer as rosy. Doubts also linger about South Korea's immediate future.

What has made that difference? The underlying economic structures could not have changed so fast as to create almost the mirror image of the former picture. What changes in the environment, the perception and some economic variables could have brought the sudden shifts in fortune? In this chapter we will examine how the rosy picture emerged and how it could have changed so completely in such a short time. More fundamentally, we ask how the emerging world environment allows such radical changes in economic fundamentals or perceptions to take place. The analysis may suggest how to respond to the opportunities, and mitigate the dangers, in the emerging world environment.

The logic of financial globalisation

Global financial integration

In the last few decades the increase in global trade has also resulted in much greater financial flows. Although net flows of global capital may be smaller than at the turn of the century, gross international financial flows are much bigger, i.e. total financial trade has increased tremendously although this has coincided with economies borrowing and lending from each other (Figure 10.1).

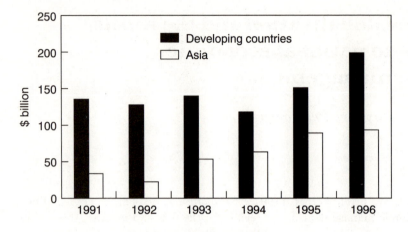

Figure 10.1 Net private capital flows, 1991–6

Another dimension of this phenomenon is the rapid development in financial instruments and technology. Data show that while growth in trade has increased at slightly higher than 5 per cent from 1980 to 1996, trading in bonds and equities and trading in currencies have increased by close to 25 per cent annually (see Tables 10.1 and 10.3).

Starting in the 1970s, the restrictions on international capital movements slowly became loosened. During most of that decade private flows of capital, largely through commercial banks to governments in developing countries, increased tremendously in order to take advantage of the perceived security of sovereign risk. This was partly in response to the 'recycling problem' of the petro-dollars that oil-producing countries had been accumulating. The succeeding 'debt problem' of the 1980s took away trust in sovereign risk and there was a short hiatus in capital flows.

Gradually, though, the dismantling of capital and exchange controls in the 1980s, accelerating in the 1990s, coincided with an intense period of deregulation of domestic financial markets. The technological innovations in telecommunications and financial techniques mentioned earlier enhanced the impact of the policy changes. The resulting liberalisation of financial markets together with the decline in transactions costs and the emergence of new financial instruments resulted in a dramatic growth in cross-border financial transactions (IMF 1997).

Table 10.1 shows the increase in cross-border transactions in bonds and equities. For some advanced countries, this increased by at least 1,500 per cent as a share of gross domestic product between 1980 and 1996. Among other factors, this represents an explosion in the participation by developed country private investors and investment funds in emerging markets, indicating increased interest in financing business activities in other parts of the world.

Table 10.1 Cross-border transactions in bonds and equities (in percentage of GDP)

Country	1970	1975	1980	1985	1990	1995	1996
United States	2.8	4.2	9.0	35.1	89.0	135.3	151.5
Japan	–	1.5	7.7	63.0	120.0	65.1	82.8
Germany	3.3	5.1	7.5	33.4	57.3	169.4	196.8
France	–	–	8.4	21.4	53.6	179.6	229.2
Italy	–	0.9	1.1	4.0	26.6	252.8	435.4
United Kingdom	–	–	–	367.5	690.1	–	–
Canada	5.7	3.3	9.6	26.7	64.4	194.5	234.8

Source: Bank for International Settlements (BIS).

This flow of equity and loan capital has been reflected by increased (out-ward) direct foreign and portfolio investment (Table 10.2). Indicating the expansion of the international activities of multinational enterprises, this growth in foreign direct investment as a proportion of the country of origin's gross domestic product is a reflection of the increasing globalisation of business in recent years.

To service the increasing financial interaction among market players in the world, the currency markets have also increased at an accelerating rate. Table 10.3 shows how global currency turnover has increased by 600 per cent in the ten-year period, 1986–95.

Table 10.2 Gross outward Foreign Direct Investment plus outward portfolio invest-ment (in percentage of GDP)

Country	1970–4	1975–9	1980–4	1985–9	1990–5
Belgium-Luxembourg		3.4	5.1	14.3	41.5
Canada	1.7	3.4	3.6	6.1	7.2
Denmark		0.6	0.9	3.5	7.2
France		1.3	2.1	4.1	7.2
Germany	1.2	1.3	1.7	5.2	6.3
Italy	0.9	0.3	0.6	1.7	5.7
Japan		0.6	2.6	5.9	3.7
Netherlands	7.3	4.7	6.0	10.9	11.1
Norway		5.6	0.4	6.6	2.1
Portugal		0.4	1.0	3.6	6.3
Spain		0.7	1.2	3.1	6.7
Sweden	1.0	1.2	1.7	5.0	7.0
Switzerland		4.5	9.4	14.7	12.8
United Kingdom	3.6	4.0	5.4	14.4	11.9
United States	1.0	1.5	1.4	2.9	3.3

Source: Bank for International Settlements (BIS).

Table 10.3 Foreign exchange trading (in billions of US$ and in percentages)

	1979	1986	1992	1995
Global estimated turnover	188	590	820	1190
As a ratio of:				
World exports of goods and services	7.4	15.8	17.4	19.1
Total reserves minus gold (all countries)	36.7	75.9	86.0	84.3

Sources: Bank for International Settlements; and International Monetary Fund.

It is interesting to compare this episode of capital market integration with the previous episode that occurred in the gold standard era before 1914. During that period, capital flows from Great Britain represented about 9 per cent of gross national product with similar proportions for France, Germany, and the Netherlands. Much of the flows went into bonds financing railroads and other infrastructure in the new world (especially the United States and Canada). In contrast, the peak current account surpluses of Japan and Germany in the mid- and late-1980s represented only 4–5 per cent of gross domestic product (IMF 1997: 165).

The difference in the character of the financial integration during the two episodes is significant (see also the chapters by Jessop and Friedman in this volume). From initial appearances, this most recent episode is characterised by a pronounced dominance of currency transactions over capital flows. This indicates the fundamental change in the character of enterprises and production technology: driven by lower transportation, communication and computing costs, firms have increased their ability to combine the lowest production costs located at far-flung geographical points in order to attain the cheapest total cost of production. This has led to lower production costs all around and, because of the increased competition resulting from the same developments, lower prices for customers. It has also increased competition among more producers in a much larger global market, leading to heightened insecurity for firms and workers.

Capital flows to developing countries and the Asia-Pacific

International financial flows have included developing countries among their destinations although this has been lopsided in favour of some developing areas. Technological innovations and the abolition of capital controls coincided with depressed economic conditions, low interest rates and a relative dearth of investment opportunities in the OECD economies. Combined with relatively high-expected returns on equities in Asian markets, these made conditions ripe for dramatic shifts in the allocation of investment funds

Table 10.4 Aggregate resource and net private capital flows to developing countries (in US$ billion)

Category	1990	1991	1992	1993	1994	1995
Total private	44.0	61.6	100.3	154.2	158.8	167.1
Portfolio investment	6.7	20.4	27.3	83.9	67.1	55.7
Debt flows	3.0	12.8	13.2	38.3	32.2	33.7
Equity flows	3.7	7.6	14.1	45.6	34.9	22.0
Foreign direct investment	25.0	35.0	46.6	68.3	80.1	90.3
Commercial banks	1.7	2.5	13.8	−4.9	9.2	17.1
Other private	10.6	3.7	12.6	6.9	2.4	4.0
Aggregate net long-term resource flows	101.9	127.1	155.3	207.2	207.4	231.3
Private capital flows as a percentage of aggregate net long-term flows	43.2	48.5	64.6	74.4	76.6	72.2

Source: Various World Bank Reports.

around the world. Table 10.4 shows that aggregate net long-term resource flows to developing countries have more than doubled from 1990 to 1995. Total private capital flows during that period have increased four times during the same period.

The increase in net long-term resource flows to developing countries has been at a phenomenal rate – external resource inflows have increased from 2 per cent of the GNP of developing countries in 1988 to 4.2 per cent in 1995. Figure 10.1 compared the net private capital flows to all developing countries and to Asia. This indicates that there has also been a response to the increasing bright prospects for future growth in Asia. For example, in 1994 developing countries in Asia grew by an average of 8.2 per cent.

A similar pattern is manifested in foreign direct investment flows. Table 10.5 shows that flows of foreign direct investment to developing countries grew two and one-half times from 1990 to 1995. However, during the same period, the flows to East Asia and the Pacific grew three and one-half times, implying that other developing areas were not as desirable destinations for foreign investment. In contrast, flows towards Sub-Saharan Africa and the Middle East have been limited by political instability, while South Asia is only now starting to relax extensive regulations and open up its economies to the international market. The lopsided nature of capital flows is manifested in the size of net resource flows in proportion to the gross national products of countries in East Asia and the Pacific, especially the ASEAN four (Table 10.6).

The larger portion of the increase has resulted from a surge in private capital flows towards the private sector in recipient countries. Private capital

Table 10.5 Annual average FDI flows to developing countries, by region (US$ million)

Region	1990–2	1993–5	1994	1995
All developing countries	35,532	79,576	80,120	90,346
Of which:				
Sub-Saharan Africa	1,396	2,309	2,987	2,187
Asia	16,024	46,427	44,279	55,749
East Asia and Pacific	15,509	44,871	43,037	53,703
South Asia	515	1,376	1,242	2,046
Europe and Central Asia	4,254	9,727	8,362	12,482
Eastern Europe and Central Asia	2,340	7,978	6,684	10,595
Rest of Europe	1,914	1,749	1,678	1,887
Latin America and the Caribbean	11,638	18,104	20,811	17,799
Middle East and North Africa	2,221	3,189	3,681	2,129

Source: Various World Bank Reports.

has dominated the inflows, accounting for about 75 per cent of the region's net external inflows from 1991–4. Foreign direct investment and portfolio equity investment have been the most important forms of private capital flows. Net foreign direct investment increased from $12.1 million in 1991 to $54.8 in 1994, while net portfolio investment grew from $0.5 billion in 1991 to $9.2 billion in 1994. The share of multilateral and bilateral official sources of finance has declined sharply from 38 per cent in 1991 to 15 per cent in 1994. These flows have been mediated by the equity and debt markets of recipient countries that have enjoyed bullish behaviour over the last few years. For example, the East Asian[1] stock markets, measured in US dollars, have seen their capitalisation increase by 241 per cent from 1990 to 1994. East Asian economies attracted 82 per cent of the net long-term external resource flows into Asia in the 1990s. In contrast, South Asian economies have continuously relied on official sources of finance.

Table 10.6 Aggregate net resource flows as percentage of GNP

Region/Country	1980	1994	1995
East Asia and the Pacific	2.9	–	7.8
Philippines	3.9	6.9	5.2
Thailand	6.5	3.3	6.1
Indonesia	2.5	5.4	6.8
Malaysia	8.7	10.2	14.7

Source: World Development Report 1996, 1997.

Financial liberalisation: 'the baby . . .'

It is perhaps important to remember why liberalisation and market-orientation are undertaken in the first place. In a recent paper in *The Economist*, Sachs (1997b) stated that 'openness was decisive for rapid growth. Open economies grew 1.2 percentage points per year faster than closed economies, controlling for everything else'. Krugman (1987), one of the foremost 'new trade economists' who have provided the arguments for theoretical deviations from free trade, has asserted that, given all the uncertainties introduced by lags and imprecision about information, recognition, and implementation, freer trade would still be the best guide for economic management. The record of several ASEAN economies and the newly-industrialised economies (NIEs) since the Second World War (and that of the Philippines in the past few years) attest to the advantages of allowing freer commerce with the rest of the world and letting the market determine the allocation of resources.

Liberalisation and the flow of capital funds have been very beneficial for developing countries including the Philippines. Liberalisation facilitates the flow of goods and services which transmits the benefits of specialisation, economies of scale and other benefits of freer trade. Private funds provide much-needed capital allowing these countries to bypass the temporal inconsistency of having very high-return projects including infrastructure at the same time that they lack the resources to undertake them. Their integration to international capital markets allows them to smooth the temporal imbalances between the need and availability of investment resources. For a country with large and expanding social service needs, this allows the government to plan heavy investments while reducing the need to contract social services.

Among the many consequences of the Philippine economic recession more than ten years ago was a drastic reduction in the investment and saving rates that are slowly recovering only now. Capital flows provide a source of spontaneous, private sector funds for the much-needed capitalisation and re-tooling for our economy. In the Philippines, substantial short-term capital flows were attracted in the 1990s, averaging a little over $10 billion per annum and resulting in, among other things, a rapid accumulation of foreign exchange reserves. It also enriches the available instruments and strengthens the environment for the mobilisation of domestic resources.

Financial integration also provides some benefits on the financial front. Three immediately come to mind. First, it helps develop the financial sector itself. The resulting lower cost of capital and efficiency in financial services are expected to benefit the economy as a whole. Second, it broadens the financial instruments available to firms and individuals for efficiently achieving their desired portfolio balances. It also provides clear signals to economic managers as to how their decisions and plans are perceived. Finally, the flow of capital will enable economies to unbind their consumption and financial decisions. For example, financial integration facilitates the ability of countries to undertake significant investments during their early growth phases, when most probably they have not yet attained the income level corresponding to the required saving rate.

The illogic of financial globalisation: '. . . and the bath water'

Employed in productive activities, capital flows permit higher investment in excess of current domestic saving. However, every silver lining has a cloud. Large foreign capital inflows have negative as well as positive effects. The turmoil in Southeast Asian foreign exchange markets in the last year high-lights some of the consequences of open economies and integrated financial markets: 'global capital markets . . . are dispassionate, brutally calculating and . . . fickle . . .' (Hirsh and Powell 1997). Smooth and rapid movements in one direction can suddenly reverse, catching individuals and firms un-prepared. Those caught with the wrong judgements can suffer large losses. While these markets provide economic activity and resources, economic managers need to be nimble enough to adjust to their unpredictable ways.

One of the sources of unpredictability stems from the possibility that domestic markets will be affected by what happens in other countries, in the same way that the Mexican peso crisis and the overall currency movements in Southeast Asia today have affected Philippine financial markets. This phe-nomenon of contagion among countries has increased in frequency since the increase in financial integration of emerging markets in the 1980s. Techno-logical innovations in communication, information processing and trans-portation now allow investors to operate in financial markets around the world, allowing them to accomplish portfolio allocation around the world throughout the day. In fact, large banks and financial firms now do this as a matter of course.

Advances in financial theory have allowed a much-expanded array of financial instruments. This has led to increased ability by firms to pass on the financial chore to third parties and concentrate on their core activities, lead-ing to increased specialisation and efficiency. The availability of financial instruments also reduces the cost of liquidity and capital. The tradeoff is that financial firms now operate at much thinner margins (good) and with higher leverage (bad), sometimes imperceptibly. That is, new financial instruments allow entities to participate at much smaller entrance costs but also increase the possibility that market reversals will rapidly eat into core capital. These new instruments also increase the ways that market actors can evade direct control of financial symptoms by policy makers (as contrasted with the management of fundamentals). The combination of wider financial reach, speedier transactions, more complicated and numerous financial instruments and the possibility of higher leverage, have all combined to increase the probability of rapid financial market meltdowns spreading globally or within geographic regions.

The international financial market players

The changes in the international financial market are absorbed by a framework that includes the market players. Table 10.7 shows the balance of payments of the Philippines for 1997, but it also summarises the main types of actors operating in the foreign currency and financial markets.

Table 10.7 Philippines balance of payments, 1997[2] (US$ million)

Current account	
A Trade	−5,383
Goods	−11,127
Exports	25,228
Imports	36,355
Services	5,744
Recipts	22,835
Payments	17,091
B Transfers	1,080
Inflow	1,670
Outflow	590
Current account overall	−4,303
Capital and Financial account	
A Medium and long-term loans	4,688
Availment	7,427
Repayment	2,739
B Trading bonds in the secondary market	−676
Resale of bonds	3,072
Purchase of bonds	3,748
C Investments	766
Non-resident investments in the Philippines	847
Resident investment abroad	81
D Short-term capital	495
E Change in Commercial Banks' NFA	1,191
Capital and Financial Account, Net	6,464
Others	−360
A Monetisation of gold	105
B Revaluation adjustments	−465
Net unclassified items	−5,164
Overall BOP position	−3,363

Source: Bangko Sentral ng Pilipinas.

The first balance, the trade account, summarises the activities of exporters and importers who buy and sell goods in the world market. Both types of players respond in the medium- and long-term to changes in the real effective exchange rate – i.e. some benchmark exchange rate between the domestic currency and the world currency (currently, primarily the US dollar) adjusted for changes in the relative cost of doing business (as indicated by the changes in relative price indices). However, as dates for settling transactions and obligations approach, they start to second-guess the market exchange rate in an effort to pinpoint the best time to implement their payments.

The international sales and purchases of services together with unilateral net transfers (e.g. bequests and gifts) are added to the trade account in order to arrive at the current account. For the Philippines, a large portion of the services inflow comes from the earnings of overseas Filipino workers. These workers generally base their decisions on the level of compensation abroad relative to their expected domestic income. But just like exporters and importers, they also speculate on the exchange rate to time their remittances to the Philippines. Most of the other services income is made up of financial, insurance and telecommunications services.

The next portion of the balance of payments is the capital account. The main components are long- and short-term investments and loans. An important part of long-term investments is foreign direct investments. The main factors involved are the long-term consideration of doing business in the country, such as political, labour and policy stability and comparative cost of doing business. On the other hand, portfolio investments from abroad depend mostly on the differential between the international and domestic returns adjusted for expected changes in the exchange rate. Expectations about exchange rate changes introduce volatility in the flow of capital funds in largely the same manner that it affects the short-term behaviour of exporters, importers and overseas workers. Slight changes in market sentiment sometimes result in large fluctuations as individuals rush to correct the composition of their holdings. International fund managers who manage the major portion of these funds are able to propagate very rapidly the implementation of these market changes.

The integration of the international financial market is most articulated in the activities of the international investment funds. While there are various types of funds – classified by tenure (i.e. long- or short-term), by industry, type of instrument (bonds, equities, etc.) and others – the strategy of investing in the global market is roughly similar for all. At the centre of each fund or umbrella group is an international investment committee that allocates funds by geographical region. Research studies, country manager reports and other information flow to the investment committee that may then revise its allocation. If these investment funds implement their revisions coincidentally or nearly so, an individual country's currency markets may experience substantial fluctuations. Furthermore, very short-term speculation on the movements of individual currency exchange rates is one instrument in the income generating paraphernalia of these funds. When the conditions are appropriate, these fund movements may actively or unintentionally undermine specific exchange rate levels.

In the presence of the increased volatility, the ability of national economic managers to directly control the fluctuations has been eroded. The instruments left for the policy makers are those for strengthening the fundamentals of the currency market. This may include provisions for greater transparency, stable policies and prudent behaviour by financial and related institutions.

Multilateral financial institutions such as the International Monetary Fund (IMF) and the World Bank, as well as countries like the United States, may be able to provide support for the effective management of the currency exchange rates. The IMF, tasked with the maintenance of an effective international payments mechanism often intervenes with short-term financing to allow countries to ride over temporary difficulties. Recently, it has also orchestrated international rescues for countries under severe exchange difficulties, as in the 1994 Mexican crisis and 1997–8 Asian currency crisis. The World Bank with its loan portfolio available for development projects has also used its macroeconomic adjustment programmes to assist in currency rescue operations.

The phenomenon of contagion

A recent example of the increasing danger of currency meltdowns due to contagion is the Asian currency crisis. Political problems in Thailand in late 1996 exacerbated doubts about the sustainability of its high growth rate. A series of speculative attacks on the baht that soon followed were at first held at bay by using the country's relatively large international reserves. A full-blown assault on the currency in May 1997 was repulsed with the participation of neighbouring ASEAN central banks. However, incessant probes finally succeeded on 2 July 1997 when Bank of Thailand was forced to free the baht from its effective peg to the US dollar. The Philippines soon followed on 11 July. These events initiated a continuing series of exchange rate corrections among ASEAN currencies and the South Korean won.

The way the turmoil spread within the region has induced interest in newer explanations of contagion in international financial markets. Calvo (1995) analysed the impact of investor herd behaviour in international financial markets due to asymmetric information across national borders. When an initial exchange rate correction is experienced within a region, foreign investors who invest on the basis of broad regional indicators and have not gone into more detailed analysis of individual countries are unable to distinguish between currencies. There is a tendency to escape from the region as a whole rather than make distinctions between individual currencies.

Frankel and Schmukler (1996) have also studied contagion through changes in the net asset values of investment funds and the resulting portfolio re-allocating. As exchange rate corrections reduce the net asset value of the portfolio, investment managers are induced to liquidate investments in some regions in order to realise gains to balance reductions in 'losing' regions. Other researchers have also studied how fundamentals can change with shifts in market perception.

The speed of contagion in the recent Southeast Asian turmoil has been ascribed to competitive devaluation, not by policy makers but as self-fulfilling expectations by market players (given the stability of the exchange rate of these currencies to the US dollar and the slowdown in the growth of their exports). There had been widespread speculation that these countries had lost competitiveness over the last few years. When the US dollar appreciated substantially relative to the German DM and the Japanese yen during the first six months of 1997, the expectations for exchange rate corrections became acutely heightened.

The Asian currency turmoil has now spawned a line of research based on market reactions and expectations of competitive devaluation by market players. The speed of contagion and the indeterminateness of the final outcome are the main concerns in this line of enquiry.

Impact on macroeconomic management

The integration of financial markets, manifested among other things by perceived increase in susceptibility to currency disturbances and by the speed of contagion, also changes the effectiveness of monetary and other macroeconomic policies. In a nutshell, monetary and credit control is diminished, the degree of diminution depending on the exchange policy chosen, and more use of fiscal and related policies have to be resorted to. A changing menu with varying proportions among the major policy components – monetary, fiscal, trade and others – requires more sophisticated financial markets as well as analysis and planning.

Two immediate issues immediately come to mind. First, an economy needs to decide how to handle the flow of funds through national borders in response to variations in market confidence about a country's immediate or intermediate prospects. Even in the case of inflows, the knowledge of what could happen when market sentiments reverse pose difficult dilemmas for economic managers. Second, the practice of macroeconomic management itself may have to change in the emerging economic environment.

Market perception and the sequence of economic liberalisation

The experience of the Southern Cone economies in the early 1980s and recent research (e.g. McKinnon 1993) imply that as economies go through economic restructuring and stabilisation, the market value of domestic firms increases and, if investment rules and foreign exchange transactions are liberalised, become attractive to foreign investors. Private investors and domestic borrowers often underestimate the risks of credit laxity as they jostle to be ahead of the pack. Both lenders and borrowers are caught in a collective myopia about how much more borrowing the economy can afford. The system limits can sometimes be opaque to market participants. Further, moral hazard problems posed by deposit insurance may induce banks to lend more than safe limits. The result can be the phenomenon that McKinnon and Pill (1995) call the over-borrowing syndrome, leading to the possibility of 'Dutch disease' in the real structure of the economy and over extension in the financial sector.

In what is now called the 'Dutch disease', an overly strong inflow of foreign exchange leads to a very strong domestic currency that reduces the competitiveness of domestic products in world markets. The cause of the original inflow could come from newly discovered resources such as the North Sea oil fields in the original case of the Netherlands or, as in the recent case of emerging markets, a revival of confidence by investors in newly-reforming countries. The resulting demise of export industries (and domestic import-substituting firms) seriously hamstrings the country when market sentiments reverse and the problem is now an outflow and a dearth of foreign exchange. The over-borrowing syndrome, as is now seen in the case of Southeast Asia, leads to weak financial and banking sectors which also threaten economic stability when the flow of funds reverses direction.

Effectiveness of macroeconomic policy tools

The literature on open economy macroeconomics has provided managers with some answers on how market openness and financial integration modify the expected effects of the various monetary instruments. For example, college students now know that with fixed foreign exchange rates, monetary authorities essentially lose effective control over the volume of money supply. With full financial integration, domestic control over interest rates becomes weak. Thus, the influence over economic activity of most of the monetary instruments is much reduced. Other approaches to foreign exchange management modify this result but the conclusion remains; in an integrated global environment monetary micro-management by the government loses much of its force.

One implication on economic management, and the one most often quoted in undergraduate texts, namely, that under fixed exchange rates 'monetary policy becomes ineffective and fiscal policy becomes important' (and that under flexible exchange rates 'fiscal policy is weak and monetary policy is powerful'), can actually be dangerously overstated. While each policy is relatively more important than the other under different exchange rate regimes, the fact is that with full financial integration both policies are weakened by the increased ability of economic resources to relocate and avoid the effects of policies. The corollary is that these policies may have unwanted side effects that economic managers ignore only at their own risk.

The second implication has to do with the character of monetary and exchange management. Before, economic managers could and often did directly control capital and other flows through regulations and directives. With increased integration and innovative financial instruments, the ability of residents and foreign investors to balance their portfolio among local and foreign assets has eroded the authorities' control over monetary, credit and currency flows.

Under these circumstances, economic managers can no longer expect to control monetary and currency magnitudes as tightly as before. Market actors are now able to respond independently to prices and underlying trends. They find ways around restrictions that are inconsistent with market signals and economic resources now rapidly migrate according to market intentions. This implies that economic managers can no longer command and must shift towards keeping the fundamentals right. The whole framework of policy making must now turn towards keeping the prices, structures and institutions conducive for market activities instead of trying to influence the volume of flows directly. One may characterise the best way to manage the economy as the 'back to basics' approach.

The practice of economic management

A period of 'retrenchment' and reflection is now needed by economic managers. This is especially true in the face of the seeming inevitability and irresistibility of the recent currency crisis. Managers now need to know exactly what they can do and what they will have to leave to the market and to the normal course of economic activity. A whole new agenda of research for economic managers seems to have opened up in the face of the changing world economic environment.

Among the first things economic managers need to find out are what the remaining monetary, fiscal and other instruments are left for them to use and how effective each of these is under different circumstances. Given the instruments at their disposal, what should be the objectives of macroeconomic policy? While it may still be useful to think about the same broad objectives of stability, low inflation, growth, equity and others which we had before the significant changes in the environment, the intermediate and operational targets may have to be modified.

Current economic ideas as well as institutional and market realities combine to influence how macroeconomic management is carried out. For example, with many exceptions one can generalise monetary management in the late 1960s and 1970s as interest rate targeting. In the 1980s, this shifted to money supply targeting. Now in the 1990s, there are suggestions to formally describe it as inflation targeting, especially in the face of many central banks being reorganised and given specific mandates to keep inflation low. Considering the new circumstances, there seems to be no doubt that the character of economic management has to change. For example, in the face of financial integration, how sustainable would an interest rate target diverging from world interest rates be in the medium and long term? While a high saving rate would still be desirable in order to remain on a high growth path, the return incentive may have to be stated in a slightly different way (for example through differential taxation between consumption and saving) and the means of achieving that may be different. In the same way, inducements for domestic and foreign direct investments may take the form of better infrastructure and efficient support services.

In such an environment, the objectives of macroeconomic management need to be modified. Some direct objectives may no longer be sustainable in the long run. For example, a government's ability to set tax levels in order to shape its tax structure may be curtailed by the consideration of how this may affect saving and investment rates in the economy. While this has always been a consideration, the limits are narrower in a world where individuals' ability to revise their portfolios is greatly enhanced.

The effect on economic managers' ability to control and their flexibility in the short run is unambiguous: these are severely curtailed in the new environment. The ultimate effects on long-run economic effectiveness could go either way. The beneficial results could come in two forms. First, because leeway in economic actions (for example, contractionary or expansionary) is restricted, the degree of reversal and the attendant pain of adjustment are also dampened. Second, the restriction of leeway reduces the temptation for economic managers to achieve short-term gain at the expense of long-run deterioration, known in the economic literature as the 'time inconsistency problem'. Both these factors could lead to less frequent and less pronounced fluctuations, making the environment more stable and predictable for individual market players.

In sum, however, these changes portend less flexibility and control on the part of economic managers. On the downside, managers have fewer powers available to judiciously counteract business cycles.

Effects on economic institutions

The implications of the new environment for policy-making have already been inducing changes in economic institutions. Governments, seeing the benefits accorded by financial integration, may be willing to incur some of the costs. One form of these costs is reduced freedom and flexibility in the design of economic institutions, including laws and regulations pertaining to how economic activity is carried out. Ahead of all these are the requirements for 'transparency' and 'openness' in government processes (including how they make and implement decisions). Countries have also started to modify their institutions in order to conform to internationally accepted forms of regulation and monitoring. For example, more and more developing countries are setting up stock and other financial exchanges together with their regulating institutions such as securities and exchange commissions. Maxfield

(1997) has also documented how developing countries have been passing legislation to make their central banks legally 'independent' (also see Sassen, this volume).

The institutional changes required by financial integration have implied, first, that governments now have less leeway in the design of their economic institutions and, second, that some form of uniformity in the structure of economic institutions may be expected to take place. How these will curtail government's ability to respond to the unique requirements of their culture and traditions is still to be seen.[3] How individual countries and populations respond to the rapidly increasing uniformity of economic institutions is still another issue that will only become clearer in the next few years.

A further response to the danger of intercountry impact and contagion are the growing calls for coordination among governments or among branches of governments such as central banks (see Paderanga 1997a). The recent call for an Asian Currency Stabilisation Fund is an example of this emerging need in the face of the new world environment (see Higgott, this volume). As economic managers look at the issues involved, however, they discover that the benefits can only be acquired by giving up some flexibility and prerogatives. For example, financiers and managers of an international fund would need to be satisfied that a country using its access to the fund would institute the reforms needed to negate further or continuous need to return. This will require that the fund's or other countries' representatives examine and analyse the borrower's reports and policies. Thus, some sovereignty and flexibility will have to be given up. Any other international arrangement will require some similar loss of sovereignty in order to overcome what economists call the 'incentive incompatibility problem.' That is, if you are given the resources to ease your difficulties why will you work hard to get out of your situation?

Still another suggestion is to impose a tax or penalty for flows of very short-term funds across borders. Most prominent among these is the 'Tobin tax' proposed by Nobel economics laureate James Tobin of Yale University as early as 1978. The scheme aims to 'put sand in the wheels' of international capital flows by imposing a minuscule tax – the initial proposal is for 0.2 per cent – on every international transfer of capital. At that level, the tax will be immaterial for long-term investments but would grow heavier as the tenure of the funds being transferred became shorter. For example, it would be equivalent to a 105 per cent annual tax if the funds are lent or transferred only for a day (compounded daily over 360 days). Thus, it would leave foreign direct investment and long-term loans and placements virtually untouched while making short-term speculation more expensive. Certain sectors have opposed it because it would lessen the efficiency of the international financial market, hamstringing its disciplinary aspects. Implementation may require that enough countries impose it; otherwise, the isolated number of economies imposing it may be avoided by the financial market, to their detriment. At the same time, it is fiscally attractive for countries with government revenue constraints because of the ease of collection.

Another method of control is the imposition of reserve requirements (to be held with banks) on short-term capital flows, effectively reducing the rate of return on domestic short-term investments for foreign investors. This will hold back some of the more volatile inflows of funds which can be unstable. The central bank of Chile currently imposes the reserve requirement on all inflows but returns the amount kept in reserve as soon as some threshold time period is reached. Thus, the administrative cost of trying to distinguish between short- and long-term flows is eliminated while the objective is still served.

Conclusion: economic nationalism and the state

In this chapter we have seen how globalisation and international financial integration are changing the volume and modes of international and financial interaction. Increased interaction results in beneficial effects for the world economy and individual countries. At the same time, these two related developments pose dangers to markets and individual participants. In order to minimise the dangers, governments need to: adjust their intermediate policy objectives towards less control; use new or modified instruments; and, change their style of managing their economies. Economic institutions, laws and regulations and even government instrumentalities may require modification.

The search is on for more instruments to allow policy makers some control over the massive flows and reversals of funds. Thus while the benefits of financial integration are inducing governments and the private sector to accede to the requirements of the emerging financial environment, parallel changes are occurring in economic institutions and government flexibility and control. To the extent that these efforts succeed in calming the markets and introducing more stability into the system, they may lead to more flows and more growth for the world economy. The result will also depend, however, on the extent to which this can be done without completely blocking the role of markets to instil discipline and efficiency in all participants, including policy makers who will need to focus on transparency, predictability and fundamental structural reforms.

In this context, some traditional concepts such as nationalism, state and citizenship may also undergo profound change. With the need to show a level playing field for all market players, the design of programmes for specific groups in the economy will become more stringent. In addition, questions regarding the design of national taxation and benefit systems will become more complicated as it is difficult to determine who should be counted as 'citizens'. The problems posed by multinational corporations such as transfer pricing, among others, will become more ubiquitous. As several other chapters in this volume suggest, the implication is that the concept of the state is undergoing substantial changes as financial globalisation continues. As economic institutions change in response to external events and requirements, and as countries join more international cooperative agreements requiring some loss of sovereignty and flexibility, the concept of the state, and particularly its role in economic management, will need to be re-examined.

Notes

1 In this instance, this includes China, Hong Kong, Indonesia, Korea, Malaysia, Philippines, Singapore and Thailand.
2 Preliminary.
3 For example, how the increasing independence of central banks will affect the coordination among the different macroeconomic agencies could depend on how the other institutions (e.g. laws and procedures) are configured in each country. The issue of 'over steering' by both monetary and fiscal authorities in the face of central bank independence and its impact on internal policy coordination has been raised.

Part IV
Global lives

11 Class formation, hybridity and ethnification in declining global hegemonies

Jonathan Friedman

Introduction

This chapter seeks to explore the complex of relations linking changing configurations in the world economy to changes in hegemony, social organisation, cultural identities and representations. The thrust of the argument is that increasing ethnic fragmentation and a polarisation between emergent global elites and nationally downwardly mobile lower classes are phenomena characteristic of the declining hegemonic centres of the world system, i.e. Europe and the United States as well as weaker zones of the global peripheries. The new elites are linked by the emergence of a matrix of globalising discourses of which hybridity has gained in dominance. The latter is used in an attempt to redescribe the world and as such is a candidate for what is classically known as a dominant ideology. It is reinforced by its opposition to the clear and often violent cultural and social fragmentation which characterises the middle- and lower-class levels of what appears to be declining Western nation states. These processes are not globally salient, but are, on the contrary, regionally specific since they are generated by declining hegemony. They do not apply directly to East and Southeast Asia, although the long stagnation of the Japanese economy bears evidence of analogous tendencies. Until this latest crisis, however, it is argued that the processes typical of this region were quite the opposite to those occurring in the West, that is, there was a tendency towards consolidation and even integration of formerly conflictual ethnic divisions into larger units, the integration if not eradication of indigenous groups and the strengthening of nationalism, national elites and regional identity. In important respects, the processes of consolidation that have been so evident in East Asia are part of the same process that has led to decline and fragmentation in the West. This chapter explores the mechanisms involved in these inverse processes, trying ultimately to clarify the social and cultural correlates of declining hegemony.

Two models of global dynamics

There are two very different ways of conceiving the transformations in the world that have come to preoccupy so many concerned with the dangers or glories of globalisation in the past several years. One belongs to a tradition that is clearly expressed in the work of Braudel (1984), and more recently of Wallerstein (1974, 1991), Arrighi (1997), and Frank and Gills (1993). It might be called the shifting hegemony model and is in turn linked to longer term historical models in which world history can be characterised in terms of the pulsation of centres of wealth accumulation that go back to the Bronze Age commercial civilisations (see Denemark *et al.* 1998; Frank and Gills 1993). The other model is decidedly more evolutionistic than cyclical. It conceives of the current situation as the emergence of a new global economy and a globalised world in which the transnational has achieved dominance over the national which in a previous era had achieved dominance over a more local, perhaps feudal, organisation (if we forget about empires for the moment). Rather than discussing these models in depth, I propose, simply, to deal with the economic processes on which they are based in order to see how they might be combined.

The first economic process is one that relates the growth and decline of centres of capital accumulation to the shift in such centres as a cyclical phenomenon. This is the kind of process referred to above. It is organised in the following algorithmic form:

1   Strategic position within a larger system as potential monopolist over trade or other flows of capital is a precondition of expansion.
2   Expansion of trade and conquest, if necessary, of larger territory.
3   Emergence of a world-workshop syndrome in which a rising centre produces final consumption goods for the larger region.
4   Accumulation of capital in the centre and the forging of centre/periphery relations.
5   Increasing wealth in centre leads to increasing costs of reproduction in the centre, partly offset by increasing productivity.
    (a) Here the pivotal ratio is between the rate of accumulation of capital and the rate of increase in productivity.
6   Wealth of the centre eventually becomes a relative problem insofar as capital accumulation becomes increasingly profitable in other parts of the system relative to the centre itself.
7   Capital export, first within a smaller region, i.e. within the centre zone itself, then within the global system as a whole, turning former peripheral areas into 'sub-peripheries' and rising new centres. By this time, the centre has entered into a long-term decline.
8   The decline is based on the export of capital itself, which leads to:
    (a) declining productive base and share of the total world market in the production of final consumption goods;
    (b) increasing percentage of imports in local consumption; and
    (c) shift capital from productive to non-productive investment.
9   In this situation, other parts of the system make important inroads into the worlds of final consumption. They accumulate capital, first, in the

form of increasing foreign investment, but then increasingly local/regional investment. Growth rates in the new rising centres are high relative to the rest of the world. They are very much focused on production where the returns are high because of competitive advantage. There are important variations here which depend on the global state of the system, i.e. in the contemporary case, the ratio of total liquidity in the system (which may be far in excess of the total capacity of the system to absorb goods and services).

10 This kind of process leads to a shift in capital accumulation in the global arena with its numerous consequences at the local and regional levels.

This model is one that generates cyclical expansion and contraction processes that involve shifting accumulation over time and space. It has been common throughout the history of commercial civilisations. One of the specific characteristics of capitalist reproduction is the general contradiction between financial and 'real productive' accumulation. While these are difficult categories to define, there are generally acceptable differences between a process of expansion of financial capital, or even what might be called fictitious capital, and a process that proceeds via production and services that are necessary for the maintenance of a given level of social reproduction. In any capitalist economy, there is a certain tendency for monetary or fictitious capital to grow faster than real capital. This is because the forces of expansion of capital as liquidity are built into the very structure of the monetary form as credit itself, while the reproductive cycle of industrial capital depends on heterogeneous factors related to final demand and levels of competition. The divergent properties of money capital and the larger cycle of industrial accumulation is one of the major mechanisms of business cycles,[1] as well as of the longer and steeper cycles that are generated by longer term forms of credit. The relation between the model of shifting accumulation and the business cycle is complex. The business cycles form longer cycles that are characterised by tendencies towards increasing differentiation of costs within the larger system. Increasing standards of living are fundamental here since they lead to increasing diversion of capital from productive to more speculative investment, increasing the ratio of fictitious to productive capital. Periods of increasing rates of fictitious investment are also periods of increasing transnational productive investment. This is one way of understanding globalisation.

In contrast to the cyclical model of shifting accumulation is the globalisation model which stresses the emergence of a new transnational global economy. The obvious aspects of the globalisation process are the multinationalisation of production via the development and dominance of transnational corporations. There is a steady increase in the importance of transnational corporations (TNC) in international trade, and an increasing vertical integration of various sectors within single firms. In the mid-1980s, foreign direct investment (FDI) increased three times faster than export trade. One understanding of this is that there is a movement from a structure of national production coupled to international trade, to an international-isation of production itself. This change is often linked to the explosive speed-up enabled by new transportation and information technologies. Much of the globalisation debate focuses on what is perceived as the newness of this situation, the loss of control by nation-states over their own inter-nationalising economies or the benefits that might be reaped by entering the new postnational world. This, however, might well be the product of the way intellectuals have experienced the most recent spate of transnationalism. After all, capital has been quite international from the very beginning. It has been estimated that as much as 30 per cent of investment in the English industrial revolution was Dutch and Italian. The British export of capital in the last part of the nineteenth century is a clear example of globalisation. It is estimated that more than half of Britain's net investment went abroad in the period 1885–94. FDI reached 9 per cent of world output in 1913, a pro-portion that was not surpassed until the early 1990s (Bairoch and Kozul-Wright 1996: 10), and it was followed after the First World War by a period of 'de-globalisation', the contraction of world trade and investment. One might argue that the main difference from the contemporary situation is that the breadth and mass of capital export has increased and the relation between portfolio and direct investment has been reversed (at least before the late 1980s). This change is expressed in the formation of multinational industrial production. Instead of exporting manufactured goods, it is productive capital itself that is exported. It is also clear that outsourcing and vertical integration of production processes has become global in a new ways. But in a more general sense, globalisation can be understood as a process of geographical decentralisation of capital accumulation based on various forms of capital export and linked to the differential conditions of accumulation in the world economy.

The process of globalisation in the sense of the formation of a larger inte-grated whole and the process of shifting accumulation are clearly related. Those who have argued for a sharp discontinuity in the current situation have stressed what we have called 'speed up', or 'time space compression' and the rapid integration of financial markets and globalised industrial pro-duction (via verticalisation and outsourcing). The question is whether the second process has replaced the first, or whether the two are related within a single cyclical model. My position, based on long-term historical research, has gravitated to the latter, but this remains an open question. Arrighi (1997: 2) has made the latter argument central to his historical understanding of the present. The world was clearly unified in former eras and a recent article in *The Economist* goes so far as to claim that 'in some respects the world economy was more integrated in the late nineteenth century than it is today' (1998: 73).

The massive development of financial markets is an important phenom-enon to understand. It has been explosive since the beginning of the 1980s, financial assets increasing 250 per cent faster than the 'aggregate GDP of all the rich industrial economies' (Sassen 1996: 40). The current global financial markets are estimated to be worth about 75 trillion dollars and it is forecasted that this may rise to 83 trillion by 2000, i.e. three and a half times the OECD's aggregate GDP (Sassen 1996a: 41). While it is debatable to what extent this is the product of the successful struggle of capital against the nation-state, it is not debatable that technological changes have made the movement of capital an instantaneous process in which sensitivity to conditions of accumulation have increased logarithmically. If this increase is related to the general model of the growth of fictitious capital in periods of declining profitability of industrial production, it might be suggested that the current growth of finance capital (generated in the West) combines such tendencies with a new information technology that raises the rate of speculative turnover exponentially, thus accounting for the appearance of 'global glut'.

The regional shift

Whether or not one conceives of global process in terms of shifting accumulation or the formation of a new globalised economy, there is a *de facto* emergence of a new powerful economic region. And in spite of the current crisis, there is no doubt that there has been a redistribution of shares in the world economy in favour of the Asia-Pacific.

The state, however, still defines the territorial zone of investment, and the level of welfare is still a national phenomenon, i.e. the degree to which capital investment tends to concentrate in one place rather than another. It is this clustering that makes it possible for Porter (1990) to argue for a comparative advantage of states in an era of globalisation. In 1956, the United States had 42 of the top 50 corporations, a clear sign of hegemony over world production. In 1989 that number had dropped to 17. Europe as a whole has a larger number (21) of the 50 top firms today than the US. This would imply that the globalisation of capital is a temporally delimited phenomenon or phase within a larger system rather than a general evolutionary phenomenon. It would in this case be related to the breakup of hegemonies, a process of fragmentation and decentralisation of accumulation of wealth in the larger system. Now in the contemporary situation, there are clear markers of this process. While production and export have increased unabated since the 1960s, the developed market economies decreased their share of total world production from 72 to 64 per cent while developing countries more than doubled. Between 1963 and 1987 the US has decreased its share of world manufacturing from 40.3 per cent to 24 per cent. Japan increased its portion from 5.5 per cent to 19 per cent in the same period. West Germany is stable around 9–10 per cent, but the United Kingdom (UK) declined from 6–5 per cent to 3.3 per cent. France, Italy and Canada also declined somewhat in this period (Dicken 1998: 27), and while there are quite significant increases in Spain, Brazil and India, the Asian newly industrialising countries have been the major benefactors of the decentralisation of capital accumulation and especially of manufacturing (ibid.). Countries such as Hong Kong, Taiwan, Korea and China have moved up rapidly on the rank list of manufacturing export countries at the same time as the leading advanced economies have lost ground in this arena, some of them by significant amounts, such as the UK and the US.

And it is the centre that is the target market for this new production. Between 1978 and 1998 manufacturing exports to the US increased from 17.4 per cent to 31.8 per cent. The process here is one where exported capital produces products that are re-imported to the centre. The trend here is towards increasing competition, decentralisation and a clear shift of capital accumulation to the East (Bergesen and Fernandez 1995: 24). The model for this argument, stated above, is that rapid multinationalisation of capital is a general characteristic of periods of hegemonic decline.

The view that we are heading towards an increasingly integrated world, a globalised economy, is certainly a tendency in economic terms, but it does not necessarily mean that we are entering a new kind of world. The world of transnational capital and accompanying transnational institutions, clubs, classes and elites is certainly a part of the globalisation process, but this does not account for the changes in regional distribution of accumulation and power in the world. Globalisation, in other words, does not mean unification or even integration in any other way than coordination of world markets. TNCs are, in important respects, the agents of decentralisation of wealth rather than its geographical concentration. It might be suggested that the current crisis has been generated by this shift, insofar as the current industrial growth in Asia has not been matched by the capacity of Western markets to absorb its products leading, in turn, to increasing competition and a credit crunch.

The redistribution of manufacturing in the world system has led to a more or less three way division of the world, with the developed Asian countries becoming the leading region while the US and Europe have declined. So while there is clearly the emergence of a global structure of capital accumulation, the very rationality of the accumulation process is predicated on geographical shifts of capital. While transnational capital represents a truly global force, the geographical decentralisation of accumulation still leads to declining hegemony in some areas and increasing hegemony, however short-lived, in others. The ultimate question, suggested earlier, is to what degree a threshold of qualitative change is achieved in which entirely new structures establish themselves, in this case, an institutionalisation of global order via political re-organisation. The emergence of global cities may be a sign of this kind of restructuring, but it is far from complete.

On the other hand, there is clearly an increase in the regionalisation of capital, the formation of three great blocks of investment. The major investors in China have been Hong Kong, Taiwan, Singapore and the Chinese overseas communities. According to some estimates, the Chinese diaspora which constitutes only 4 per cent of the total population is an enormous economy in its own right (equivalent to two-thirds of China's GDP) and is an important investor in China (three-quarters of China's 28,000 firms) (Camilleri 1997: 22).

Another process that should be noted is the internal differentiation within the region itself. There are countries like Japan that have quickly moved from exporters of goods to exporters of capital and importers of goods, often of their own exported capital, a pattern linked to the decline of other major economic powers. Hong Kong has become a major investor in Shanghai real estate and in Guangdong industries, displacing a significant portion of its own home investment to the mainland (see Dicken and Yeung, this volume).

Box 11.1

Can the general discussion above be applied to the current crisis in East Asia? The current collapse of markets throughout the region is the subject of intense discussion. There have been those who have raised the more general issue of global overcapacity as the central problem. East Asia has led the increase in world production since 1991, accounting for more than half of the total. This has been part of a definite industrial policy financed by a combination of massive investment in the form of direct foreign investment and a very high level of loans. It might be argued that the expansion of final market goods, especially in the automotive, computer chip and other components, and clothing industries has outstripped world demand, putting increasing pressures on prices and generating a potential deflationary spiral. Some economists, like Paul Krugman have countered that the problem is not overproduction but a certain lack of effective demand and that this normal phenomenon can be remedied by lowering interest rates. This kind of analysis is astonishingly functionalist, as if there were no tendencies to generate situations in which demand and supply are structurally incongruous in a capitalist market. The discussion of the crisis in the economic press has tended to blame it all on mismanagement and even incompetence, claiming that credit has quite simply been too easy and citing the high levels of 'non-performing loans' in this part of the world.

Most of the financial mess is of Asians' own making, and nowhere is this clearer than in South Korea. For years, the government has treated the banks as tools of state industrial policy, ordering them to make loans to uncreditworthy companies and industries.

(*The Economist*, 15–23 November 1997: 19)

Now this kind of moralising does not give an adequate account of the mechanisms involved. After all we are talking about economies that have grown extremely rapidly and that today are the locus of the largest economic region in the world. Certainly there has been massive credit based investment, and it has indeed led to growth. The question is why it doesn't work just now and how this is related to the crisis. I think that some of the suggestions made above might help in this. If we describe a region as an *attractor* of capital due to its generally advantageous rate of potential capital accumulation relative to other areas, then the transformation of the structure of total capital might be adequate in itself to account for the current crisis. The movement of capital to Asia was not a mere question of industrial investment, although the rate of gross fixed investment is between 30 and 35 per cent of the GDP compared to the advanced capitalist countries where it is around 20 per cent. Even in such a situation the relative weight of financial capital is so enormous relative to industrial capital that any region lucky enough to get the stuff gets it in proportions that are bound to lead to overcapitalisation and high rates of speculation.

I have argued here that globalisation is not a new phenomenon, nor that it even represents the kind of massive change that would accord it the status of a new era. Globalisation would seem rather to be the product of two processes, one cyclical and the other secular. Globalisation occurs in periods of hegemonic decline, but it might also be on the verge of becoming a permanent state, due to the changing conditions of accumulation affected by the last round of time-space compression predicated on information technology. Globalisation, whether temporary or permanent, generates mobility and in the contemporary high-tech world, highly integrated communicating elites. These are the elites that produce much of the discourse of the postnational and the hybrid which are prevalent in the West as new dominant ideologies.

Social structuration of the global system

In previous publications (Friedman 1996, 1998), I have suggested that there are two parallel social processes currently at work in the old hegemonic centres of the global system. The first of these is a process of fragmentation, both cultural and political, which takes the form of indigenisation, regionalisation, nationalisation (in the sense of nationalism) and the ethnification of immigrants. The other process is what I have referred to as a 'lift-off' at the apex of society, an increase in class polarisation which includes the globalisation of the world's upper classes and elites. These two processes are simultaneous aspects of the transformation of the world system but they are also highly uneven processes. Vertical and horizontal polarisation discussed below have occurred primarily in declining hegemonic networks, while in

East and Southeast Asia, the converse has been the norm, i.e. national and regional consolidation. The rise of indigenous movements, while globally orchestrated by an array of new international institutions and facilitated by international media and web sites, has not been successful in East and Southeast Asia, where increasingly powerful states have combined violence and accommodation in their strategies of integration. In the following discussion, I have concentrated primarily on the Western sector, emphasising the contrasting nature of developments in Asia.

Global processes are best understood as vectors, force fields that channel strategies and processes of identification. The globalisation of tribal elites, national and business elites is organised by the vectors of the same social field. If the same globalisation produces different results, this is because the local structures are very different from one another. Similarly, the horizontal polarisation or fragmentation that characterises so many national societies today produces different results depending on the state–society structures that are articulated to the global processes. While I begin with an analytical separation of the horizontal and vertical processes, they are, in reality, intertwined in ways that are crucial for understanding the current state of the world.

Parameters of globalisation I: horizontal fragmentation

The decline of hegemony of the advanced industrial centres has led to a process that I have previously described in terms of fragmentation. It relates the decline of modernist identification and an increase in 'rooted' forms of identity, whether regional, indigenous, immigrant-ethnic or national. If the modernist nation-state is based on the identification of a subject population with a national project that defines its members principally in terms of equality and political representativity, and which is future-oriented and developmentalist, when this project ceases to function as an attractor, its subjects must look elsewhere. The modern nation-state is founded on a massive transformation of the world system in which a homogenising, individualising and democratising process in the centre is combined with and dependent upon a hegemonic expansion in the rest of the world, the formation of a centre–periphery organisation. The modernist state is one in which the ethnic content of the nation is usually secondary to its function as a citizenry-based development project, in which cultural assimilation is necessary to homogenise former regional and contemporary immigrant difference that might weaken the unity of the national project. The decline of hegemony is also the decline in the unifying force of its mechanisms of identification. Those who were partly integrated and stigmatised move to establish themselves and those who were totally assimilated must search for new forms of collective belonging. This leads to a range of cultural identifications that fragment and ethnify the former political units, from ethnic to religious to sexual, all in the vacuum left by the disappearance of the future.

The process of fragmentation is expressed in the growth and strengthening of sub-national and transnational identities, indigenous, regional, immigrant, but national identity is also increasingly 'indigenised', i.e. transformed from formal political citizenship into a culturally rooted collectivity. While these new identifications are often opposed to one another, they have emerged as aspects of the same process of dehomogenisation.

1   Indigenous populations have increased in size since the mid-1970s, not as a matter of biology but of identity choice. The number of self-identified North American Indians more than doubled from 1970 to 1980 after more than a century of steep decline and there are at least five 'new' tribes. My work on Hawaiians demonstrates a similar tendency to re-identification. Indigenous groups have both re-appeared where they had more or less disappeared or begun to re-assert their rights where they have been marginalised. It is estimated that there are perhaps 350 million indigenous people that have become increasingly organised and have won a series of battles over land and cultural autonomy.

2   Sub-national regionalism is also, since the mid-1970s, on the increase, and forms, for example, a powerful lobby in Europe today, aiming for a combination of a strong centralised Europe and a decentralised nation-state.

3   Migration is once again a massive phenomenon in a destabilised world. But immigrants no longer come to their new countries simply to become good citizens. Rather, the ethnification of such groups has led to a strong tendency to diasporisation and to a cultural politics claiming recognition in the public sphere. That is, rather than becoming assimilated to declining nation-states they maintain and develop transnational identities, cultures and social existences.

4   National identity has also become increasingly ethnified in this period. This is expressed in the emergence of nationalist movements, and xenophobic ideologies that are themselves partially generated by economic crisis and downward mobility (see next section).

This process cannot be understood without placing it in the context of a weakened nation-state structure as a specific form of relation between people and their representative governmental bodies. The decline of modernism is very much a product of the weakening of the state machine, its tendency towards bankruptcy and its general instability largely a result of the accelerating mobility of capital and taxable income. The transformation of the state is an issue in itself to which we must return. What is crucial here is that the focality of the state in identity formation is giving way to competing identities, from indigenous, regional and migratory populations. This has also implied a decentralisation of resources within the state, along broadly ethnic/regional lines and an increasing division of powers, between the state as representative of the nation and the sub-groups that tend to displace it. This might be understood as a temporary phenomenon, since earlier periods of our history are filled with debates concerning assimilation versus weaker forms of integration or even the formation of more federal structures. Kallen (1924) suggested during the early debates of this century that ethnic minorities ought to be given more autonomy as social entities and that the US could become a kind of ethnic consociational democracy. In any case, assimilationism became dominant policy. Current tendencies are much more serious. Wieviorka (1977) has reminded us that ethnic fragmentation is merely an aspect of a much broader cultural fragmentation including gender, age, religion and most of the other cultural categories that constitute modern society.[2]

It is worth noting the difference between previous tendencies to multi-ethnicity, at the turn of the century, and the current situation. While there was vivid debate in the US on the reconstitution of society in multicultural terms, the same kind of debate was not present in Europe where assimilation was simply taken as given. Europe was still organised around the combination of a strongly ethnic state and a colonial world structure in which coming to the metropole was immediately understood as social mobility, implying a will to assimilate to the superior. This was structured strongly enough to be more or less obvious to nationals as well as immigrants, regionals and indigenous peoples. While there were clearly differences in the constitution of nation-states, such as the *jus sanguinis* of Germany and the *jus solis* of France, the process of assimilation was powerful in both cases. The high proportion of Polish labourers in German industrial development led to their eventual absorption into German national identity. The legal and cultural processes were not necessarily equivalent. While the conditions of assimilation are difficult to ascertain, I would argue that the ideological situation in earlier parts of the century was strongly nationalist while this situation has become reversed in the past decades. This reversal or ideological inversion is an important aspect of the general situation. Gitlin (1995) has argued for the same identity shift in the US. Earlier in the century, immigrants came to become part of the country whereas today, they come to remain part of their countries of origin (see Glick Schiller, this volume). Immigration in the current situation harbours strong tendencies to diasporisation, which must be understood in terms of a set of practices in which identification with a homeland is the basis for the organisation of cultural, economic and social activities that transgress national borders.

Consolidation in East and Southeast Asia as an expression of hegemonic restructuring

An important contrast here is that while fragmentation is occurring in the old centres, Asia would seem to be heading in the opposite direction. With ideologies of the state and of development on the rise rather than in retreat, this area of the world is clearly more future oriented than the West. The rise of nationalism is itself a potential problem in the region, and, of course, processes of homogenisation remain very fragile. On the other hand, there is little or no tolerance for separatism, nor for tendencies to establish conditions of Western style democratic confrontation. This is no mere cultural difference. One has only to return to the nineteenth century, to Victorianism, to Bismark, to ascertain the degree to which national growth was independent of democratic politics and all tendencies to political fragmentation. On the contrary, there are striking parallels between the ideology of Victorian England and neo-Confucianism. I would suggest that these ideologies can be understood in structural and historical terms rather than in purely cultural terms. Indonesia, a country that has become increasingly consolidated after decades of internal strife, has a national 'discipline' movement, *Gerakan, Disiplin Nasional* (Hill 1994), and is actively engaged in forcefully integrating its internal others. The clear opposition to Western values and investment in an Asian way has led to consolidation within states rather than the fragmentation that has characterised the West. Even a society such as Singapore, founded on a colonial structure of pluralism, has struggled increasingly toward cultural unity, which in the 1980s has been referred to 'communitarian inclusionism' (Perry *et al.* 1997: 84). There is also a kind of 'vacuum cleaner' effect in the growth process which draws youth away from their local environments to centres of increasing employment and new forms of life. This includes both push and pull effects, but it is clearly expressed in the 100 million internal migrants in China. There have been innumerable interpretations of the relation between cultural and political economic processes in the region. The 'Asian Values' approach has been interpreted in simple cultural terms by business economists of the past decades, i.e. a more efficient way to run capitalism. But it is perhaps best seen as part of the content of the nationalisation process itself. If I have stressed the similarities with Victorianism and the larger family of nationalist ideologies associated with industrialism, this is not to deny the vast and various differences in real cultural forms, but to stress the strategic commonalities in the global system (see Robison 1995; Khoo 1995; Rodan 1995; Tu 1991; Tønnessson and Antlöv 1996). Certainly, the role of kinship networks in the structuring of all aspects of life implies a very different structure of the nation than that in the West. A recent article by Jayasuriya (1997) suggests that 'Asian values' represent a form of 'reactionary modernism' (Herf 1982) in their combination of national-cum-traditionalist and authoritarian values with the ideology of industrial development. The implication that this ideology has something in common with fascism is certainly interesting in structural terms, but it does not take into consideration the historical reaction to liberalism embodied in fascism, nor its working class and egalitarian core. The Victorian or even Bismarkian model thus seems better. It is important to note the degree to which Western discourse on Asia is so entirely ahistorical in this respect, assuming quite innocently that Western industrialism was somehow a product of the kind of liberal society to be found there today. Any political history of Europe demonstrates, on the contrary, that industrialisation proceeded in an 'illiberal' regime until quite late.

The economic crisis reveals the degree to which nationalisation has occurred. In Indonesia, there was clearly a nationalist mobilisation against Suharto, leading to his resignation in late May 1998. In Korea, the working class strikes and demands for state responsiveness are examples of a nationalisation of the population. Numerous calls by the state for discipline and even prayer (as in Thailand) have led to broad response at a national level. The close relation between state and capital in many of the crisis ridden countries has been much discussed since the massive increase in easy credit was clearly channelled through these often quite personal networks. While this may be a socially specific aspect of the economies of the region accountable in terms of the history of the political structures involved (but a thorough comparative analysis is necessary here), it was not recognised as a cause of the crisis until after the fact. The internal political conflicts that ensue from the crisis as well as the possibility of a growing regionalism and nationalism in face of the threat of global takeovers and other forms of intervention should be staked out as an important area of research that might reveal deeper insights into the nature of social and political structures in the region.

Parameters of globalisation II: vertical polarisation

While cultural and social fragmentation is occurring with various degrees of confrontation and violence in the former hegemonic regions of the world system, there is another process that has been discussed widely. Class stratification in these areas is on the increase and often in quite astounding proportions, not least in these areas of the world system. This is not, of course, a simple process and is definitely not limited to a combination of impoverishment and the enrichment of a capitalist class. The stratification process includes significant elites connected to public institutions, international bureaucracies and professional classes, all of whom depend in varying degrees on tax funds, their speculative growth and other sources of income that have been in one way or another transferred to the public sphere. I refer to this as the 'global porkbarrel' phenomenon,[3] which plays an important role in consolidating global class identities and novel cultural discourses. The economic parameters of this process in these areas of the world system are well known through variations on common themes. Countries like Sweden with limited class differentiation and countries like the US with much higher levels, have experienced the same transformational vectors in the past decade, vectors that are common properties of a global dynamic. While the ratio of richest to poorest in Sweden is 2.7 as opposed to 5.9 for the US, the same kinds of changes have occurred. These are the economic vectors discussed in the first part of the chapter; the combination of global shift, speed-up and the changing composition of capital. The US is the exemplar of this kind of change where downward mobility since the 1970s has been a common denominator of the period. Flexible labour regimes have expanded leading to a larger proportion of working poor. Incomes have stagnated or declined and mobility has become increasingly limited. In Europe unemployment has reached alarming proportions. In Sweden, it was above 12 per cent in the mid to late 1990s and has now declined, primarily due to public sector spending and make-work programmes. The private sector has seen continuous decline in employment that began in the 1970s.

The articulation of vertical polarisation and horizontal fragmentation takes on a variety of forms. At one extreme there is a cultural minimal state which is approximated in the United States, where individualism and a sacred private sphere have entailed a certain disinterested tolerance for cultural difference as long as it is not politicised. In continental Europe, on the other hand, the nation-state has a much stronger cultural character and multiculturalism here appears as a stronger threat to the former social contract which has always been considerably weaker in the United States. The economics of this are clearly expressive of the different variants of the nation-state. In Europe, the percentage of the population below the poverty line that was raised above the minimum in 1986 was between 35 per cent and 60 per cent, with the Scandinavian countries approaching 100 per cent. The equivalent figure for the US was 0.5 per cent (Mingione 1996: 35). The US sports an official poverty rate of over 15 per cent for the nation as a whole, jumping to considerably more than 20 per cent in some states. If one calculates in terms of families and raises the income to $25,000, which seems to be a more adequate definition of the threshold of subsistence adequacy, then the figure rises to 28 per cent (Hacker 1997: 229). In both Europe and the US, the rate of ghettoisation has been extreme and the formation of underclasses of mixed ethnic origins has implied unemployment rates that are often several times higher than those of the native born. Here, of course, there is a significant difference between polar extremes such as Sweden where in the relatively well off welfare supported ghettos, unemployment is commonly more than 50 per cent, and states like California where immigrants, not least undocumented ones, play a crucial role in the economy.

The economic transformation has been accompanied not only by downward mobility, but by an upward mobility among sections of the middle and upper classes. The polarisation is evident in the enormous incomes of the elites and the proliferation of scandals surrounding misuse of credit cards, double salaries, nightclub visits and vacations on national expense accounts, all leading to a crisis of confidence. The rift between 'the people' and the elites is expressed in emergent patterns in the European Union (EU) where declining accountability and increasing perks form an uncomfortable pair.

This kind of development at the regional and international level has produced new kinds of experiences for those involved. A person with such a career is more bound to his or her equivalents in the system, than to members of his own territorial unit. The position may also take on a new moral posture.

The cosmopolitan is promoted to a new kind of legitimacy. It is increasingly associated with a postnational agenda of global citizenship. In a formerly homogenising nation-state like Sweden, elite discourse stresses the slogans of multiculturalism, democratisation and globalisation as the new goals of world society. In recent interviews on the concept of people and peoplehood, or *folk*, an inversion of values is evident. While it is, in fact, the case that the notion of *folk in folkhem* or 'people's home' was taken over from the conservatives by the social democrats in the 1930s, it became associated with notion of the people's will, with plebiscite, with concepts and symbols that expressed the notion of the 'captured state' or the 'captured elite', a dominant class that had been domesticated by the working class. 'Nationalism' was associated with the progressive in the 1950s through the 1970s, with a people's control over its conditions of existence, but today the notion of 'people' is associated with reaction, nationalism and essentialism. In my interviews, 'plebiscite' was understood as dangerous, the concept of *folkhem* was highly suspect, and the combination 'people's will' 'smelled' of the 1930s. In this ideological inversion, multiculturalism has replaced older elite ideals of socialism. In other European states, a formerly nationalist elite who may have seen 'the people' as a motley foreign mixture, today identifies itself as hybrid and views 'the people' as dangerous purists.

Hybridity and class

The 'revolt of the elites' is characteristic of the formation of the new cosmopolitan identity. Hybridity is of top-down vision produced by this new positioning. Looking down on the new imploding urban zones with their diasporic minorities crowded into ethnic neighbourhoods, the new elites can marvel at a new-found cultural globalisation. Here they can consume the entire world, in the form of foods, and feasts of sight, from clothing to language to music. Cosmopolitan desires can be realised in the new internationalised urbanity. The only difficulty lies in the social realities of this celebrated world: the ghettoisation, marginalisation and criminalisation that underlie the more celebratory image. The latter can be circumvented by remaining mere consumers and observers in a world of gated enclaves. What is good for eating might not be so pleasant in the kitchen.

The discourse of hybridity has an interesting logical structure (Friedman 1997). It is at once cosmopolitan and postmodernist in its refusal of modernism. It is thus a re-investment of relativised cultures in a global scheme of cultural meetings. The new structure is a cultural ecumene, one that can only be understood from above. The new encompassing cosmopolitan elite is thus one that incorporates all the differences in the world, transforming them into the identity of the new authorities of the world.

There are numerous contradictions in this position which are not difficult to exemplify. One of the most salient images of hybrid identity is found in the much discussed book by Gloria Anzaldúa, *Borderlands/La Frontera: The New*

Mestiza (1987), which details an identity based on border-crossing and mixture, ethnic, national and sexual. The notion of the border as something to be straddled so as to be perpetually on both sides, is very different, of course, from the daily lives of real border-crossers, especially the undocu-mented immigrants who cross over at great danger and whose life histories are replete with aversion and fear of precisely the border (Milla 1995). There is clearly a class division in representations here. While there is a verit-able culture industry among academics that has grown up around the border-crossing identity, the story at the lower end of the scale is quite different (Friedman 1997). In Guatemala, there is a 'new mestizo' ideology that is rather widespread in Central America (Canclini 1995). This is also an elitist movement that harbours a logic that is implicitly anti-Indian, who, in the case of Guatemala, make up the majority of the population. Maya can now be told that they are not pure and that all Guatemalans are part Indian. This implies, of course, that the legitimacy of Mayan land claims can be nullified. In Australia, perhaps the most immigrant-dense country in the world, the government, some years ago, launched a multicultural policy programme and a book called *Creative Australia* which was meant to recreate unity out of increasing diversity. On one occasion, a representative literary scholar went to talk to a group of Aboriginal artists and intellectuals, pre-sumably to entice them into the new multicultural project. He went on for some time about how mixed the Aborigines were as a population and that any other view of themselves was tantamount to *essentialism*, that favourite word of cultural studies. When he was through, an older man rose, looked the hybridist straight in the eyes, and said,

'I'm an essentialist mate, and if you don't like it you can bugger off!'

There is clearly a conflict between hybridising elites and those who identify as indigenous. Canada, another state that has declared itself multicultural, has faced similar opposition from Indians who refuse to be classified as just another ethnic minority. They are the First Peoples, and this, of course, is more than cultural distinctiveness. It is about rights to land and political autonomy.

There is little evidence that hybridity works on the ground. There have been interesting developments in attempts to establish 'bi-racial' identity in the US. The bi-racial movement is primarily a middle-class activity and con-tains a strong strategy of distinction making in which class mobility leads to attempts to separate oneself from a preceding, in this case, lower status identity. The attractor in this is 'whiteness'. The logical contradiction in this kind of identification lies between individual and collective identities. Every individual has a specific genealogy and is thus a very particular mixture. Collective creole identities in the past have always and continue to be closed ethnic identities just as 'non-mixed' identities. The bi-racial movement split several years ago when Asian bi-racials protested at the dominance of African

Americans. The new group took on the title, *Hapa* Forum, *hapa* being the Hawaiian word for 'half'. This is a normal product of the above contradiction. Any attempt to form a collectivity must also create boundaries and constitute the particular constituents of that identity. Hybrid identity only works as a generalised discourse or as an individual identity. It is thus most suitable for elites where the only commonality of the identity is that it is positioned above the fragmenting multi-ethnic world below.

In previous work (Friedman 1997, 1998), I have discussed the logic of hybridity, arguing that it can be understood as a postmodern cosmopolitanism that combines an international identity with a revived culturalism, a kind of 'leaky essentialism'. The problems of the fragmenting world are equivalent to the essentialising of differences. To solve this problem, we have only to reconceive the world in terms of mixtures of such essential things. Cosmopolitans in the earlier years of this century were true modernists who identified with a future of expanding knowledge, rationality, and experimentation, whether in arts or sciences. The new cosmopolitans are absorbed by issues of identity. This has strong parallels with an older racialism in its obsession with embodied identity: 'before we were pure but now we are mixed.' The discourse of hybridity tends to conflate race and culture in ways that echo the discussion of the last century. Hybridity as a concept does not solve the issue of essentialism. Rather it reifies it by its very structure. The only way to identify a hybrid category is by specifying its genealogy, the origins of its constituents. Thus hybridity logically entails genealogical thinking and cultural genealogies necessarily reify cultural identities, the accumulation of cultural traits.

However, as stated above, hybridity can indeed function as a class or elite identity in which the particularity of mixtures is never at issue. There is some evidence to suggest that hybridity among intellectuals is in some sense a reaction to multicultural politics in which difference became a divisive issue threatening the unity of the elite. Gilroy, for example, in his attempt to define a Black Atlantic identity as opposed to Afro-centric models has argued hybridity against those who invest in African roots. But this kind of identity is itself a social differentiation argued in strangely objectivist terms. 'We trans-Atlantic blacks are not representatives of the African. We have more, we are a new combination, representatives of the post-colonial conditions of the world. Just as the new mestizos we represent a new people, dare I say "race", that shall inherit the earth, or at least point the way to the future.' Homi Bhabha (1994) is perhaps the purest representative of hybridity as a new class ideology and his use of the term is much more generalised to practically all forms of in-betweeness to which he refers to as the 'third space'.

The connection between the restructuring of global classes and the emergence of hybridity has been made previously (Dirlik, 1994a; Friedman 1997, 1998). I would argue that there is a truly massive ideological transformation involved here that I have referred to as cosmological inversion. This includes some of the phenomena described above which are included in the discourse of post-nationalism, anti-essentialism, multiculturalism and hybridity. In a certain sense this is a reversal of the ideology of common goals and super-ordinate social projects common to a former left and a nationalism which was part of both left and right ideologies. The lift off of the state defines a new populism that appears as reactionary, but which, in reality, is very much more complex. It re-imagines the former left as the new conservatism. As democracy, globalisation and multiculturalism become slogans of self-identified progressive politicians, it becomes reactionary to demystify the structural adjustment inherent in such projects.

The issue of hybridity is primarily a product vertical polarisation in con-ditions where modernism is on the decline. It consists of a cosmopolitan identification that is based on cultural rootedness, i.e. a melange of cultures (Friedman 1997). One would not expect this kind of identification in periods of expansion which tend, instead, to be focused on the future rather than the past. Thus, in East Asia, such identification ought to be rather weak. That several of the spokespeople for hybridity are Indians is less interesting here than that they are very much established in the West rather than at home.

Paradoxes of globalisation

The globalising tendencies, including massive capital flows and the increasing possibility of rapid communication, interact in crucial ways with the process of fragmentation, often splitting it into new micro-classes. Indigenous groups such as the Sami and the Maori and increasingly, North American Indians demonstrate the degree to which financial and legal advantages have led to internal differentiation. Rata (1997) has demonstrated the way in which 'tribal capitalism' was established among the Maori organised within the framework of their own social structures. Indigenous leaders have been sucked into international organisations that have both provided a needed voice for rights, but also created a new global elite stratum in the world system. This has created internal friction and has tested the strength of relations of representativity in such groups.

At the same time, indigenisation has been a powerful factor of identification among the marginalised populations and underclasses of the declining hege-mons. The ideologies of the New Rights in Europe and the militia groups in the US are evidence of this. Many of these groups have strongly indigenous ideologies, invoking anti-universalism, local autonomy, nationhood over citizenship, 'tribal' religion and anti-modernist holism. There are African American Indian tribes such as the Washitaw who are allied with the Repub-lic of Texas, and numerous examples of cooperation between Black Power organisations and the Klu Klux Klan, primarily under the common banner of anti-statism, anti-cosmopolitanism and separatism.

These tendencies, summarised in Figure 11.1, are not isolated from one another. They all interact on the internet and are thoroughly embedded in the world systemic processes that we have discussed. The world processes

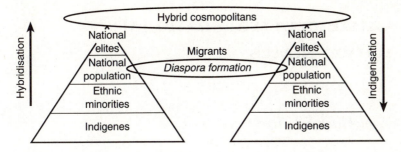

Figure 11.1 Hybridity

that become salient in this model are the combined and seemingly contra-dictory phenomena of increasing cultural fragmentation in substantial parts of the world at the same time as there is an apparent increase in global unity in the form of communication, capital flows and global elite formations. These simultaneities are organised by a single nexus of global political eco-nomic processes and form the basis for the differential identity politics that are sometimes referred to as 'glocalisation', the globalisation of the local and the localisation of the global. The latter metaphors, however, are not expres-sions of cultural processes in themselves but aspects of more powerful forces of local/global articulation. Class and ethnicity, vertical and horizontal polarisation, are the two contradictory formations that emerge from the dynamics of globalisation.

Notes

1 This issue is discussed in some mathematical detail in a paper by Friedman and Sugita (ms).
2 This generalised fragmentation is clearly expressed in the deconstruction of gender identities, both in intellectual discourse and in much middle class experimentation. Here, roles are reversed and varied in the extreme and identities are reduced to acts. Butler (1990) has gone so far as to suggest that there are no gender identities other than those that are imposed externally by the State or related Foucauldian power structure.
3 The term 'global porkbarrel' refers to a situation in which huge amounts of primarily public funds are made available to well positioned global actors who use the funds to reproduce and reinforce their positions and increase their power of consumption (see Friedman 1997, 1998).

12 Citizens in transnational nation-states

The Asian experience

Nina Glick Schiller

Transmigrants and the logic of nation-state building[1]

The 1990s was a period in which political leaderships in several Asian states and in the United States (US) were accused of corrupt practices. But while the charges in Japan, Korea and Indonesia were about internal corruption, in the US charges of foreign influence on domestic affairs, including the election of a President, were central to a campaign-financing scandal. Johnny Chung, a naturalised US citizen born in Taiwan, was accused of illegally funnelling almost $300,000 to the US Democratic Party in order to finance the re-election of President Clinton in 1996 (Gerth and Sanger 1998). Almost $100,000 of that money was alleged to have come from a high-ranking military official and member of the Central Committee of the Communist Party of the People's Republic of China (Gerth 1998: 1). The allegations appearing in headlines of the *New York Times* that a 'Democratic Party Fund-Raiser' had a 'China Tie' represented the most recent chapter in a generations-old story about the transnational political activities of immigrants from many regions of the world and the targeting of Asian immigrants because of such activities. As such, the uproar about 'the China connection' was also a story about the construction of both US and Asian national identities in past periods of capitalist expansion and in the present era of globalisation.

In this chapter, I argue that from their inception many nation-state building projects have been transnational in scope.[2] In both late nineteenth- and late twentieth-century mass migrations, immigrants who established transnational networks and lived their lives across international borders have played an important but often unacknowledged role in nation-state building. An analysis of transnational migration and the transnational networks of immigrants, past and present, contributes to the emerging scholarship of the relationship between processes of globalisation and nation-states. It also allows us insight into the ways in which contemporary globalisation processes differ from those of the previous periods.

Rethinking paradigms of the relationship between nations, states and international migration

Before I develop the argument of this paper several definitions are necessary. I employ the word 'transnational' to discuss political, economic, social and cultural processes that (1) cross the borders of one or more states; (2) include actors that are not states; but (3) are shaped by the policies and institutional practices of particular states.[3] Migrant networks that cross the borders of several states can be said to be transnational. Persons who live their lives across borders, developing social, familial, political, economic and religious networks that incorporate them into two or more states can be considered to be 'transmigrants' (Glick Schiller *et al.* 1992: 1).

The term 'state' indicates a sovereign system of government within a particular bounded territory. In contrast, 'nation' evokes the sense of peoplehood that a particular population uses to distinguish itself from other national groups. Nation-state building is therefore identified as 'a set of historical and affective processes that link disparate and heterogeneous populations together and forge their loyalty to and identity with a central government apparatus and institutional structure' (Fouron and Glick Schiller 1997: 281).

Since its inception, capitalism as a mode of production, distribution and consumption has been global in its reach. Yet, when I use the term globalisation I intend it to mean more: that we are currently living in a period in which capitalist processes are being restructured in fundamental ways in relationship to the rapid and deregulated flows of capital (Mittleman 1996b: 230–1).

There is much that is useful in the emerging paradigm of globalisation. It provides fresh perspectives on political, economic, social, and cultural processes. However, a number of weaknesses have also emerged in the scholarship on globalisation. In the first place, globalisation has both 'subjective' and 'objective' connotations (Mittleman 1996b: 230). The concept functions as an ideology as well as a description of the restructuring and intensification of global connection (Smith 1997; Turner 1990). Moreover, as the unit of analysis has moved from the nation-state to the globe, some scholars, educators, political leaders and the media magnify the scope and the novelty of contemporary global processes and ignore or minimalise the continuing significance of the state (Canclini 1995; Hannerz 1992). Others, while acknowledging the continuing presence of the state, have leapt from the evidence of globalisation to the conclusion that the current historical conjuncture is marked by a subversion of 'the hyphen that links the nation to the state' (Appadurai 1990: 304). We have been told that 'the boundary of the power to impose differences . . . is being eroded by transnational developments causing the structure of the nation-state to become problematic' (Kearney 1991: 52).

In response to the initial panegyrics about global flows, a new scholarship of the state has emerged which argues that rather than 'dithering away'

(Turner 1997), states are undergoing a 'metamorphosis' (Beck 1997: 139). New relationships are being established between the structures and institutions of various states and the regional and global processes within which capital is accumulated, invested, commodified, and allocated (Sassen 1996a; Camilleri and Falk 1992; Stallings 1995). 'To realise material gain from globalisation, the state increasingly facilitates this process, acting as its agent' (Mittleman 1996a: 7). In their efforts to maintain a structure of law and compete for greater shares of capital and markets, multinational corporations are finding new ways to use the legal structures and military or police capacities of states (Jessop 1994; Panitch 1997; Rosecrance 1996; Sassen 1996a). States that are not powerful nor locales of global cities are also affected by current trends but their degree of sovereignty, always tentative, is being further reduced.

However, this new scholarship of the relationship between state structures and globalisation has had little to say about the continuing significance of territorially-based national identities, rhetorics, and political processes. Theorists of the state in the new global order have yet to fully address the degree to which the class forces which are transforming contemporary states are also continuing to engage in nation-state building processes. Nor has the current growing body of data on contemporary transnational migration been incorporated into the debate about the restructuring of state powers and functions.

Before we can ascertain whether current processes of globalisation are disrupting the interest or capacity of leaders of states to continue nation-state building projects and eroding the allegiance that populations have to territorially based states, a historical comparison is in order. We need a more historicised view of the relationship between global processes of capitalism, nation-state building, and international migration. Central to this historical comparison are three questions: (1) How new is transnational migration?; (2) What was the relationship between migration and nation-state building during the late nineteenth century, an era of nation-state building in Asia, Europe, and Latin America?; and (3) What is the current status of nation-state building projects, given the heightened level of globalisation? In the remainder of this chapter I will offer some tentative answers to these questions using examples from nineteenth- and twentieth-century Asian emigration from China, Japan, Korea and the Philippines to the US and from the twentieth-century regional migration in Asia. In both time periods, I will show that these Asian emigrants are best understood as transmigrants, living their life across international borders and participating in the social, economic, cultural and political processes of two or more states. Asian emigrants to the US emerge as key players in nineteenth/early twentieth-century discourses about national identity in the US and in the construction of national identities in their homelands. In the late twentieth century, we need research that explores the role that emigrants continue to play in the political and economic processes of their homelands. My preliminary conclusion is that a

significant sector of contemporary emigrants are transmigrants who participate in the political processes of more than one state. At the same time,
through their presence in other lands, these transmigrants serve as racialised
others against whom political leaders can develop narratives that link state
and nation and unite an engaged citizenry in an age of globalisation.

How new is transnational migration? The Asian experience

Within the last few years, researchers have begun to argue that the com-
puters, satellites, and rapid transportation technologies which have been a
dramatic aspect of globalisation have produced a new form of migration.
Immigrants as well as corporations are now transnational, maintaining
multiple ties across international borders (Wakeman 1988; Smith 1998;
Portes 1997). But transnational migration from both Asia and Europe to the
US dates back to the nineteenth century (Glick Schiller 1999, forthcoming).
Most emigrants intended to return and organised their incorporation into
their new land around the sending of remittances to their old home. The
transnational migration of the past was prompted in Asia, as it was in
Europe, by global transformations in the organisation and deployment of
capital that disrupted local economies and made life insecure in both sending
and receiving societies (Bodnar 1985).

Chinese emigrants fled from a weak imperial state that experienced war,
foreign debt and political upheaval as a result of European and US penetration. Although until 1894, the punishment for leaving was death, by 1880,
105,465 Chinese people had entered the US (Takaki 1990: 216; Wong
1982). By 1875, Chinese workers made up almost a quarter of the male work-
force of California (Kwong 1987). In Japan, the Meiji Restoration of 1868
led to intensive taxation, industrialisation and urbanisation. In an environment of both social disruption and the search for new knowledge, both
workers and students began to depart even before the legalisation of emigration in the 1880s. Between 1881 and 1930, 275,308 Japanese immigrants
arrived in the US with almost half of this population settling in Hawaii
(Spickard 1996: 20, 162). After about 70,000 labourers emigrated to
Hawaii, Korean emigration to the US was restricted by the Japanese government which annexed Korea in 1910. However, more than 2,000 Koreans,
primarily refugees from Japanese rule, arrived in the US between 1910 and
1924 (Kim 1981: 21). Beginning in 1903, Filipinos also began migrating to
both Hawaii and to the US mainland. However, their large scale migration
began in the 1920s when US law restricted all other Asian and most Southern
and Eastern European migration.

In all cases, emigrants generally planned to return. The Japanese emigrants saw themselves not as *teiju* (emigrating permanently) but as *dekasegi*
(going-out to work) (Spickard 1996: 20). Plans to return were reinforced by
the conditions emigrants found in the US. While Irish, Eastern and Southern

European immigrants settling in the US in the nineteenth century were seen as racially different from the white US mainstream, the colour line drawn against Asian immigrants was more impenetrable and embedded in law, as well as rhetoric and social practice. The Naturalisation Act of 1790 allowed naturalisation only to whites. In a series of court cases beginning in 1878 when a federal court declared that 'a native of China, of the Mongolian race, is not a white person' immigrants from China, Japan and Korea found themselves part of the US labour force but not part of the body politic.

Even if they had wealth or education, their racialisation limited their social mobility since many states excluded persons who could not become naturalised from public employment, land ownership and the practice of medicine, dentistry, bank directing, embalming, nursing, teaching and plumbing (Wong 1982). Although the attacks were first directed towards the Chinese, over time, these restrictions and legal and defacto segregation in education and public accommodation were extended to other Asians.[4] Cultural practices were also targets beginning with the 1875 California law against the wearing of *ques* by Chinese immigrants (Wong 1982). In 1913, the California legislature passed the Alien Land Act that kept all those who were ineligible for citizenship from owning land. Asians could not testify against whites in court or intermarry with whites. In addition, legal steps were taken to end Asian emigration beginning in 1882 with the exclusion of Chinese workers.

A 1922 ruling against a Chinese immigrant states the prevailing US ethos.

> The yellow or bronze racial colour is the hallmark of Oriental despotisms. It was deemed that the subject of these despotisms, with their fixed and ingrained pride in the type of their civilisation, which works for its welfare by subordinating the individual to the personal authority of the sovereign, as the embodiment of the state, were not fitted and suited to make for the success of a republican form of government. Hence they were denied citizenship.
>
> (Lopez 1996: 56)

For the Asian immigrants who were building lives for themselves in the US, these legal rulings carried potent messages not only about race but also about nation.

In reaction to their racialisation and legal exclusion from American citizenship and political participation, many Asian immigrants returned home. Between 1908 and 1943, 90,199 Chinese left the US (Chun 1990: 5). However studies of immigrant communities indicate that many Japanese and Chinese responded to the discrimination and exclusion by keeping their stake in America but also maintaining their home ties through a complex system of cultural practices. They returned home to marry when at all possible, even if their spouses could not legally emigrate. Chinese and Japanese immigrants would often send a son born in the US home to preserve the ties of family and culture (Spickard 1996; Wong 1982). Chinese clan identifications and associations and the Japanese family system facilitated the maintenance and continuation of home ties and simultaneous incorporation into businesses and associational life in the US (Wong 1982; Spickard 1996). Chinese immigrants also invested in social status in their home village by building schools and ancestral temples (Chun 1990: 45). There is some indication that Chinese, Japanese and Korean immigrants also reacted to their racialisation and exclusion by beginning to identify with the state and nation from which they emigrated.[5]

The relationship between migration and nation-state building: the nineteenth century

In the nineteenth century, most rural folk left home with their sense of self defined in terms of locality and family rather than in national terms. Observers of US immigration have noted that it was within the process of settling in the US that European immigrants adopted national identities (Park 1974 [1925]; Glazer 1954). It seems clear that Asian immigrants also began to develop allegiances to their ancestral homeland through the process of emigrating and then finding themselves excluded, stigmatised and defined as racially different (Espiritu 1996; Lowe 1997; Takaki 1989; Rafael 1995). During this same period, Asian intellectuals and political leaders formulated ideologies of race and nation in relationship to their own experiences of exile, migration and exclusion. These processes of constructing and popularising Asian national identities are best understood as transnational. That is to say, the late nineteenth-century emergence of national identities in Asia, the adoption of national identities by Asian immigrants, as well as reiterations of US national identity during that period all were situated within relationships that stretched beyond the territory of the various states. Consequently, while researchers have tended to differentiate between 'internal racism' and 'external racism' (Balibar 1991), it would be more productive to explore the racialisation of Asian immigrants, transnational migration and nineteenth-century nation-state building within a single analytical framework (Glick Schiller *et al.* 1992, 1995; Chuch 1996).

We do know that emerging national leaderships in China and Korea spent significant periods of their life outside the territorial boundaries of their state, surviving as racialised strangers in a strange land while maintaining ties to home. Even after the immigration of Chinese and Japanese workers was discontinued, the children of powerful families obtained foreign education. 'By 1939 56.2 per cent of the highest ranking figures in the Chinese nationalist government, academic institutions, and the military had received advanced degrees in the US' (Kwong 1987: 16). In turn, Korean political refugees used their transnational networks to build an opposition to the Japanese occupation and create an independent and modern nation-state. Syngman Rhee, elected the first president of the Republic of Korea in 1848, studied at George Washington, Harvard and Princeton Universities in the US.

Sun Yat-Sen, the founder of the Chinese Kuomintang Party, lived for sixteen years in the US, Japan and Europe enmeshed in transnational political efforts to build the Chinese nationalist movement. In his efforts to organise the Confucian ethos that legitimated the Chinese imperial state, he popularised the notion that national identities have racial foundations. His influential statement 'Three Principles of the People' delivered in China in 1923 uses the language of blood ties as the basis of unity of the Chinese people. 'The greatest force is common blood. The Chinese belong to the yellow race because they come from the blood stock of the yellow race. The blood of ancestors is transmitted by heredity down through the race, making blood kinship a powerful force' (quoted in Dikötter 1997a: 4). In stating that nations were racial communities, Sun was reflecting and contributing to a worldwide academic and political discourse that was hegemonic before the Second World War. Japanese formulations of national identity used a similar language of blood informed by the study of anthropology and experiences of Japanese elites abroad (Dikötter 1997b).

That is not to say that the nationalism that emerged was only a 'derivative discourse' (Chatterjee 1986). Each nation-state built on embedded folk beliefs and indigenous schools of thought about hierarchy, kinship and identity. But beginning in the middle of the nineteenth century, Asian reformers and modernisers found legitimation for their political projects in social Darwinism, de Gobineau and the scientific racism of nineteenth-century anthropology. These ideas were simultaneously disseminated within European and US colonial projects in Asia and brought back home by Asian nationalist leaders who had lived abroad and remained part of transnational political projects (Dikötter 1997b; Weiner 1997).

These ideologies were reflected in a series of state practices and political actions through which Asian political leaders made claims to their emigrant populations settled abroad. That is to say, China and Japan extended their governmental functions to encompass populations that lived far beyond the territorial boundaries of their states while Korean nationalist leaders included Koreans abroad as part of the movement to build an independent Korea. In effect, the conception of the state with which these leaders operated was one of a transnational nation-state.

From the very beginning of legal emigration, the Japanese national and prefectural governments imposed regulations to insure that those living abroad would not bring disgrace to the nation (Spickard 1996). The state made family at home responsible for those living abroad, using state power to reinforce transnational networks. Through transactions with Japanese functionaries both in Japan and abroad, Japanese who emigrated learned that the Japanese government, rather than their home village, was their homeland.

The fact that persons born in Japan, China or Korea could not become US citizens reinforced the continuing link that Asian immigrants in the US had to their home government. However, it should be noted that those home governments also saw themselves as representing the descendants of their emigrants who were born in the US and were US citizens. The Japanese government used its consuls in the US to closely monitor Japanese immigrants (Harrington 1980). Organisations of Japanese immigrants in the US were given consular functions (Spickard 1996: 53). The Chinese nationalist state was weaker but it also worked closely with Chinese settled in the US. After the Kuomintang Party consolidated its power in China in 1927, it set up an Overseas Affairs Bureau because the new government 'recognised the political and economic importance of the overseas Chinese' (Kwong 1987: 101). In light of the current debates about transnational migration and deterritorialisation, it is important to note that these transnational political movements that began in the nineteenth century and extended up until the Second World War were still very much about territory. Transmigrants were thought to maintain allegiance to state governments which were territorially based.

Chinese nationalist leaders worked to encourage the flow of emigrant remittances and saw populations settled abroad as a source of capital as well as political support.

> The KMT was pragmatic; it wanted to ensure that it would receive the continued financial support of the overseas Chinese, particularly the regular remittances to families in China. Chinatown residents were also seen as investors in Chinese industries.
>
> (Kwong 1987: 101)

The nationalist projects of both Chinese and Japanese political leaders found support among emigrant populations. Overseas Chinese sent funds to support Sun Yat Sen and the Kuomintang's resistance to the Japanese invasion of China (Ong 1993).

> Many overseas identified China's fortunes with their own and attributed their mistreatment in the US to the low status of their homeland. They wanted to see a stronger China, and so overseas Chinese were particularly patriotic. They have consistently shown extraordinary concern for the welfare of their homeland and have contributed, both spiritually and financially, to strengthen China.
>
> (Kwong 1987: 101)

Chinese and Korean immigrants in the US and elsewhere participated in political movements 'back home.' From 1910–45 Koreans settled in the US raised money for the liberation of Korea from Japan (Harrington 1980: 112).

These connections were reinforced by US policies that distinguished between immigrants from Europe and Asia. As the US moved to challenge the transnational loyalties of its European immigrants after the First World War through Americanisation and naturalisation campaigns, it reinforced the distinction between European immigrants and those from Asia who were not eligible for citizenship. The differential treatment of German and Japanese immigrant populations during the Second World War reinforced the equation of Japanese racial identity with an immutable connection to the Japanese state. Both Japanese immigrants and persons of Japanese descent born in the US and therefore citizens were equally suspect of loyalty to Japan and stripped of their freedom and property.

Transnational migration and nation-state building in the era of globalisation: the Asian experience revisited

After the Second World War a new conception of the relationship between nation-states and populations became hegemonic among political leaders around the world and emigrating populations. In this new conceptualisation, the entire globe was depicted as the discrete domain of nation-states. A government's sovereignty was restricted to within the territorial borders of its state. Each person belonged to a state and each person could have only one state. Scholars of immigration ignored or forgot the continuing transnational connections of immigrants and portrayed them as uprooted persons who had abandoned home and family for their new land (Handlin 1973 [1951]). The institutionalisation of the United Nations and the replacement of colonial empires by newly independent states served to popularise this new conception of the human condition.

In reality, states varied in the degree to which they abandoned dual citizenship policies and instituted the practice of territorially-restricted nation-states.[6] Although Asian immigrants were accorded citizen rights in the US after the Second World War, both the governments of South Korea and the Republic of China continued to regard emigrant populations as part of their state and maintained close supervision of its emigrants settled in the US throughout the Cold War. Kim (1981) reported that 'It is no exaggeration to say the Korean Consulate General is the informal government of New York's Korean community and that the consul general is its "mayor".' In the context of the Cold War the US government encouraged Korea and the Chinese government in Taiwan to pursue the same types of transnational political representation that had made the Japanese immigrants so suspect before the Second World War. On the other hand, after the founding of the People's Republic of China, overseas Chinese found their transnational family networks and economic activities on the mainland barred by policies of both the PRC and the US.

By the 1990s, however, large scale migration had become the order of the day in many regions of the world, emigrants were once again building transnational networks, and the relationship between emigrants and their ancestral lands was being addressed by increasing numbers of states. Putting aside the dominant assumption that the province of state power is confined to the territorial boundaries of the state except at times of war, a growing number of political leaders began to assert that their states existed wherever members of their population and their descendants had settled. Noting these developments in Latin America, the Caribbean, Europe, and Asia my colleagues and I took them to be an indicator of the global restructuring of capital and declared that something unprecedented was taking place, the growth of the 'deterritorialised nation-states' (Basch *et al.* 1994).[7] We identified three aspects of the current historical conjuncture that were contributing to the development of such states: (1) the growth of a new wave of transnational migration; (2) global economic insecurities; and (3) the continuing necessity for states to legitimate their governance. We were wrong about the novelty of the political stance of these states and our choice of terms was unfortunate because a national and bounded territory still remains an important part of the imagery of the transnational nation-state. However, it is becoming increasingly evident that such states are re-emerging, that they are different in significant ways from previous transnational state practices, and that these differences reflect the nature of contemporary processes of globalisation.[8] A variety of states including Mexico, the Dominican Republic, Colombia and Haiti are developing government practices, official offices or ministries, and even constitutional changes to incorporate their emigrant populations living abroad (Fouron and Glick Schiller 1997; Graham 1996; Guarnizo 1998, forthcoming; Smith 1997; Sanchez 1997).

Asia has not stood removed from this trend although little research on transnational nation-state building has been done there. There is certainly evidence that in Asia, 'the death of the nation-state is much exaggerated' and that 'those transnational theorists telling us to stop talking about the state might well be advised to direct some of their attention to Southeast Asia' (Dusenbery 1997: 250). In the remainder of this paper, I will sketch some of the emerging trends and issues in Asia that warrant further research.

Within the last few decades, as a result of uneven economic development within Asia and changes in the US immigration law in 1965 which made Asian immigration possible, there has been significant migration within Asia and between a number of Asian states and the US. By the 1980s the Philippines, China, and Korea were among three of the four states that sent the largest number of immigrants to the US (DeSipio and de las Craza 1998). Locations in Asia such as Singapore, Japan, Hong Kong and Taiwan have also emerged as destinations of mass migration. By the 1990s, the 350,000 foreign workers in Singapore make up 20 per cent of the nation's labour force (*Migration News* 1997). Foreign Asian domestic workers in Hong Kong in 1995 made up the majority of domestic workers in the city (Noble 1997: 3).

Whatever their destination, Asian migrants have found that they face both economic and political insecurity. In Asia, migrant workers are generally excluded from permanent settlement. In the US, while Asian immigrants can now obtain permanent resident status and become US citizens, they have continued to face discrimination, as well as the economic uncertainties that have accompanied the replacement of US industrial production with a low waged service economy. Despite the growth of a visibly wealthy sector of Chinese and Indian immigrants, 'since 1965 the profile of Asian immigration has consisted of low-wage, service sector workers as well as "proletarianised" white-collar professionals' (Lowe 1997: 15).[9] Labelled as a model minority, Asian immigrants have found that they continue to be distinguished from the US body politic and bear the brunt of the anger of both black and white Americans who are displaced by the restructuring of the US economy (Takaki 1990; Lowe 1997; Ong 1997b). As Lowe (1997: 4) points out, 'The American *citizen* . . . [continues to be] defined over against the Asian *immigrant*'. Meanwhile Asian immigrants are also being racialised within Asian states where they are employed on a temporary basis. Noble (1997), for example, reports that in the 1980s, the Chinese in Hong Kong used the word 'Filipino girl' interchangeably with 'maid' or 'servant'. Filipino women were defined as racially different from the Chinese and naturally suited to be servants.

The racialisation experienced by Asian immigrants can be seen as an indicator of the economic instabilities unleashed in various economies by the forces of globalisation. However, the targeting of Asian immigrants is also a reflection of the way in which nationalism and nation-state building processes continue to be salient within the globalising economy. The process of racialisation of immigrants continues to be a central mechanism through which national identities are linked to state structures. Citizens learn to identify with their state by distinguishing themselves from persons who are seen as foreign to that state. Asian immigrants, whether they live in other countries in Asia or elsewhere, are central actors in these definitional processes. We need more research to understand the extent to and ways in which current day Asian immigrants' experiences of racialisation abroad precipitate or reinforces their establishment of transnational family networks, their identification with their ancestral land, and their engagement in home country politics. Certainly there is evidence that Indian immigrants have turned to 'long distant nationalisms' and have been major contributors to the Hindu communalist movement that in 1998 were able to win the political leadership in India (Anderson 1992; Lessinger 1995).

Migrants working on contract in Singapore, Hong Kong or Taiwan leave home knowing that permanent settlement is unlikely. They migrate in search of money that can support family left behind, as well as capital that can be invested in land, housing and businesses back home (Noble 1997). Although permanent settlement has been possible in locations such as the US, Asian immigrants also often emigrate to support family and economic activities in their homeland and form transnational family networks (Kim 1981; Spickard 1996; Kwong 1987; Chen 1992; Chun 1990; Lessinger 1995).

At the same time, the political leaderships of some Asian countries are reaching out to their past and contemporary emigrant populations and reclaiming them as members of their ancestral states. Labour-exporting states such as the Philippines are contributing to the contemporary revitalisation of transnational nation-state by reclaiming populations abroad, whether they have departed as temporary labourers or have become citizens of other countries. Beginning with President Marcos, Filipino leaders developed a rhetoric which embraced Filipinos abroad as part of the Philippine state and nation and as responsible for its welfare. With two-thirds of its citizens below the poverty line in the 1980s, the Philippine government began an official policy of exporting workers and remittances emerged as a major component of the Philippine economy. The state directly entered into the process of labour contracting, making money from fees and exit taxes. By 1990, there were over one and a half million Filipinos emigrants working in 120 countries. The average migrant supports five persons in the Philippines (Noble 1997). According to the Philippine government, the country is the world's largest exporter of labour and remittances make up its largest source of foreign currency. Overseas contract workers sent home US$4.9 billion in remittances in 1995 (Tadiar 1997).

Philippine citizenship is accorded by *jus sanguinis* and therefore children of Philippine citizens born abroad have dual citizenship (Pido 1986: 109), in order to encourage emigrants with dollars to return to visit and retire. Beginning in 1973, the Philippine government took further steps to reach out to its emigrants by giving them special tax exemptions and property rights (Basch *et al.* 1994). In 1978 the Filipino legislature introduced a law granting dual citizenship to persons who had become US citizens (Pido 1986: 109).

Chinese political leaders in China and abroad have developed a nationalist rhetoric of inclusion that seeks to encompass a population that extends far beyond China's borders. After 1978, China again emerged as a major exporter of labour. The Ministry of Foreign Trade and Economic Cooperation reported that remittances from the 200,000 migrant workers outside China in 1994, together with Chinese-supplied materials used in foreign projects, generated $8 billion for China in 1994 (*Migration News* 1997). However, the discourse of Chinese identity that is being developed reaches out not just to these recent migrant workers but to the broader population of 'overseas Chinese', persons of Chinese descent who are well incorporated into other states.

There is contestation between overseas Chinese capitalists and the government of China about how their relationship is to be framed and about what constitutes the nature of Chineseness and no single narrative has emerged (Dirlik 1997; Ong 1997b; Smart 1997). Chinese leaders who engage in this discourse are interested not only in insuring a flow of remittances to China but also in encouraging overseas Chinese with considerable amounts of

capital to invest in China and protect Chinese commercial interests globally.[10] To accomplish this task, China has not made constitutional changes
but there are indications that officials and the press are reviving the language
of race, utilised by Sun Yat-Sen and the nationalists who first sought to build
a modern Chinese state.

> [T]he 1990s are marked by an inward/outward turning towards the
> racial/cultural self, a reinvention of Chinese essence that transcends time
> and space. Overseas Chinese, returning in Western trappings and bear-
> ing capital, but still physically Chinese (as expressed in phrases like
> 'black eyes and yellow skin'/*hei yanjing, hwang pifu*; 'our own bones and
> flesh'/qin gurou; 'our very own people'/ wo zijideren), become a symbolic
> affirmation of Chinese singularity, and at the same time, the transnatio-
> nalisation of Chinese essence.
>
> (Ong 1994: 17)

For another set of Asian states including Singapore, Japan, Malaysia and
South Korea, the initial stages of capitalist restructuring brought prosperity
and the continuation of a developmentalist state. Those Asian states which
prospered in the 1980s and 1990s found themselves importing rather than
exporting labour. The flows of both capital and labour across the borders of
these states was met not by breaking the bonds between state and nation but
a renewed nationalist rhetoric and efforts to consolidate a national population
that could continue to legitimate the state. These states have been interested
in regulating the labour flow tightly so as not to be overwhelmed by
immigrants making claims on the state or destabilising the fragile political,
economic and social contracts that bind together these societies. Political
rhetoric that racialises the social contract is being reintroduced. For example,
Japanese media and corporations justify the Japanese Immigration Law that
prohibits the entry of unskilled [foreign] workers by explaining that 'such an
influx might endanger the racial harmony of Japanese society' (Yoshino
1997: 210–11).[11]

At the same time, even these states have found occasion to incorporate
emigrant populations who live beyond the territorial boundaries of their
state. Japanese corporations have responded to labour shortages not by
legalising 'foreign workers' but by recruiting Brazilians whose parents or
grandparents were Japanese immigrants. According to Yoshino (1997: 211)
who has studied 'the discourse of blood and identity in Japan', the Japanese
media . . . do not problematise the racialised nature of the [recruitment] . . . –
'one will always be Japanese by virtue of blood' (also see Kong, this
volume).[12] As in the case of China, the Japanese are reviving and rehabili-
tating the older nationalist language of belonging which based citizenship
not on residence within the territorial boundaries of the state, but on an
inheritance of identity based on blood ties.

By 1998 structural adjustment policies were being imposed on many of the Asian 'tiger' states. These policies reduce governmental engagement in national economies, reduce price supports on food and fuel and cut back on government spending on education and health care. In other words, they reduce or eliminate aspects of the developmentalist state policies that have allowed some Asian states to maintain the political stability and integration. In light of these changes, and the real attacks they bring on the living standards of working people, the political leaderships of these states may be forced to search for alternative means of legitimating their state to an increasingly impoverished working class. At this juncture, states such as South Korea, with a sizable emigrant population and with a dual nationality law that dates back to the 1970s, may move more aggressively towards portraying themselves a transnational nation-state.[13]

The reconfiguration of political, military, and economic power in the world that has followed from the end of the Cold War and the emergence of the US as the sole military superpower and a central player in the formulation and implementation of World Bank policies is also contributing to the renewed significance and visibility of transnational nation-states. These trends may be affecting nation-state building in Asia.

In a global economy in which the US has emerged as one of the institutional bases for the organisation and circulation of capital, it has become increasingly important for foreign governments and corporations to influence US state policy. While US law limits foreign lobbies, citizens can serve as important protectors and mediators of the interests of their ancestral states and its corporate interests. Transmigrants may again appear as key actors and emigrant populations, if organised as transnational constituencies, can provide political support.

And so we return to Johnny Chung who is now in prison in the US for making illegal contributions to President Clinton's 1996 campaign. Immigrant political action in which US citizens often act in concert with political leaders of their home country is neither novel nor confined to Asian immigrants. However, for several reasons, the case of Johnny Chung is significant for the analysis of transnational nation-state building in an age of globalisation. The details behind the exchange of money reveal the ever-growing interlocking of corporate interests so that US and Chinese executives worked to subvert or change American laws and trade regulations that limited the export of US defence technology (Gerth and Sanger 1998). However, in the US media, these interlocking interests were portrayed as a 'China tie.' Despite the panegyrics to the global economy and the rhetoric of multicultural America by some US political leaders, the US media continue to fuel US nationalism by confronting it with a menacing Asian presence (Clinton 1996; Gerth 1998; Gerth and Sanger 1998: 1, 18; Ong 1997b).

Work has yet to be done to ascertain whether there will be a distinctive Asian configuration of these transnational political practices and their accompanying rhetoric. We do know that states such as Singapore have promoted a narrative of capital which envisions the development of an alternative Asian modernity (Dirlik 1997; Nonini and Ong 1996; Ong 1997a). We also know that as Ong (1997a: 33) stated:

> In Asia today, state projects of modernity are engaged in the production of national subjects, whereas alternative modernities associated with flexible accumulation celebrate self-propelling subjects. A major theme in this negotiation of modernity is the tension between the nation and its subjects.

What remains to be seen is whether Asian political leaders and emigrant populations will increasingly embrace reiterations and further developments of the ideology and practices of the transnational nation-state in response to this tension.

Whether the current resurrection and rehabilitation of concepts of the transnational nation-state is a positive or negative development depends on the social, political, and economic position of the evaluator. Even in this preliminary overview, it is clear that this particular package of both ideological construction and political practices brings differential benefits to those who participate in this political process or are affected by it. As with any nation-state building project, transnational nation-states are cross-class enterprises. For immigrants of varying classes settled abroad who are engaged in family strategies of transnational migration, the protection and representation of the transnational nation-state may assist them against anti-immigrant and racial attacks. This type of state formation may also assist immigrant entrepreneurs in their efforts to invest back home or develop transnational businesses. However, there are also a number of serious problems in such ideologies which are of concern to those of us whose interest is building the struggle for social justice and against economic exploitation and disparities. First of all, transnational nation-state building can serve to revitalise nationalist ideologies among middle and impoverished classes, in a period of disillusionment with post-colonial nationalism. The transnational spaces carved by immigrant networks but legitimated by ideologies of transnational nation-state become the locale within which immigrants imagine a brighter future. Their political energies are channelled away from struggles to change the politically oppressive and economically disparate circumstances within their national territory. Instead, poor and middle-class immigrants become supporters of a renewed transnational nation-state building that maintains and benefits the classes and individuals who currently hold power. Moreover the popularisation of nationalist ideologies among immigrant populations often fosters and reinforces patriarchal ideologies that restrain the freedom and equality of women (Espiritu 1996a).

There is also the problem of essentialism. The concept of the transnational nation-state, both past and present, are based on ideas of the fixed and biological bonds of descent that link emigrating populations to an ancestral territory and its state. These are bonds that go beyond culture and language. According to this conception of a national population, the descendants of immigrants, although they no longer speak the language of their ancestral country nor are familiar with its culture and history, may still be part of a national diaspora with claims to their 'homeland'. The designation of nationality on the basis of ancestry divides the world into racially distinct and forever separate populations. It has proven an ideology that has great political potency and a potency which political leaders have used historically as a justification for war and genocide. The transnational nation-state is built on exactly these ideas about race and nation.

While I have argued that nation-states are continuing to play roles within the globalising economy and that once again some nation-states are being constituted as transnational, my purpose is not to endorse these developments. On the contrary, I offer my analysis of these global trends as a call to confront both the language and the structures of essentialised differences that are re-emerging in the present historical conjuncture.

Notes

1 This chapter is the result of the support and encouragement of a number of individuals and institutions. Institutional support for research upon which the theoretical framework of this paper is based has been provided by the Rockefeller Foundation through a grant to Instituto de Filosofia e Ciências Humanas, UNICAMP, the Mellon Foundation through a grant to Yale University, the Graduate Dean's Research Fund and the Center for the Humanities of the University of New Hampshire and the Wenner Gren Foundation. Among the people who have provided encouragement and contributed intellectually to this paper and whom I thank are Linda Basch, Cristina Szanton Blanc, Josh DeWind, Bela Feldman-Bianco, Georges Fouron, Luis Guarnizo and Stephen Reyna. I am particularly grateful to Lily Kong, Kris Olds and Henry Yeung for the encouragement to address the Asian experience and present a paper at the conference they organised in Singapore in 1997. The paper builds on a framework about transnational migration and the deterritorialised nation-state which I developed jointly with Linda Basch and Cristina Szanton Blanc between 1987 and 1993.

2 Transnational nation-state building involves people from all classes and engages the energies of both men and women. More research needs to be done on how class and gender affect immigrant participation in transnational political activities.

3 This distinction has been emphasised by Mato (1997).

4 In the years after 1898 when the Philippines became a US colony, Filipinos were made 'nationals' of the US and regarded as 'wards' with rights of unlimited entry until 1935. However, they faced much discrimination and the general anti-Asian sentiments, and were prohibited from becoming US citizens and owning land. Their efforts to differentiate themselves as racially different from Asians and not subject to the same segregation were unsuccessful. For example, after Filipinos won exemption from miscegenation laws on the basis that they were Malays rather than Mongolian, California altered miscegenation laws to add Malay race to those prohibited from marrying whites (Pido 1986: 69).

5 The first wave of Filipino immigrants seems to have maintained relatively fewer transnational networks (Pido 1986). However Filipino intellectuals abroad were significant contributors to the development of the Filipino nationalist movement

that contested first Spanish and then US colonial rule, as well as to a literature connecting the immigrant experience to Philippine history and politics (Rafael 1998; Bacho 1997).

6 For several decades after the war, the Japanese government's primary concern was in reconstituting the basis of its legitimacy within its own territory. After their traumatic experience during the Second World War, persons of Japanese descent in the US kept their distance from the Japanese government, although they re-established their family networks. During this period, newly independent governments, such as that of the Philippines sought to build a national economy, and discouraged 'the brain drain' rather than seeking connections with emigrant populations.

7 See also Feldman-Bianco's (1992, 1994) work on Portugal as a 'global nation'.

8 I explore these differences in Glick Schiller (1998 and forthcoming).

9 Those immigrants who have been economically successful often have arrived with a relatively high degree of education (Chen 1992; Lessinger 1995). Even many of the highly educated immigrants experience downward social mobility, at least initially, because of their inability to speak English well.

10 Ong and Nonini have pointed out that overseas Chinese may employ rhetorics of transnational Chineseness without identifying with China as a nation-state (Ong 1993; Ong and Nonini 1996).

11 Japan actually has utilised a large number of illegal workers as well as having a large number of Koreans who are long-term residents of Japan or who were born there (Yoshino 1997).

12 By claiming its second and third generation immigrants settled in Brazil, Japan is creating a connection to the Brazilian and Latin American economy. At the same time, Brazil has found it useful to utilise its population of Japanese descent as a link to Asian economies and has recently changed its citizenship laws to allow dual citizenship to emigrants. This human bridge of Brazilian-Japanese (or Japanese-Brazilians) became the subject of direct negotiations between Brazil and Japan in 1997 (Feldman-Bianco personal communication).

13 When the South Korean government focused on political surveillance of its emigrants living in the US, the US did not challenge the transnational politics of South Korea. However South Korean participation in US politics was targeted in the 1980s when Koreans entered into the US political process, as have many immigrant groups and their home countries. Koreans were accused of trying to buy political influence (Awanohara 1994).

13 Globalisation, transmigration and the renegotiation of ethnic identity[1]

Lily Kong

Introduction: rethinking globalisation

Despite voluminous research on globalisation, there is growing acknowledgement that insufficient attention has been paid to 'globalisation from below'. Specifically, there is growing recognition of globalisation as a dynamic, contingent and contested process that impinges on and is in turn impinged upon by individual actors and social groups beyond the huge, imposing and overpowering structures of economy (Giddens 1996). In this chapter, I wish to emphasise the contingent nature of globalisation, that is, that it is not an 'out there' phenomenon, but 'an "in here" phenomenon' which involves 'transformations in the very texture of everyday life . . . , affecting even intimacies of personal identity' (Giddens 1996: 367–8). While much of the literature has focused its attention on globalisation in large metropolises, functioning as command and control centres, economic motors and knowledge-bases (Amin 1997), there is equally well a need to understand the experiences of individuals who people these metropolises that are constantly undergoing changes associated with globalisation. My particular aim here is to illustrate, through my empirical work on Singaporean transmigrants negotiating their sense of ethnic (Chinese) identity, the dynamic, contingent and contested nature of ethnic identity as it is constructed and reconstructed in a global context. I wish therefore to draw the literature on globalisation away from the study of formal, macroscale and quantifiable transnational processes to focus on the informal, microscale and qualitative experiences of everyday people (Boden 1994).

Specifically, my empirical questions centre on Singaporean Chinese transmigrants working in China, and their negotiation of Chinese identity. I ask the question: what happens to the sense of ethnic (Chinese) identity among Singaporean Chinese when confronted with transnational conditions in a predominantly Chinese context? What are the local and global forces that impinge on the ongoing (re)construction of ethnic identity of these Singaporean Chinese? In addressing the empirical questions, the larger theoretical answers that will emerge from this examination centre primarily on the nature of ethnicity in a world of increasingly intense and extensive social, cultural, economic and political interconnections,[2] and secondarily, on the nature of 'hybridity' and 'third cultures'.

Theoretical developments

Questions of identity

The issue of 'identity' is a slippery one. Simplifying from the vast literature, one view suggests an unproblematic conception of identity while another acknowledges that identity comprises unstable formations and sites of differences. As an illustration of the former, in liberal discourse, identity is assumed to be something that unproblematically connects individuals to society, with individuals who share some common trait thereby having an 'identity' as members of a particular group in society (Rouse 1995). On the other hand, recent developments in critical anthropology, feminism and cultural studies argue that identities are 'unstable formations constituted within webs of power relations' (Nonini and Ong 1997: 24). Identity, in this sense, is relational and conjunctural, and does not exist as an 'essence'. It is thought of as becoming rather than being (Hall 1989), as non-locatable in time and space (Shotter 1993), and as socially constructed (Jackson and Penrose 1993). The passage from an unproblematic conception of identity as the shared possession of 'norms' to the socially constructed, contested multiplicities of identity is closely bound up with the forces of globalisation. As increasing acknowledgement is given to the intersection of global capital and cultural flows on the one hand, and the local responses to and (re-)constitution of such flows, on the other, it becomes increasingly clear that identity – who one is, where one belongs, what one's place in the world is – cannot be understood as stable and static elements but as constantly balancing global patterns and local conditions.

Issues of ethnic identity

The long-standing division in views of ethnicity may be summarised as the primordialist and situationist positions. The former argues that ethnicity is ascribed, 'deeply rooted, given at birth and largely unchangeable' (van den Berghe 1978: 401). The situationist view argues that ethnicity is a phenomenon emerging from 'a constantly evoking interaction between the nature of the local community, the available economic opportunities and the national or religious heritage of a particular group' (Yancey *et al.* 1976: 397). In this view, the human being is 'seen as an active agent selectively and strategically presenting and displaying his [*sic*] ethnic emblems in ways he sees fit. Ethnic identity is merely 'a thing' subjected to manipulation and differential presentation; it is not a reflection of the true self' (Chan and Tong 1993: 143).

Rosaldo (1988), however, is careful to argue that ethnicity is 'neither completely expressive (and primordial) nor completely instrumental (and situational)'. Rather, it is usually both. Indeed, Chan and Tong (1993) take the argument further and suggest that there are specific times and situations when ethnicity tends towards being 'expressive' or 'instrumental'. They posit that the ethnic actor has a 'primary, core ethnic identity', a 'master identity' that is 'best expressed and nurtured in private' (the centre), which is expressive, but he/she also has a secondary ethnic identity that is expressed in public/the periphery, which tends towards the instrumental (Chan and Tong 1993: 146). In this sense, ethnic affiliation is more usefully seen as being located along a 'continuum of ways in which people organise and categorise themselves, ranging from chosen affiliation at one end to given membership at the other' (Horowitz 1975: 55), supporting Fishman's (1977) view of ethnicity as a phenomenological interplay between ascription and self-selection.

Interrogating Chinese identity

The literature on Chinese identity rivals that on globalisation, transnationalism and identity in volume, and at the risk of simplification again, the positions within it may be cast as those which adopt a unitary, if developmental view of Chinese identity, as against those which interrogate the multiplicity and instability of Chinese identity. The former is well illustrated in Wong's (1982) treatment of Chinese Americans, for example, in which he traces the generational development of their sense of ethnic identity. He argues that there is a sense of linear movement from one state of identity to another (from 'old overseas Chinese' or '*lo wah kiu*' to 'Chinese Americans' in which there is an increasing sense of 'merging' of 'Chineseness' and 'Americanness'). Within each state/stage though, Wong assumes a static notion of identity, and ignores any sense of conflict and negotiation, much less multiplicity and instability. In a parallel way, Gosling's (1983) work on Chinese identity in Southeast Asia similarly assumes that Chinese either adapt, accommodate or assimilate with their 'host' cultures. His call for total acculturation reflects the thinking about the nature of ethnic identity that was still popular in the early 1980s where there was little room for constantly shifting identities as it is understood in a global postmodern world.

Wang's (1988) discussion of changing Chinese identities in Southeast Asia moves the conception of identity along when he acknowledges explicitly the multiplicity of identities – historical, nationalist, communal, national (local), cultural, ethnic and class-based. He also adopts the notion of Chinese identity as underpinned by several norms, such as physical attributes, political loyalty, class interests and cultural values. This idea of ethnicity as possession of certain norms and values has been disputed in more recent literature.

One example of the arguments in this emerging literature is Nonini and Ong's (1997: 3–4) work on Chinese transnationalism as an alternative modernity, in which they argued that Chineseness is not about the possession of norms or values but about relations of persons to forces and processes of globalisation:

> 'Chineseness' is no longer, if it ever was, a property or essence of a person calculated by that person's having more or fewer 'Chinese' values or norms, but instead can be understood only in terms of the multiplicity of ways in which 'being Chinese' is an inscribed relation of persons and groups to forces and processes associated with global capitalism and its modernities.
>
> (Nonini and Ong 1997: 3–4)

Thus, instead of adopting the view of much of the traditional studies of 'overseas Chinese' in which Chinese in Hong Kong, Taiwan, Southeast Asia, North America and elsewhere are regarded as residual and imperfect replications of the 'real' Chinese culture in China, there is a need to acknowledge and investigate the nature of modern 'diasporic'[3] Chinese who have multiple orientations, possibly forming a third culture. They have more than a 'double consciousness' (Gilroy 1993), facing

> many directions at once – toward China, other Asian countries, and the West – with multiple perspectives on modernities, perspectives often gained at great cost through their passage via itineraries marked by sojourning, absence, nostalgia, and at times exile and loss.
>
> (Nonini and Ong 1997: 12)

Singaporeans in China: increasing transmigration in a global world

Fawcett and Carino (1987) have pointed out the shift in the global system of international migration in the last few decades of the twentieth century as one in which Asia and Latin America have taken over from Europe as the dominant regions of origin of migrants. The movement of populations from Asia has primarily been to destinations in Canada, the US and Australasia, the result of increased international linkages, increased prosperity and increased demands for political freedom (Skeldon 1994: 177–8). At the same time, within Asia, there have been significant population movements, particularly to areas of high economic growth. Right up till the early 1990s, the main destinations were South Korea, Taiwan, Hong Kong, Singapore and Japan. In the last few years, however, significant movements to China are evident with the rapid opening up of the China market. Singapore has certainly been responsible for a rapid increase in capital investments in China. While US$8.6 billion was invested in China between 1979 and 1994, in 1995 alone, a total of US$8.67 billion worth of new direct investment contracts were signed. The investments are in the provinces of Guangdong, Fujian, Jiangsu, Liaoning, Shandong, Yunnan and Sichuan (Chan and Tong 1996: 1). This has led to the increase in the numbers of Singaporeans working in China.

It is estimated that there are currently 1,000 Singaporeans based in Beijing although a far larger and inestimable number commute from Singapore frequently on short trips of a few days to a few weeks each time for work purposes. This trend of an increasing number of Singaporean transmigrants who straddle home and at least one other country for work has been encouraged by the government particularly in the 1990s with the drive to regionalise the economy. This has involved Singapore-based companies moving their operations to regional locations, a strategy aimed at enhancing their competitiveness and expanding Singapore's economic space beyond its limited geographical boundaries. While particularly active in the 1990s, this regionalisation drive in fact originated in 1986 when an Economic Committee, charged with charting economic directions for future growth, suggested measures to create a niche for regional operational headquarters and the export of services (Hui 1997).

Singapore companies responded to these exhortations by investing in the region, evidenced in the establishment of industrial parks in various countries: China, India, Indonesia and Vietnam. But beyond these industrial parks, many entrepreneurs also independently invested and set up operations overseas. In 1993 alone, 3,174 companies were established abroad, 33 per cent more than in 1990 and three times more than in 1981. China experienced the greatest increase in the number of Singapore companies established, from zero in 1981 to 16 in 1985 and then 181 in 1993 (Hui 1997: 112).

The empirical material for my subsequent discussion was collected in August 1997 in Beijing, a location chosen for a variety of reasons. Beijing is estimated to have the largest concentration of Singaporeans in China. Here may be found Singaporeans from a broad range of backgrounds and work experience, since they had independently sought out Beijing as a work and business destination, as opposed to the government-led Suzhou Industrial Park further east. As one of the major historical, political and cultural hearths of China with its 5,000 year history and tradition, Singaporeans in Beijing would have to negotiate their Chinese identity within a context where Beijing Chinese thought themselves to be 'superior Chinese', the centre of the Chinese 'kingdom' (see later discussion).[4]

Renegotiating ethnic identity in a global condition

Redefining ethnic markers

The markers of ethnicity are best understood not as universals, but as grounded in the particularities of specific contexts and everyday lives. I will argue that as contexts and conditions change with transmigrations, people re-evaluate and cope with their changing circumstances in a global world by constantly shifting their conceptions of ethnicity, and indeed, simultaneously adopting quite contradictory conceptions of ethnic identity.

My starting point is the question of how the ethnicity of Chinese in Singapore is understood. Clammer (1982) suggests, in thinking particularly about the Peranakan Chinese,[5] that religion, language and place of origin are all neither necessary nor sufficient conditions for ethnic identity. He argues:

> The key to Chineseness is . . . descent and appearance. Culture – speaking Chinese, eating Chinese food, etc. – may reinforce this basically racial self-concept, but these things do not constitute it, nor does their absence in the case of any given individual deny it.
>
> (Clammer 1982: 129)

Clammer's analysis, unfortunately, is not grounded in ethnographic work, and while logically correct, it will quickly become apparent in my empirical discussion that there are multiple logics, and that while people may recognise that which Clammer suggests, other logics suggest contradictions that they negotiate at an everyday level.

This sense of multiple constructions of ethnicity is evident in Tong and Chan's work (1994: 25), where they argue that 'what it means to be Chinese in Singapore is contested terrain'. Drawing on ethnographic material, they begin by arguing that ascriptive ethnic identity is most common: one is 'born' a Chinese, and the phenotypical attribute of skin colour takes precedence in the definition of a Chinese. This, they suggest, is because of Singapore's multiracial society[6] and the clearly different skin colours. At the same time, religion, language and education have become increasingly amorphous as markers of ethnicity. Some Chinese, for example, are Christians and are not confined to Taoism or 'Chinese religion'.[7] A large proportion of Singaporeans, regardless of ethnicity, speak English; and all the different groups share access and exposure to the same education. The single ascribed principle of birth (descent and origin) for ethnic group membership thus 'emphasises the "fact" of immutability and unchangeability of one's Chineseness' (Tong and Chan 1994: 12). Yet, at the same time, Tong and Chan also acknowledge that different groups of Chinese emphasise different ethnic markers. Thus,

> while the Chinese-educated felt a Chinese must speak, read and write Chinese, and follow all the customs and rituals, the English-educated tended to be more concerned with what they regarded as core values, the most often cited being 'filial piety', and the performance of key rituals, such as the celebration of Chinese New Year or Mid-Autumn Festival.
>
> (Tong and Chan 1994: 16)

In implicitly drawing attention to the contradictions between 'immutability' and instability of Chinese identity, Tong and Chan's (1994) analysis serves as the springboard to my empirical discussion in this section, in which I interrogate specifically the instability and contradictions of ethnic identity and ethnic markers, particularly when people are confronted with contexts and conditions other than ones they had originally developed their ethnic constructions in.

The questioning begins with Edward's[8] expressed perplexity: 'How is it that although we are of the same genetic link, we are still very different?' A year into his job in Beijing, Edward has come to question if his descent is what makes him Chinese, in immediate contrast to the primacy of descent that Tong and Chan (1994) identified as significant for Chinese in Singapore. The importance of phenotypical attributes has also receded now that Edward and other Singaporean transmigrants in Beijing find themselves in a context other than the multiethnic one in which they originally developed their ethnic constructions, particularly one in which most people are characterised by the same phenotypical characteristics.

In renegotiating their conceptions of Chineseness, interviewees most frequently called upon three ethnic markers: language, value systems and cultural practices defined as the practice of traditions and customs, and the engagement in Chinese arts. Rather than unquestioning adoption of these indicators as ethnic markers, they were expressed in contradictory terms: sometimes they were embraced as crucial markers of Chineseness; at other times, they were denied significance.

One of the characteristics most frequently mooted as a marker of ethnicity was language, and in particular, Mandarin. The sheer ability to speak a common language with the vast Chinese population in the 'heart of the motherland', as Edward put it, was enough to assure him of his Chinese identity. For John, the ability to communicate in Mandarin with 'the Chinese' makes him realise his roots: 'that I *am* Chinese'. Despite theoretical discourse which rejects the liberal position that identity is about the sharing of some common trait, interviewees clearly still adopt this position, and language becomes an important ethnic marker for interviewees. That it is Mandarin which these interviewees refer to points to the particularities of the contexts in which they are negotiating their ethnicity: Beijing, where Mandarin is the *lingua franca*, and Singapore, where 'Speak more Mandarin, less dialect' campaigns have sought to establish Mandarin as the *lingua franca* amongst Chinese. While similarity in substantive terms allows language to be identified as a common resource, it does raise the question of whether the lack of similarity in specific language ability in some other context would cause the importance of language as ethnic marker to recede.

This potential mutability is borne out even by some of the interviewees, who question the value of language as an ethnic marker. Meng Hao, who had earlier declared his sameness with the Chinese,[9] nevertheless is keen to emphasise that while he can speak the language, it does not indicate his mind-set and orientation because in actual fact, he thinks in English and translates into Mandarin. This is expressed in a variety of ways among interviewees, who indicated that true communication was not just about facility with a language but about the communication of meanings, the nuances and subtleties that are couched in history and steeped in culture. This is most pointedly expressed by Reuben who declares: 'You can understand Chinese, but you may not understand the Chinese'. This supports Chambers' (1994: 22) argument that language is not primarily a means of communication but above all, 'a means of cultural construction in which our very selves and sense are constituted'. Yet, Reuben has little difficulty in claiming Chineseness for himself despite his limited ability in the language, thus discounting in one breath the importance of language as an ethnic marker, which he had earlier asserted. It does not occur to interviewees that their constructions of ethnicity are inherently contradictory, and I would suggest that it is their transnational condition that contributes to this mutability. On the one hand, the heightened consciousness of ethnic identity that Singaporeans generally feel, the result of the institutionalisation and bureaucratisation[10] of ethnicity in Singapore and a historical legacy from colonial ideology[11] (Benjamin 1976; Clammer 1982; Siddique 1990; Tong and Chan 1994), stays with these interviewees even as they relocate. These interviewees thus recognise themselves as 'Chinese', and when confronted with the question of what makes them so, seek markers, including language. Yet, they also see, from their transnational location in Beijing that their language ability does not make them like the Chinese, whose language ability is better and extends beyond superficial communication. Sometimes, they are even confronted with a situation in which Caucasians (because of their transnational location) speak better Mandarin than they themselves do. They then have to re-evaluate the usefulness of language as a marker.

The same disharmony is apparent in the way in which interviewees attempt to come to terms with value systems and cultural practices as ethnic markers. Interviewees were quick to indicate how they had always conceived of the Chinese as conservative and filial, tradition-bound and custom-led, and steeped in Chinese arts, culture and history. These were the Chinese whom one encountered 'in the books', as Victor pointed out, 'the pre-communist, and particularly, pre-Cultural Revolution sort'. This construction clearly arises because their exposure to and contact with China was primarily through their parents and/or grandparents whose understanding of China in turn stemmed from the pre-Cultural Revolution days. Interviewees were keen to hold on to such values and traditions as ethnic markers and had gone to China thinking they would encounter the Chinese thus, perhaps even recovering some of their own Chineseness in the process. Yet, these indicators were no longer useful to define Chineseness because the Chinese no longer behaved in that way. Interviewees recognised that it was because they had gone through the Cultural Revolution while Singaporeans were still 'more traditional', continuing to uphold certain customs and festivals, maintain strong and close parent–child relationships, and embrace more conservative values. Some also recognised that while the traditions were not strongly apparent in Beijing, they may well be in more provincial and rural, or in Southern China. Nevertheless, in confronting Chineseness in their everyday settings in Beijing, interviewees were faced with several questions: Was Chineseness defined by what the present-day Beijing Chinese were, what the Singaporean Chinese thought they were, or what characterised the Singaporean Chinese themselves?

In confronting this dilemma, many interviewees adopted one or both of two negotiated stances to define Chinese identity. The first was to redefine what constituted a valid ethnic marker, thus choosing to define Chineseness in terms of what the Chinese are now. Various interviewees, for example, suggested that value systems were not indicative of a person's ethnicity. Second, a large proportion of interviewees indicated that they thought Singaporean Chinese to be 'more Chinese than the Chinese', in terms of the 'culture and thinking', 'of art and culture', 'rituals and customs', and 'morals and value system'. They thus chose to define the Chinese in terms of their pre-Beijing conceptions of Chineseness and even in their own Singaporean terms. Daphne articulated the views of many when she said:

> There are certain things that I find the local Chinese are even more liberal and less conservative in than me. So when that happens, it makes you feel that maybe you are even more Chinese than them. . . . Let's say, certain festivals like Chinese New Year. There are certain things that they don't do which we practise. And you think, how come? They are from the mainland so they should be more traditional than we are, but they tell you, no, we don't do things like that. It's old-fashioned already. So when such things happen, you find that there's a discrepancy in terms of practices between you and the local Chinese here. That makes me feel that, hey, maybe I am more Chinese than them. So for me, I think the Chineseness is equated with being conservative, being traditional.

The discrepancy that Daphne refers to may be attributed to the 'hybrid time'[12] (Pieterse 1994: 167) in which interviewees operate. Their constructions of Chinese identity are anchored in different historical moments. What they have been used to are constructions of Chineseness based on pre-Cultural Revolution China. Their location in Beijing now forces them to confront a different experience of Chineseness. Yet, for some, the desire to continue holding on to previous constructions prompts them to re-evaluate the Chineseness of the Chinese, thus 'disembedding'[13] themselves from the Chinese in two ways. First, they become disembedded from the Chinese in that they recognise the two 'ethnicities' are different and yet both are Chinese (in other words, they deny the value of various ethnic markers). Second, they become disembedded from the Chinese whom they see to be 'less than Chinese', thus valorising those very markers of ethnicity that they also simultaneously seek to deny. Such is the irony of the transnational condition.

Constructing multiplicities and hierarchies of Chineseness

Another way in which interviewees confront their Chinese identity in their specific transnational condition is to embrace the notion of multiplicities and hierarchies of Chineseness. They then situate themselves at different points in the hierarchy at different times in different contexts. This coping strategy is triggered when interviewees, having taken for granted their Chineseness in Singapore, now find themselves in a context where their Chinese identity must be questioned. As Edward confessed, 'Now I'm a bit confused because being a Chinese in Singapore and being a Chinese in China are completely different'.

Interviewees' response of calling upon the notion of multiplicities of Chineseness is constructed upon the hierarchies that Beijing Chinese are themselves said to believe in. As several interviewees point out, Beijing Chinese regard Chinese from other provinces as *wai di ren* (foreigners), 'looking down on them' from an 'elite' posture. Singaporean and other Chinese from outside China are looked upon in a different way, sometimes as the *hua qiao* (overseas Chinese) 'returning to the fold' of the 'mother dragon' (Reuben), sometimes as *wai guo ren* (foreigners) who happen to be *hua ren* (Chinese). The nomenclature is not incidental but indicates how positively or negatively one is being regarded. Interviewees suggest that the former is less fondly regarded than the latter. *Hua qiao*, having abandoned China, are currently returning now that the 'mother dragon' is opening up and doing well again. The latter, on the other hand, symbolise 'the best of both worlds', according to Reuben because

> locals like to be associated with expatriates. But whereas a Caucasian expatriate is culturally too far away, and there is no association, between Chinese and Chinese, you have an association, and there is the halo effect, so it's quite positive.

Interviewees adopt the concept of multiplicities of Chineseness quite readily, turning it to their advantage, because it provides them with the wherewithal to deal with the enigma of being Chinese and unlike the Chinese at the same time.

Searching for 'authenticity': maintaining and recovering 'Chineseness'

A third way in which interviewees confront their ethnicity is to search for a particular form of 'authentic' ethnic identity that they have constructed for themselves. This entails, first, an attempt to maintain an 'authentic' Chinese identity, which is rooted in Chinese rituals, traditions and customs common in Singapore, and second, to recover a 'lost' Chinese identity, that 'quintessential' Chineseness that was conceived prior to their arrival in Beijing.

The most common evidence of the attempt to maintain Chineseness is the simulation of Chinese traditions and ceremonies commonly practised in Singapore, even if these traditions are no longer widely practised in Beijing. One example is the celebration of the mid-autumn Festival, which the Singapore Club in Beijing[14] organises. Considering the singularity of climatic seasons in Singapore, the mid-autumn festival is a particularly misplaced practice there, but it continues to be celebrated with the consumption of mooncakes, and the parading of lanterns by children. This practice is re-imported into Beijing because as Edward puts it,

> We Singaporeans tend to remember. What we have back home is all this. So we tend to import it here.

This revival of a tradition (Featherstone 1993: 177) is a way of asserting a sense of Singaporean Chineseness that being away seems to prompt. It is a way of recreating a sense of place, what Dürrschmidt (1997) calls 'constructing familiarity around fragments' and what Chan (1994: 312) suggests is 'reproducing homeland culture'. It underscores the importance of the recreation of rituals and performances in maintaining meaning and identity (Connerton 1989, cited in Featherstone 1993).

The maintenance of Chineseness is not only achieved by importing rituals, it is as commonly, if not more commonly, the case that Singaporean Chinese return to Singapore to partake in a revalorisation of ethnic identity. The single most important festival in the Chinese calendar is the Chinese New Year, for which interviewees religiously make their 'pilgrimages' back to Singapore. The strength of conviction expressed to explain the need to return is stark. Peng Hong sees it as a need to return to his 'family home' so that his children may visit him and pay their respects at the 'family hearth'. Matthew and Wen Mei promised their respective mothers that they would be home yearly for the celebrations. Judy, Wee Kok and Chin Chin, who all visit Singapore twice a year, choose Chinese New Year as their only definite point of return, while the time of the second visit is always variable. For Anthony and Jane, the special significance lies in making it to the New Year's Eve reunion dinner when families traditionally gather together from wherever they may be. This is the sort of anchor that Wei Peng talks about, for

> someone who is international, who has lived abroad for many, many years. At the end of the day, you still need to have an anchor, and my anchor was being Chinese. That is where my culture is, my experiences and my outlook stems from being a Chinese.

Beyond seeking to maintain Chineseness through ritual performance and tradition maintenance, interviewees also attempted to recover a 'lost' ethnicity, often the 'Chineseness' that they conceived of prior to their arrival in Beijing. These 'culture building' efforts entailed engagement in activities to improve competence in Chinese arts, culture and history. This attempt stemmed from what they perceived themselves to be short on. As Michael articulated,

> When I was in Singapore, I didn't want to know about Chinese culture. I was not interested. But when I came here, it's a very rich history. The Chinese have a long history. When somebody tells me something about history, I listen . . . whereas in Singapore, I couldn't be bothered. I was more interested in Western things.

It also stemmed from their enhanced sense of pride at being a Chinese. For Shirley,

> I feel proud as a Chinese here. Everybody is Chinese here and I can see they are so proud to be Chinese. So I can sense that kind of pride.

In practical terms, it has prompted many of the interviewees to engage in activities that would enhance their 'Chineseness', such as learning to play a Chinese instrument, developing calligraphic skills, taking up Chinese painting, and learning classical Mandarin. Many hire tutors to help them. Others build up their library of books about things Chinese, visit museums, mine the media for programmes on Chinese history, arts and culture, thus managing to 'fill some of [their] hunger for finding out [their] Chinese roots' (John).

Acknowledging hybridities

Apart from negotiating their Chinese identity, interviewees also discuss the intersection of their Chinese and other identities, reflecting the hybrid space (Pieterse 1994) or 'translocalities' (Appadurai 1996) that they occupy (see also Friedman, this volume). This hybridity is apparent at two levels. First, Singaporeans acknowledge that they are hybrids to start off with, as Chinese who draw on 'Western lifestyles, Western schools of thought, Western education' (Matthew). Second, they become yet a different type of hybrid as a result of their transmigration, plugged in as they are in Beijing to an international community, a local Chinese community and a Singaporean community simultaneously. I will examine briefly each of these states of hybridity below.

Interviewees were quick to acknowledge that they were hybrids to start off with in Singapore. As Henry articulated, reflecting the views of many others, 'although I'm a Chinese, we live in a society that is greatly influenced by Western culture, and I feel that I'm a combination of East and West'.

Indeed, in the process of becoming more Westernised, Wei Peng is of the opinion that Singaporeans have 'lost some of their Chineseness'. This hybrid creature called a Singaporean Chinese represents a greater melange of cultures than the Taiwanese and Hong Kong Chinese, according to Wei Peng. Underneath a 'Western veneer', he argues that the Taiwanese and Hong Kong Chinese are still 'very, very Chinese' whereas 'Singaporeans, on the other hand, have become more Americanised, in that they have lost some of their Chineseness in their attempt to become a Westerner' (see also Li *et al.* 1995, for a brief discussion of the distinction between Hong Kong Chinese and mainland Chinese). Further evidence of this Westernised Chinese is borne out for Edward in the way in which he feels he relates better to those Beijing Chinese who have been exposed to education in the West. Some interviewees lament this state of hybridity that Singaporeans are thought to embody, suggesting that hybridity is a state in which people lose some of what they were before but gain less in turn in terms of what other people are. Victor articulates this less-than-ideal in-betweenness most pointedly in talking about Singaporeans' language ability:

> No matter how good we are in our so-called *pu tong hua* [Mandarin], we will never be able to match their language here. Likewise, even when we speak English when we go to England, the type of English we speak is quite different from what the local people speak. So in terms of language, there is always this difference. . . . Singaporeans are neither good for this nor that, language-wise. I mean, we don't speak English like the English, and we don't speak Mandarin like the Chinese people. So we are like half-castes, and they never respect us.

In this sense, a certain loss is implied, echoing Pieterse's (1994) notion of hybridity as a form of interstitiality that detracts from prelapsarian purity. It almost negates the value of a 'cosmopolitan culture' that Hannerz (1990) celebrates, a 'third culture' which allows people to communicate with like persons from around the world (Featherstone 1993).

Interviewees also recognise that they have developed a post-Singapore hybridity conditioned on their transnational existence in Beijing. This has had cultural as well as social implications. Culturally, a sense of confusion sometimes confronts them, as in the case of Meng Hao:

> I was thinking, 'Am I speaking English or Chinese?' . . . My daily language that I use now is Mandarin, but I can't write. So I am quite mixed-up. I prefer to read in English, but I converse in Mandarin the whole day and night. And then in my mind, I am wondering what it is I speak now? I am at that crossroads now, because I have lost my 'feel' with English, and I need to [improve] my Chinese. . . . So what am I? I am in transition. I am neither good here nor there. It's a very uncomfortable feeling at this moment. So when I meet Singaporeans,

I will be like, wow, the English is there. . . . When I compare with the Taiwanese and they start speaking Mandarin, I am like, I am not up there either. So it is a loss of something. You know you are losing grip with something, and hoping it's a transition. Either I classify myself as not a fully Chinese-speaking Singaporean or . . . but I don't think I want to classify myself as that now. So this is the difficulty.

This in-betweenness is also reflected in a sense of placelessness that inter-viewees expressed. Lam Kwong expressed this in terms of how when he was in Singapore, he missed Beijing, and how the converse was also true. In that sense, he felt that he was 'neither here nor there now', a condition which Chambers (1994: 17) described thus: 'One foot is here and the other always elsewhere, straddling both sides of the border'.

Socially, however, their transnationalism is a source of celebration, as Chin Chin and Wen Mei bear out. Their social relations are integrally intertwined with an international community of expatriates working in Beijing, ranging from British to Canadian to Taiwanese to Malaysians, while embracing the Singaporean community as well. For them, as for others, the experience gives them an 'outlook, a mentality' that is 'more open and not so inward-looking' (Chin Chin), which they variously describe as 'international' (John) and 'global' (Matthew). In denying that this outlook and mentality is completely Western or Eastern, they provide support for the argument that a 'third culture' develops in transnational situations, one in which trans-migrants 'become more flexible, and more able to adapt to different conditions' (John).

Exploiting ethnicity

While interviewees negotiate who they are in their transnational context, sometimes revealing a certain confusion and contradiction, they are neverthe-less clear about how they may exploit their ethnicity to their advantage, thus tipping the economic and power relations in their favour. This is an important question to address in examining how Singaporean Chinese renegotiate their ethnic identity, as so much of the literature indicates the fact that ethnic relations and interaction are not only about the articulation of similarities and differences in social symbols or cultural attributes, but about power relations, the ways in which symbols and attributes are produced and manipulated within the context of divergent material conditions, class interests and asymmetrical relations of power (Kakakios and van der Velden 1984). This is represented, for example, in the struggle for political, cultural and economic rights and access to social benefits (Fried 1983), often thought of in majority–minority dimensions. What I hope to illustrate in this section is that the manipulation of ethnic attributes also occurs 'intra-ethnically', between the Beijing and Singaporean Chinese. My empirical material suggests that Chinese identity is a 'resource' that is 'mobilised' even amongst Chinese, often for economic ends (see also Glick Schiller, this volume).

Interviewees were candid about two main ways in which they attempted to manipulate their Chineseness for economic gain. At an everyday level, when shopping for daily needs and when visiting tourist places, many choose to use their Chineseness to bargain and to pay local rates. Even while their accent might reveal them to be non-Beijing locals, many are happy to claim that they are from south China where the accents bear greater similarity to those of Singaporean Chinese. At another level, in the world of business and capital movements, many seek to emphasise their affinities with the Chinese in several ways. Some seek to accentuate the ability to communicate, arguing that 'when they are more comfortable in communication, it's easier because they will trust you more' (Edward). Others, through engaging in Chinese cultural activities, find a platform for facilitating opportunities and negotiating business deals. Participating in Chinese cultural clubs such as the *Qing Huang Dao Ju Le Bu* for Peng Hong is one example. Yet others highlight family and ancestral ties, such as Meng Hao:

> The way you do business is you have to find affinity, common ground. So [one of] my . . . strongest grounds [is that] my brother is in Fujian and I am half-local.

Finally, there are those who call on Chinese history, politics and culture for material ends. Meng Hao's appropriation of the Red Book and Long March provides the most interesting example. To motivate his mainland Chinese staff to achieve targets, he produced his own version of Mao's Red Book, replete with exhortations to perform. He also organised a 'Long March' and encouraged his staff to participate as testimony of their ability to persevere and achieve what appears impossible.

While ethnicity is a resource that is mobilised for gain, there are also times when the reverse happens, that is, when one's phenotypical attributes give one away as Chinese, which in turn elicits negative treatment. At an everyday level, being Chinese may mean that one is not given the same service as a non-Chinese (particularly Caucasian) foreigner because, as Choon Yong explained

> Beijingers are basically very proud. They don't want to serve another Chinese, especially southerners. Sometimes when you talk to them in Mandarin, they just don't bother. When you speak to them in English, you get better service.

Being a Chinese superior at the workplace may also mean that employees try to take advantage and make demands (of extra employment benefits) which they would not make on a non-Chinese foreigner. As Victor argues, the rationale is that 'you are my kind, so you understand my needs. I am poor, so you must make up for it'. In Richard's words, 'they treat us like a gold mine'. Indeed, Mark is of the opinion that there is no such thing as 'we are all Chinese' because 'there is no real advantage to being Chinese'. In fact, there may be outright problems in being Chinese, because of the resentment that builds up against other Chinese who have obviously done well economically. Whereas it seems more acceptable that Caucasians are better off, on the assumption that they have skills the Chinese do not, Beijing Chinese sometimes react to Singaporean Chinese rancorously because they feel 'whatever you can do, I can do better. Why must you be my boss? I can do the job here' (Choon Yong). Thus, precisely because of their obvious Chinese attributes, Singaporean Chinese are sometimes treated worse than if they were not 'obviously' Chinese. For this reason, transmigrants oftentimes do not attempt to translate their social and economic positions from Singapore to social and cultural capital in Beijing, evidence that is contrary to the findings of Glick Schiller *et al.* (1992: 12), because to do so would be tantamount to flaunting what they have, thus inviting negative reactions. This divergent conclusion stems simply from the fact that the transmigrants that have primarily been studied so far are poor migrants from Third World contexts and are mainly relocating to developed countries where per capita income is generally higher, while the reverse is true in my study. What this points to is a need to pay greater attention to the rapidly emerging type of transmigrant in a global world – not an unskilled 'labour migrant' who is escaping from the poverty of the homeland, but a highly skilled professional person bringing his/her expertise elsewhere (Mitchell 1993, 1997; Olds 1998).

Conclusions

In examining transmigration rather than abstract cultural flows or representations, I have explored the ways in which transnational processes are located within the life experience of individuals, making up, as Glick-Schiller *et al.* (1992: 50) say, 'the warp and woof of daily activities, concerns, fears, and achievements'. The importance of examining globalisation as shaping and being shaped by the experiences of individuals cannot be over-emphasised. The debates on globalisation must not only acknowledge the need for this micro-level of analysis but also engage more actively in such detailed empirical investigation. In focusing on the renegotiation of ethnic identity amongst transmigrants, I have illustrated how transmigration is a dynamic process of cultural heterogeneity and improvisation rather than a timeless site of cultural loss (Rosaldo 1989). What is evident from my empirical discussion is that transmigrants are active agents who both shape and react to global conditions.

To summarise, Singaporean Chinese transmigrants in Beijing negotiate their Chineseness in various ways. First, where appropriate, they deny or valorise the salience of certain ethnic markers (language, value systems and cultural practices), thus allowing them to claim Chineseness when they desire. Second, they endorse the Beijing Chinese conceptions of multiplicities and hierarchies of Chineseness, but overturn it by sometimes claiming to be 'more Chinese than the Chinese'. Third, they seek 'authentic' Chinese practices to maintain and recover their Chinese identity. In that sense, they are constantly looking between Beijing and Singapore for their ethnic identity, and this runs against the view of many migration studies that migrants either hold on to identities of their place of origin or abandon them and adopt new ones consonant with their destinations (Rouse 1995: 353). As I have illustrated, neither are totally true, nor entirely false. What the evidence does suggest is that constructions of ethnicity are historically and place contingent, as when Singaporeans expect to see the China of their pre-communist, pre-cultural revolution history books, or when they regard Chineseness as being that which they are familiar with in Singapore. This reflects Marsella *et al.*'s (1985) view that ethnic identity is shaped by the places where people have lived, particularly in their early years. By place, what is meant is not just the location, but also its history (Singapore's colonial legacy and its institutionalisation of ethnicity, or Beijing's 5,000 year history and its chequered role on the world stage) and its cultural practices (for example, in Singapore, the use of Mandarin, the practice of certain traditions and the celebration of certain festivals, or the lack of these traditions and customs in Beijing). To this extent, the reassertion of such constructions of Chinese identity suggest that place-based identity is sometimes revalorised rather than relegated to obscurity. This parallels Watts' (1996: 64) suggestion that globalisation is sometimes about reterritorialisation, not deterritorialisation. It may then be argued that particularity is a global value and what is taking place is a 'universalisation of particularism' or 'the global valorization of particular identities' (Robertson 1992: 130; 1994; see also Friedman, this volume).

Yet, my empirical material also suggests that place-based notions of ethnicity are sometimes challenged. When that happens, people are then confronted by a sense of dislocation. Under such circumstances, they begin to reconceive ethnicity as an arena of invention and reinvention, developing transnational affiliations and acquiring multiple identities. This is when ethnic identity cannot be simply regarded as a division of people into 'Us' and 'Other' because there is no simple straightforward conception of what constitutes 'Us' and what constitutes 'Other'.

Apart from renegotiating their Chinese identity, I have also dealt with two other issues pertaining to interviewees' identity negotiation. First, they address the question of their identities by thinking through the intersection of Chinese and other influences on themselves. In so doing, they confront their hybrid condition, and simultaneously celebrate and condemn it, further evidence of the lack of a master narrative in a global, transnational age, in this case, a master narrative that defines good and bad, authentic and inauthentic, pure and impure. Second, and similarly reflecting this constant contradiction, is the issue of ethnicity and its relationship to material conditions. While their Chinese identity is sometimes patently exploited for material gain, at other times, it can work against them materially. Thus, although the 'positionality' of individuals in social and power relationships (Li *et al*. 1995: 343) may be related to how ethnicity is appropriated, it is not a clearcut situation where ethnic 'belonging' suggests material benefit.

In sum, what I have examined in a specific empirical context is how ethnic identities are reproduced, negotiated, transformed and appropriated with transmigration. In theoretical terms, what I have illustrated is that ethnicity cannot be essentialised nor totalised, but in its multiplicity and trans-nationality, intermixture and hybridity, reflects instead the new circum-stances with its interplay of global and local, past and present, class and power relations. The result is the formation of 'new ethnicities' of sorts.

Notes

1 This chapter was written while I was Visiting Fellow at the Department of Geography, University of Melbourne. I wish to gratefully acknowledge Dr Jane Jacobs for facilitating the visit and the National University of Singapore for giving me time off.
2 As a shorthand, I refer to this reconstituted world as a 'global world' throughout the chapter.
3 I use the term simply to mean Chinese scattered across the globe. I do not take on board the implication that diasporic people 'imagine themselves as a nation out-side a homeland' (Kearney 1995: 553).
4 In-depth interviews were conducted with 30 Singaporean Chinese, four in small group contexts (with an average of four persons per group) and the rest as indi-viduals. The combination of techniques was necessary for practical purposes (to facilitate logistical arrangements) and useful for theoretical reasons since they allowed for situations where potentially sensitive and personal insights could be shared on an individual basis, as well as for the re-creation of social situations in which interaction may spark off particular discussions and insights amongst par-ticipants. All interviews were in English, with periodic injections of Mandarin and Chinese dialects. They were taped and transcribed. Interviewees ranged in age from their mid-20s to early 60s. Their length of stay in Beijing ranged from half a year to seven years, although in general, most had been there for about a year. There were 19 males and 11 females, an imbalance that reflects the general pattern among Singaporean transmigrants. While some of them were on corporate assignments, others were running their own businesses.
5 These are Straits-born Chinese who have mixed Malay and Chinese ancestry. They often speak a patois that combines Malay, Hokkien and English words and practise a form of 'Chinese' religion.
6 Singapore's population comprises about 77.3 per cent Chinese, 14.1 per cent Malays, 7.3 per cent Indians and 1.3 per cent 'Others' (*Yearbook of Statistics*, 1996).
7 See Kong (1991) for a characterisation of 'Chinese religion' in Singapore.
8 All interviewees have been given pseudonyms to protect their anonymity.
9 Henceforth, 'the Chinese' or 'mainland Chinese' is used to refer to Beijing Chinese in particular. I am not assuming similarities among Chinese in different parts of China and am aware of the dangers of essentialising and totalising.
10 The state in Singapore uses ethnicity as a primary social form of identification and the main form of socio-cultural classification.

11 When Sir Stamford Raffles, the founder of modern Singapore, designed Singapore's town plan in 1822, for example, he divided the city into quarters based on ethnic lines.

12 Vargas (1992) adopted the term from the Latin American *tiempos mixtos* and used it to mean the coexistence and interspersion of premodernity, modernity and postmodernity.

13 Amin (1997: 12) refers to 'disembedding' as the maintenance of lifestyles and life routines in new places by migrants. Tong and Chan (1994: 27) refer to it in the specific context of Singaporean Chinese as their act of distancing from the Chinese history, culture, tradition and heritage of mainland China, and a distancing from the local community in Singapore, where ethnicity, they argue, has become individualised and personalised, defined in terms of personal and family history.

14 This is a club for Singaporeans, run by volunteers. It organises social and sports events as well as business talks and luncheons. It has a membership of about 300, representing about 30 per cent of the estimated Singaporean population resident in Beijing. Although another 70 per cent of Singaporeans in Beijing are not members, a significant proportion attends the activities organised by the club periodically. It is also not uncommon that a member of the club has a spouse who joins in the activities but is himself/herself not an officially registered member.

14 Globalisation, postcolonialism and new representations of the Pacific Asian metropolis

Dean Forbes

The metropolis has been at the centre of both the economic growth and financial crisis that have characterised the Pacific Asian region in the 1990s. It has also occupied the centre stage of political events; been cultivated as home to the key symbols of nationhood; is disproportionately influential in the production and reproduction of culture; and embraces the tense social relations of modernising societies. Pacific Asian metropolises are, therefore, at the forefront of the globalisation process. The transparency of the urban landscape reveals the extent to which incorporation in a global economy, with its attendant cultural traits, value systems and routines of everyday life, sculptures that with which it intersects.

There are a variety of globalisation perspectives, inevitably providing a particular interpretation on the contemporary city, prioritising some processes and ignoring others. Two that are of some importance in understanding Pacific Asian cities are the political economy and postcolonial approaches. Political economy approaches highlight growing global economic integration and its impact on urban processes. Dimensions of urban change, from economic through to cultural relations, which either endure or emerge in subtly hybrid forms weakly linked to globalisation, tend to be neglected. Postcolonial approaches help identify and recover the underlying complexity of the metropolis.

Thus, political economy and postcolonial approaches together constitute two necessary, complementary approaches to a multidimensional understanding of the contemporary metropolis. However an imbalance between the emphasis given to the two approaches in recent literature needs to be addressed, and the balance recovered through greater emphasis on, albeit problematical, postcolonial approaches. The chapter begins by critically exploring contemporary representations of the Pacific Asian metropolis, with special attention to Singapore. The emphasis of these representations is on the political economy aspects of globalisation and, consequently, they risk neglecting other transient and enduring characteristics of the metropolis.

The role of cinema in representations of the city is the focus of the second part of the chapter. Two films of Vietnamese director Tran Anh Hung are used to look at contrasting representations of Ho Chi Minh City. The final part of the chapter seeks to explore ways of reconciling these different perspectives of the metropolis.

Globalisation, postcolonialism and the metropolis

> Globalisation as a concept refers both to the compression of the world and the intensification of consciousness of the world as a whole.
>
> (Robertson 1992: 8)

> Post-colonialism is the synthesis of what was imposed and what survived.
>
> (Thompson 1997)

In probing the significance of representations of Pacific Asian metropolises the concept of globalisation needs to be defined, and the political economy and postcolonial approaches to globalisation explored further. These approaches have distinct attributes, yet at the same time they overlap at the edge. More importantly, though, political economy and postcolonialism are inseparable.

The term globalisation has acquired layers of new meaning in the last few years, and is now the contemporary expression, albeit transformed, of many earlier debates. Notable among these strands, globalisation counts among its predecessors the Marxist and neoMarxist theories of development and under-development which emerged in the 1960s and 1970s and which centred on the expansion of capitalism and its articulation with precapitalist modes of production. It also draws on world systems theory and other variations of an essentially materialistic view of history. Thus political economy has become the dominant strand of analysis of globalisation. However contemporary usage of the term globalisation has acquired greater breadth and depth of meaning. Robertson (1992) stresses that it signifies neither a recent, nor an exclusively economic, closing together of societies.

The term postcolonialism likewise has a long history, and has been embellished over the years. In my usage postcolonialism is an approach intended 'to achieve an authentic globalization of cultural discourses . . . abolish all distinctions between center and periphery . . . and to reveal societies globally in their complex heterogeneity and contingency' (Dirlik 1994: 329). Thus postcolonialism is especially entwined with the search for identity, meaning and perspective. Yet it is not synonymous with poststructuralism, with its rejection of metanarratives, for supporters of postcolonial approaches 'still consider it vital to understanding the nature of power and privilege in the (post)modern world' (Jacobs 1996: 30).

Thus political economy and postcolonialism are mutually dependent approaches to globalisation. The economic dimension of imperial expansions (be they colonial or 'newly' global) is undeniable, as are the uneven divisions of power and privilege they produce. But explanations that rest too heavily upon this logic work only to re-centre the metropole by incorporating 'the world', and all that happens in it, into the accumulative logic of the core. The contingency of this logic, its need to negotiate an often reluctant and almost always transformative periphery, is clearly lost within narrow political economy accounts (Jacobs 1996: 16–17). Agency, the capacity of the 'periphery' to resist or transform is the essential dimension which post-colonialism highlights.

Postcolonial perspectives have been brought to illuminate the city in several prominent studies. Jacobs' (1996: 14) concern is primarily resistance (and 'complicity, conciliation, even blind disregard') to the dominant culture, expressed in aboriginal attempts to leave an imprint on the landscape of contemporary Australian cities.

What is common to these [postcolonial] perspectives is an attention not to the formal geopolitics of imperialism nor to a single political economy of 'the world', but a sensitivity to the culture of imperialism and those formations that might register as counter-colonial or postcolonial.

Representations of space and the metropolis

Globalisation has encouraged distinctive views about the production and reproduction of space, in which the urban is a vital part (Wilson and Dirlik 1995; King 1995; Dirlik this volume). It reflects the concern of scholars that the way in which places (or spaces) are defined, labelled and represented has a significant influence on the assumptions that are made about those places.

Arguments have evolved about the process by which global economic restructuring, the most powerful catalyst of restructuring within Pacific Asia,[1] is bringing about a 'borderless world'. This political economy perspective, often associated with the writings of Ohmae (1995), is also evident in a clutch of business books (e.g. Dobbs-Higginson 1994; Rohwer 1995) which are proliferating throughout the region. Implicit in this work is an emphasis on concepts of the corporation or the enterprise, financial transfers and flexible production. In this perspective, Pacific Asia is constituted by a string of production (and service) centres. These sites change with great rapidity as production is organised and reorganised in response to costs of production and constantly evolving consumer demand. In this view of economic restructuring particular places have less meaning; localities, in the sense of a complex web of distinctive interactions, are not important.

Among the most striking consequences of the impact of the global economy on the production of space within Pacific Asia has been the accelerated creation of new urban forms (Forbes and Thrift 1987; Lin 1994). A polarisation of development in a limited number of urban regions has occurred, encouraging the idea of the city-region rather than the city *per se*. Rohwer

(1995: 42) argues that these city-regions, like the other border-spanning regions which are important in Pacific Asia, through generating their own financial resources and striking agreements with foreign investors, have emerged as key economic actors. Moreover, they are becoming increasingly independent of central government economic control, except in terms of money supply and foreign trade policy.

The concept of the extended metropolitan region (EMR) highlights the penetration of large metropolises into their hinterlands to create new urban structures (Ginsburg *et al.* 1991; McGee and Robinson 1995). The evolving international division of labour has created new urban centres of capital accumulation in Pacific Asia which are extending their dominance further into their surrounding hinterlands, urbanising the countryside and enmeshing villagers into the urban economy. Huge EMRs comprising large cities and hinterlands of mixed rural and non-rural activities and incorporating transport corridors are a feature of the spatial transition in Asia.

In tandem with the expansion of the metropolis has been the impact of the global economy on the creation of 'world city' services within Pacific Asia (Friedman 1986: 72; 1995; Lo and Yeung 1996). Yeung (1995) argues that a new functional city system is emerging within Asia, hierarchically arranged with regard to urban services, not population. In his formulations Yeung includes Tokyo, Osaka, Nagoya, Seoul, Taipei, Hong Kong, Manila, Bangkok, Kuala Lumpur, Singapore and Jakarta within this network.

These world cities, it is further argued, form an emerging megaurban corridor linking together the major coastal urban regions of Pacific Asia (see Figure 14.1). The megaurban corridor is centred on air, surface and sea transportation corridors and telecommunication linkages (Rimmer 1993, 1995, 1996, 1997; Douglass 1995; Yeung 1995; Yeung and Lo 1996; McGee 1997). A cluster of cities and corridors focus on northeast Asia. The Bohai Rim region draws together major cities such as Tokyo, Osaka, Seoul, Pusan, Beijing, Tianjin and Shanghai (Choe 1996). Another megaurban region is based on southern China and Taiwan, connecting Hong Kong, Guangzhou and the Zhujiang River delta region, together with Taipei and the adjacent Chinese mainland cities such as Xiamen. Yet another megaurban corridor links the major Southeast Asian cities along the corridor that runs from Bangkok, down the Malay Peninsula incorporating Kuala Lumpur and Singapore, and along the Sumatran coast and through Java. These representations of a new space economy somewhat overstate the tangible links between places within these corridors.

Singapore as global hub and world city

Within southern Pacific Asia Singapore is repeatedly claimed to be the most global of the metropolises. This representation of Singapore as a world city and hub of an evolving megaurban region (and global network of cities) is

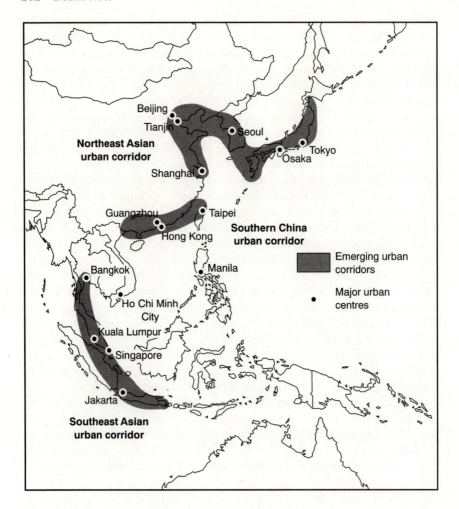

Figure 14.1 Emerging Asian Pacific urban corridors
Sources: Based on Douglass 1995: 54; Rimmer 1993: 198; Yeung 1995: 83.

often elaborated, with remarkable consistency, in government, business and
scholarly literature. The consistency of this representation is helping to construct a very powerful image of the island state, albeit not an uncontested one.

Although the city-state's prominence in services predates independence,
credit is generally given to the People's Action Party (PAP) government,
and its long-term leader Lee Kuan Yew, whose advice is now sought in the
globalising economies of China and Vietnam. Singapore's regional and
global role continues to be strongly steered by government policy, evoked in
the term 'a developmental city state' (Perry *et al.* 1997). Government statements are a significant means of establishing and reinforcing an image of

Singapore, especially in embellishing Singapore's world city aspirations. No other Southeast Asian government has succeeded in emulating Singapore's harnessing together of its image-making and economic development strategy, although the Malaysian government, through such high profile developments as the Multimedia Super Corridor, has tried to do so.

Prime Minister Goh Chok Tong has used the metaphor of 'the next lap' in order to both establish continuity with, and differentiate between, the present regime and the PAP strategies under the leadership of Lee Kwan Yew. Goh's intention is clearly stated: 'Singapore is positioning itself as a hub for high value-added manufacturing, international business services and innovation' (Goh Chok Tong 1996). The metaphor of the hub has become central to Singapore's world city status in current government literature, and is a very prominent feature of the public face of the Singapore government.

The powerful and very influential Economic Development Board has launched a strategy titled International Business Hub 2000, which it calls 'a framework for promoting the services sector based on a cluster approach [which] aims to develop Singapore into an international business hub and a service gateway into the Asia-Pacific' (Ministry of Information and the Arts 1997b: 117). The four service clusters of the programme are education and healthcare, communications and media, logistics (which is to shift emphasis from asset-based to knowledge-based management) and the expansion of the establishment in Singapore of regional headquarters (Economic Development Board 1997).

The Ministry of Information and the Arts (1997a), which has a key role in the construction of the image of Singapore, defines its mission as being:

> To help inform, educate and entertain, as part of our national goal to make Singapore a hub city of the world and to build a society that is economically dynamic, socially cohesive and culturally vibrant.

Parallel themes are echoed throughout the city-state. The National Computer Board (NCB) (1997) is responsible for the Information Technology 2000 masterplan, which is a core feature of a world city strategy. The NCB expresses its vision around the global hub concept:

> Singapore, the Intelligent Island, will be a global centre for science and technology, a high-value location for production and a critical node in global networks of commerce, communications and information.

Perhaps the clearest, and least critical celebration of Singapore's merits as a hub city suitable for international business permeates the popular business literature. The city seems to have successfully incorporated so-called 'Asian values' into flexible Western business strategies (see Thrift, this volume). Singapore regularly scores highly on measures of attractiveness to international business executives, its location and infrastructure providing an almost unbeatable combination (Perry *et al.* 1997: 18). This image is reinforced in numerous publications celebrating the recent economic progress within Pacific Asia.[2] Rohwer (1995: 37), for example, enthuses about a city 'which is richer than half of Europe and ticks as precisely and pristinely as Frankfurt or Zurich'. Dobbs-Higginson (1994: 335–6) refers to:

> this diamond-shaped island [which] glitters as one of Southeast Asia's brightest economic gems . . . the country works like a well-managed small business, epitomising the best of the Chinese character . . . things hum in Singapore. The place is clean, orderly and prosperous.

While the terminology differs, the scholarly literature on the political economy of globalisation also focuses on Singapore's hub status. The island's recent economic history has been dominated by its trading and entrepot role, but this has masked several shifts of economic strategy. One of the most important, in terms of defining Singapore's location within the global economy, was the shift from import-substitution oriented to export oriented industrialisation in the 1960s (Huff 1987).

Singapore was designated an emerging world city in the initial formulations of the concept by Friedman (1986). In recent years, scholars have given more attention to Singapore's evolution as a world city (see Yuan and Choo 1995; Chua 1996; Forbes 1996: 43–7; Macleod and McGee 1996; Perry *et al.* 1997: 15–22). Arguments supporting Singapore's position as a 'world city' largely centre on its high order service sector functions. The Singapore economy is among the most internationalised in the world, with very high levels of foreign direct investment relative to GDP. Aided by the uncertainty created about Hong Kong following its re-absorption into China, it has also become an important centre for foreign multinationals to establish regional centres from which to springboard into other Pacific Asian economies. A late 1996 estimate by the Singaporean Economic Development Board suggested approximately 2,000 companies have established regional offices in Singapore (Perry *et al.* 1997: 17).[3]

The strategy by Singapore to provide a base for overseas investment has taken several different forms. First, the Singapore growth triangle, which links together Singapore with the Riau Islands in Indonesia and Malaysia's province of Johor is a distinctive form of metropolitan expansion (Macleod and McGee 1996; Perry 1998). The rationale underpinning the region is that it combines Singapore's capital, technology and managerial talent with the land and labour resources of southern Malaysia and island/coastal Sumatra, thus sharing development between the three participant regions. Second, significantly the Singaporean government and corporate sector has also expanded well beyond its immediate hinterland. High profile, targeted investments in China include development by the Jurong Town Corporation of a 7,000 hectare industrial park in Suzhou and a 1,000 hectare industrial park in Wuxi, which each form the centrepiece of so-called industrial town-ships. While these focused investments have yet to live up to expectations, they illustrate the way in which the Singaporean state has sought to accelerate Singapore's economic integration with Pacific Asian countries. Third, the Singapore government has sought to establish the city as a regional tourist hub, hoping to simultaneously expand tourist income and also promote the regionalisation of the Singapore economy (Chang 1998).

Singapore's services performance and infrastructure have provided the impetus for its world city role (Perry *et al.* 1997: 15–22). Financial services are well developed, particularly in terms of foreign exchange dealing and commodity trading. Intracity and international transport and communica-tions are effective, with information technology a particular priority (Wong 1996). Government is stable and untainted by the serious corruption that plagues neighbouring countries, especially Indonesia. The developmentalist, hub city orientation of the city has had to be supplemented by explicit atten-tion to the city's bio-physical environment, although these competing ideolo-gies have sometimes clashed (see Ho 1998). Nevertheless, an improved environmental orientation has added to the direct business related services and created a high quality of life for the well remunerated, as a result of good standards of housing, health, education, recreation and consumer services. Illustrative of the attitude to planning and its representation within academic discourse is Yeung's (1987) description of Singapore (and Hong Kong) as 'cities that work'.

Representing the Pacific Asian metropolis – as a world city or part of an emerging megaurban region – is an important departure from past images of the city. These consciously constructed 'imaginative geographies', illustrated by the portrayal of Singapore, attempt to outline the dimensions of the impact of globalisation on Pacific Asia's metropolises. In the case of Singapore, the representations are cumulative; they build and reinforce the image of a dynamic, world city, poised to become a significant hub in the global economy. Singapore's shortcomings, such as the restricted availability of labour which makes it dependent on short-term immigrant sources, excessive government control of information circulation (most recently, Singapore has led moves to censor use of the Internet), and the very high cost of land and building space, have done little to affect the construction of this world city image.

Singapore's aspirations to be, and characterisation as, a 'hub city', or a 'world city', is closely connected to its ability to forge a niche in the global economy. The political economy approach to globalisation highlights the emergence of a representation that centres on the success with which the city has begun to exploit that niche. To provide a contrast, and pursue other aspects and interpretations of globalisation, I will now consider a different dimension of representation of a different city, through a different medium, and attempt to explore postcolonial perspectives of the Pacific Asian city.

Representation of the metropolis in cinema

Representations of cities in film[4] are a particularly important, and fertile, source of insight (Clarke 1997). In contrast to the overtly political economy emphasis on globalisation in the earlier discussion, cinematic representations of the city highlight the life of the individuals who inhabit the city rather than the urban space itself. Individual responses to their circumstances take precedence over the structural contexts that provide boundaries for their behaviour. As an illustration, Hutnyk (1996) uses writing, photography and film to explore the way in which the 'rumour of Calcutta' is composed and transmitted by Western 'travellers'. These

> technologies of representation give focus to the imagery which enframes Western views of Calcutta: decay is not simply there, it is sought out, fore-grounded, represented, and becomes a tourist attraction.
>
> (Hutnyk 1996: viii)

Film is of some importance in understanding the ways in which geographies are constructed, and is becoming increasingly influential in the representation of Asian societies, replacing the literature of Maugham and Kipling in its influence on public perception. Hutnyk (1996: 178) makes the somewhat ambitious claim that 'film offers the closest mimetic approximation of an "unmediated" human perception'. However, film is not a transparent medium, any more than any other text, such as a travel book or scholarly text. Moreover the production of film is itself complex and value-laden, and the political economy of production and distribution of considerable signifi-cance to the effect film has on its audience.

The films of Tran Anh Hung

Asian cinema in general, and Vietnamese cinema in particular (see Charlot 1994), is an important way of helping to identify fragments of an emerging postcolonial perspective on the urban. Two recent films by Vietnamese director Tran Anh Hung have made their presence felt in Western cinemas. *The Scent of the Green Papaya* (1993) and *Cyclo* (1995) are of interest to an under-standing of the way in which cities in Vietnam function because they are an indigenous construction of urban Vietnam, told through a story of the rhythms of daily life in Saigon/Ho Chi Minh City. Such an explicit, yet critical, reading of a major Vietnamese city at different points in time, makes these two films unique. Unlike many of the contemporary films pro-duced by Vietnamese filmmakers, under the close supervision of government agencies, they maintain a greater distance from the influences of state ideology. Moreover they give us a perspective on globalisation from the inside out; that is, they provide a postcolonial viewpoint that does not overtly privilege the global, but nevertheless does not ignore it.

Saigon/Ho Chi Minh City is a city whose citizens have maintained significant linkages with the outside world. The French colonial administration which controlled the city from the 1880s to the 1940s imposed not only a bureaucratic structure but left their imprint on the urban landscape (the architecture) and the people (the food, language). America's flirtation in the 1960s and 1970s was much briefer, but just as intense, as the material of war was packed into an expanding city filling up with the refugees from rural battles. Beginning in the mid-1970s the city briefly turned in on itself as liberation and socialism were imposed before Vietnam's economic reform (doi moi) in the late 1980s opened the city once again to integrate back into the regional and global economy. Saigon/Ho Chi Minh City's residents might justifiably feel at the forefront of the globalisation process, yet they retain a sense of Vietnamese-ness that Tran Anh Hung deftly explores.

Tran Anh Hung was born in Vietnam in 1962, before leaving for Paris with his family in 1975. He made two short films in 1988 and 1991 before his two major efforts, both of which were French co-productions. *The Scent of the Green Papaya* was shot on a set designed with considerable attention to detail by Tran Anh Hung in Paris, whereas *Cyclo* was filmed in Ho Chi Minh City, with, of course, the approval of government.

Both films have won international recognition. *The Scent of the Green Papaya* won the Camera d'Or Award at the Cannes Film Festival Awards and was the first Vietnamese film submitted for the Best Foreign Film competition (and was subsequently nominated) at the Academy Awards. *Cyclo* was Winner of the Golden Lion for Best Film at the Venice Film Festival (1995), among other prizes. Despite their critical acclaim, these are both essentially 'art-house' movies, which of course limits their impact, just as Satyajit Ray's depictions of Calcutta are less influential than Roland Joffe's in *City of Joy* (Hutnyk 1996: 177).

Both Tran Anh Hung films centre on a poor, working class character struggling to cope with a demanding urban existence. *The Scent of the Green Papaya* is set in Saigon during 1951 and 1961. A young woman (Mui) makes her way to the city and is employed as a domestic servant in a middle-class household. The quiet, brooding atmosphere within the house is the backdrop to the routine chores of everyday life and the subtle, but tense, relationships between the servant, her co-worker and the family. The patient execution of routine daily tasks, such as the preparation of the green papaya which is chopped in pieces and eaten as a vegetable, conveys the feeling of everyday household life. The daily rhythms are dominated by cooking, cleaning and disjointed snatches of conversation with family members and neighbours. Sparse dialogue symbolises the importance of non-verbal communication among household members, contributes to the moody atmosphere and highlights the significance of daily chores in the lives of the key characters.

The second part of the film switches to 1961. Mui is now in her 20s and is employed in the household of Khueyen, a composer of music with a passion for Chopin and Debussy. Khueyen's fiancée is highly Westernised and becomes more and more jealous of Khueyen and Mui, even though no overt relationship exists between the two. Eventually the fiancée departs, raising the question of whether this symbolises the rejection by Khueyen of the West, represented by his fiancée. Khueyen and Mui grow closer, eventually falling in love. The director explains: 'Western seduction is based on a very dynamic game of force, of bumping into one another . . . The other form, which is more Asian, is what I call impregnation. It's very different. First of all, people avoid one another. Then they create opportunities to be in the same place, to meet one another. Little by little, they become indispensable to each other' (Cross 1993: 35).

'Globalisation' impinges on the lives of the characters in the films, but in carefully defined ways. The placidness of domestic life is juxtaposed with the off-screen turmoil of the city. The servant leaves her rural home to migrate to Saigon, but the film gives no clues as to why this occurred. Only infrequently does the turmoil of the city, created by the fighting between the Vietnamese nationalists and the French, and later between north and south, briefly intrude on the film. Tran Anh Hung explains that 'big picture history' cannot coexist with 'the little story', even though they are the same in the French language: he chose 'the little story'.

Does Khueyen's spurning of his fiancée and eventual expression of love for Mui symbolise a rejection of the West and an embracing of Asia? Probably not. Khueyen himself is urbane, Westernised and fascinated by Western music. He is no hero of the director, who describes Khueyen as 'kind of a shifty guy who, inside himself, is weak' (Cross 1993: 35). Moreover, in the closing sequences Mui puts on Western lipstick, mimicking Khueyen's fiancée. This is no rejection of the West, just a shake of the cherry tree.

Cyclo is also set in Saigon, though it is now the early 1990s and it is called Ho Chi Minh City. The city is at the forefront of Vietnam's economic renovation, the population responding with alacrity to the possibilities of private enterprise and joint ventures with eager foreign investors. The bureaucracy struggles to maintain control, but is defeated by its own need to become more entrepreneurial to survive. Corruption is rampant, and illegal economic activities are growing in significance.

The cyclo is a trishaw, or pedicab, and once a common feature of Asian cities. There were about 40,000 cyclos (or trishaws) operating in Ho Chi Minh City in 1995. Life is a hard grind for trishaw riders and made more difficult by city authorities who have recently banned cyclos from 50 streets within the city centre. A cyclo riders' association argues for greater support for the riders unable to continue earning enough in the outer parts of the city.

Cyclo recounts the story of an un-named 18-year-old cyclo driver who scrapes a living with remarkable grit on the busy streets of Ho Chi Minh City, until the theft of his vehicle deprives him of his means of support. The first part of the film dwells on the life of the cyclo rider and his links with his family and friends. He spends most days on the streets peddling his poor and middle-class customers around the inner city beneath a stifling sun. The cyclo's parents are both dead, his father, also a cyclo rider, having been killed in a vehicle accident. He now lives with his grandfather who mends bicycle tyres, a younger sister who shines shoes after school, and an elder sister who carts water to the market. They are part of Ho Chi Minh City's underclass, their home a gloomy wooden structure of two rooms. As in *The Scent of the Green Papaya* Tran Anh Hung patiently allows his characters to reveal themselves through their routine tasks.

When the cyclo's vehicle is stolen from him life spirals downwards. Unable to pay the owner (the Boss Lady) the young man is forced to become more closely involved with local thugs and is lured into crime. His elder sister is likewise driven into prostitution by the family's poverty, her pimp also being the leader of her brother's criminal gang. The film is as violent as *The Scent of the Green Papaya* was placid, and a sharply different picture of the city, dwelling on the criminal underbelly, emerges. The ending is ambiguous, with the cyclo tipping paint over himself and holding a goldfish between his lips, perhaps signalling his descent into madness.

The off-screen environment of the city is very different from that portrayed in Tran Anh Hung's other film. The fighting with the French and the civil war has ended but now the characters are buffeted by a rampantly marketising economy. Cyclo riding is one of the few legal occupations open to young men from poor families, or those whose families were identified with the government of the South during the Vietnam War. Their day-to-day struggle to earn a living on the streets typifies the rapid expansion of the informal sector in Vietnam since the late 1980s. At the same time the expansion of criminal activity is a product of the restructuring of power within the city that accompanied economic reform, while the demand for drugs is a continuation of the drug trade during the American presence in Vietnam in the 1960s and early 1970s. All cash transactions between the characters are in American dollars, symbolising an underlying theme of globalisation.

There are several important themes implicit in both these filmed representations of Saigon/Ho Chi Minh City. The first is the significance of the routines of everyday life captured by the patient documentation and slow moving camera shots and exquisite visual framing of the film maker. Tran Anh Hung's two films are exceptional in this regard: he is seemingly unimpressed by the need for pace, action or dialogue, and instead confident in the arresting quality of the characters' mundane tasks. This minimalist, 'little story' approach, stands in sharp contrast to scholarly writing on the Asian city.

The second is the understatement of the external environment represented almost exclusively by off-screen events. The viewer is acutely aware that 'globalisation' is a backdrop, but the rhythm of urban life continues, given shape as much by routines and individual relationships as by the cataclysmic changes which we associate with globalisation. This is not an argument against the 'big picture' approach. Quite the contrary. The point is that the 'big picture' does not take precedence.

Third, Tran Anh Hung displays an ambivalence about the West. He over-simplifies in his implicit references to an Asia–West dualism. And he has been accused of naiveté (even phallocentricity) in his portrayal of women, apparently oblivious to contemporary feminism. Though *The Scent of the Green Papaya* is dominated by its female characters, and the Boss Lady is a strong figure in *Cyclo*, the women in his films are seemingly less in control than controlled. Tran Anh Hung replies that his aim is to show the suffering of women, and with historical veracity. He says: 'What was important for me was to create a specific rhythm, to find the very movement of the Vietnamese soul' (Cross 1993: 35). Perhaps his struggle is with himself, as after years in Paris he seeks to reconcile auteur and identity in his representation of Vietnam and the Vietnamese.

New perspectives on the metropolis

Accelerating globalisation, in its economic, social and political sense, has provided an impetus to the creation of new, imaginative representations of Pacific Asian urban areas. Yet it is the economic dimensions of globalisation which provide the dominant, underlying architecture of current representations, exemplified by the discussion of Singapore and the world city. As a result, the political economy approach to the city almost always prevails in current academic discourse. However, it is argued in this chapter that these need to be broadened and diversified, as the limitations of the approach become apparent. Accounts of the contemporary Pacific Asian metropolis draw on modernist traditions which originated in Western social science, and especially political economy. These arguments embody an assumption that the economic features of globalisation have precipitated a process of restructuring within Pacific Asia resulting in continued growth and expansion of the metropolises and the forging of increased links along urban corridors.

This pattern of urban change is consistent with the high levels of inter-regional economic integration within Pacific Asian economies (Forbes 1997a: 15–17; see also Higgott, this volume). Corporations, it is argued, have been able to exploit locally the advantages of the product cycle, shifting production from country-to-country within Pacific Asia as costs of production change and new low-cost centres are sought out. The emerging urban corridors within Pacific Asia, and these metropolises' connections with other world cities, are patterned on the economic linkages which have emerged between nations.

The political economy approach to globalisation is often biased by assumptions of top-down determination, in which capitalism and modernity simultaneously homogenise and differentiate. The representation of the metropolises and urban corridor growth which are emerging in Pacific Asia highlight the features which help to differentiate them from large cities in other parts of the world. In themselves, many of the characteristics of the Pacific Asian metropolis, such as their very large size or emergent world city characteristics, are not unique. However these cities are acquiring new, distinctive characteristics. Singapore is a good example of this. The government's commitment to developing as a regional hub through, for example, the Growth Triangle, and a global hub through its attractiveness as a site for regional corporate headquarters, is helping to fashion new space economies that reconfigure economic linkages and transcend national boundaries. The articulation of these expressions of new kinds of regional identity herald the emergence of postcolonial space.

The political economy approach to the metropolis, as Jacob's (1996: 6–17) alluded to in the quotation cited earlier in this chapter, is an essential part of explanation. However postcolonialism points to the inadequacy of essentialising understanding as 'the accumulative logic of the core'. Hence the argument upon which this chapter is predicated, of the need to draw interpretations of globalisation from both political economy and postcolonialism. Yet how can the political economy and postcolonial perspectives be reconciled? By exploring issues of authorship, representation, everydayness and resistance.

Authorship is important because postcolonialism pushes scholars to search out the different sources of representation of a metropolis. Knowledge of the contemporary Pacific Asian metropolis has been disproportionately the product of Western academic social scientists, supplemented by consultants and staff from international development agencies. Increasingly, though, Pacific Asian scholars are providing significant inputs to the accumulating knowledge about cities. Moreover, so too are politicians and bureaucrats helping to shape the debate about the metropolises, the proactive Singapore government among the most important. Almost all of these perspectives on the Pacific Asian cities are characterised by hybridity, in which Westernised concepts (narrative, statistical analysis, the text as preferred medium of expression) and the English language are used to stamp an indigenous interpretation of urban development on this research field.

Yet hybridity and the reconceptualisation of space, which are essential to this project, also create new questions about identity and ownership. In a region rapidly reconfiguring, in which metropolises and their networks provide spaces separate from the nation, who is entitled to authorship? It could be argued that the continuing input of Western academics is an imposition, an attempt to conceptualise and hence appropriate Pacific Asia's urban future. Yet this argument ignores the fluidity and reconceptualisation of postcolonial space itself. Pacific Asia is, after all, a transient, contested construct. In a reconfigured postcolonial space, in which questions of identity have become more complex and disputed, inevitably the imagining of new urban forms will come from many different sources.

There is evident in much of the writing on the new metropolises a lack of consciousness of the problematical nature of representation (Hutnyk 1996). That is, little attention is given to a critical assessment of the assumptions which underpin different perspectives of the metropolis, and the way these reinforce (or sometimes subvert) particular images of the city. An intriguing question, yet to be adequately addressed, is how are Pacific Asian metropolises and megaurban corridors being represented in order to make them palatable to their residents? Although a plethora of studies over many decades have established the importance of cash incomes and net economic gains in attracting migrants to large cities, few have asked why people want to remain in very large, congested, and generally expensive metropolises.

The Singapore government devotes much attention to creating the appropriate images of Singapore, both for domestic consumption and to enhance the city's attractiveness as a hub. In this it seems remarkably successful. However other major cities within the Pacific Asian region have generally more negative images. This raises the question of what attracts people to places such as Ho Chi Minh City (or Jakarta), and what keeps them there? Most scholarly accounts, quite correctly, centre on the economic opportunities that are concentrated in the metropolises and reinforced by the kind of globalisation that the region is experiencing. Cultural issues are a significant dimension of the globalisation argument, but largely absent from the literature describing the new urban forms.[5] Thus we need to understand what it is about the social and cultural environment of the metropolises which complement their economic drawing power and make them such magnets to people. The breadth and diversity of urban sub-cultures can be explored through different mediums of representation, such as film and literature. The cinema, as illustrated by the work of Tran Anh Hung, with its sub-text of representation of the urban, provides a perspective of the city totally absent from other accounts and inaccessible to most scholars.

Globalisation changes the parameters of urban life, but the resilience of cities and their residents, and the otherwise ignored urban landscapes, also need to be identified. A postcolonial approach to Asian cities calls for serious, critical attention to the expression of alternative representations of continuity and of change. An important aspect of Tran Anh Hung's films was their ability to balance continuity and change, perhaps best exemplified by Mui's comment towards the end of *The Scent of the Green Papaya* that 'however the cherry trees change, they keep the shape of the cherry tree'. Though it is tempting to dismiss this statement as a cliché, the way in which Hung interweaves ritual, such as the cutting of the papaya, with the inevitable changes which urban residents experience, whether due to changes in their life cycle or the political and economic circumstances of the city, balances continuity and change in a way not usually found in political economy approaches to globalisation.

Postcolonial studies also highlight resistance to the globalisation process. The emergence of new forms of the Pacific Asian metropolis has not generally been represented as resistance to capitalism *per se* but instead is portrayed as the embracing and restructuring of capitalism, giving it a distinctive Asian face. Enthusiasts for the uniqueness of Asian business practices have perhaps been temporarily subdued by the Asian financial crisis, but are bound to bounce back. Their arguments challenge the pre-eminence of the old core centres of the global economy, at the same time as perpetuating the capitalist world system, albeit in a reconfigured space. The metropolises, of course, are central to this position. They subvert by taking control, becoming centres of growth economies.

Alternative patterns of resistance in the urban landscape can also be identified through postcolonial approaches. Jacobs (1996) has demonstrated this in the Australian context, where aboriginal imprints on the cities are often contested or worse, go entirely unrecognised. Tran Anh Hung's *Cyclo* explores the milieu of the criminal gang, itself a means of avoiding government and, perhaps unintentionally, subverting the market economy by bringing it into disrepute. City studies in the 1970s and 1980s often focused on the informal sector and squatter communities, as part of an overall emphasis on the poor. But in recent years there is little of a substantive nature about sites of urban resistance. The Pacific Asian metropolis is all too often homogenised, its space undifferentiated.

A reconciliation of the insights that can be derived from political economy and postcolonial approaches to globalisation will not necessarily lead to a seamless perspective – or theory – of the metropolis. Pacific Asian cities are too large, complex and contradictory to achieve that form of coherence. However, examining the styles of representation of the city, whether through a conscious attempt to create and reinforce a particular image, or through a more incidental imagining in the context of a popular medium such as film, is important to achieving a more multidimensional grasp of the new metropolis.

Acknowledgements

This argument elaborates upon ideas first mentioned in an earlier published paper (Forbes 1997a). I am grateful for the help of Cecile Cutler in the preparation of successive drafts, and for the comments and discussion of participants in the Logic(s) of Globalisation Workshop at the National University of Singapore.

Notes

1 I use the term Pacific Asia in preference to other terms to represent the arc of countries from Japan and Russia in the north through East and Southeast Asia to Australia and New Zealand. This is an unconventional use of the term Pacific Asia.
2 A contrastingly cautious, even negative view of Singapore's financial markets is contained in Daly and Logan (1989: 239–43).
3 A statement by Prime Minister Goh Chok Tong in October 1996 claimed more than 4,000 multinational corporations are established in Singapore.

4 The representation of the city in contemporary Pacific Asian literature (and in travel guides, *pace* Hutnyk 1996) is another theme worth exploration. A list of readings, many by outsiders, was an endearing feature of McGee's (1967) landmark *The Southeast Asian City*.

5 Though the importance of culture is clearly established in writing on cities, including the Pacific Asian city. See, for example, Askew and Logan (1994), Kim *et al.* (1997).

References

Abo, T. (1996) 'The Japanese production system: the process of adaptation to national settings', in R. Boyer and D. Drache (eds) *States Against Markets: The Limits of Globalization*, London: Routledge.

Adam, B. (1994) *Timewatch*, Cambridge: Polity.

Adler, E. and Crawford, B. (eds) (1991) *Progress in Post War International Relations*, New York: Columbia University Press.

Aggarwal, R. (ed.) (forthcoming) Special Issue on Multinationals from Emerging Countries, *International Business Review*, 6.

Agnew, J. and Corbridge, S. (1995) *Mastering Space: Hegemony, Territory and International Political Economy*, London: Routlege.

Altvater, E. and Mahnkopf, B. (1997) *Grenzen der Globalisierung. Ökonomie, Ökologie und Politik in der Weltgesellschaft*, Münster: Westfälisches Dampfboot.

Aman, A. C. Jr (1995) 'A global perspective on current regulatory reform: rejection, relocation, or reinvention?', *Indiana Journal of Global Legal Studies* 2: 429–64.

Amin, A. (1997) 'Placing globalisation', *Theory, Culture and Society* 14: 123–37.

Amitav A. (1997) 'Ideas, identity and institution building: from ASEAN way to Asia-Pacific way', *The Pacific Review* 10, 3: 319–46.

Anderson, B. (1992) 'The new world disorder', *New Left Review* May/June: 2–13.

Angel, D. P. (1994) *Restructuring for Innovation: The Remaking of the U.S. Semiconductor Industry*, New York: The Guilford Press.

Anzaldúa, G. (1987) *Borderlands/La Frontera: the New Mestiz*, San Fransisco: Aunt Lute Books.

Appadurai, A. (1990) 'Disjuncture and difference in the global cultural economy', *Public Culture* 2, 2: 1–24.

Appadurai, A. (1996) 'Sovereignty without territoriality: notes for a postnational geography', in P. Yaeger (ed.) *The Geography of Identity*, Ann Arbor: The University of Michigan Press.

Arrighi, G. (1994) *The Long Twentieth Century. Money, Power, and the Origins of Our Times*, London: Verso.

Arrighi, G. (1997) 'Globalisation, state sovereignty, and the "endless" accumulation of capital', Revised version of a paper presented at the Conference on 'States and Sovereignty in the World Economy,' University of California, Irvine, 21–23 February 1997.

Askew, M. and W. Logan (eds) (1994) *Cultural Identity and Urban Change in Southeast Asia: Interpretative Essays*, Geelong: Deakin University Press.

Awanohara, Susumu (1994) 'Spicier melting pot: Asian-Americans come of age politically', in J. Kromkowski (ed.) *Race and Ethnic Relations* 94/95, Guillford, CT: Dushkin Publishing Group.

Bacho, P. (1997) 'The tragic sense of Filipino history', in M. Root (ed.) *Filipino Americans: Transformation and Identity*, Thousand Oaks, CA: Sage.

Bairoch, P. and Kozul-Wright, R. (1996) 'Globalisation myths: some historical reflections on integration, industrialisation and growth in the world economy', United Nations Conference on Trade and Development Discussion Paper #113.

Balibar, E. (1991) 'Racism and nationalism', in E. Balibar and I. Wallerstein (eds) *Race, Nation, and Class: Ambiguous Identities*, London: Verso.

Basch, L., Glick Schiller, N., and Szanton Blanc, C. (1994) *Nations Unbound: Transnational Projects, Postcolonial Predicaments, and Deterritorialised Nation-States*, New York: Gordon and Breach.

Bauman, Z. (1990) 'Modernity and ambivalence', *Theory, Culture and Society* 7, 2–3: 143–69.

Beck, U. (1997) *The Reinvention of Politics: Rethinking Modernity in the Global Social Order*, M. Ritter (tr) Cambridge: Polity Press.

Bello, W. (1997a) 'Addicted to capital: the ten-year high and present-day withdrawal trauma of Southeast Asia's economies', http://focusweb.org/focus/library/addicted_to_capital.htm, accessed 1 June 1998.

Bello, W. (1997b) 'The end of the Asian miracle', http://www.stern.nyu.edu/~nroubini/asia/miracle.pdf, accessed 18 May 1998.

Benjamin, G. (1976) 'The cultural logic of Singapore's multiculturalism', in R. Hassan (ed.) *Singapore: Society in Transition*, Kuala Lumpur: Oxford University Press.

Bergesen, A. and Fernandez, R. (1995) 'Who has the most Fortune 500 firms?: A network analysis of global economic competition, 1956–1989', *Journal of World-Systems Research* 1, 12: 1–28 (this is an internet journal so all articles are self-contained with respect to page numbers).

Berman, N. (1995) 'Economic consequences, nationalist passions: Keynes, crisis, culture, and policy', *The American University Journal of International Law and Policy* 10, 2 (Winter): 619–70.

Bernanke, B. S. and Mishkin, F. S. (1997) 'Inflation targeting: a new framework for monetary policy?', *Journal of Economic Perspectives* 11, 2: 97–116.

Bernard, M. (1997) 'Ecology, political economy and the counter-movement: Karl Polanyi and the second great transformation,' in S. Gill and J. Mittelman (eds) *Innovation and Transformation in International Studies*, Cambridge: Cambridge University Press.

Bernard, M. and Ravenhill, J. (1995) 'Beyond product cycles and flying geese', *World Politics* 47: 171–209.

Bhabha, H. K. (1990) 'DissemiNation: time, narrative and the margins of the modern nation', in H. K. Bhaba (ed.) *Nation and Narration*, London: Routledge.

Bhabha, H. K. (1994) *The Location of Culture*, London: Routledge.

Bhagwati, J. (1998) 'The capital myth', *Foreign Affairs* 77, 3: 7–12.

Biersteker, T. (1995) 'The "triumph" of liberal economic ideas in the developing world', in B. Stallings (ed.) *Global Change, Regional Response: The New International Context*, Cambridge: Cambridge University Press.

Blanck, D. (1992) 'The impact of the American academy in Sweden', in R. Lunden and E. Asard (eds) *Networks of Americanisation: Aspects of the American Influence in Sweden, Studia Anglistica Upsaliensia* 79: 80–93.

Boden, D. (1994) *The Business of Talk: Organizations in Action*, Cambridge, MA: Polity Press.

Bodnar, J. (1985) *The Transplanted: A History of Immigrants in Urban America*, Bloomington, IN: Indiana University Press.

Boisier, S. (1994) 'Regionalisation process: past crises and current options', *CEPAL Review* 52: 177–88.

Bourdieu, P. (1977) *Outline of a Theory of Practice*, Cambridge: Cambridge University Press.

Bowker, G. and Star, S.L. (1994) 'Knowledge and infrastructure in international information management', in L. Bud-Frierman (ed.) *Information Acumen: The Understanding and Use of Knowledge in Modern Business*, London: Routledge.

Bowles, P. (1997) 'ASEAN, AFTA and the new regionalism', *Pacific Affairs* 70, 2: 219–33.

Braganza, B. (1996) Research Scientist, Environmental Research Division of the Institute of Environmental Science for Social Change (formerly the Manila Observatory). Interview with the author, Quezon City, Philippines, 2 March.

Braudel, F. (1984) *The Perspective On The World*, New York: Harper and Row.

Brenner, N. (1997) 'Trial By Space: Global City Formation, State Territorial Restructuring and the Politics of Scale', Paper presented to Cities in Transition Conference, Humboldt University, Berlin, 20–22 July.

Brosius, J. P. (1997) 'Endangered forest, endangered people: environmentalist representations of indigenous knowledge', *Human Ecology* 25, 1: 47–69.

Brown, M. F. (1997) *The Chanelling Zone*, Cambridge, MA: Harvard University Press.

Buck-Morss, S. (1995) 'Envisioning capital: political economy and display', in L. Cooke and P. Wollen (eds) *Visual Display: Culture Beyond Appearances*, Seattle: Bay Press.

Budnivich, C. and Le Fort, G. (1997) 'Capital account regulation and macroeconomic policy: two Latin American experiences', Working Paper No. 6, Marco: Banco Central de Chile.

Bull, H. (1977) *The Anarchical Society*, London: Macmillan.

Butler, J. (1990) *Gender Trouble*, London: Routledge.

Cable, V. (1995) 'The diminshed nation state?', *What Future for the State? Daedalus* 124, 2: 23–53.

Calvo, G. (1995) 'Varieties of capital market crises', unpublished manuscript, University of Maryland: Center for International Economics.

Camagni, R. (1991) *Innovation Networks: Spatial Perspectives*, London: Belhaven Press.

Camagni, R. (1995) 'The concept of *innovative milieu* and its relevance for public policies in European lagging regions', *Papers in Regional Science* 74, 4: 317–40.

Camilleri, J. (1997) 'Regionalism and globalism in Asia-Pacific', paper presented at Toda Institute for Global Peace and Policy Research, Honolulu, Hawaii 1997. Title of conference: 'Human Security and Global Governance in the Asia-Pacific'.

Camilleri, J. and Falk, J. (1992) *The End of Sovereignty? The Politics of a Shrinking and Fragmented World*, Aldershot: Edward Elgar Publishing.

Canclini, N. (1995) *Hybrid Cultures: Strategies for Entering and Leaving Modernity*, C. Chiappari and S. Lopez (tr) Minneapolis, MN: University of Minnesota Press.

Cannon, T. and Zhang, L-Y. (1996) 'Inter-region tension and China's reforms', in I. Cook, M. Doel and R. Li (eds) *Fragmented Asia*, Aldershot: Avebury.

Caprio, G. Jr and Honahan, P. (eds) (1991) *Monetary Policy Instruments for Developing Countries*, Washington, DC: World Bank.

Caprio, G. Jr and Klingebiel K. (1997) 'Bank insolvency: bad luck, bad policy, or bad banking?', in M. Bruno and B. Peskovic (eds) *Annual World Bank Conference on Development Economics, 1996*, Washington, DC: World Bank.

Carrier, J. G. (ed.) (1995) *Occidentalism: Images of the West*, Oxford: Oxford University Press.

Carrier, J. G. (ed.) (1996) *Meanings of the Market*, Oxford: Berg.

Carrier, J. G. and Miller, D. (eds) (1998) *Virtualism: The New Political Economy*, Oxford: Berg.

Cartier, C. L. (1995) 'Singaporean investment in China: installing the Singapore model in Sunan', *Chinese Environment and Development* 6, 1/2: 117–44.

Casey, E. S. (1993) *Getting Back into Place: Toward a Renewed Understanding of the Place-World*, Bloomington, IN: University of Indiana Press.

Castells, M. (1996) *The Rise of the Network Society*, Oxford: Blackwell.

Castree, N. (1995) 'The nature of produced knowledge: materiality and knowledge construction in Marxism,' *Antipode* 27, 1: 12–48.

Chambers, I. (1994) *Migrancy, Culture and Identity*, London and New York: Routledge.

Chan, K. B. (1994) 'The ethnicity paradox: Hong Kong immigrants in Singapore', in R. Skeldon (ed.) *Reluctant Exiles? Migration from Hong Kong and the New Overseas Chinese*, New York and Hong Kong: Sharpe and Hong Kong University Press.

Chan, J., Sculli, D. and Si, K. (1991) 'The cost of manufacturing toys in the Shenzhen Special Economic Zone in China', *International Journal of Production Economics*, 25: 181–90.

Chan K. B. and Tong C. K. (1993) 'Rethinking assimilation and ethnicity: the Chinese in Thailand', *International Migration Review* 27: 140–68.

Chan K. B. and Tong C. K. (1996) 'Singaporean Chinese doing business in China', paper presented at the International Academic Workshop on 'Chinese Business Connections in Global and Comparative Perspective', Beijing, 10–12 September.

Chang, T. C. (1998) 'Regionalism and tourism: exploring integral links in Singapore', *Asia Pacific Viewpoint* 39, 1: 73–94.

Charlot, J. (1994) 'Vietnamese cinema: first views', in W. Dissanayake (ed.) *Colonialism and Nationalism in Asian Cinema*, Bloomington, IN: Indiana University Press.

Chatterjee, P. (1986) *Nationalist Thought and the Colonial World: A Derivative Discourse*, London: Zed Books.

Chen, H. (1992) *Chinatown No More: Taiwan Immigrants in Contemporary New York*, Ithaca, NY: Cornell University Press.

Cheng, C. Y. (1992) 'Greater China common market', *World Journal* 26 July: C2–4 (in Chinese).

Cheng, C. Y. (1997) 'Economic relations across the Taiwan Straits: progress, effects and prospects,' *American Asian Review*, XV, 1: 91–118.

Chesneaux, J. (1992) *Brave Modern World: The Prospects for Survival*, tr. by Diana Johnstone, Karen Bowie and Francisca Garvie, London: Thames and Hudson.

Childs, B. J. (1994) 'The value of transcommunal identity politics,' *Z Magazine*, July/August: 48–51.

Chin, C. B. N. and Mittelman, J. H. (1997) 'Conceptualising resistance to globalisation', *New Political Economy* 2, 1: 25–37.

Choe, S. C. (1996) 'The evolving urban system in North-East Asia', in F. C. Lo and Y. M. Yeung (eds) *Emerging World Cities in Pacific Asia*, Tokyo: United Nations University Press.

Christopher, M. (1992) *Logistics and Supply Chain Management*, London: Pitman Publishing.

Chua, B. H. (1996) 'Singapore: management of a city-state in Southeast Asia', in J. Ruland (ed.) *The Dynamics of Metropolitan Management in Southeast Asia*, Singapore: Institute of Southeast Asian Studies.

Chuch, K. (1996) 'The transnation and its pasts', *Public Culture* 9: 93–112.

Chun, S. (1990) 'European and Asian immigration into the US in comparative perspective, 1820s to 1920s', in V. Yans-McLaughlin (ed.) *Immigration Reconsidered: History, Sociology, and Politics*, New York: Oxford.

Chung, C. Y. (1997) 'Division of labour across the Taiwan Strait: macro overview and analysis of the electronics industry', in B. Naughton (ed.) *The China Circle*, Washington, DC: Brookings Institution Press.

Clammer, John (1982) 'The institutionalization of ethnicity: the culture of ethnicity in Singapore', *Ethnic and Racial Studies* 5, 2:127–39.

Clarke, D. (ed.) (1997) *The Cinematic City*, London: Routledge.

Clinton, W. J. (1996) *Weekly Compilation of Presidential Documents* 33, 45: 1735–45.

Clough, R. (1993) *Reaching Across the Taiwan Strait: People-to-People Diplomacy*, Boulder, CO: Westview Press.

Conley, T. (1996) 'The wit of the letter: Holbein's Lacan', in T. Brennan and M. Jay (eds) *Vision in Context: Historical and Contemporary Perspectives on Sight*, London: Routledge.

Conti, S. (1993) 'The network perspective in industrial geography', *Geografiska Annaler*, 75, B: 115–30.

Cooper, R. K. and Sawaf, A. (1997) *Executive EQ: Emotional Intelligence in Business*, London: Orion Business Books.

Corbridge, S. and Thrift, N. (1994) 'Money, power and space: introduction and overview', in S. Corbridge, R. Martin and N. Thrift (eds) *Money, Power and Space*, Oxford: Blackwell.

Corsetti A., Pesenti, P. and Roubini, N. (1998) 'What caused the Asian currency and financial crisis', http://www.stern.nyu.edu/~nroubini/asia/AsianCrisis.pdf, accessed 4 June 1998.

Coulson-Thomas, J. (ed.) (1994) *Business Process Re-engineering*, London: Nicholas Brealey.

Cowles, M. G. (1995) 'Setting the agenda for the new Europe: the European round table and EC 1992', *Journal of Common Market Studies*, 33, 4: 501–26.

Crainer, S. (1997a) *Corporate Man to Corporate Skunk: The Tom Peters Phenomenon*, London: Capstone Publishing.

Crainer, S. (1997b) 'Get me a writer!', *Silver Kris* December: 36–8.

Crosby, T. W. (1996) *The Measure of Reality. Quantification and Western Society, 1250–1600*, Cambridge: Cambridge University Press.

Cross, A. (1993) 'Portraying the rhythm of the Vietnamese soul; an interview with Tran Anh Hung', *Cineaste* 20, 3: 35.

Cyclo (Xich Lo). Les Productions Lazennec, 1995. Vietnamese, with subtitles. Director Tran Anh Hung.

Dacumos, V. (1996) Chairman, Guardians of the Environment for the Future of Youth. Interview with the author. Gabaldon, Nueva Ecija, Philippines, 9 March.

Daly, M. and Logan, M. (1989) *The Brittle Rim*, Melbourne: Penguin.

de Geuss, A. (1997) *The Living Company*, London: Nicholas Brealey.

de Guzman, A. (1996) Parish priest and President, Confederation of Nueva Ecijanons for the Environment and Social Order, Inc. Interview with the author. Cabanatuan City, Nueva Ecija, Luzon, Philippines, 9 March.

del Castillo, R. A. (1996) Professor of Forest Resources and Director, University of the Philippines Los Banos Agroforestry Program. Interview with the author. Los Banos, Laguna, Philippines, 11 March.

dela Torre, E. (1996) President, Folk Philippine-Danish School. Interview with the author. Quezon City, Philippines, 12 March.

Deconde, A. (1992) *Ethnicity, Race, and American Foreign Policy*, Boston, MA: Northeastern University Press.

Denmark, F. J., Gills, B. and Modelski, G. (eds) (1998) *World System History: The Science of Long Term Change*, Walnut Creek: Altamira Press.

Dent, C. M. and Randerson, C. (1996) 'Korean foreign direct investment in Europe: the determining forces', *The Pacific Review* 9, 4: 531–52.

DeSipio, L. and de la Garza, R. O. (1998) *Making Americans, Remaking America: Immigration and Immigrant Policy*, Boulder, CO: Westview.

Dicken, P. (1992) 'International production in a volatile regulatory environment: the influence of national regulatory policies on the spatial strategies of transnational corporations', *Geoforum* 23: 303–16.

Dicken, P. (1994) 'Global-local tensions: firms and states in the global space-economy', *Economic Geography* 70, 2:101–28.

Dicken, P. (1998) *Global Shift: Transforming the World Economy*, Third Edition, London: Paul Chapman; New York: Guilford.

Dicken, P. and and Miyamachi, Y. (1998) 'From noodles to satellites: the changing geography of the Japanese sogo shosha', *Transactions of the Institute of British Geographers* 23, 1: 55–78.

Dicken, P., Peck, J. and Tickell, A. (1998) 'Unpacking the global', in R. Lee and J. Wills (eds) *Geographies of Economies*, London: Arnold.

Dicken, P., Tickell, A. and Yeung, H. W. C. (1997) 'Putting Japanese investment in Europe in its place', *Area*, 29, 3: 200–12.

Dieter, H. (1997) 'APEC and the WTO: cooperation or collision?' *The Pacific Review* 10, 1: 19–38.

Dikötter, Frank (1997a) 'Introduction', in F. Dikötter (ed.) *The Construction of Racial Identities in China and Japan*, Honolulu: University of Hawaii Press.

Dikötter, Frank (1997b) 'Racial Discourse in China: Continuities and Permutations', in F. Dikötter (ed.) *The Construction of Racial Identities in China and Japan*, Honolulu: University of Hawaii Press.

Dirlik, A. (1993a) 'Introducing the Pacific' in A. Dirlik (ed.) *What is in a Rim? Critical Perspectives on the Pacific Region Idea*, Boulder, CO: Westview Press.

Dirlik, A. (ed.) (1993b) *What is in a Rim? Critical Perspectives on the Pacific Region Idea*, Oxford: Westview Press.

Dirlik, A. (1994a) 'The postcolonial aura: third world criticism in the age of global capitalism', *Critical Inquiry* Winter: 328–56.

Dirlik, A. (1994b) *After the Revolution: Waking to Global Capitalism*, Hanover and London: Wesleyan University Press.

Dirlik, A. (1997) 'Critical reflections on Chinese capitalism as a paradigm', in N. Glick Schiller (ed.) *Narratives of Capitalism*, special issue of *Identities: Global Studies In Culture and Power* 3, 3: 303–30.

Dirlik, A. (ed.) (1998) *What is in a Rim? Critical Perspectives on the Pacific Region Idea*, revised edition, Maryland: Rowman and Littlefield Publishers.

Dobbs-Higginson, M. S. (1994) *Asia Pacific: Its Role in the New World Disorder*, Melbourne: Mandarin.

Dobson, A. (ed.) (1991) *The Green Reader: Essays Toward a Sustainable Society*, San Francisco: Mercury House.

Dornbusch, R. (1997) 'World economic trends,' in *World Economic Trends*, VI, 4, Ramsey, NJ: Trans-National Research Corporation.

Douglass, M. (1995) 'Global interdependence and urbanization: planning for the Bangkok mega-urban region', in T. G. McGee and I. M. Robinson (eds) *The Mega-Urban Regions of Southeast Asia*, Vancouver: UBC Press.

Douw, L. (ed.) (1997) *Unsettled Frontiers and Transnational Linkages: New Tasks for the Historian of Modern Asia*, Amsterdam: VU University Press for the Centre for Asian Studies.

Dumaine, B. (1997) 'Asia's wealth creators confront a new reality', *Fortune*, December 8: 42–55.

Dunning, J. H. (1993) *Multinational Enterprises and the Global Economy*, Reading, MA: Addison Wesley.

Dunning, J. H. (1995) 'The global economy and regimes of national and supra-national governance', *Business & The Contemporary World* 7, 1: 124–36.

Dunning, J. H. (1998) *Globalisation and FDI in Asian Developing Countries*, Paper Presented at the Conference on Global Change: The Impact of East Asia in the 21st Century, Manchester Metropolitan University, April 1998.

Dürrschmidt, J. (1997) 'The delinking of locale and milieu: on the situatedness of extended milieux in a global environment', in J. Eade (ed.) *Living the Global City*, London: Routledge.

Dusenbery, V. (1997) 'Diasporic Imaginings and the Conditions of Possibility: Sikhs and the State in Southeast Asia', in V. Rafael and I. Abraham (eds) *Sojourn, Special Focus Issue on Southeast Asian Diasporas* 12, 2: 226–60.

East Asia Analytical Unit (1995) *Overseas Chinese Business Networks in Asia*, Parkes, Australia: Department of Foreign Affairs and Trade.

Eccleston, B. (1996) 'Does North-South collaboration enhance NGO influence in deforestation policies in Malaysia and Indonesia?', *Journal of Commonwealth and Comparative Politics* 34, 1: 66–89.

Eccleston, B. and Potter, D. (1996) 'Environmental NGOs and Different Political Contexts in South-East Asia: Malaysia, Indonesia and Vietnam', in Parnwell, M. and Bryant, R. (eds) *Environmental Change in South-East Asia*, London: Routledge.

Economic Development Board (1995) *Regionalisation 2000: Singapore Unlimited*, Singapore: EDB.

Economic Development Board (1997) 'Services sector registers growth in 1997', EDB, Singapore. (http://www.sedb.com)

Edwards, S. (1996) 'Exchange rates and the political economy of macro economic discipline', *American Economic Review* 86, 2: 159–63.

Elgar, T. and Smith, C. (eds) (1994), *Global Japanization? Transnational Transformation of the Labour Process*, London: Routledge.

Escobar, A. (1995) *Encountering Development: The Making and Unmaking of the Third World*, Princeton, NJ: Princeton University Press.

Espiritu, Y. L. (1996a) *Asian American Women and Men: Labour, Laws, and Love*, Thousand Oaks, CA: Sage.

Espiritu, Y. L. (1996b) 'Colonial oppression, labour importation, and group formation: Filipinos in the US', *Ethnic and Racial Studies* 19, 1: 29–48.

Fang, S. (1992) 'A proposal for establishing a Mainland-Taiwan-Hong Kong Economic Commission', *Jingi Ribao* 24 June: 4 (in Chinese).

Fawcett, J. T. and Carino, B. V. (eds) (1987) *Pacific Bridges: The New Immigration from Asia and the Pacific Islands*, New York: Center for Migration Studies.

Featherstone, M. (ed.) (1990) *Global Culture: Nationalism, Globalisation and Modernity*, London: Sage.

Featherstone, M. (1993) 'Global and local cultures', in J. Bird *et al.* (eds) *Mapping the Futures: Local Cultures, Global Change*, London and New York: Routledge.

Feldman-Bianco, B. (1992) 'Multiple layers of time and space: The construction of class, race, ethnicity, and nationalism among Portuguese immigrants', in N. Glick Schiller, L. Basch, and C. Blanc-Szanton (eds) *Towards a Transnational Perspective on Migration*, New York: New York Academy of Sciences.

Feldman-Bianco, B. (1994) *The State, Saudade and the Dialectics of Deterritorialisation and Reterritorialisation*, Paper Delivered at Wenner Gren Symposium 117, Mijas, Spain, June.

Financial Times, 1997.

Fishman, J. A. (1977) 'Language and ethnicity', H. Giles (ed.) *Language, Ethnicity and Inter-Group Relations*, London: Academic Press.

Florida, R. (1995) 'Toward the learning region', *Futures* 27, 5: 527–36.

Foister, S., Roy, A. and Wyld, M. (1997) *Holbein's Ambassadors*, London: National Gallery.

Forbes, D. K. (1996) *Asian Metropolis: Urbanisation and the Southeast Asian City*, Melbourne: Oxford University Press.

Forbes, D. K. (1997a) 'Metropolis and megaurban region in Pacific Asia', *Tijdschrift voor Economische en Sociale Geografie* 88, 5: 457–68.

Forbes, D. K. (1997b) 'Regional integration, internationalisation and the new geographies of the Pacific', in R. Watters and T.G. McGee (eds) *Asia Pacific: New Geographies of the Pacific Rim*, London: C. Hurst.

Forbes, D. K. and N. J. Thrift (1987) 'International impacts on the urbanisation process in the Asian region: a review', in R. Fuchs, G. Jones and E. Pernia (eds) *Urbanisation and Urban Policy in Pacific Asia*, Boulder, CO: Westview Press.

Foucault, M. (1970) *The Order of Things: An Archaeology of the Human Sciences*, London: Tavistock Publications.

Fouron, G. and Glick Schiller, N. (1997) 'Haitian identities at the juncture between diaspora and homeland', in P. Pessar (ed.) *Caribbean Circuits: Transnational Approaches to Migration*, Staten Island: Center for Migration Studies.

Franck, T. M. (1992) 'The emerging right to democratic governance', *American Journal of International Law* 86, 1: 46–91.

Frank, A. G. and Gills, B. (1993) *The World System: Five Hundred Years or Five Thousand*, London: Routledge.

Frankel, J. A. (1996) 'Recent exchange rate experience and proposals for reform', *American Economic Review* 86, 2: 153–8.

Frankel, J. and Sergio S. (1996) 'Crisis, contagion, and country funds: effects on East Asia and Latin America', *Pacific Basin Working Paper No. PB96-04*. Center for Pacific Basin Monetary and Economic Studies, Federal Reserve Bank of San Francisco.

Fried, C. (1983) 'Introduction', in C. Fried (ed.) *Minorities: Community and Identity*, Report of the Dahlem Workshop on Minorities: Community and identity, Berlin: Springer-Verlag.

Friedman, J. (1996) 'The implosion of modernity', in M. J. Shapiro and H. Alker (eds) *Challenging Boundaries: Global Flows, Territorial Identities*, Minneapolis: University of Minnesota Press.

Friedman, J. (1997) 'Global crises, the struggle for cultural identity and intellectual pork-barreling: cosmopolitans, nationals and locals in an era of de-hegemonisation', in P. Werbner (ed.) *The Dialectics of Hybridity*, London: Zed Press.

Friedman, J. (1998) 'The hybridisation of roots and the abhorrence of the bush', in M. Featherstone and S. Lash (eds) *Spaces of Culture: City, Nation, World*, London: Sage.

Friedman, J. and Sugita, K. (1973) 'Underconsumption theory and the rate of profit' ms.

Friedman, T. (1996) 'Balancing NAFTA and Neighborhood,' *Rocky Mountain News* (from *The New York Times*) 13 April 1996: 44A.

Friedmann, J. (1986) 'The world city hypothesis', *Development and Change* 17, 1: 69–84.

Friedmann, J. (1995) 'Where we stand: a decade of world city research', in P. Knox and P. Taylor (eds) *World Cities in a World System*, Cambridge: Cambridge University Press.

Fu, L. (1992) 'Hong Kong-Macau and Both Sides of the Taiwan Strait: a Chinese economic sphere', *Journal of Beijing University, Social Science Edition* 5: 85–92 (in Chinese).

Fuchs, L. (1990) *The American Kaleidoscope: Race, Ethnicity, and the Civic Culture*, Hanover, NH: University Press of New England.

Garnaut, R. (1997) *Open Regionalism in the Pacific*, London: Routledge.

Gereffi, G. (1996) 'Commodity chains and regional divisions of labour in East Asia', *Journal of Asian Business* 12: 75–112.

Gereffi, G. and Korzeniewicz, M. (eds) (1994) *Commodity Chain and Global Capitalism*, London: Praeger.

Gerth, J. (1998) 'Democrat Fund-Raiser Said to Name China Tie', *New York Times* May 15: A1, A20.

Gerth, J. and Sanger, D. (1998) 'How Chinese Won Rights to Launch Satellites for US', *New York Times* 17 May 1,18.

Gibson-Graham, J. K. (1996) *The End of Capitalism (as we knew it): A Feminist Critique of Political Economy*, Oxford: Blackwell.

Giddens, A. (1996) 'Affluence, poverty and the idea of a post-scarcity society', *Development and Change* 27: 365–77.

Gill, S. (1995) 'Globalisation, market civilisation and disciplinary neo-liberalism', *Millenium: Journal of International Studies* 24,3: 399–423.

Gilroy, P. (1993) *The Black Atlantic: Modernity and Double Consciousness*, Cambridge, MA: Harvard University Press.

Ginsburg, N., Koppel, B. and McGee, T. G. (eds) (1991) *The Extended Metropolis: Settlement Transition in Asia*, Honolulu: University of Hawaii Press.

Gitlin, T. (1995) *The Twilight of Common Dreams: Why America is Wracked by Culture Wars*, New York: Henry Holt.

Glazer, N. (1954) 'Ethnic groups in America: From national culture to ideology', in M. Berger, T. Abel and C. H. Page (eds) *Freedom and Control in Modern Society*, New York: D. Van Nostrand Company.

Glick Schiller, N. (1995) 'The implications of Haitian transnationalism for US–Haiti relations: Contradictions of the deterritorialised nation-state', *Journal of Haitian Studies* 1, 1: 111–23.

Glick Schiller, N. (1998) 'Who are these guys: A transnational reading of the US Immigrant Experience', in L. Goldin (ed.) *Identities On the Move*, Austin, TX: University of Texas Press.

Glick Schiller, N. (forthcoming, 1999) 'Transmigrants and nation-states: something old and something new in the US immigrant experience', in J. De Wind, P. Kasinitz, and C. Hirshman (eds) *America Becoming, Becoming America*, New York: Russell Sage.

Glick Schiller, N., Basch, L. and Szanton Blanc, C. (1992) 'Transnationalism: A new analytic framework for understanding migration', in N. Glick Schiller, L. Basch and C. Szanton-Blanc (eds) *Towards a Transnational Perspective on Migration: Race, Class, Ethnicity and Nationalism Reconsidered*, New York: New York Academy of Sciences.

Glick Schiller, N., Basch, L., and Blanc-Szanton, C. (1992) 'Transnationalism: a new framework for understanding migration', *Annals of the New York Academy of Sciences* 645: 1–24.

Glick Schiller, N., Basch, L. and Szanton Blanc, C. (1995) 'From immigrant to transmigrant: theorising transnational migration', *Anthropological Quarterly* 68: 48–63.

Glick Schiller, N. and Fouron, G. (1997) 'Blood lines: racial foundations of the transnational nation-state', *Globalisation, State, Identities, Special issue of Revista Crítica Ciêncians Sociala* 48, Junho: 33–66.

Global Crisis, Local Struggles. Special Issue, *Social Justice* 20, Fall–Winter 1993: 3–4.

Goh Chok Tong (1996) 'Speech at the Belgian Business Forum, 15 October 1996', Ministry of Information & The Arts, Singapore.

Goodman, D. (1995) 'New economic elites', in R. Benewick and P. Wingrove (eds) *China in the 1990s*, Basingstoke: Macmillan.

Goody, J. (1971) *The Domestication of the Savage Mind*, Cambridge: Cambridge University Press.

Goody, J. (1987) *The Interface Between the Written and the Oral*, Cambridge: Cambridge University Press.

Goody, J. (1996) *The East in the West*, Cambridge: Cambridge University Press.

Gosling, L. A. P. (1983) 'Changing Chinese identities in Southeast Asia: an introductory review', in L. A. P. Gosling and L. Y. C. Lim (eds) *The Chinese in Southeast Asia: Identity, Culture and Politics*, vol. 2, Singapore: Maruzen Asia.

Graham, P. (1996) 'Nationality and political participation in the transnational context of Dominican migration', in P. Pessar (ed.) *Caribbean Circuits: Transnational Approaches to Migration*, Staten Island, New York: Center for Migration Studies.

Gramsci, A. (1971) *Selections from the Prison Notebooks of Antonio Gramsci*, Hoare, Q. and Smith, G. N. (eds) New York: International Publishers.

Granovetter, M. (1985) 'Economic action and social structure: the problem of embeddedness', *American Journal of Sociology* 91: 481–501.

Greenhalgh, S. (1994) 'De-orientalizing the Chinese family firm', *American Ethnologist* 21, 4: 746–75.

Greenspan, A. (1997) 'Testimony of Chairman Alan Greenspan before the Committee on Banking and Financial Services, U.S. House of Representatives', 13 November 1997, http://www.bog.frb.fed.us/boarddocs/testimony/19971113.htm, accessed 18 May 1998.

Greenspan, A. (1998) 'Mr. Greenspan discusses the ascendance of market capitalism', *BIS Review* 29.

Guarnizo, L. E. (forthcoming) 'The rise of transnational social formations: Mexican and Dominican State responses to transnational migration', *Political Power and Social Theory*.

Guarnizo, L. E. and M. P. Smith (1998) 'The locations of transnationalism', in M. P. Smith and L. E. Guarnizo (eds) *Transnationalism from Below*, New Brunswick: Rutgers University Press.

Gurmit Singh K. S. (1997) Executive Director, Centre for Environment, Technology and Development, Malaysia. Interview with the author. Petaling Jaya, Malaysia. 15 November.

Hacker, A. (1997) *Money: Who Has How Much and Why*, New York: Scribner.

Hall, S. (1989) 'Cultural identity and cinematic representation', *Framework* 36: 68–81.

Hall, S. (1990) 'Cultural identity and diaspora', in J. Rutherford (ed.) *Identity: Community, Culture, Difference*, London: Lawrence and Wishart.

Hamel, G. and Prahalad, C. K. (1994) *Competing for the Future*, Boston, MA: Harvard Business School Press.

Hamilton, Gary G. (ed.) (1996a) *Asian Business Networks*, Berlin: de Gruyter.

Hamilton, Gary G. (1996b) 'Competition and organization: a re-examination of Chinese business practices', *Journal of Asian Business* 12,1: 7–20.

Hammer, M. and Champy, J. (1993) *Re-engineering the Corporation. A Manifesto for a Business Revolution*, London: Nicholas Brealey.

Hampden-Turner, C. and Trompenaars, L. (1997) *Mastering the Infinite Game. How East Asian Values are Transforming Business Practices*, London: Capstone Press.

Handlin, O. (1973) [1951] *The Uprooted*, second edition, Boston, MA: Little, Brown.

Hannerz, U. (1990) 'Cosmopolitans and locals in world culture', *Theory, Culture and Society* 7, 2–3: 237–52.

Hannerz, U. (1992) *Cultural Complexity: Studies in the Social Organisation of Meaning*, New York: Columbia University Press.

Harries-Jones, P., Rotstein, A. and Timmerman, P. (1992) *Nature's Veto: UNCED and the Debate over the Earth*, University of Toronto, unpublished paper.

Harrington, M. (1980) 'Loyalties: Dual and Divided', in M. Walzer, E. Kantowicz, J. Higham and M. Harrington (eds) *The Politics of Ethnicity*, Cambridge, MA: Harvard University Press.

Harvey, D. (1982) *The Limits to Capital*, Oxford: Blackwell.

Hatch, W. and Yamamura, K. (1996) *Asia in Japan's Embrace: Building a Regional Production Alliance*, Cambridge: Cambridge University Press.

Heberer, T. (1995) 'The political impact of economic and social changes in China's countryside', *China Studies* 1 (Autumn): 49–92.

Heelas, P. (1996) *The New Age*, Cambridge: Polity Press.

Heisler, M. (1986) 'Transnational migration as a small window on the diminished autonomy of the modern democratic state', *Annals* (American Academy of Political And Social Science) 485: 153–66.

Henkin, L. (1990) *The Age of Rights*, New York: Columbia University Press.

Herf, J. (1982) *Reactionary Modernism*, Cambridge: Cambridge University Press.

Higgott, R. (1997a) '*De facto* and *De jure* regionalism: the double discourse of region in the Asia-Pacific', *Global Society* 11, 2: 165–83.

Higgott, R. (1997b) 'Ideas and identity in the interntional political economy of regionalism: the Asia-Pacific and Europe compared', *Kokusai Seiji* 114:14–48.

Higgott, R. (1998) 'The politics of east Asian economic crises of 1997/8', *Business Challenges and Opportunities in the Asia-Pacific Region*, London: Royal Institute of International Affairs, 30 March 1998:1–20.

Higgott, R. and Nossal, K. R. (1997) 'The international politics of liminality: relocating Australia in the Asia-Pacific?', *Australian Journal of Political Science* 32, 2: 169–86.

Higgott, R. and Stubbs, R. (1995) 'Competing conceptions of economic regionalism: APEC versus EAEC', *The Review of International Political Economy* 2, 3: 549–68.

Hill, H. (ed.) (1994) *Indonesia's New Order: The dynamics of socio-economic transformation*, Honolulu: University of Hawaii Press.

Hill, R. C. and Fujita, K. (1996) 'Flying geese, swarming sparrows or preying hawks? perspectives on East Asian industrialization', *Competition and Change* 1: 285–97.

Hirsh, M. and Powell, B. (1997). 'Hunting tigers,' *Newsweek* September 17: 58–9.

Hirst, P. (1997) 'The global economy – myths and realities,' *International Affairs* 73, 3: 409–25.

Hirst, P. and Thompson, G. (1996) *Globalization in Question: The International Economy and the Possibilities of Governance*, Cambridge: Polity.

Hiscock, G. (1997a) 'Asia's next wealth club', *World Executive's Digest* December: 19–22.

Hiscock, G. (1997b) *Asia's Wealth Clubs: Who's Really Who in Business – The Top 100 Billionaires in Asia*, London: Nicholas Brealey.

Hitz, Keil, Lehrer, Ronneberger, Schmid, Wolff (eds) (1995) *Capitales Fatales*, Zurich: Rotpunkt Verlag. (Please note that the editors listed themselves thus, no first names, no initials.)

Ho, H. C. (1997a) 'A value orientation for nature preservation in Singapore', *Environmental Monitoring and Assessment* 44: 91–107.

Ho, H. C. (1997b) Senior Lecturer, Department of Philosophy, National University of Singapore, Interview with the author, Singapore, 5 December.

Ho, K. C. (1998) 'From port city to city-state: forces shaping Singapore's built environment', in W. B. Kim, M. Douglass, S-C. Choe and K. C. Ho (eds) *Culture and the City in East Asia*, Oxford: Clarendon Press.

Hobsbawm, E. (1975) *The Age of Capital*, New York: Charles Scribner's Sons.

Hobsbawm, E. (1992) *Nations and Nationalism Since 1780*, second edition, New York: Cambridge University Press.

Hodder, R. (1996) *Merchant Princes of the East: Cultural Delusions, Economic Success and the Overseas Chinese in Southeast Asia*, Chichester: John Wiley.

Holston, J. (ed.) (1996) Cities and Citizenship. A Special Issue of *Public Culture*.

Hone, A. (1974) 'Multinational corporations and multinational buying groups: their impact on the growth of Asia's exports of manufactures – myths and realities', *World Development* 2: 145–9.

Horowitz, D. (1975) 'Ethnic identity', in N. Glazer and D. P. Moynihan (eds) *Ethnicity: Theory and Experience*, Cambridge, MA: Harvard University Press.

Hotta, M. (1996) President, Alter Trade Japan, Inc., Interview with the author, Tokyo, 25 February.

Howell, J. (1993) *China Opens its Doors: the Politics of Economic Transition*, Hemel Hempstead: Harvester Wheatsheaf.

Hu, Y. S. (1992) 'Global firms are national firms with international operations', *California Management Review* 34, 2: 107–26.

Hu, Y. S. (1995) 'The international transferability of the firm's advantages', *California Management Review* 37, 4: 73–88.

Huang, C-L. (1989) *Hong Kong into the Twenty-First Century*, Hong Kong: Chung Wah Publishing (in Chinese).

Huber, T. (1994) *Strategic Economy of Japan*, Boulder, CO: Westview Press.

Huczynski, T. (1993) *Management Gurus. What Makes Them and How to Become One*, London: Routledge.

Huff, W. G. (1987) 'Patterns in the economic development of Singapore', *The Journal of Developing Areas* 21, 3: 305–25.

Hui, W. T. (1997) 'Regionalization, economic restructuring and labour migration in Singapore', *International Migration* 35, 1: 109–28.

Hutnyk, J. (1996) *The Rumour of Calcutta: Tourism, Charity and the Poverty of Representation*, London: Zed Books.

Inoue, R. (1996) Director, Pacific Asia Resource Center, Interview with the author, Tokyo 24 February.

International Chamber of Commerce and UNCTAD (1998) http://www.unicc.org/unctad/en/pressref/bg9802en.htm, accessed 13 May 1998.

International Monetary Fund (IMF) (1997) *World Economic Outlook* Washington, DC: IMF.

International Monetary Fund (IMF) (1998) *World Economic Outlook* May, Washington, DC: IMF.

Ip, R. (1995) 'Hong Kong's manufacturing industry – moving upward to succeed', Hong Kong Science Park Symposium organized by the Chinese University of Hong Kong, 14 December.

Jackson, P. and Penrose, J. (eds) (1993) *Constructions of Race, Place & Nation*, London: UCL Press; Minneapolis: University of Minnesota Press.

Jackson, T. (1997a) 'Not all rubbish', *Financial Times* 24 December: 14.

Jackson, T. (1997b) *Inside Intel*, London: Macmillan.

Jacobs, J. (1996) *Edge of Empire: Postcolonialism and the City*, London: Routledge.

Jarillo, J. C. (1988) 'On strategic networks', *Strategic Management Journal* 9: 31–41.

Jayasuriya, K. (1997) 'Asian values as reactionary modernization', in *Nordic Newletter of Asian Studies* 4: 19–27.

Jessop, R. (1990) *State Theory: Putting Capitalist States in their Place*, Cambridge and University Park PA: Polity and Pennsylvania State University Press.

Jessop, R. (1993) 'Towards a Schumpeterian workfare state', *Studies in Political Economy* 43: 7–39.

Jessop, R. (1994) 'Post-Fordism and the State', in A. Amin (ed.) *Post-Fordism: A Reader*, Oxford: Blackwell.

Kakakios, M. and van der Velden, J. (1984) 'Migrant communities and class politics: the Greek community in Australia', in G. Bottomley and M. M. de Lepervanche (eds) *Ethnicity, Class and Gender in Australia*, Sydney: George Allen & Unwin.

Kallen, H. (1924) *Culture and Democracy in the United States*, New York: Arno Press.

Kaminsky, G., Lizondo, S. and Reinhart, C. (1997) 'Leading indicators of currency crises', Working Paper, Washington, DC: IMF.

Kao, J. (1997) *Jamming*, Boston, MA: Harvard Business School Press.

Kaplan, R. S. and Norton, D. P. (1997) *The Balanced Scorecard*, Boston, MA: Harvard Business School Press.

Katzenstein, P. and Shiraishi, T. (eds) (1997) *Network Power: Japan and Asia*, Ithaca, NY: Cornell University Press.

Kayatekin, S. and Ruccio, D. (1998) 'Global fragments: subjectivity and class politics in discourses of globalisation', *Economy and Society* 27, 1: 74–96.

Kearney, M. (1991) 'Borders and boundaries of the state and self at the end of empire', *Journal of Historical Sociology* 4, 1: 52–74.

Kearney, M. (1995) 'The local and the global: the anthropology of globalization and transnationalism', *Annual Review of Anthropology* 24: 547–65.

Kelly, P. (1997) 'Globalisation, power and the politics of scale in the Philippines', *Geoforum* 28, 2: 151–72.

Kelly, P. (1999) 'The Geographies and Politics of Globalisation', *Progress in Human Geography* 23.

Kennedy, D. (1992) 'Some Reflections on 'The Role of Sovereignty in the New International Order', in *State Sovereignty: The Challenge of a Changing World: New Approaches and Thinking on International Law* 237 (Proceedings of the 21st Annual Conference of the Canadian Council on International Law, Ottawa, October.

Khoo, B. T. (1995) *The Paradoxes of Mahathirism*, Kuala Lumpur: Oxford University Press.

Khor, M. (1998) 'A poor grade for the IMF', *The Far Eastern Economic Review* 15 January.

Kim, I. (1981) *New Urban Immigrants: The Korean Community in New York*, Princeton, NJ: Princeton University Press.

Kim, W. B., Douglass, M., Choe, S. C. and Ho, K. C. (eds) (1997) *Culture and the City in East Asia*, Oxford: Clarendon Press.

King, A. D. (1995) 'Re-presenting world cities: cultural theory/social practice', in P. Knox and P. Taylor (eds) *World Cities in a World System*, Cambridge: Cambridge University Press.

Kleiner, A. (1996) *The Age of Heretics. Heroes, Outlaws and the Forerunners of Corporate Change*, New York: Doubleday.

Knox, P. and Taylor, P. (eds) (1995) *World Cities in a World-System*, Cambridge: Cambridge University Press.

Kong, L. (1994) 'Environment as a social concern: democratising public arenas in Singapore?', *Sojourn* 9, 2: 277–87.

Kotkin, J. (1991) *Tribes: How Race, Religion and Identity Determine Success in the New Global Economy*, New York: Random House.

Kratochwil, F. (1986) 'Of Systems, Boundaries and Territoriality', *World Politics* 34: 27–52.

Kristof, N. (1998) 'Financial crisis reshaping Asian politics, too', *International Herald Tribune* 20 May: 1.

Krugman, P. (1987) 'Is free trade passé?', *Journal of Economic Perspectives* 1, 2: 131–44.

Krugman, P. (1998a) 'Asia: what went wrong', *Fortune*, 2 March http://www.pathfinder.com/fortune/1998/980302/fst8.html, accessed 23 March.

Krugman, P. (1998b) 'Will Asia bounce back?', speech for Credit Suisse First Boston, Hong Kong, March, http://web.mit.edu/krugman/www/suisse.html, accessed 4 June.

Kwong, P. (1987) *The New Chinatown*, New York: Hill and Wang.

Latour, B. (1986) 'Visualisation and cognition', in H. Kuclick (ed.) *Sociology of Knowledge: Studies in the Sociology of Culture Past and Present* 6: 1–40.

Latour, B. (1987) *Science in Action*, Milton Keynes: Open University Press.

Latour, B. (1988) 'Opening one eye while closing the other. . . a note on some religious paintings', in G. Fyfe and J. Law (eds) *Picturing Power: Visual Depiction and Social Relations*, London: Routledge.

Latour, B. (1993) *We Have Never Been Modern*, Brighton: Harvester-Wheatsheaf.

Lefevbre, H. (1991) *The Production of Space*, Oxford: Basil Blackwell.

Leung, P. K. (1997) 'Cities of memory – cities of fabrication', *Rendition* 47/48: 93–104.

Lessinger, J. (1995) *From the Ganges to the Hudson*, New York: Allyn and Bacon.

Leyshon, A. (1997) 'True stories? Global dreams, global nightmares, and writing globalisation,' in R. Lee and J. Wills (eds) *Geographies of Economies*, London: Arnold.

Li, F. L. N., Jowett, A. J., Findlay, A. M. and Skeldon, R. (1995) 'Discourse on migration and ethnic identity: interviews with professionals in Hong Kong', *Transactions, Institute of British Geographers* 20: 342–56.

Lim, K. W., Chai, R. and Yee, M. F. (1998) *Hidden Agenda*, Kuala Lumpur: Limkokwing Integrated.

Lim, L. (1997) 'The Southeast Asian currency crisis and its aftermath', *Journal of Asian Business* 13, 4: 65–83.

Lin, G. C. S. (1994) 'Changing theoretical perspectives on urbanisation in Asian developing countries', *Third World Planning Review* 16, 1: 1–24.

Ling, L. (1996) 'Hegemon and the internationalising state: a post-colonial analysis of China's integration into Asian corporatism', *Review of International Political Economy* 3, 1: 1–26.

Lo, F. C. and Yeung, Y. M. (eds) (1996) *Emerging World Cities in Pacific Asia*, Tokyo: United Nations University Press.

Lopez, I. H. (1996) *White By Law: The Legal Construction of Race*, New York: New York University Press.

Low, L., Ramstetter, Eric D. and Yeung, H. W. C. (1996) *Accounting for Outward Direct Investment from Hong Kong and Singapore: Who Controls What?*, Working Paper No. 5858, National Bureau of Economic Research, Washington, DC.

Low, L., Toh, M. H., Soon, T. W., Tan, K. Y. and Hughes, H. (1993) *Challenge and Response: Thirty Years of the Economic Development Board*, Singapore: Times Academic Press.

Lowe, L. (1997) *Immigrant Acts: On Asian Cultural Politics*, Durham, NC: Duke University Press.

Lu, D. and Zhu, G. (1995) 'Singapore direct investment in China: features and implications', *ASEAN Economic Bulletin* 12, 1: 53–63.

Mack, A. and Ravenhill, J. (eds) (1994) *Pacific Cooperation: Building Economic and Security Regimes in the Asia-Pacific Region*, Sydney: Allen and Unwin.

Macleod, S. and McGee, T. G. (1996) 'The Singapore-Johore-Riau growth triangle: an emerging extended metropolitan region, in F. C. Lo and Y. M. Yeung (eds) *Emerging World Cities in Pacific Asia*, Tokyo: United Nations University Press.

Manila People's Forum on APEC (1996) *Hidden Costs of Free Trade: Statement of the Philippine PO-NGO Summit on the APEC*, unpublished document, Quezon City, Philippines, 6 July.

Marcos, Sub-Commandant (1997) 'Why are we fighting: the Fourth World War has begun', in *Le Monde Diplomatique*, August/September 1997.

Mark, J. P. (1987) *The Empire Builders: Power, Money and Ethics inside the Harvard Business School*, New York: William Morrow.

Marsella, A. J., De Vos, G. and Hsu, F. L. K. (1985) *Culture and Self*, New York and London: Tavistock.

Martin, H-P. and Schumann, H. (1997) *The Global Trap: Globalisation and the Assault on Democracy and Prosperity*, London: Zed Books.

Mason, M. (1992) 'The origins and evolution of Japanese direct investment in Europe', *Business History Review* 66: 435–74.

Massey, D. (1994) *Space, Place and Gender*, Minneapolis, MN: University of Minnesota Press.

Mato, D. (1997) 'On Global Agents, Transnational Relations, and the Social Making of Transnational Identities and Associated Agendas in 'Latin' America', *Identities: Global Studies in Culture and Power* 4, 2: 167–212.

Maxfield, S. (1997) *Gatekeepers of Growth: The International Political Economy of Central Banking in Developing Countries*, Princeton, NJ: Princeton University Press.

Mayntz, R. (1993) 'Modernisation and the logic of interorganisational networks', in J. Child, M. Crozier, R. Mayntz *et al. Societal Change Between Market and Organisation*, Aldershot: Avebury.

McDermott, M. C. (1992) 'Taiwan's electronics companies are targeting Europe', *European Management Journal* 24, 9: 934–48.

McDonough, W. J. (1996) 'A framework for the pursuit of price stability', *Economic Policy Review* 3, 3: 1–8.

McGee, T. G. (1967) *The Southeast Asian City*, London: Bell.

McGee, T. G. (1997) 'Globalisation, urbanisation and the emergence of sub-global regions: A case study of the Asia-Pacific region', in R. Watters and T. G. McGee (eds) *Asia Pacific: New Geographies of the Pacific Rim*, London: C. Hurst.

McGee, T. G. and Robinson, I. M. (eds) (1995) *The Mega-Urban Regions of Southeast Asia*, Vancouver: UBC Press.

McKinnon, R. (1993) *The Sequence of Economic Liberalisation*, New York: Cambridge University Press.

McKinnon, R. and Pill, H. (1995) 'The 'over borrowing syndrome'', typescript, Department of Economics, Stanford University, California.

Messner, D. (1996) *Die Netzwerkgesellschaft*, Köln: Weltforum Verlag.

Micklethwait, J. and Wooldridge, A. (1996) *The Witch Doctors. What the Management Gurus are Saying, Why it Matters and How to Make Sense of It*, London: Heinemann.

Migration News October 1997, University of California at Davis (accessible at http:// migration.ucdavis.edu).

Milla, M. (1995) Interview material.

Miller, D. (1996) *Capitalism: An Ethnographic Approach*, Oxford: Berg.

Miller, P. and Rose, N. (1997) 'Mobilising the consumer: assembling the subject of consumption', *Theory, Culture and Society* 14: 1–36.

Mingione, E. (1996) 'Urban poverty in the advanced industrial world: concepts, analysis and debates', in E. Mingione (ed.) *Urban Poverty and the Underclass*, Oxford: Blackwell.

Ministry of Information and the Arts (1997a), Mission Statement, Singapore. (http:// www.gov.sg).

Ministry of Information and the Arts (1997b) A Review of 1996, Singapore.

Mishkin, F. S. and Posen, A. S. (1996) 'Inflation targeting: lessons from four countries', *Economic Policy Review* 3, 3: 9–110.

Mitchell, K. (1993) 'Multi-culturalism, or the united colors of capitalism', *Antipode* 25: 263–94.

Mitchell, K. (1995) 'Flexible circulation in the Pacific Rim: capitalisms in cultural context', *Economic Geography* 71: 364–82.

Mitchell, K. (1997) 'Transnational discourse: bringing Geography back in', *Antipode* 29, 2: 101–114.

Mittelman, J. H. (ed.) (1996a) *Globalisation: Critical Reflections. Yearbook of International Political Economy* Vol. 9, Boulder, CO: Lynne Reinner Publishers.

Mittelman, J. H. (1996b) 'Rethinking the "New Regionalism" in the context of globalisation', *Global Governance* 2, 2: 189–213.

Mittelman, J. H. (1996c) 'The Dynamics of Globalisation', in J. Mittleman (ed.) *Globalisation: Critical Reflections*, Boulder, CO: Lynne Reinner.

Mittelman, J. H. (1996d) 'How Does Globalisation Really Work?', in J. Mittleman (ed.) *Globalisation: Critical Reflections*, Boulder, CO: Lynne Reinner.

Mittelman, J. H. (1997a) *Globalisation, Peace and Conflict*, Bangi, Malaysia: Universiti Kebangsaan Malaysia Press.

Mittelman, J. H. (1997b) 'Rethinking Innovation in International Studies: Global Transformation at the Turn of the Millennium', in S. Gill and J. Mittleman (eds) *Innovation and Transformation in International Studies*, Cambridge: Cambridge University Press.

Mittelman, J. H. (2000) *The Globalization Syndrome: Transformation and Resistance*, Princeton: Princeton University Press.

Morales, H. 'Boy.' (1996) President, Philippine Rural Reconstruction Movement, Interview with the author, Quezon City, Philippines, 13 March.

MPF (1996) 'Proposed Philippine PO-NGO Position' *Executive Summary. Manila People's Forum (MPF) on APEC 1996*, unpublished document. Manila.

Munday, M., Morris, J. and Wilkinson, B. (1995) 'Factories or warehouses? A Welsh perspective on Japanese transplant manufacturing', *Regional Studies* 29, 1: 1–17.

Muto, I. (1994) 'PP21: A Step in a Process', *AMPO Japan-Asia Quarterly Review* 25, 2: 47–53.

Muto, I. (1996) Pacific Asia Resource Center, Interview with the author, Tokyo, 25 February.

Muto, I. and Kothari, S. (n.d.) *Towards Sustainable Systems*, unpublished discussion paper for PP21, Tokyo.

Nathan, D. and Kelkan, G. (1997) 'Collective villages in the Chinese market', *Economic and Political Weekly* May 3/10: 951–63.

National Computer Board (1997) 'Transforming Singapore into an Intelligent Island', Singapore, (http://www.ncb.gov.sg).

National Council of Women of the Philippines (1996) 'APEC and the Women: Catching the Next Wave', *GO-NGO Forum on Women*, unpublished document, 16 July.

Nee, V. (1992) 'Organisational dynamics of market transitions: hybrid forms, property rights, and mixed economy in China', *Administrative Science Quarterly* 37: 1–27.

Ng, F. and Yeats, A. (1996) 'Open economies work better! Did Africa's protectionist policies cause its marginalisation in world trade?', Policy Research Working Paper No. 1636, The World Bank, International Economics Department.

Noble, C. (1997) *Maid to Order in Hong Kong: Stories of Filipina Workers*, New York: Cornell University Press.

Nonaka, H. and Takeuchi, I. (1995) *The Knowledge-Creating Company*, Oxford: Oxford University Press.

Nonini, D. M. and Ong, A. (1997) 'Chinese transnationalism as an alternative modernity', in A. Ong and D. Nonini (eds) *Ungrounded Empires: The Cultural Policits of Modern Chinese Transnationalism*, New York and London: Routledge.

O'Brien, R. (1992) *Global Financial Integration: the End of Geography*, London: Pinter.

Ohmae, K. (1990) *Borderless World*, New York: Harper Perennial.

Ohmae, K. (1995) *The End of the Nation State: The Rise of Regional Economies*, New York: HarperCollins and The Free Press.

Oi, J. (1992) 'Fiscal reform and the economic foundations of local state corporatism in China', *World Politics* 45 (Cot.): 99–126.

Olds, K. (1998) 'Globalization and urban change: tales from Vancouver via Hong Kong', *Urban Geography* 19, 4: 360–85.

Olds, K. and Yeung, H. W. C. (1998) *Reshaping 'Chinese' Business Networks in a Globalising Era*, Paper Presented at the Workshop on 'Asian business Networks', Department of Sociology, National University of Singapore, 31 March–2 April 1998.

Olds, K. and Yeung, H. W. C. (1999) '(Re)shaping "Chinese" business networks in a globalising era', *Environment and Planning D: Society and Space* 17.

Ong, A. (1993) 'On the edge of empires: Flexible citizenship among Chinese in diaspora', *Positions* 1, 3: 745–78.

Ong, A. (1994) 'Cultural capital, cultural citizenship: The work of signs in the age of flexible accumulation', Paper prepared for Symposium 117, Wenner Gren Conference Transnationalism, Nation-State Building, and Culture, Mijas, Spain, June.

Ong, A. (1997a) 'A momentary glow of fraternity: Narratives of Chinese nationalism and capitalism', in *Special Issue on Narratives of Capitalism*, N. Glick Schiller (ed.) *Identities: Global Studies in Culture and Power* 3, 3: 331–66.

Ong, A. (1997b) '"A Better Tomorrow"? The struggle for global visibility sojourn', in V. Rafael and I. Abraham (eds) *Special Focus Issue of Sojourn on Southeast Asian Diasporas* 12, 2: 192–225.

Osborne, J. and Rose, N. (1997) 'In the name of society, or three theses on the history of social thought', *History of the Human Sciences* 10: 87–104.

O'Shea, J. and Madigan, C. (1997) *Dangerous Company. The Consulting Powerhouses and the Businesses They Save and Ruin*, London: Nicholas Brealey.

Paderanga, C. Jr (1996) 'Philippine financial development, 1980–95', in E. Esguerra and I. Kazuhisa (eds) *Financial Sector Issues in the Philippines*, Tokyo: Institute for Developing Economies.

Paderanga, C. Jr (1997a) 'Economic interdependence and macroeconomic coordination', in C. Paderanga, Jr (ed.), *The Philippines in the Emerging World Environment: Globalisation at a Glance*, Quezon City: University of the Philippines Press.

Paderanga, C. Jr (1997b) 'Roots and responses to the ASEAN currency crisis', Paper prepared for the Forum on the Currency and Haze Crises in Southeast Asia, ASEAN Economic Forum, 13 November 1997, sponsored by the Institute for Southeast Asian Studies, Singapore.

Panagariya, A., Quibria, M. G. and Rao. N. (1996) 'The emerging global trading environment and developing Asia', Asian Development Bank, Economic Staff Paper No. 55, Manila: Asian Development Bank, July.

Panitch, L. (1997) 'Rethinking the Role of the State', in *Globalisation: Critical Reflections*, J. Mittelman (ed.). Boulder, CO: Lynne Reinner.

Paul, J. R. (1994) 'Free Trade, Regulatory Competition and the Autonomous Market Fallacy', *The Columbia Journal of European Law* 1, 1: 29–62.

Pauly, L. W. and Reich, S. (1997) 'National structures and multinational corporate behavior: enduring differences in the age of globalization', *International Organization* 51, 1: 1–30.

Park, R. (1974 [1925]) 'Immigrant Community and Immigrant Press and its Control', reprinted in *The Collected Papers of Robert Park*, New York: Arno Press.

Peck, J. A. and Tickell, A. (1994) 'Searching for a new institutional fix: the after Fordist crisis and global-local disorder', in A. Amin (ed.) *PostFordism: a Reader*, Oxford: Blackwell.

Pellegram, A. (1997) 'The message in paper', in D. Miller (ed.) *Material Cultures: Why Some Things Matter*, London: UCL Press.

PEO/Structure, Pacific Economic Cooperation Council (1997) *Exchange Rate Fluctuations and Macroeconomic Management*, Japan Committee for Pacific Economic Outlook Kansai: Japan Committee.

Peraldi, M. and Perrin, E. (eds) (1996) *Réseaux Productifs et Territoires Urbains*, Toulouse: Presses Universitaires du Mirail.

Perry, E. (ed.) (1996) *Putting Class in Its Place: Worker Identities in East Asia*, Berkeley, CA: Institute of East Asian Studies, University of California.

Perry, M. (1998) 'The Singapore growth triangle in the global and local economy', in V. R. Savage, L. Kong and W. Neville (eds) *The Naga Awakens: Growth and Change in Southeast Asia*, Singapore: Times Academic Press.

Perry, M., Kong, L. and Yeoh, B. (1997) *Singapore: A Developmental City State*, Chichester: John Wiley & Sons.

Pessar, P. (1995) *A Visa for a Dream*, Boston, MA: Allyn and Bacon.

Petri (1993) 'The East Asian trading bloc: an analytical history', in J. Frankel and M. Kahler (eds) *Regionalism and Rivalry: Japan and the United States in Pacific Asia*, Chicago: University of Chicago Press.

Phillips, N. (1997) *Reality Hacking*, London: Heinemann.

Pido, A. (1986) *The Philipinos in America*, Staten Island, NY: Center for Migration Studies.

Pieterse, J.N. (1994) 'Globalisation as hybridisation', *International Sociology* 9, 2: 161–84.

Pigg, S. L. (1992) 'Inventing social categories through place: social representations and development in Nepal', *Comparative Study of Society and History* 34, 3: 491–513.

Piven, F. (1995) 'Is it global economics or neo-laissez-faire?', *New Left Review* 213: 107–14.

Polanyi, K. (1957) *The Great Transformation: The Political and Economic Origins of Our Time*, Boston, MA: Beacon Press.

Polanyi, K. (1968) *Primitive, Archaic and Modern Economies: Essays of Karl Polanyi*, G. Dalton (ed.) New York: Anchor.

Pollock, J. (1993) 'The United States in East Asia: holding the ring', in *Conference Papers on Asia's International Role in the Post-Cold War Era*, Part I, Adelphi Paper 275, London: International Institute of Strategic Studies: 69–82.

Porter, M. (1990) *The Competitive Advantage of Nations*, Basingstoke and New York: Macmillan and Free Press.

Porter, T. M. (1995) *Trust in Numbers. The Pursuit of Objectivity in Science and Public Life*, Princeton, NJ: Princeton University Press.

Portes, A. (1997) 'Immigration Theory for a New Century: Some Problems and Opportunities', *International Migration Review* 31, 4: 799–825.

Portes, A. and Rumbaut, R. (1990) *Immigrant America: A Portrait*, Berkeley, CA: University of California Press.

Poster, M. (1995) *The Second Media Age*, Oxford: Blackwell, Polity.

Power, J. and Sicat, G. (1971) *The Philippine Industrialisation and Trade Policies*, London: Oxford University Press.

Radelet, S. and Sachs, J. (1998) 'The onset of the East Asian financial crisis', 30 March http://www.hiid.harvard.edu/pub/other/asiacrisis.html, accessed 18 May 1998.

Rafael, V. (ed.) (1995) *Discrepant Histories: Translocal Essays on Filipino Cultures*, Philadelphia, PA: Temple University Press.

Rafael, V. (1998) 'Embodying Translation: Castilian and the Origins of Nationalism in the Philippines', Paper delivered at the Symposium 'Borders/Partitions/Statism,' Trinity College, Hartford, Connecticut, March.

Rata, M. (1997) 'Global capitalism and the revival of ethnic traditionalism in New Zealand: The emergence of tribal-capitalism', Ph.D. thesis University of Auckland.

Rebugio, L. L. (1996) Professor and Dean, College of Forestry, University of the Philippines Los Banos. Interview with the author. Los Banos, Laguna, Philippines. 11 March.

Reid, A. (1988) *Southeast Asia in the Age of Commerce, Vol. 1: The Lands below the Winds,* New Haven, CT: Yale University Press.

Reid, A. (1993) *Southeast Asia in the Age of Commerce, Vol. 2: Expansion and Crisis,* New Haven, CT: Yale University Press.

Riddle, D. I. (1986) *Service-Led Growth: The Role of Service Sector in World Development,* New York: Praeger.

Rimmer, P. J. (1993) 'Transport and communications in the Pacific Economic Zone during the early 21st Century', in Y. M. Yeung (ed.) *Pacific Asia in the 21st Century: Geographical and Developmental Perspectives,* Hong Kong: Chinese University Press.

Rimmer, P. J. (1995) 'Moving goods, people, and information: putting the ASEAN megaurban regions in context', in T. G. McGee and I. M. Robinson (eds) *The Mega-Urban Regions of Southeast Asia,* Vancouver: UBC Press.

Rimmer, P. J. (1996) 'International transport and communications interactions between Pacific Asia's emerging world cities', in F. C. Lo and Y. M. Yeung (eds) *Emerging World Cities in Pacific Asia,* Tokyo: United Nations University Press.

Rimmer, P. J. (ed.) (1997) *Pacific Rim Development: Integration and Globalisation in the Asia-Pacific Economy,* Sydney: Allen and Unwin.

Robertson, R. (1992) *Globalization, Social Theory and Global Culture,* London: Sage.

Robertson, R. (1994) 'Glocalisation: Space, Time and Social Theory', *Journal of International Communication* 1: 1.

Robison, R. (1995) 'Ideology and the politics of Asian values', *The Pacific Review* 9, 3: 309–27.

Rodan, G. (1995) *Political Oppositions in Industrialising Asia,* London: Routledge.

Rodan, G. (1996) 'Theorising political opposition in East and Southeast Asia,' in G. Rodan (ed.) *Political Oppositions in Industrialising Asia,* London: Routledge.

Rodrik, D. (1997) Has Globalisation gone too far?, *California Management Review* 39, 3: 29–53.

Rohwer, J. (1995) *Asia Rising,* London: Nicholas Brealey Publishing.

Rosaldo, R. (1988) 'Ethnic concentration: the Ilongots in Upland, Luzon', in A. T. Rambo, K. Gillogly and K. L. Hutterer (eds) *Ethnic Diversity and the Control of Natural Resources in Southeast Asia,* Michigan Papers on South and Southeast Asia, Centre for South and Southeast Asian Studies, the University of Michigan.

Rosaldo, R. (1989) *Culture and Truth: The Remaking of Social Analysis,* Boston, MA: Beacon Press.

Rosamond, B. (1996) 'European regional identity & international political economy of European integration', Utrecht: Conference of the International Society for the Study of European Ideas, 1–12 August.

Rosecrance, R. (1996) 'The rise of the virtual state', *Foreign Affairs* 75, 4: 45–56.

Rosen, F. and McFadyen, D. (eds) (1995) *Free Trade and Economic Restructuring in Latin America,* (A NACLA Reader), New York: Monthly Review Press.

Rosenau, J. N. (1997) *Along the Domestic-Foreign Frontier: Exploring Governance in a Turbulent World*, Cambridge: Cambridge University Press.

Rouse, R. (1992) 'Making Sense of Settlement: Class Transformation, Cultural Struggle, and Transnationalism among Mexican Migrants in the US', in *Towards A Transnational Perspective on Migration: Race, Class, Ethnicity, and Nationalism Reconsidered*, N. Glick Schiller, L. Basch and C. Blanc-Szanton (eds.) New York: New York Academy of Sciences.

Rouse, R. (1995) 'Questions of Identity: personhood and collectivity in transnational migration to the United States', *Critique of Anthropology* 15, 4: 351–80.

Ruggie, J. G. (1993) 'Territoriality and beyond: problematising modernity in international relations', *International Organisation* 47, 1: 139–74.

Sachs, J. D. (1996) 'Economic transition and the exchange-rate regime', *American Economic Review* 86, 2: 147–52.

Sachs, J. D. (1997a) 'The wrong medicine for Asia', *New York Times*, 3 November, http://www.stern.nyu.edu/~nroubini/asia/AsiaSachsOp-EdNYT1197.html, accessed 24 May 1998.

Sachs, J. D. (1997b) 'Nature, nurture and growth', *The Economist* June: 19–22.

Salacuse, J.(1991) *Making Global Deals: Negotiating in the International Marketplace*, Boston, MA: Houghton Mifflin.

Sanchez, A. I. (1997) 'Transnational Political Agency and Identity Formation Among Colombian Immigrants', paper presented at the Conference on Transnational Communities and the Political Economy of New York, New School for Social Research, New York, February.

Sassen, S. (1988) *The Mobility of Labour and Capital: A Study in International Investment and Labour Flow*, New York: Cambridge University Press.

Sassen, S. (1996a) *Losing Control? Sovereignty in an Age of Globalisation*, The 1995 Columbia University Leonard Hastings Schoff Memorial Lectures. New York: Columbia University Press.

Sassen, S. (1996b) 'The state and the global city: notes towards a conception of place-centered governance', *Competition and Change* 1, 1: 31–50.

Sassen, S. (1998a) *Globalisation and its Discontents. Selected Essays*, New York: New Press.

Sassen, S. (1998b) 'Data Set on Innovative Cross-border Financial Deals, 1994–1998. Project on Governance and Accountability in the Global Economy', (On file with author at Department of Sociology, University of Chicago, USA).

Sassen, S. (ed.). (forthcoming) *Cities and their Cross-border Networks,* Institute for Advanced Studies, United Nations University, Tokyo, Japan.

Sato, Y. (1993) 'The Salim Group in Indonesia: the development and behaviour of the largest conglomerate in Southeast Asia', *The Developing Economies* 31, 4: 408–41.

Schaeffer, R. (1997) *Understanding Globalisation: The Social Consequences of Political, Economic, and Environmental Change*, Lanham, MD: Rowman and Littlefield.

Scholte, J. (1997) 'Global capitalism and the state', *International Affairs* 73, 3: 427–52.

Scott, J. C. (1990) *Domination and the Arts of Resistance: Hidden Transcripts*, New Haven, CT: Yale University Press.

Serrano, I.R. (ed.) (1994) 'Civil Society in the Asia-Pacific Region', in CIVICUS: World Alliance for Citizen Participation *Citizens: Strengthening Global Civil Society*, Washington, D.C., CIVICUS: 271–317.

Serrano, I. R. (1996) Vice President, Philippine Rural Reconstruction Movement. Interview with the author. Quezon City, Philippines, March 13.

Shapiro, E. (1995), *Fad Surfing in the Boardroom*, San Francisco: Addison Wesley.

Shapiro, M. (1993) 'The globalisation of law', *Indiana Journal of Global Legal Studies* 1: 37-64.

Shaw, M. (1994) 'Civil Society and Global Politics: Beyond a Social Movements Approach', *Millennium: Journal of International Studies* 23, 3 (Winter): 647–67.

Shotter, J. (1993) *Cultural Politics of Everyday Life*, Buckingham: Open University Press.

Siddique, S. (1990) 'The phenomenology of ethnicity: a Singapore case study', *Sojourn* 5, 1: 35–62.

Simon, D. F. (ed.) (1995) *Emerging Technological Trajectory of the Pacific Rim*, Armonk: M. E. Shape Inc.

Skeldon, R. (1994) 'East Asian migration and the changing world order', in W. T. S. Gould and A. M. Findlay (eds) *Population Migration and the Changing World Order*, London: John Wiley.

Sklair, L. (1994) 'Global sociology and global environmental change', in M. Redclift and T. Benton (eds) *Social Theory and the Global Environment*, London: Routledge.

Sklair, L. (1997) 'Social Movements for Global Capitalism: The Transnational Capitalist Class in action', *Review of International Political Economy* 4, 3: 514–38.

Smart, J. and Smart, A. (1991) 'Personal relations and divergent economies: a case study of Hong Kong investment in South China', *International Journal of Urban and Regional Research* 15, 2: 216–33.

Smith, A. (1990) 'Towards a global culture?' *Theory, Culture and Society* 7, 2–3: 171–92.

Smart, A. (1997) 'Capitalist story-telling and hegemonic crises: some comments', *Identities: Global Studies in Culture and Power* 3, 3: 399–412.

Smith, M. P. (1992) 'Postmodernism, urban ethnography, and the new social space of ethnic identity', *Theory and Society* 21, 4: 493–531.

Smith, N. (1997) 'The satanic geographies of globalisation: uneven development in the 1990s', *Public Culture*, 10, 1: 169–89.

Smith, N. J. (1988) 'The region is dead! Long live the region!', *Political Geography Quarterly* 7, 2: 141–52.

Smith, R. (1998) 'Transnational migration, assimilation and political community', in M. Crahan and A. Vouvoulias Bush (eds) *The City and the World: New York City in Global Context*, New York: Council on Foreign Relations.

Songco, D. (1996) National Coordinator, CODE-NGO. Interview with the author. Quezon City, Philippines, 13 March

Spickard, P. (1996) *Japanese Americans: The Formation and Transformations of an Ethnic Group*, New York: Prentice Hall.

Stallings, B. (1995) *Global Change, Regional Response: The New International Context of Development*, Cambridge: Cambridge University Press.

Storper, M. J. (1996) 'The resurgence of regional economies: ten years later', *European Urban and Regional Studies* 2, 3: 191–221.

Storper, M. J. (1997) 'Territories, flows, and hierarchies in the global economy', in K. R. Cox (ed.) *Spaces of Globalisation: Reasserting the Power of the Local*, New York: Guilford.

Storper, M. J. (1997) 'The city: centre of economic reflexivity', *Service Industries Journal* 19, 1: 1–27.

Straits Times, 8 May 1998: 67.

Sum, N-L. (1994) *Reflections on Accumulation, Regulation, the State, and Societalisation: a Stylised Model of East Asian Capitalism and an Integral Economic Analysis of Hong Kong*, Ph.D. Dissertation submitted to the Department of Sociology, University of Lancaster.

Sum, N-L. (1995) 'More than a "war of words": identity politics and the struggle for dominance during the recent "Political Reform" period in Hong Kong', *Economy and Society* 24, 1: 69–100.

Sum, N-L. (1996a) 'Strategies for East Asia regionalism and the construction of NIC identities in the post-Cold War era', in A. Gamble and A. Payne (eds) *Regionalism and World Order*, Basingstoke: Macmillan.

Sum, N-L. (1996b) '"Greater China" and the global-regional-local dynamics', in I. Cook and R. Li (eds) *Fragmented Asia*, Aldershot: Avebury.

Sum, N-L. (1998) 'The making of the "Greater China" subregion', in G. Hook and I. Kearns (eds) *Subregionalism and World Order*, Basingstoke: Macmillan (in print).

Sum, N-L. (1998) 'Theorising export-oriented economic development in East Asian newly-industrialising countries: a regulationist perspective', in I. Cook, M. Doel, R. Li and Y. Yang (eds) *Dynamic Asia*, Aldershot: Avebury.

Sung, Y. W. (1997) 'Hong Kong and the economic integration with the China Circle', in B. Naughton (ed.) *The China Circle*, Washington, DC: Brookings Institution Press.

Tadiar, N, (1997) 'Domestic Bodies of the Philippine', in V. Rafael and I. Abraham (eds) *Special Focus Issue on Southeast Asian Diasporas*, 12, 2: 153–91.

Takaki, R. (1989) *Strangers From a Different Shore*, New York: William Morrow.

Takaki, R. (1990) *Iron Cages: Race and Culture in Nineteenth-Century America*, New York: Oxford University Press.

Tan, C. H. (1995) *Venturing Overseas: Singapore's External Wing*, Singapore: McGraw-Hill.

Tan, C. Z. (1997/98) *Investment Strategies and Overseas Chinese Business Networks: A Study of Singaporean Firms in Hainan Province*, Unpublished Academic Exercise, Department of Geography, National University of Singapore.

Taylor, P. J. (1995)'World cities and territorial states: the rise and fall of their mutuality', in P. Knox and P. J. Taylor. (eds) (1995) *World Cities in a World-System*, Cambridge: Cambridge University Press.

Tenbruck, F. (1990) 'The dream of a secular ecumene: the meaning and limits of politics of development', *Theory, Culture and Society* 7, 2–3: 193–206.

Tengco, G. J. C. (1996) Project Coordinator, Institute of Environmental Science for Social Change (formerly Environmental Research Division of the Manila Observatory), Interview with the author, Cabanatuan City, Nueva Ecija, Luzon, Philippines, 9 March.

The Economist (1997) 'One World?', 18–24 October: 99–100.

The Economist (1998) 'The Century the earth stood still', 20 December 1997–2 January 1998: 71–3.

The Economist (1998) 'Frozen miracle: A Survey of East Asian economies', 7 March.

The Nikkei Weekly, 9 February 1998.

The Scent of the Green Papaya (Mui Du Du Xanh). Les Productions Lazennec, 1993. Vietnamese, with subtitles. Director Tran Anh Hung.

The Straits Times, 6 December 1997.

The Sunday Times, London, 15 March 1998.

Thompson, C. (1997) *The Weekend Australian*, 7–8 June 1997.

Thrift, N. J. (1984) 'Flies and germs: a geography of knowledge', in D. Gregory and J. Urry (eds) *Social Relations and Spatial Structures*, London: Macmillan.

Thrift, N. J. (1995) 'A hyperactive world?', in R. J. Johnston, P. Taylor and M. Watts (eds) *Geographies of Global Change*, Oxford: Blackwell.

Thrift, N. J. (1996a) 'Shut up and dance: or, is the world economy knowable?', in P. Daniels and W. Lever (eds) *The Global Economy in Transition*, Harlow: Longman.

Thrift, N. J. (1996b) 'New urban eras and old technological fears: reconfiguring the goodwill of electronic things', *Urban Studies* 33: 1463–493.

Thrift, N. J. (1996c) *Spatial Formations*, London: Sage.

Thrift, N. J. (1997) 'The rise of soft capitalism', *Cultural Values* 1: 29–57.

Thrift, N. J. (1998a) 'The rise of soft capitalism', in A. Herod, G. O'Tuathail and S. Roberts (eds) *An Unruly World?: Globalisation, Governance and Geography*, London: Routledge.

Thrift, N. J. (1998b) *Cities and Global Economic Change*, London: Routledge.

Tong, C. K. and Chan K. B. (1994) 'One face, many masks: the singularity and plurality of Chinese identity', Paper presented at the Conference on 'The Last Half Century of the Chinese Overseas (1945–1994): Comparative Perspectives', University of Hong Kong, 19–21 December. Paper forthcoming in *Diaspora*.

Tønnessson and Antlöv (eds) (1996) *Asian forms of the nation*, Richmond Surrey: Curzon.

Tort, P. (1989) *La Raison Classificatoire: Quinze Etudes*, Paris: Ambier.

Tu, W. (ed.) (1991) *The Triadic Chord: Confucian Ethic, Industrial East Asia and Max Weber*. Singapore: Institute of East Asian Philosophy.

Turner, B. (1990) 'The Two Faces of Sociology', in M. Featherstone (ed.) *Global Culture: Nationalism, Globalisation and Modernity*, London: Sage.

Turner, T. (1997) 'The Dithering Away of the State', Paper delivered at Guggenheim Conference on Globalisation, Hawaii, June.

UNCTAD (United Nations Conference on Trade and Development) (1995) *World Investment Report, 1995*, New York: United Nations.

UNCTAD (1996a) *Sharing Asia's Dynamism: Asian Direct Investment in the European Union*, New York: United Nations.

UNCTAD (1996b) *Trade and Development Report, 1996*, New York: United Nations.

UNCTAD (1996c) *World Investment Report 1996: Investment, Trade and International Policy Arrangements*, New York: United Nations.

UNCTAD (1997) *World Investment Report 1997*, Geneva: UNCTAD.

UNCTC (1992) *World Investment Directory 1992: Foreign Direct Investment, Legal Framework and Corporate Data. Volume 1: Asia and the Pacific*, New York: United Nations.

United Nations Research Institute for Social Development (1995) *Global Citizens on the Move*, UNRISD: Geneva, Switzerland.

van den Berghe, P.L. (1978) 'Race and ethnicity: a sociological perspective', *Ethnic and Racial Studies* 1, 4: 401–11.

Vargas, V. (1992) 'The Feminist Movement in Latin America: Between Hope and Disenchantment', in J. P. N. Pieterse (ed.) *Emancipations, Modern and Postmodern*, London: Sage.

Veltz, P. (1996) *Mondialisation: villes et territoires: l'économie archipel*, Paris: Economica.

Wade, R. (1990) *Governing the Market: Economic Theory and the Role of Government in East Asian Industrialization*, Princeton, NJ: Princeton University Press.

Wade, R. and Veneroso, F. (1998a) 'The Asian crisis: the high debt model versus the Wall Street-Treasury-IMF complex', *New Left Review* March/April: 3–25.

Wade, R. and Veneroso, F. (1998b) *The Asian Financial Crisis: The Unrecognised Risk of the IMF's Asia Package*, New York, Russell Sage Foundation, mimeo.

Wakeman, F. (1988) 'Transnational and comparative research', *Items* 42, 4: 85–8.

Walder, A. G. (1994) 'The decline of communist power: elements of a theory of institutional change', *Theory and Society* 23, 2: 297–324.

Walker, R. B. J. (1993) *Inside/Outside: Internatinal Relations as Political Theory*, Cambridge: Cambridge University Press.

Walker, R. B. J. (1994) 'Social Movements/World Politics', *Millennium: Journal of International Studies* 23, 3: 669–700.

Wallerstein, I. (1974) *The Modern World System*, New York: Academic Press.

Wallerstein, I. (1991) *Geopolitics and Geoculture*, Cambridge: Cambridge University Press.

Walpole, P. W. (1996) Executive Director, Institute of Environmental Science for Social Change (formerly Environmental Research Division of the Manila Observatory). Interview with the author, Quezon City, Philippines, 12 March.

Walsh, C. (1995) 'Optimal contracts for central bankers', *American Economic Review* 85 (March): 150–67.

Wang G. W. (1988) 'The study of Chinese identities in Southeast Asia', in J. W. Cushman and G. W. Wang (eds) *Changing Identities of the Southeast Asian Chinese since World War II*, Hong Kong: Hong Kong University Press.

Wang, S. (1994) 'Central-local fiscal politics in China', in H. Jia and Z. Lin (eds) *Changing Central-Local Relations in China: Reform and State Capacity*, Boulder, CO: Westview.

Wapner, P. (1996) *Environmental Activism and World Civic Politics*, Albany: State University of New York Press.

Warne, F. J. (1913) *The Immigration Invasion*, New York: Dodd, Mead, and Co.

Watts, M. (1996) 'Mapping identities: place, space, and community in an African City', in P. Yaeger (ed.) *The Geography of Identity*, Ann Arbor: The University of Michigan Press.

Weber, C. (1996) *Writing Sovereignty*, Cambridge: Cambridge University Press.

Wee C. H., Lee K. S. and Hidajat, B. W. (1991) *Sun Tzu: War and Management: Application to Strategic Management Thinking*, Singapore: Addison Wesley.

Weidenbaum, M. and Hughes, S. (1996) *The Bambook Network: How Expatriate Chinese Entrepreneurs Are Creating a New Economic Superpower in Asia*, New York: The Free Press.

Weiner, M. (1997) 'The invention of identity: Race and nation in pre-war Japan', in F. Dikötter (ed.) *The Construction of Racial Identities in China and Japan*, Honolulu: University of Hawaii Press.

Weiss, L. (1997) 'Globalisation and the myth of the powerless state,' *New Left Review* 225: 3–27.

Wells, L. T. Jr (1983) *Third World Multinationals: The Rise of Foreign Investment from Developing Countries*, Cambridge, MA: MIT Press.

Wendt, A. (1992) 'Anarchy is what states make of it', *International Organisation* 46, 2: 391–425.

Wendt, A. (1994) 'Collective identity formation and the international state', *American Political Science Review* 88, 2: 384–97.

Wensley, M. (1997) 'The politics of exclusion: Australia, Turkey and the definition of regionalism', *The Pacific Review* 10, 4: 523–55.

Wesson, T. (1990) 'Towards a fuller understanding of foreign direct investment: the example of Hyundai's investment in the U.S. personal computer industry', *Business & the Contemporary World* 3: 123–35.

Whitley, R. (1992) *Business Systems in East Asia: Firms, Markets and Societies*, London: Sage.

Wieviorka, M. (1977) 'Un nouveau paradigme de la violence', in M. Wieviorka (ed.) *Un nouveau paradigme de la violence*, Paris: l'Harmattan.

Williams, K. (*et al.*) (1992) 'Against lean production', *Economy and Society* 21: 321–54.

Williamson, J. (1996) 'Globalisation and inequality then and now: the late 19th and early 20th centuries', National Bureau of Economic Research, Working paper 5491.

Wilson, R. and Dirlik, A. (eds) (1995) *Asia/Pacific as Space of Cultural Production*, Durham: Duke University Press.

Wolf, M. (1996) 'A country divided by growth', *Financial Times* 20 February: 14.

Women's Forum (1996) 'Women's Forum for the APEC Manila Process', *Manila People's Forum on APEC*, unpublished document. Manila, 3 July.

Wong, B. P. (1982) *Chinatown: Economic Adaptation and Ethnic Identity of the Culture*, New York: Holt, Rinehart and Winston.

Wong, C. P. W. (1991) 'Central-local relations in an era of fiscal decline: the paradox of fiscal decentralisation in post-Mao China', *The China Quarterly* 128: 691–715.

Wong, T. C. (1996) 'Information technology and its spatial impact on Singapore', *Review of Urban and Regional Development Studies* 8: 33–45.

Wooldridge, A. (1997) 'Trimming the fat. A survey of management consultancy', *The Economist*, 22 March, Survey.

World Bank (1997a) *Global Economic Prospects and the Developing Countries*, Washington, D.C.: World Bank.

World Bank (1997b) *World Development Report, 1997: The State in a Changing World*, Washington, D.C.: World Bank.

Wyman, M. (1993) *Round-Trip to America: The Immigrants Return to Europe, 1880–1930*, Ithaca, NY: Cornell University Press.

Xu, X. (1994) 'Taiwan's economic cooperation with Fujian and Guangdong: the view from China', in G. Klintworth (ed.) *Taiwan in the Asia-Pacific in the 1990*, St. Leonards: Allen and Unwin.

Yan, Y. (1996) *The Flow of Gifts*, Stanford: Stanford University Press.

Yancey, W. L., Ericksen, E. P. and Juliani, R. N. (1976) 'Emergent ethnicity: a review and reformation', *American Sociological Review* 41: 391–403.

Yang, M. (1989) 'The gift economy and state power in China', *Comparative Study of Society and History* 31: 25–54.

Yang, M. (1994) *Gifts, Favours, and Banquets: the Art of Social Relationships in China*, Ithaca, NY: Cornell University Press.

Yates, J. (1994) 'Evolving information use in firms, 1850-1920: ideology and information techniques and technologies', in L. Bud-Frierman (ed.) *Information Acumen. The Understanding and Use of Knowledge in Modern Business*, London: Routledge.

Yates, J. and Orlikowski, W. J. (1992) 'Genres of organisational communication', *Academy of Management Review* 17: 299–326.

Yearbook of Statistics (1996) Singapore: Department of Statistics.

Yeung, H. W. C (1994a) 'Third World multinationals revisited: a research critique and future agenda', *Third World Quarterly* 15, 2: 297–317.

Yeung, H. W. C. (1994b) 'Transnational corporations from Asian developing countries: their characteristics and competitive edge', *Journal of Asian Business* 10, 4: 17–58.

Yeung, H. W. C. (1997a) 'Business networks and transnational corporations: a study of Hong Kong firms in the ASEAN region', *Economic Geography* 73, 1: 1–25.

Yeung, H. W. C. (1997b) 'Cooperative strategies and Chinese business networks: a study of Hong Kong transnational corporations in the ASEAN region', in P. W. Beamish and J. P. Killing (eds), *Cooperative Strategies: Asia-Pacific Perspectives*, San Francisco, CA: The New Lexington Press.

Yeung, H. W. C. (1998a), 'Service transnational corporations from Hong Kong: an emerging competitor in the regional and global marketplace', *International Business Review* Vol. 6.

Yeung, H. W. C. (1998b) *Transnational Corporations and Business Networks: Hong Kong Firms in the ASEAN Region*, London: Routledge.

Yeung, H. W. C. (1998c) *Under Siege? Globalisation and Chinese Business in Southeast Asia*, Paper Presented at 'Workshop on Southeast Asia under Globalization', Academia Sinica, Taipei, 9–12 April 1998.

Yeung, H. W. C. (1998d) 'The political economy of transnational corporations: a study of the regionalisation of Singaporean firms', *Political Geography* 17, 4: 389–416.

Yeung, H. W. C. (1998e) 'Capital, state and space: contesting the borderless world', *Transactions of the Institute of British Geographers* New Series, 23, 3: 291–309.

Yeung, H. W. C. (1998f) 'The social-spatial constitution of business organisations: a geographical perspective', *Organization* 5, 1: 101–28.

Yeung, H. W. C. (1998g), 'Transnational economic synergy and business networks: the case of two-way investment between Malaysia and Singapore', *Regional Studies* 32, 8: 687–706.

Yeung, H. W. C. (1999a) 'Under Siege? Economic globalisation and Chinese business in Southeast Asia', *Economy and Society* 28, 1: 1–31.

Yeung, H. W. C. (1999b) 'The internationalization of ethnic Chinese business firms from Southeast Asia: strategies, processes and competitive advantage', *International Journal of Urban and Regional Research* Vol. 23, 1: 103–27.

Yeung, H. W. C. (1999c) 'Regulating investment abroad? The political economy of the regionalisation of Singaporean firms', *Antipode* 31.

Yeung, Y. M. (1987) 'Cities that work: Hong Kong and Singapore', in R. Fuchs, G. Jones and E. Pernia (eds) *Urbanization and Urban Policies in Pacific Asia*, Boulder, CO: Westview Press.

Yeung, Y. M. (1995) 'Pacific Asia's world cities in the new global economy', *Urban Futures* 19: 81–7.

Yeung, Y. M. (ed.) (1993) *Pacific Asia in the 21st Century: Geographical and Developmental Perspectives*, Hong Kong: Chinese University Press.

Yeung, Y. M. and Lo, F. C. (1996) 'Global restructuring and emerging urban corridors in Pacific Asia', in F. C. Lo and Y. M. Yeung (eds) *Emerging World Cities in Pacific Asia*, Tokyo: United Nations University Press.

Yoshino, K. (1997) 'The discourse on blood and racial identity in contemporary Japan', in F. Dikötter (ed.) *The Construction of Racial Identities in China and Japan*, Honolulu: University of Hawaii Press.

Yuan, L. L. and Choo, M. L. L. (1995) 'Singapore as a global city: strategies and key issues', *Urban Futures* 19: 90–6.

Zawiah Y. (1994) *Resisting Colonialist Discourse*, Bangi, Malaysia: Universiti Kebangsaan Malaysia Press.

Zhao, L. and Aram, J. (1995) 'Networking and growth of young technology-intensive ventures in China', *Journal of Business Venturing* 10, 5: 349–70.

Zweig, D. (1995) '"Developmental Communities" on China's coast: the impact on trade, investment, and transnational alliances', *Comparative Politics* 27, 3: 253–74.

Zysman, J., Doherty, E. and Schwartz, A. (1997) 'Tales from the 'global' economy: cross-national production networks and the reorganisation of the European economy', *Structural Change and Economic Dynamics* 8, 1: 45–85.

Name index

Subject index

Bold indicates main entry

Schumpeterian 32
separatism 200
Singapore 5, 6, 12, 73, 78, 80, 109, 135,
244; 'developmental city state' 242; as
global hub and world city 241–5;
growth triangle 244, 251 (*see also*
growth triangles); Singapore-Suzhou
Township Development Company
(SSTDC) 123; transmigrants in
China 223
social relations: globalisation of 11;
network of 41
sogo shosha 112, 122
South Korea 5, 6, 7, 14, 79, 94, 95, 102,
103, 109, 154, 188, 208
Southeast Asia 2, 3, 5–6, 14, 49, 54, 95,
99
space 20, 132, 141; economic 36;
electronic 130, 131, 132–3, 141–2; of
flows 129; geographical 3; politics of
145; production and reproduction
of 240; social construction of 42;
subnational 151
Special Economic Zones (SEZs) 135–6,
137
state 149; definition of 203; guarantor of
rights of global capital 159;
mechanisms **151–3**; and new
populism 200; and privatised
governance 155
sub-regional economic zones 131
supranational organisations 151

Taiwan 5, 6, 68, 94, 95, 103, 109,
135–8, 140–1, 143, 188
territory 2; globalised forms of 12

Thailand 6, 7, 9, 79, 84; King Bhumibol
Adulyadej 54
'third cultures' 220
'third space' 199
Third World 50, 79; multinationals 107
time-space: compression 21, 186;
dimensions 132–3; distantiation 21–2;
envelope 24; governance **129–34**, 145;
tensions in 142–4
Tobin tax 22, 178
township–village enterprises (TVEs)
137–9, 141–3
transnational corporations 10, 20, 22,
34, 45, 51, 68, 139, 204
transnationalisation 47, 203; of classes,
genders, ethnicities 50; of culture 48
transnationalism 50, 186
triads 24, 34, 74, 112, 115

United Nations Conference on Trade
and Development (UNCTAD) 5,
107, 110–11
United States 11, 20, 22, 28, 34, 48, 51,
94, 102, 104, 109, 135, 187
urbanisation 3

Vietnam 11, 32, 73, 78
virtualism 57

'whiteness' 198
Women's Forum 84
World Bank 22, 28, 83, 93, 215
World Trade Organisation (WTO) 93,
100, 109, 155

Yen 6